It is rare for a distinctively confessional
tradition but those of the church catholi
Doctrine Malcolm Yarnell demonstrates what is at stake in the Baptist witness that
attempts to speak the truth in love to the broader Christian community. Irenic and yet uncompromising, one can only be grateful for the clarity of his free-church perspective that mines the wealth of doctrine and discipleship in service of the gospel of Jesus Christ. Indeed the reproach that the free church lacks theological depth or an adequate ecclesiology will be silenced. Those who engage Yarnell will discover a formidable interlocutor and one worth wrestling with, yielding blessings rich in both understanding and piety. And as for ecumenical prospects, while surely eschewing a magisterial mantle, Yarnell presents his fellow Christians (and maybe not a few Baptists) with spiritual meat that is as formative as it is instructive. One senses a profound loss in the manifold wisdom of Christ if such a witness were not borne or articulated. While Yarnell trusts the Lord for the former, his readers are in his debt for the latter.

Ralph Del Colle, PhD
Associate Professor of Systematic Theology
Marquette University

If you are a participant in the "Baptist Experiment," Malcolm Yarnell's *The Formation of Christian Doctrine* is the most important book in the past fifty years. More important, this volume is the most significant guide for navigating the confusing waters of the contemporary tempest. If you are not a Baptist but maintain the slightest curiosity about why Baptists have charted a dissenting and exclusive, to say nothing of lonely, path, here is the tome that will not only answer your questions but also precipitate the thoughtful stroking of your academic beard. If I could prevail upon every pastor in Baptist life to read just one book, I would plead that it be this volume.

Paige Patterson, PhD
President
Southwestern Baptist Theological Seminary

Learned in its analysis, theologically and spiritually astute, and deferential to the judgment of the gospel, this study of the foundation and development of Christian doctrine from the perspective of the believers' church will enrich its own tradition and provide much food for thought to others.

John Webster, PhD, DD, FRSE
Professor of Systematic Theology
King's College, University of Aberdeen

The Formation of Christian Doctrine is a masterful introduction to the study of theology and theological method by one of Southern Baptists' most brilliant thinkers. Malcolm Yarnell provides a wide-ranging survey of the various theological traditions and models, enabling his readers to see the issues and challenges in each approach, while developing a thoroughgoing approach to theology consistent with the best of the believers' church tradition. Yarnell rightfully contends that theology must be in conversation with the academy, while calling for Baptist theology to be confessional, unapologetically biblical, and offered in service to the church. This book will not only help advance the work of theology in Baptist life but will impact discussions regarding the self-identity and mission of Baptists in general and Southern Baptists in particular. I heartily commend this volume.

David S. Dockery, PhD
President
Union University

While I would take a somewhat different path than Malcolm Yarnell proposes in this book, I regard it as a major contribution in the emerging scholarly discussion on Baptist identity and Christian theology. Malcolm is a well-trained theologian who digs deeply and reads widely, and I especially appreciate his engagement here with several major non-Baptist theologians. This is the kind of theological scholarship that serves well the Church of Jesus Christ.

Timothy George, PhD
Dean, Beeson Divinity School
Samford University

Books about doctrine are, unfortunately, not very popular with most Christians. However, nothing is more important than developing solid Christian theology in our colleges and seminaries to produce powerful preachers who can refute theological error. We need the same profound teaching in our churches to produce growing Christians who will make disciples among unbelievers. And we need the same doctrines on the mission field to produce healthy converts who will defend the gospel against sects and cults. Recognizing these needs, Malcolm Yarnell addresses the foundation and development of Christian teaching from the perspective of the evangelical free churches. He shows that the confession of the sufficiency of the inerrant Holy Scriptures, the correcting guidance of the Holy Spirit, and dependence upon other illuminated believers are the best prerequisites for engaging in theology and formulating Christian proclamation. This book is both a challenge for theologians and an encouragement for believers who love the Scriptures and the church and know that true Christian doctrines are fundamental for reaching our multiethnic and multicultural society with the gospel of Jesus Christ.

Friedhelm Jung, Dr. theol.
Gründungsrektor des Masterprogramms, und
Dozent für Deutsch, Griechisch und Systematische Theologie
Bibelseminar Bonn e.V., Bornheim, Germany

Malcolm Yarnell is one of the brightest lights of contemporary Baptist theology. This book, an exploration of theological method and the development of doctrine, demonstrates why our churches are grateful to Christ for the gift of Yarnell's mind and heart. Yarnell in this volume seeks to apply the free-church commitments of the right wing of the Anabaptist movement to today's theological discussions. Even (and perhaps especially) those of us who start in a more Reformed or revivalist direction will do well to follow the example of Yarnell's rigorously thoughtful, pastorally applied method to our own patterns of thinking about our triune God and His revelation to us through Jesus.

Russell D. Moore, PhD
Dean, School of Theology, and Senior Vice President for Academic Administration
The Southern Baptist Theological Seminary

Vibrant, urgent, learned, repentant—and above all resolutely loyal to Scripture—this is living theology for a living church. Firmly rooted in the believers' church tradition, this remarkable essay makes a genuinely original contribution to the recent literature on the development of doctrine. By turns quietly persuasive and deliberately provocative, it is a welcome reminder that the first and last word in Christian theology belongs to the Lord: "Follow Me."

Donald Wood, DPhil
Lecturer in Systematic Theology
King's College, University of Aberdeen

An essay in fundamental theology by an erudite and convinced Baptist historian and theologian cannot but be intriguing. Written in a spirit of love for Christ and with clarity of conviction, *The Formation of Christian Doctrine* is enlightening, stimulating, and stirring, an honest and forthright contribution to ecumenical discussion committed to the lordship of Christ.

John Yocum, DPhil
Associate Professor of Theology
Loyola School of Theology, Ateneo de Manila University

THE FORMATION OF CHRISTIAN DOCTRINE

MALCOLM B. YARNELL III

Nashville, Tennessee

978-0-8054-4046-1

Published by B&H Publishing Group
Nashville, Tennessee

Dewey Decimal Classification: 230
Subject Heading: CHRISTIANITY—DOCTRINES

1 2 3 4 5 6 7 8 9 10 11 12 • 15 14 13 12 11 10 09 08 07
VP

CONTENTS

Chapter 3
The Foundation of Doctrine: A Believers' Church Proposal 73

Chapter 4
The Development of Doctrine: Biblical and Historical Considerations 107

PREFACE

THEOLOGY AS FRIENDLY BUT FRANK CONVERSATION

One of the great joys and great problems in the theological enterprise is its necessarily conversational dimension. From a believers' church perspective, this entails conversation and judgment within the local church, conversation and recommendation within one's own tradition, and conversation and proselytism with those outside. Rich benefits may result from such theological conversations, as may misunderstandings. In writing this book on theological method, it has become clearer to me that theology, especially theology that focuses upon first principles, is an enterprise pregnant with possibilities and fraught with dangers. My prayer is that this book will foster frank but fruitful discussions both within and without the free-church tradition and that it will avoid as much as possible the conflicts that inevitably come with explorations of fundamental truth.

In a book defending free-church principles in the last century, a British Baptist by the name of Henry Townsend made two successive statements that indicate the difficult dilemma faced by the irenic theologian exploring fundamental truths. On the one hand, he was clear about the uniqueness of his tradition: "Free Church principles are rooted and grounded in the crisis of New Testament Christianity." The implication is that the principles of other church traditions are, in some significant sense, *not* rooted and grounded in the New Testament. But, on the other hand, immediately afterwards, Townsend made crystal clear that his convictions came from a heart seeking truth with humility. "If I appear to deal harshly with Institutional Religion it will be that I must present the facts which alone explain the existence and witness of the Free Churches: there is no harshness in my mind nor in my heart."[1]

Similarly, although this writer exposes for examination the undercarriages of various theological traditions within Christianity, this exposure is meant more to increase understanding than to cement division. Yet there seems little doubt that such an exposition will result initially in increased tension both between the traditions and among certain sectors within the free-church tradition that tend rather insecurely toward an alien paradigm. It is hoped, however, that the exposition will lead in the second place to a renewed appreciation for the contributions of the free-church theological tradition both within my tradition and among proponents of other traditions. As a free churchman, I am committed to the ontological supremacy of Jesus Christ as epistemologically revealed by the Word of God

[1] Henry Townsend, *The Claims of the Free Churches* (London: Hodder & Stoughton, 1949), 19.

illumined by the Holy Spirit to the free churches. In other words, although I might have written it better, I could not have written this book with any substantive difference, precisely because the foundational and developmental principles delineated herein are what we believe have been established by God through the Bible. Admittedly, the free churches could be wrong and this writer even more so, but it will take the Spirit's illumination of the biblical text to convince otherwise. Until then we invite the reader to join the free churches in catechizing and enacting the truth of Scripture.

THEOLOGICAL PREVIEW

On my desk today are five books that do not figure prominently in the discussion that follows. However, they could just as easily have been included. A review of their contents may prepare the reader for what to expect in the text. First, there is the first book written by Joseph Ratzinger in his role as Benedict XVI, the bishop of Rome. Appropriately, the book concerns the early ministry of Jesus Christ, and the foreword discusses some fundamental principles of New Testament interpretation. As Benedict tackles the problems created by the acids of the modern historical-critical method, he is careful neither to appropriate that method uncritically nor to jettison it entirely. Historical criticism is "an indispensable tool," but one must "recognize the limits" of the method. Benedict's careful appropriation of this method while calling for an appreciation of the "deeper value" of the Bible, understood according to "canonical exegesis" and a "Christological hermeneutic" alongside an affirmation of an early high Christology, is most appreciated.[2]

And yet, in spite of the appreciation that a believers' church biblicist must freely and willingly grant to the current pope, he recognizes an indisputable problem. Benedict argues that the Bible emerged from within the people of God and that it "lives within this same subject." The ecclesial nature of biblical exegesis presented by the pope is indeed worthy of lauds, but the captivity of Scripture to the church is worthy of admonition. The living, active subject in Benedict's paradigm of God, church, and Scripture is the church itself: she is "a collective subject" or "the living subject of Scripture" that is "the deeper 'author' of the Scriptures."[3] Once again, the pope's architectonic ecclesiology has subtly but significantly replaced the Holy Spirit with the church. This subversion is not a mere peccadillo; it represents a longstanding shift in the foundation of Roman theology with the elevation of ecclesiology at the expense of theology.

Second, there is an interesting book written by Maurice Wiles before his death. This giant of theological liberalism relates the stories of his two grandfathers, both of whom were Christian ministers. *Scholarship and Faith: A Tale of Two Grandfathers* is both a well-written piece of historical theology and a heartwarming tale of theological developments. Even into his last days, the clarity,

[2] Joseph Ratzinger (Benedict XVI), *Jesus of Nazareth: From the Baptism in the Jordan to the Transfiguration*, trans. Adrian J. Walker (New York: Bloomsbury, 2007), xi–xxiv.

[3] Ibid., xxi.

conciseness, and compelling nature of this scholarly mind is evident. Interestingly, one of his grandfathers, Joseph Pitts Wiles, was a leading free churchman, a Strict and Particular English Baptist, who challenged the extreme predestination teachings in his denomination. The other grandfather, John Herbert Wilkinson, was an Anglican parish priest who wanted to be a scholar but was waylaid by a debilitating handicap. Both of his grandfathers were scholarly and pious though of relatively different traditions.

While Wiles initially followed the evangelical path blazed by his Anglican grandfather, he took that forefather's scholarship much further than Wilkinson, an irenic defender of biblical truth, would probably have appreciated. The last chapter summarizes the theological development of Wiles himself, showing how he began as an evangelical Christian and moved toward the liberal position he consistently advocated in his productive years. If this free churchman hoped to witness a return to a high view of Scripture and classic understanding of the Godhead by this superb scholar before his death, he was sorely disappointed. Wiles apparently remained to the end of his life skeptical regarding the Bible and optimistic regarding human philosophy. Nevertheless, in spite of this personal spiritual disappointment, I put down the book with an even greater appreciation for Wiles, especially regarding the subtlety of his mind and the humility of his character.[4]

The third book is written by one of my own teachers, an English systematic theologian by the name of John Webster. Webster was Lady Margaret Professor of Divinity at the University of Oxford during my time there but has now moved on to a similar role at the University of Aberdeen, Scotland. Webster is an evangelical theologian in both the classical and modern senses of that adjective. The second volume of his *Essays in Christian Dogmatics* contains an interesting essay entitled "On Evangelical Ecclesiology." Webster wrote this essay after hearing me deliver a paper on ecclesiology in the Theology Seminar at Oxford. While Keith Ward, Regius Professor of Divinity at Oxford, had characteristically decried the exclusivism he (correctly) detected behind my paper, and Richard Cross, a professor of philosophical theology at Oxford, had characteristically merely tolerated a less-than-philosophical piece, John felt compelled to interact. He sent me a copy of his essay, written soon after my paper, seeking comments. A few years later, he published his essay, initially with a new journal, *Ecclesiology*, after presenting it at an evangelical conference in Wheaton, Illinois.[5]

I have belabored this small piece in the historical development of recent theology because where John and I previously considered ourselves as participating in the same theological project, his essay and this book will doubtless open a breach between us. You see, although John's evangelicalism was initially attractive, I have increasingly come to believe that Baptists must distance themselves

---

[4] Maurice Wiles, *Scholarship and Faith: A Tale of Two Grandfathers* (Cambridge: Biograph, 2003). Appreciation is extended to David Wiles, Maurice's son, for making this rare book regarding his family and his father available.

[5] John Webster, "On Evangelical Ecclesiology," *Ecclesiology: The Journal for Ministry, Mission and Unity* 1 (2004): 9–35.

from evangelicalism.[6] John issued a personal call with this good word: "But these things can only happen if evangelicals take the time to reacquaint themselves with the deep exegetical and dogmatic foundations of the traditions to which they belong; and, more important still, they can only happen if evangelicals demonstrate the supreme ecumenical virtue of acknowledging that we also need to change."[7] Following John's sage advice, I explored my tradition's foundations; going beyond his call, I explored my tradition's doctrine of historical development, too. Unfortunately, in spite of John's hope for an ecumenical rapprochement, it seems that a clearer and bolder line than ever must be drawn between our traditions over the doctrine of the church. John's fundamental prioritization of divine election and the invisible church are as equally anathema to this free churchman as Benedict's fundamental prioritization of the Roman magisterium and extrabiblical tradition.

This brings us to the fourth and fifth books on my desk that preview the discussion to come. Walter Klaassen has an illuminating subtitle to his book on Anabaptism: "Neither Catholic nor Protestant." As the subtitle suggests, Klaassen concluded that those free churches affiliated with the sixteenth-century Anabaptists are equally distant from Protestants as from Catholics.[8] Sjouke Voolstra put the matter in equally provocative though opposite terms. Voolstra sees Anabaptists as being "both Catholic and Protestant."[9] Perhaps the truth lies somewhere between the two statements. Anabaptist and other free churches are neither Catholic nor Protestant at the same time that they are both Catholic and Protestant. There are doctrinal issues that separate the free churches as much from the evangelicals as join them with the Catholics, and vice versa. To some free churchmen, such a statement may come as a surprise, for free-church theologians in the United States have begun to measure themselves to a great degree according to evangelicalism, whatever that means.

DEFINING EVANGELICALISM

The reasons for the conflation of American free churches with evangelicalism are historically complex. Suffice it to say that due to the American context and the general malaise of European Christianity, the evangelical churches, in some ways, have moved toward the free churches in their ecclesiology. Similarly, the free churches have moved toward the evangelicals in their theology as a result of their deepening interest in theological discourse and their unexpected influence upon the broader American culture. The old European dividing line of the magisterial churches versus the free churches has been confused by the American disestablishment of all the churches yet cultural hegemony of some free churches; and the

---

[6] Yarnell, "Are Southern Baptists Evangelicals? A Second Decadal Reassessment," *Ecclesiology* 2 (2006): 195–212.

[7] Webster, *Confessing God* (New York: T&T Clark, 2005), 192.

[8] Walter Klaassen, *Anabaptism: Neither Catholic nor Protestant*, 3rd ed. (Kitchener, ON: Pandora, 2001).

[9] Sjouke Voolstra, "Hetzelfde, maar anders," in *De doorwerking van de Moderne Devotie*, ed. C. Graafland, A. Y. Yelsma, and A. G. Weiler (Netherlands: Holdersum, 1988), 119–33; cited in C. Arnold Snyder, *Following in the Footsteps of Christ: The Anabaptist Tradition* (Maryknoll, NY: Orbis, 2004), 27.

old dividing line of theological speculation versus lived piety has been confused by the growing theological sophistication of the free churches and the increasing piety of the evangelical churches.

Further confusing the matter is the fact that evangelicalism that offered ready-at-hand conceptual tools to those free churches, including within the Southern Baptist Convention, who sought to fight their way past the dominance of theological liberalism. Members of modern American evangelical churches and free churches found themselves co-belligerents in defending the inspired text. Indeed, many free churchmen, including the current author, consider themselves more at home with the evangelicals than with free church liberals, especially with regard to the doctrine of Scripture. Yet biblical inspiration and inerrancy do not stand alone as foundational doctrines. This is as true for evangelicals as it is for the free churches.

The definition of *evangelical* used in this book thus deserves some comment. Many American readers understand the term *evangelical* only in its modern sense as those affiliated in some way with the legacies of Billy Graham and Carl Henry, both of whom were simultaneously Baptist and evangelical. The term is, however, much older than the mid-twentieth century. James Leo Garrett Jr. conveniently traces the common beliefs of those who have been known as "evangelicals" since the sixteenth century. Those common beliefs include justification by grace alone, biblical authority, and a simple yet orthodox Christology. Yet Garrett's definition effectively elides the significant separation between the older free churches and the older evangelicals, a matter concerning which his scholarship is otherwise fully aware.[10]

The classic definition of *evangelical* was primarily as a descriptor of the magisterial Reformation churches,[11] while the modern definition of *evangelical* included the successor churches of both the magisterial Reformation churches and the successor churches of the radical Reformation churches. Moreover, the twentieth-century definition of *evangelical* was used to make distinctions within the various traditions and denominations. In the modern era *evangelical* no longer indicated distinct churches but an opposition party to that of the liberals who inhabited the same churches and denominations. The German language actually has two different adjectives to distinguish classical evangelicalism (*evangelische*) from modern evangelicalism (*evangelikale*), the latter especially indicative of an Anglo-American influence.[12] The English language does not offer such a distinction, and the shift in the meaning of "evangelical" from the classic to the modern definitions is significant.

---

[10] James Leo Garrett Jr., "Who Are the 'Evangelicals'?" in *Are Southern Baptists "Evangelicals"?* ed. Garrett, E. Glenn Hinson, and James E. Tull (Macon, GA: Mercer University Press, 1983), 33–63.

[11] Regarding a specifically English historiographical use of the term, see Diarmaid MacCulloch, *Thomas Cranmer: A Life* (New Haven, CT: Yale University Press, 1996), 2.

[12] Friedhelm Jung, *Die deutsche Evangelikale Bewegung: Grundlinien ihrer Geschichte und Theologie*, 3rd ed. (Bonn: Verlag für Kultur und Wissenschaft, 2001); idem, "American Evangelicals in Germany," trans. Siegfried Schatzmann, *Southwestern Journal of Theology* 47 (2004): 13–26.

Unfortunately, there is currently still another shift in the meaning of "evangelical" underway. By the beginning of the twenty-first century, "evangelical" came to mean a fairly broad subset of American Christianity and its use is now co-opted by often disparate groups. Moreover, the detachment of "evangelical" from any discernable ecclesiology means that the word may become essentially useless, a point stridently made by Darryl Hart. Hart opines that "evangelicalism" is little more than a marketing construct demanding a minimalist understanding of the Christian faith.[13] Hart's complaint strikes this author as prescient. In other words, the term has lost the substantive meaning it once possessed. In light of these etymological problems, I have chosen to use *evangelical* primarily in its classical sense as a description of the magisterial Reformation theologians and their theology. Similarly, those who intentionally follow their beliefs are also described as "evangelical." Because the modern sense of *evangelical* is becoming largely meaningless due to its instability, the classic sense must receive renewed priority.

The problem of an endlessly shifting definition of evangelicalism is no doubt exasperated by the weak ecclesiology latently inherent within the magisterial Reformers' speculative conception of the church as invisible. An even more debilitating problem is that many young free-church theologians have begun to move toward classical evangelical theology due to their initial attraction to modern evangelical theology. Indicative of the deeply unstable and destabilizing nature of modern American evangelicalism is the fact that it is increasingly serving the role of a way station for free-church Christians who desire new or renewed submission to Rome or affiliation with the Eastern Orthodox. This has been exemplified by no less than the sitting president of the Evangelical Theological Society and a professor at Baylor University, a traditionally Texas Baptist institution. Frank Beckwith, a deservedly respected scholar and a personal acquaintance of the author, recently converted to Roman Catholicism. Perhaps most shockingly, though not unexpectedly, the conversion of this prominent evangelical raised only minor negative commentary.[14] The future stability of the free churches appears to demand a prudent distancing from the evangelical churches just as from Rome.

ACKNOWLEDGEMENTS

Above all, I wish to thank my theological soulmate, my wife of twenty years, Karen Annette. Although a capable theologian in her own right, she has often delayed her writing and teaching ministry in order to allow me the space to write and teach and preach. She faithfully ministers to the needs of her husband and our five children with a love that is absolutely Christlike. Her self-sacrificial and God-honoring life is that of a free-church heroine. Thank you, my love, for your Christian witness to me and to our children. And thank you, Truett, Matthew, Graham,

[13] D. G. Hart, *Deconstructing Evangelicalism: Conservative Protestantism in the Age of Billy Graham* (Grand Rapids: Baker, 2004).

[14] Gregory Tomlin, "ETS President Resigns, Returns to Catholicism," Baptist Press, May 9, 2007.

Kathryn, and Elizabeth, for bringing me personal joy after painful hours and days with nothing but books. May you grow to love God and His Word more than even your mother and I do. In the following acknowledgments, it should be axiomatic that the subjects may find much in this book with which they will agree as with which they will disagree. Any errors found herein, of course, are mine alone; any lauds, though probably few, of course, must be shared.

Among the living theologians who have been influential in the development of the theological method detailed in this book, I would like to thank Wayne DuBose, my pastor of many years, whose powerful preaching shaped my respect for the proclaiming power of God's Word. Also influential have been my professors of theology, including: James Leo Garrett Jr., the last of the gentleman theologians, who suggested I pursue my interest in ecclesiology; Paige Patterson, a visionary leader, who bequeathed me an unrepentant passion for biblical truth and Baptist origins as well as many a hearty laugh; Geoffrey Wainwright, an Anglo-Methodist theologian at Duke University, who was used both to humble me and teach me; Stanley Hauerwas, who fed a developing passion for the Anabaptists, strangely at the same time as he created an appreciation for Aristotle and Thomas Aquinas; Kenneth Wilson, my first supervisor at Oxford University, a Methodist educator and administrator who taught me in word and deed regarding the need for a thick anthropology; David Kirkpatrick, who taught me eschatology, served as my faculty supervisor, and then allowed me to supervise him; John Webster, mentioned above; and Oliver O'Donovan, an evangelical theologian that few evangelicals may ever properly appreciate.

Among the living professors of history, who have been influential in the development of my historical method, I would like to thank Paul Gritz, who demonstrated that the boring subject of history was inherently exciting; David Steinmetz, Amos Ragan Kearns Professor of the History of Christianity at Duke University, who patiently taught many historical theologians a significant lesson with regard to the distinction between historical theology and theological history; Paul Fiddes, the retiring principal of Regent's Park College and Professor of Systematic Theology at Oxford University, who is primarily a systematic theologian but has a keen understanding of historic Baptist theology; Judith Maltby, my second supervisor and a reader at Corpus Christi College in Oxford, a conformist who read carefully the musings of an uncompromising nonconformist regarding the English Reformation and always offered helpful commentary; Diarmaid MacCulloch, Professor of Reformation History at Oxford University, whose considerable talents and accomplishments yet personal interest both inspired and intimidated; and, Rowan Williams, the Archbishop of Canterbury, who kindly read my doctoral dissertation on historical theology and exemplified how theology most certainly may follow history.

Among my colleagues in theology, I would like to thank the following professors at Southwestern Baptist Theological Seminary, who have in various ways proved that theological iron sharpens theological iron, all of whom have an enduring interest in either theological or historical method and some of whom read portions of this book: Gerardo Alfaro, Craig Blaising, Robert Caldwell, Emir Caner, Keith Eitel, Kevin Kennedy, Jason Lee, Thomas White, and John Mark Yeats. Colleagues at other institutions who have been influential upon me with regard to theological method and denominational distinctives include Russ Moore and Steve Lemke, staunch advocates of Baptist principles who, respectively, lead the academic programs at Southern Seminary and New Orleans Seminary; Don Wood, an expert on Karl Barth and fellow Oxonian, now at Aberdeen University; Dan Keating and John Yocum, fellow Oxonians and faithful sons of the Roman church; Ralph Del Colle, a systematic theologian extraordinaire at Marquette University and conversation partner in an ongoing Evangelical-Catholic conversation; Bart Barber, an adjunct professor at Southwestern Seminary and pastor in Farmersville, Texas; and, Mark Forrest, a long-time friend and pastor in Plano, Texas.

Special thanks are extended to Madison Grace, my administrative assistant at Southwestern Seminary, a multitalented gift of God, including being a reflective sounding board for all things biblical and theological; John Landers, a tireless editor and free-church historian, who graciously stepped out of retirement to complete this project; Robert Dena, a police officer and fellow member at Birchman Baptist Church, who was always interested in my book even if he feigned ignorance regarding its contents; all those Baptist bloggers, the populist theologians of the rising generation, who alternately impress and boggle; the trustees of Southwestern Seminary, who granted me a sabbatical for the purpose of writing; and especially, my graduate students at Southwestern Seminary and the Bibelseminar Bonn, who regularly and without complaint grant me the privilege of exploring with them the fascinating intricacies of systematic theology and historical theology in light of the authoritative and life-giving pronouncements of the Word of God.

It would be remiss in a book on doctrinal formation from a free-church perspective not to mention the particular free churches that regularly display much of what is described in the following pages. I hope this book reflects well upon those communities, for it is in them that I was born again and learned to follow the Christ who died, arose, and will come again. Among these churches are Barksdale and Summer Grove and Lakeview in northwest Louisiana, Western Hills and Birchman in east Texas, and Tabbs Creek in North Carolina. God has used you as instruments to bring me rebirth and to help me walk with integrity in His ways. May all free church theologians and historians never forget the truth you teach: that theology includes the cerebral but that it is merely the reflective dimension of humans upon a greater personal, dynamic relationship with God enabled through His living and active Word glorified by the Holy Spirit in the midst of the congregation.

ABBREVIATIONS

ACW	Ancient Christian Writers
AHR	*American Historical Review*
ANF	*Ante-Nicene Fathers*. Edited by Alexander Roberts and James Donaldson. 10 vols. New York, 1885–1897
AR	*Archiv für Reformationsgeschichte*
BBC	Broadman Bible Commentary
BDCT	Patrick W. Carey and Joseph T. Lienhard, eds. *Biographical Dictionary of Christian Theologians*. Peabody, MA, 2000.
BDE	Timothy Larson, ed. *Biographical Dictionary of Evangelicals*. Downers Grove, IL, 2003
BJRL	*Bulletin of the John Rylands Library*
CC	Philip Schaff and David S. Schaff, eds. *The Creeds of Christendom: With a Preface and Critical Notes*. 6th ed. 3 vols. 1931, repr. Grand Rapids, 1993
CD	*Church History*
CGR	*Conrad Grebel Review*
CR	*Christian Renewal*
CSCD	Cambridge Studies in Christian Doctrine
CTJ	*Calvin Theological Journal*
CTR	*Criswell Theological Review*
DEC	Norman P. Tanner, ed. *Decrees of the Ecumenical Councils*. Washington, 1990
ESB	Clifton J. Allen, ed. *Encyclopedia of Southern Baptists*. 4 vols. Nashville, 1958–82
FC	The Fathers of the Church: A New Translation
FM	*Faith & Mission*
FT	*First Things*
GH	*German History*
HER	*English Historical Review*
HJ	*Historical Journal*
HTR	*The Harvard Theological Review*
HUG	*Harvard University Gazette*
IJST	*International Journal of Systematic Theology*
JAAR	*Journal of the American Academy of Religion*
JBL	*Journal of Biblical Literature*

JBR	*Journal of Bible and Religion*
JBTM	*Journal of Baptist Theology and Mission*
JEH	*Journal of Ecclesiastical History*
JETS	*Journal of the Evangelical Theological Society*
JHI	*Journal of the History of Ideas*
JR	*Journal of Religion*
JTS	*Journal of Theological Studies*
KD	*Kerygma und Dogma*
LCC	Library of Christian Classics
LW	Harold J. Grimm, ed. *Luther's Works*. 52 vols. Philadelphia, 1957
MidJT	*Midwestern Journal of Theology*
MQR	*Mennonite Quarterly Review*
NBR	*The North British Review*
NEQ	*The New England Quarterly*
NICNT	New International Commentary on the New Testament
NPNF[1]	*Nicene and Post-Nicene Fathers, Series 1*. Edited by Philip Schaff and David Schaff. 14 vols. New York, 1886–1890
NPNF[2]	*Nicene and Post-Nicene Fathers, Series 2*. Edited by Philip Schaff and David Schaff. 14 vols. New York, 1890–1900
ODNB	*Oxford Dictionary of National Biography*
PNTC	Pillar New Testament Commentary
PRS	*Perspectives in Religious Studies*
RevExp	*Review and Expositor*
RP	*Review of Politics*
RS	*Religious Studies*
RSR	*Religious Studies Review*
SBHT	Studies in Baptist History and Thought
SCES	*Sixteenth Century Essays and Studies*
SCJ	*Sixteenth Century Journal*
SWJT	*Southwestern Journal of Theology*
TDNT	*Theological Dictionary of the New Testament*. Edited by G. Kittel and G. Friedrich. Translated by G. W. Bromiley. 10 vols. Grand Rapids, 1964–1976
TM	*Theology for Ministry*
TNTC	Tyndale New Testament Commentaries
TS	*Theological Studies*
TT	*Theology Today*
VC	*Vigiliae Christianae*
WBC	Word Biblical Commentary
WTJ	*Westminster Theological Journal*
WW	*Word & World*
ZNE	*Zeitschrift für die Neutestamentliche Wissenschaft und die Kunde der Ältenkirche*

Chapter One

THEOLOGICAL METHOD AS DISCIPLINED RESPONSE TO DIVINE REVELATION

What is this book, and what makes it different enough to be considered by the theologian whose shelves are already filled with good books? It is a preliminary exercise in theological method, perhaps some would say a theological prolegomena, except that it is adamantly yielded to Jesus Christ as revealed in the Bible by His Spirit to the church, exhibiting suspicion toward the philosophical underpinnings affiliated with traditional prolegomena. This book seeks to understand how the formation of true Christian doctrine develops from a proper theological foundation. It therefore deals with two large structural aspects of theological method: the foundation of doctrine and the development of doctrine, or, respectively, the static and dynamic dimensions of theology.

This book is different in at least three ways. First, it is an admittedly unusual attempt by a Southern Baptist theologian to set forth a Christian theological method, a consideration of the foundations for the proper development of doctrine, specifically from a believers' church perspective. Baptist theologians have not generally engaged in prolegomena or fundamental theology, and those who have done so tend to follow the approaches of other traditions, including Reformed scholasticism,[1] the liberal academy,[2] or Lutheran philosophical theology.[3] The closest forerunner is perhaps the extremely short prolegomena of John Leadley Dagg, the first Southern Baptist systematic theologian, a nineteenth-century defender of slavery who offered a primarily biblical theology even if according to a rudimentary Reformed paradigm.[4]

---

[1] J. P. Boyce, a student of the Princeton theologian Charles Hodge, prefaces his systematic theology with a discussion of theology as a "science" concerned with "the investigation of facts," uncritically summarizing and applying Hodge's Reformed foundations to a Southern Baptist context. James Petigru Boyce, *Abstract of Systematic Theology* (1887; repr., Hanford, CA: Den Dulk, [n.d.]), 3–4. Charles Hodge, *Systematic Theology*, (1872; repr., Peabody, MA: Hendrickson, 2001), 1:1–17.

[2] E. Y. Mullins offers an extensive prolegomena that treats religious experience and Scripture as correlative sources of theological truth. Edgar Young Mullins, *The Christian Religion in Its Doctrinal Expression* (Philadelphia: Judson, 1917), 1–136. I have discussed elsewhere Mullins's liberal theological method, which evinces dependence upon Friedrich Schleiermacher. Yarnell, "Changing Baptist Concepts of Royal Priesthood: John Smyth and Edgar Young Mullins," in *The Rise of the Laity in Evangelical Protestantism*, ed. Deryck Lovegrove (London: Routledge, 2002), 236–52.

[3] Millard Erickson, a student of Wolfhart Pannenberg, interacts with modern philosophical trends in his prolegomena and indeed throughout his popular systematic theology. Millard J. Erickson, *Christian Theology*, 2nd ed. (Grand Rapids: Baker, 1998), pt. 1. Wolfhart Pannenberg, *Systematic Theology*, trans. Geoffrey W. Bromiley (Grand Rapids: Eerdmans, 1991), 1:1–61.

[4] Dagg begins his systematic theology with an exhortation to Bible study for the heart, then proceeds to a detailed consideration of the inspiration, transmission, and authority of Scripture. John Leadley Dagg, *A Manual*

While "prolegomena" often appears as a subsection in the broader discipline of systematic theology in the English-speaking world, the continental European academy has come to treat *Fundamentaltheologie* (foundational theology) as a separate discipline with a larger task. This movement, beginning in Prague in 1856, first became a self-standing discipline in Roman Catholic theological faculties. In spite of initial misgivings, it has subsequently become a concern for Protestants too. Gerhard Ebeling, Wolfhart Pannenberg, and Wilfried Joest made pioneering efforts in the 1970s, and the discipline is now a fruitful field for evangelical theologians. Recognizing that the Catholic penchant for a theology of nature and grace shaped by church authority must be distinguished from the Protestant regard for sin and faith shaped by revelation, Michael Roth shows how the field of foundational theology is already being treated in evangelical circles. He also proposed three tasks for an evangelical foundational theology: the traditional theological *principia*, apologetics, and encyclopedia. Because it considers the circumstances by which faith is constituted, foundational theology may serve as an integrative science among the fissiparous theological disciplines.[5]

Second, this book is a somewhat unusual prolegomena in that it takes seriously the historical shape of dogma.[6] Christian theologians share the bodily limitations of other Christians on this planet who have received only glimpses of glory. Theologians must humbly admit that any discussion of eternal truth depends upon the grace of revelation, wherein eternity has manifested itself in a specific way and for specific purposes at specific times to those who are historically framed. This grace of revelation occurred supremely in the incarnation, life, death, and resurrection of Jesus Christ. Because our access to God's goodness occurs within a historical construct that inculcates a way of thinking and living, church doctrine must be considered historically. Correct doctrine, moreover, arises while interpreting Scripture, and if we believe that the Spirit works in all Christians, then we should listen to Christians throughout history when formulating doctrine. According to the dictum of Ebeling, "Church history is the history of the exposition of Scripture."[7] It is a peculiarly modernist hubris, a conceit rooted in its mythology of progress, to consider the contributions of modern scholars to the theological conversation superior, whether as exegetes or as philosophers, to those of another period.

Finally, this book is unusual in that, while it seeks to engage the rigorous standards of academic scholarship, it is unabashedly committed to personal submission to Jesus as Lord as foundational for theology; indeed, for all of reality.

of Theology (1857; reprint, Harrisonburg, VA: Gano, 1990), 22–42.

[5] M. Petzoldt remarked, "Fundamentaltheologie—das ist doch eine Domäne katholischer Theologie! Gehört so etwas an eine Fakultät für evangelische Theologie?" (ET: "Foundational theology—that is rather a domain of Catholic theology! Does such a thing belong to an evangelical theological faculty?") Petzoldt, "Zur Frage nach der Konfessionalität der Fundamentaltheologie (1993)," in *Christsein Angefragt: Fundamentaltheologische Beiträge* (Leipzig, 1998), cited in Michael Roth, "Die Bedeutung der Fundamentaltheologie für die Evangelische Theologie," *KD* 48 (2002): 99–117.

[6] Cp. James Orr, *The Progress of Dogma* (Grand Rapids: Eerdmans, 1952).

[7] Gerhard Ebeling, *The Word of God and Tradition: Historical Studies Interpreting the Divisions of Christianity*, trans. S. H. Hooke (London: Collins, 1968), 11.

It couples the sense of "foundations" as used by Karl Rahner for an introduction to critical thinking about the faith,[8] with the sense of "foundation" used by Martin Honecker that Christian theology must be based on Christian faith. "Theology refers to faith. It lays out faith." Faith is the "precondition" of Christian theology.[9] From this basis we attempt an academic work for the church and an ecclesial work for the academy. Unfortunately these two institutions often view each other with suspicion, rather than dwelling upon what should be a common goal. This book seeks to bridge the divide between church and academy by proposing a truly ecclesial foundation for the work of the theological academy. It is therefore intended to prepare those who wish to lead others to see the intricately wondrous beauty of God who should be worshipped in both houses (though in necessarily different ways) to think critically in a theological manner about their faith. Because of this conviction, the book requires a forthright presentation of the shared faith of the author and his particular ecclesial community.

Reflecting the witness of the prologue to John's first epistle (1 John 1:1–2:2), it is hoped this book will bring glory to God by bearing witness to His truth, goodness, and beauty. If truth ultimately represents the eternal being of God, the source (*archas*) of all that is; and goodness, the righteous activity of God that grants us propitiation (*hilasmos*) through the blood of His Son; then beauty may be said to represent the light (*phos*) that engulfs the fellowship (*koinonia*) of man in the Spirit with the Father and the Son. As truth became flesh in Jesus Christ, His goodness becomes ours by confession and results in a sanctified life, and beauty is experienced as the fullness of joy (*chara*) that is nothing less than the final and blessed vision of God. This is the witness of Scripture and the desire of this theologian. Thus, this book seeks, by turns, to be theologically descriptive, prophetically prescriptive, and doxologically expressive, though it focuses primarily on the first task.

Truth, goodness, and beauty, from a personal and communal theological perspective: this was also Augustine's approach as seen, for instance, in his influential *Confessions*. The leading theologian of Western Christianity could not separate his science, his system of knowledge, from his personal commitment to God. The formal separation of faith and science is certainly a most peculiar and deceptive modern fiction. Truth and personal commitment cannot be separated, for the lack of personal commitment to truth is simply another way of preparing to tell a lie. Truth, ultimately a reference to the being of the One who is yet Three; goodness, the righteousness of the Son that becomes ours by faith and expresses its faith in responsible act; and, beauty, the Spirit-given experience of holistic harmony and proportion: these are integral to the Christian theological project. "For 'truth is what you have loved' and 'whoever enacts truth comes to the light.' I want to en-

[8] Karl Rahner, *Foundations of Christian Faith: An Introduction to the Idea of Christianity*, trans. William V. Dych (New York Crossroad, 1985), 1–13.

[9] "Theologie bezieht sich auf Glauben. Sie legt Glauben aus." Martin Honecker, *Glaube als Grund Christlicher Theologie* (Stuttgart: Kohlhammer, 2005), 80.

act the truth—before you, by my testimony; and by my writing, before those who bear witness to this testimony."[10]

The theological method offered here seeks to be faithful, as indicated, to a Christian foundation of discipleship that honors the highest authority of Scripture. Recognizing the phenomenon of the development of doctrine, its structure is also historical, engaging with events and theologians in the broader Christian conversation regarding the witness of Scripture. This historico-theological method is necessary, for Scripture is never interpreted in a vacuum. Jesus promised the apostles that the Spirit would guide them into the truth (John 14:26; 16:23). It is taken as a matter of faith that the Spirit who led the apostles and prophets to record the truth revealed to them also guided the church to respond by recognizing the authority of those writings. The church's recognition of the authority of God's Word written is evident in the existence of the biblical canon. It is also taken as a matter of faith that the Spirit has not forsaken the church but continues to lead her into the truth through illuminating the canonical text He originally inspired and subsequently gathered. Individual Christians encounter the truth that we call theology in the fold of the church as they read the Bible. The Spirit who witnesses to the church in the text lays upon her the responsibility to be a witness of its theology to the world (John 15:26–27).

A brief apology for fundamental theology may be required in light of recent claims for the superiority of a nonfoundational theology, even by theologians within the believers' church tradition.[11] Among postmodern theologians, there has been a vehement rejection of the idea of theological foundations. Fortunately nonfoundationalism or postfoundationalism is, within the guild of systematic theology, now largely an isolated phenomenon.[12] It is unfortunate, however, that postmodern philosophy, from which nonfoundationalism borrows, has permeated Western culture and thus popular Christianity. The cry that every interpretation of Scripture is equally valid is indicative of the existence of nonfoundationalism in popular theological circles.[13] "Postmodernism is a type of thinking that rebels

[10] Augustine of Hippo *Confessions* 10.1.1 (trans. Garry Wills [New York: Penguin, 2002], 211).

[11] For a preliminary discussion of free-church contributions to nonfoundationalism, see chapter 2.

[12] The movement has received only passing consideration among international systematic theologians, as evidenced in the *IJST* for the last five years. There is the odd book review devoted to the subject, but the articles and book reviews overwhelmingly concern the foundational subjects of Scripture, tradition, and philosophy. Grenz's postmodern theological method deals with the foundations of Scripture and tradition even while it emphasizes culture. Mark S. Medley, review of Stanley J. Grenz and John R. Franke, *Beyond Foundationalism: Shaping Theology in a Postmodern Context* (Louisville, KY: Westminster John Knox, 2000), in *IJST* 4 (2002): 83–90.

[13] Perhaps the most vibrant form of popular theology may be found among Internet bloggers. Take this example of postmodern theology, which, although claiming a scriptural foundation, seems to allow for an endless variety of legitimate interpretations: "There are at least two interpretations on the gifts (cessationists and continualists), there are at least two interpretations on soteriology (Calvinism and Arminianism and everything in between), there are at least two interpretations on ecclesiological government (congregational and elder rule), there are at least two interpretations on separation of church and state, there are at least two interpretations on the authority and credentials of the baptizer, there are at least two interpretations on the consequences of Adam's sin, etc. . . . I could go on, and on, and on. . . . We must be very careful that we don't get to the point where a disagreement over the interpretation of the doctrines contained in the sacred text separate and exclude one group or the other." Wade Burleson, "The Inspired, Inerrant, Infallible Bible Is Sufficient for Me (Part II)." See http://kerussocharis.blogspot.com; accessed 26 October 2006.

against any totalizing understanding of reality, against any 'grand metanarrative.' It is opposed to universalization, rationalization, systematization, and the establishment of consistent criteria for the evaluation of truth-claims." Unfortunately these attitudes fail to adequately account for the description of the faith in Scripture as a living deposit. By rejecting ultimate truth claims, postmodern nonfoundationalism makes Christianity ultimately unintelligible.[14] In the project at hand, discerning a proper means of formulating Christian doctrine, nonfoundationalism lacks a relevant basis.

A theological foundation provides the forms upon which Christians develop their understandings of God, creation, and redemption. It is evident that within Christian discourse, the issues of theological foundation and doctrinal development are intimately related. Doctrines develop from somewhere and, even when radically altered, still reflect an origin in addition to a trajectory. Conceptually we may distinguish the foundation from the development, but in an organic system, a metaphor that certainly characterizes the church (often imaged in the New Testament as a "body"),[15] continuity between a basis and its growth is required. Separating a living entity from its origin brings only death; a living faith cannot be divided into pieces for examination like a laboratory animal, or separated like bricks from a broken building. However, in approaching a doctrine of development, it is necessary to begin with a theological foundation.

Although the current author engages willingly and desirously in the broader Christian conversation, as will be seen shortly, he approaches such conversation from a specific community, a church within the Southern Baptist Convention, which holds zealously to the Word of God as the highest authority for all true doctrine. Before discussing the Southern Baptist theological authority of the Word of God, this particular vibrant tradition is placed within the broader category of the believers' churches, which share a distinct view of theological foundation and doctrinal development.

THE THEOLOGICAL METHOD OF THE BELIEVERS' CHURCHES

The theological method of the believers' churches may be described in a number of ways. What is perhaps most striking, in comparison with the alternatives outlined in the next chapter, is that method develops character as much as it develops doctrine. While indebted to the theological contributions of the early fathers and the Protestant Reformers, the believers' churches transcend them by demanding radical yieldedness and discipleship to Jesus Christ, often by reserving baptism for true believers. The theological method of the believers' churches is characterized by degrees of Christocentrism, biblicism, pneumatic hermeneutics, and congregationalism.

---

[14] Thomas G. Guarino, *Foundations of Systematic Theology* (London: T&T Clark, 2005), 6, 19.

[15] Paul S. Minear, *Images of the Church in the New Testament* (Philadelphia: Westminster, 1960), 173–220; Avery Dulles, *Models of the Church*, expanded ed. (New York: Doubleday, 1987), 50–56.

Competing Historiographies

It is not unusual to have historiographical debates in Christian circles regarding historical identity, especially with regard to the Reformation period, since it witnessed the fracturing of Western Christianity into various identities. For example, the English Reformation guild experienced a seismic upheaval as a result of criticisms of the supposedly "Whig" interpretation of A. G. Dickens.[16] Again, Anabaptist scholars have moved from a monogenetic theory of origins to a polygenetic theory, and now there are calls to move beyond that.[17] Similarly modern Southern Baptists have been embroiled in a decades-long battle over the identity of the Baptist movement. On the one side is the liberal appeal to the novel concepts of "soul competency" and "the priesthood of the believer." E. Y. Mullins popularized these doctrines at the beginning of the twentieth century. To be a Baptist, according to the liberal myth, involves the vigorous defense of one's personal rights against the encroachment of biblicism, creedalism, and ecclesiasticism. This understanding dominated the official Southern Baptist seminaries for most of the twentieth century and is still popular in the pulpit and in the pew.[18]

Pitted against the liberal myth is the conservative appeal to Scripture as the inspired, authoritative, and inerrant Word of God. A number of theologians have sought to counter the liberal myth with a conservative historiography built on Baptists' exemplary and simple submission to God's Word. They note that historical Baptists reach back beyond Enlightenment liberalism's effects upon Baptist theology to strong theological moorings in the Protestant Reformation.[19] In the debate over authority, the Baptist historiography of freedom has been pitted against the Baptist historiography of biblicism.

Unfortunately neither historiography is entirely satisfactory, for the strongest biblicists are adamant about their liberty, and the staunchest libertarians still claim Scripture is authoritative. The difference is often a matter of contrasting emphases more than a matter of outright denial. Moreover, alternative historiographies, taking the argument beyond issues of authority, are now beginning to make appeals for the Baptist heart with regard to soteriology and ecclesiology. A revived Calvinism among Baptist theologians and in some churches, which makes up for its small numbers through strident advocacy, has come into periodic conflict with a larger number of pastors and some theologians who are traditionally non-Reformed in soteriology and warmly evangelistic in activity. Moreover, some proponents of

[16] A. G. Dickens, "The Early Expansion of Protestantism in England 1520–1558," *Archiv für Reformationsgeschichte* 78 (1987): 187–221; idem, "The Shape of Anti-clericalism and the English Reformation," in *Politics and Society in Reformation Europe: Essays for Geoffrey Elton on His Sixty-fifth Birthday*, ed. E. I. Kouri and Tom Scott (London: Macmillan, 1987), 379–410; Christopher Haigh, "Anticlericalism and the English Reformation," *History* 68 (1983): 391–407; idem, "Revisionism, the Reformation and the History of English Catholicism," *JEH* 36 (1985): 394–405; idem, "The Recent Historiography of the English Reformation," *HJ* 25 (1982): 995–1007.

[17] There are now calls for movement beyond that polarization. Gerald Biesecker-Mast, "The Persistence of Anabaptism as Vision," *MQR* 81 (2007): 21–42.

[18] *Being Baptist Means Freedom*, ed. Alan Neely (Charlotte, NC: Southern Baptist Alliance, 1988); Walter B. Shurden, *The Baptist Identity: Four Fragile Freedoms* (Macon, GA: Smyth & Helwys, 1993).

[19] R. Stanton Norman, *More Than Just a Name: Preserving Our Baptist Identity* (Nashville: B&H, 2001).

seeker-sensitive churches, novel missiologies, and the emergent movement, in their desire for cultural relevancy, have darkly labeled their opponents, who promote a traditional understanding of the church, as "Landmarkists."

In light of these competing voices, where is the proper historiography? Is there a historiography that is true to the historical evidence and incorporates the variety of competing historical ideologies vying for dominance among Baptists? In other words, is there a comprehensive historiography for all Baptists? This chapter assumes that such a historiography may be found in a broader heritage cognizant of Baptist polygenesis. In other words, wherever earnest Christians have returned to God's Word and prayed for the Spirit's guidance in reading and applying it, there have appeared congregations that have Baptist characteristics. Sometimes grouped with the "Radical Reformation"[20] or "Free Churches"[21] or "Believers' Churches"[22] or "Dissenters,"[23] Anabaptists and Baptists take seriously the divine call to discipleship, beginning with the covenantal identification of water baptism for believers only.

Although the historical link between seventeenth-century English Baptists and the sixteenth-century Continental Anabaptists is largely, though not entirely, circumstantial, there is strong evidence of a theological coinherence. For instance, there was extensive communication between the two groups.[24] These communications, both written and oral, occurred between Dutch Mennonites and both branches of the English Baptists: the Waterlander Mennonites with the English General Baptists, and the Rhynsburger Mennonites with the English Particular Baptists. Taking these Mennonite-Baptist interactions into account, in addition to various English Baptist interactions, it recently has been argued that the traditional historiographical divisions between the General and Particular branches of the English Baptists require significant revision, especially with regard to the early seventeenth century.[25]

John Smyth, the pastor of the first General Baptist congregation, which he baptized while they were exiled in Amsterdam, later led a large part of his congregation to seek membership with a Waterlander Anabaptist church.[26] The smaller part of his congregation, led by Thomas Helwys, returned to England to start a vibrant if beleaguered community of churches based in London beginning near Spitalfields Market. The General Baptists were not alone in their communication

[20] George H. Williams, *The Radical Reformation*, 3rd ed. (Kirksville, MO: Sixteenth Century Journal Publishers, 1992).

[21] Winthrop S. Hudson, "Define Your Terms," *Foundations* 4 (1961): 99–101.

[22] Donald F. Durnbaugh, *The Believers' Church: The History and Character of Radical Protestantism* (Scottdale, PA: Herald, 1968).

[23] Michael R. Watts, *The Dissenters* (Oxford: Oxford University Press, 1978–1995).

[24] The lack of evidence might be accounted for by the harsh persecution of the Anabaptists, both on the Continent and in England. The frightening specter of the revolutionary Anabaptists of Münster hung over both the English Baptists and the Continental Anabaptists for centuries and was most acutely felt in the sixteenth and seventeenth centuries.

[25] Stephen Wright, *The Early English Baptists, 1603–1649* (Rochester, NY: Boydell, 2006).

[26] James R. Coggins, *John Smyth's Congregation: English Separatism, Mennonite Influence, and the Elect Nation* (Scottdale, PA: Herald, 1991); Jason K. Lee, *The Theology of John Smyth: Puritan, Separatist, Baptist, Mennonite* (Macon, GA: Mercer University Press, 2003).

with the Mennonites. The Particular Baptist who led in recovering believers' baptism by immersion, Richard Blunt, did so while communicating through letters and visitation with the Rhynsburger Anabaptists. Some earlier Baptist historians assumed Blunt had actually been baptized by the Rhynsburger Anabaptists.[27]

Thomas Helwys could not in good conscience join with the Waterlander Mennonites because he rejected their pacifism and their doctrine of the incarnation. He also rejected Smyth's desire for an ecclesial succession to reclaim properly the New Testament practice of believers-only baptism. Nevertheless, manifesting a general commonality in belief and practice, the English General Baptists maintained communication with the Waterlander Mennonites for years.[28] Although Helwys rejected membership with the Mennonites for some important reasons,[29] he seemed perfectly happy with other central doctrines that Baptists and Mennonites still share. Helwys did not reject membership with the Waterlander Mennonites because of their demand for radical yieldedness and discipleship to Jesus Christ. Helwys did not reject membership with the Waterlander Mennonites because they saw baptism as only for true believers. Like the Anabaptists, Helwys and the earliest Baptists were simply Christocentric, biblicist, Spirit led, egalitarian, and congregational. Indicating theological dependence upon the Anabaptists, Helwys praised them "because you haue been instrumets of good in discovering divers of our erors unto us, which we acknowledg to the praise of God, & with thank full harts to you."[30]

Alongside the scattered evidence regarding historical dependence of the early English Baptists upon the Mennonites, strong evidence of common doctrines remains, especially with regard to ecclesiology. Like their Continental forerunners, the English Baptists were driven to their unique positions by an overarching desire to fully obey Jesus Christ. Characteristic of their common ecclesiology, Continental Anabaptist and English Baptist alike, is the concern to follow the "rule of Christ." This led them to emphasize the correct practice of the ordinances of baptism and the Lord's Supper and the necessity of redemptive church discipline.[31] And yet these three commonalities seem to concern practical theology rather than fundamental

[27] Barry R. White, *The English Baptists of the Seventeenth Century*, rev. ed. (Didcot, Oxfordshire: Baptist Historical Society, 1996), 60–61.

[28] Ibid., 23–24.

[29] The lengthy subtitle of Helwys's treatise on the need for maintaining separation clearly indicates his reasoning. "1. That Christ tooke his Flesh of Marie, having a true earthly, naturall bodie, 2. That a Sabbath or day of rest, is to be kept holy everie First day of the weeke. 3. That ther is no Succession; nor privilege to persons in holie thinges. 4. That Magistracie, being an holy ordinance of God, debarreth not anie from being of the Church of Christ." A final section discusses Helwys's rejection of the predestinarian theology of Dutch Calvinism. Thomas Helwys, *An Advertisement or admonition, unto the Congregations, which men call the New Fryelers, in the lowe Countries, written in Dutche, And Publiched in Englis* (Amsterdam, 1611), unpaginated.

[30] "To Hans de Ries, Reynier Wybrantson, and the Congregations whereof they are," in ibid., unpaginated.

[31] Compare the radically biblical and Christ-centered ecclesiology shared by the earliest associational confessions of the Anabaptists, the Particular Baptists, and the General Baptists. The Schleitheim Confession (1527), arts. 1–3; First London Confession (1644), arts. 33–47; The Faith and Practice of the Thirty Congregations (1651), arts. 46–56. These confessions are available in the widely used *Baptist Confessions of Faith*, ed. William L. Lumpkin rev. ed. (Valley Forge, PA: Judson, 1969), 25, 165–69, 182–84. A critical edition of Baptist confessions is needed.

theology in its entirety. Though important, there was something deeper than mere confluence with regard to the ordinances of Christ that drove the Baptists and the Anabaptists to their similarly radical ecclesiologies.

Theologians and historians have sought to identify the basis of Baptist distinctiveness in a number of places. Each of these efforts points to some significant truth within Baptist life, and yet most are inadequate to explain anything beyond a certain segment of Baptist life and history.

First, B. R. White pointed to the separatist ecclesiology of the early English Baptists as seminal. White proved his point historically with regard to the seventeenth century, yet separatist ecclesiology on its own does not account for the evangelistic passion that arose among the Particular Baptists in the late eighteenth century or the individualistic freedom-orientation among many Baptists in the nineteenth and twentieth centuries.[32]

Second, Calvinistic Baptist historians often point to a common Baptist concern for divine sovereignty, both in England and in America, especially during the eighteenth and nineteenth centuries. This phenomenon is, to be sure, evident, and Baptist theology cannot be understood without reference to a strong tradition of Reformed theology within the Baptist fold.[33] However, the reference to Calvinism, on its own, is grossly simplistic. The Anabaptist and later Baptist movements share a common trajectory away from ecclesial fellowship with the Reformed churches. For similar reasons the Anabaptists came out of the Reformed church of Zürich, and the Baptists came out of the Reformed church of England. The current effort to "reform" Baptist churches along the lines of the Presbyterian's Westminster tradition should be seen as peculiar to a marginal sector of Baptist life and somewhat anachronistic.[34]

Third, others have pointed to the strong missionary and evangelistic tradition among Baptists that began in the eighteenth century. William Carey and Andrew Fuller have become icons among missionary Baptists due to their rejection of hyper-Calvinism and their fostering of the modern missions movement. Carey rejected the common Calvinist supposition that the Great Commission was limited to the apostles.[35] Yet the emphasis on missions and evangelism is too often more a matter of practice than of principle. Missions and evangelism are phenomenal evidence of a deeper theology at work.

[32] B. R. White, *The English Separatist Tradition: From the Marian Martyrs to the Pilgrim Fathers* (Oxford: Oxford University Press, 1971); Yarnell, "Changing Baptist Concepts of Royal Priesthood."

[33] Thomas J. Nettles, *By His Grace and for His Glory: A Historical, Theological, and Practical Study of the Doctrines of Grace in Baptist Life* (Grand Rapids: Baker, 1986).

[34] Nettles seeks to reform Southern Baptist life along the lines of the Second London Confession (1689), a fact hidden by his reticence to properly cite that particular confession. The Second London Confession is a successor of the Independents' Savoy Declaration (1658) and ultimately the Presbyterians' Westminster Confession (1646). Rejecting this strict Calvinistic tradition, Southern Baptists opted to revise the less Calvinistic New Hampshire Confession (1833) when constructing their own Baptist Faith and Message (1925, 1963, 2000). Nettles, *Ready for Reformation? Bringing Authentic Reform to Southern Baptist Churches* (Nashville: B&H, 2005), 6.

[35] William Carey, *An Enquiry into the Obligations of Christians, to Use Means for the Conversion of the Heathens* (London, 1792).

Fourth, as mentioned above, liberal Baptists have pointed to the longstanding emphasis upon religious liberty in Baptist life. These appeals to the Baptist penchant for liberty are historically viable but often misapplied as a result of shifting ideas being attached to the same word. Religious liberty as a principle for relating to the state is absolutely necessary; the principle of religious freedom has a long pedigree in the free churches. But freedom in the modern sense has been disjoined from its positive scriptural and historic religious meaning. American ideas of liberty and freedom, ranging from the Southerner's claim of liberty to hold slaves to Hollywood's concept of freedom as sensual gratification, have competed for the American heart.[36] After the Enlightenment, the Baptist understanding of religious freedom shifted from a positive liberty for churches to worship Christ and became a negative freedom for individuals fleeing every authority.[37] Unrestrained libertarianism is a woefully inadequate basis for the construction of a church or of a theology for the church. A stable theological foundation requires a positive rather than a negative basis, and a stable theology for a church requires a communal rather than an individualist basis.

Fifth, more recently, conservative Southern Baptists have resurrected their denomination's traditional respect for Scripture as the Word of God. Beginning in the 1960s and reaching a critical point in 1979, upon the election of Adrian Rogers as president of the Southern Baptist Convention (SBC) with a mandate for theological conservation, an important battle over the doctrine of inerrancy began. Inerrancy, as Carl F. H. Henry, its most substantial theological proponent, recognized, is a consequence of the inspiration of Scripture. And inspiration is a work of the Holy Spirit. The battle over inerrancy was ultimately about authority in theological method. Should theology be derived from Scripture or from something else, such as modern concepts of rationality, especially modern theories of history and science? The inerrantists carried the day in the convention and eventually dominated SBC denominational entities.

The current author participated in that struggle and reveled in the victory for a proper theological authority. Even so, the inerrancy of Scripture, in a strict sense, describes the perfection of Scripture. The authority of Scripture may be defined through inerrancy, but the questions of proper interpretation and application remain open. "Inerrancy" is a doctrine developed in the twentieth century that reflects the traditional understanding of most Christians in history regarding Scripture.[38] Inerrancy should be affirmed by the free-church theologian, but it is inadequate to serve as a theological foundation on its own. Beyond the inerrancy of Scripture, the sufficiency of Scripture for the entirety of Christian doctrine

---

36 David Hackett Fischer, *Liberty and Freedom* (New York: Oxford University Press, 2005), 284–89, 471–74, 510. Fischer defines the Latin *libertas* in the context of inequality and slavery, while the Indo-European *friya* indicated the rights granted in society. Both ideas demanded responsible living. Ibid., 3–8.

37 C. Emanuel Carson, executive director of the Baptist Joint Committee on Public Affairs, lamented that Baptist attention to Jefferson's Enlightenment vision of a wall of separation between the church and the state had a decidedly negative effect: "all content has often been drained out of religious freedom as a positive force." Robert T. Handy, "The Principle of Religious Freedom and the Dynamics of Baptist History," *PRS* 13 (1986): 31.

38 See the Chicago Statement on Biblical Inerrancy (1973).

should also be affirmed, as should the requirement of the Holy Spirit for illuminating the Bible. Inerrancy is one of many doctrines regarding the Bible that must be accounted for in constructing theology. If inerrancy then cannot stand alone, it also cannot serve as a sufficient theological foundation on its own. There is a deeper and wider theological reality of which inerrancy is a part.

Each of these five doctrines finds a firm historical manifestation in Baptist life. The seventeenth-century Baptists focused on ecclesiology. Eighteenth-century Baptists were consumed with the doctrine of God. Nineteenth-century Baptists brought missions to the forefront in denominational practice. Twentieth-century Baptists described their identity according to freedom and then proceeded to recover biblical inerrancy when the libertarian strains overextended into theology. If traditional ecclesiology, divine sovereignty, missions and evangelism, religious liberty, and inerrancy, though all necessary for understanding Baptists, are ultimately insufficient on their own—theologically, historically, or practically—to describe the theological foundation of Baptists, what remains? What is the fundamental, comprehensive truth that characterizes Baptists and their theological method?

The Fundamental Contribution of the Believers' Churches

Scripture and history provide clues to identifying the foundation and developmental principles of Baptist theological method. This truth is shared by other believers' churches too. The deep, comprehensive truth is discovered, among other places, in the Great Commission, most clearly stated in Matthew 28:16–20:

> But the eleven disciples proceeded to Galilee, to the mountain which Jesus had designated. When they saw Him, they worshipped Him but some were doubtful. And Jesus came up and spoke to them, saying, "All authority has been given to Me in heaven and on earth. Go therefore and make disciples of all the nations, baptizing them in the name of the Father and the Son and the Holy Spirit, teaching them to observe all that I commanded you; and lo, I am with you always, even to the end of the age."

The Great Commission has been a central passage for believers' churches since at least the sixteenth century.[39] Moreover, as will be seen in chapter 5, this passage was central in the early development of the critical Christian doctrine of the Trinity, and by extension, Christology. According to Balthasar Hubmaier, the earliest Anabaptist theologian, the Great Commission cannot be lightly considered, "for a serious command demands serious obedience and fulfillment."[40] Hubmaier's comment appeared in the most important book on baptism written in the sixteenth century. Anabaptist baptism was understood as more than a mere symbol, not in the sense of being a grace-conveying sacrament but in the sense of a personal and visible commitment to testify with a holy church to a lost world. Baptism carried

[39] Yarnell, "The Heart of a Baptist," *CTR*, n.s. 4 (2006): 73–88.

[40] Balthaser Hubmaier, *On the Christian Baptism of Believers* (1525), in *Balthaser Hubmaier: Theologian of Anabaptism*, trans. and ed. H. Wayne Pipkin and John H. Yoder (Scottdale, PA: Herald, 1989), 122.

with it "the determination to change one's life by the help of God."[41] Baptism was a symbol of commitment and a testimony of faith: "But when he receives the baptism of water the one who is baptized testifies that he has pledged himself henceforth to live according to the Rule of Christ."[42]

"Commitment," "pledge," "determination," "submission," "obedience," "fulfillment": these terms appear again and again in the great literature of the Anabaptist movement of the sixteenth century. Two German nouns capture the essence of the Anabaptist genius: *Gelassenheit* and *Nachfolge*. *Gelassenheit* was the more common word in the sixteenth century, while *Nachfolge* is the more common German word today. It is difficult to provide an exact translation of *Gelassenheit*, but "yieldedness" or "surrender," indicating the submissive attitude of a Christian disciple, seems most appropriate.[43]

Gelassenheit pictures a profound and ongoing personal commitment to Jesus Christ within His body, the church, as it witnesses to the world. The term has three interrelated aspects. First, the term is soteriological, describing the entirety of salvation. A disciple of Jesus Christ is one who has the attitude of *Gelassenheit* to Christ. Second, the term is ecclesiological, for the disciple is integrated with the body of Christ, the church. If "disciple" represents one's personal commitment to follow Christ, "discipline" represents the church's commitment to follow Christ. Third, *Gelassenheit* is apologetic in intent. Those who are yielded to Christ seek to bring others to the same relationship with Christ. *Gelassenheit* begets *Gelassenheit*. Disciples beget disciples through witness to the Lord Jesus Christ.

While *Gelassenheit* describes the attitude of a disciple of Christ, *Nachfolge* describes the essence of that disciple. Harold Bender said the "first and fundamental" point of the Anabaptist vision is "the essence of Christianity as discipleship."[44] In his book *The Anabaptist Story*, William R. Estep disclosed the roots of the Anabaptist movement within the Reformation. With the Protestant Reformers the Anabaptists embraced the cardinal Reformation doctrines of *sola scriptura*, justification by faith alone, and the priesthood of all believers. But because the Reformers refused fully to carry out their call for an earnest commitment to Christ, the Anabaptists manifested consistent discipleship through their obedience to follow Christ in believers' baptism. As a result, they formed believers' churches that depended neither on Rome nor on the state but on Christ alone. "Baptism was held obligatory for three reasons: Christ has commanded it; it is a necessary act of personal discipleship; and it is the symbol of corporate discipleship of the visible church."[45]

Durnbaugh discerned a similar commitment to discipleship among all those churches identified as believers' churches.[46] Others have also noted the commit-

---

[41] Ibid., 101.

[42] Ibid., 127.

[43] C. Arnold Snyder, *Anabaptist History and Theology: An Introduction* (Kitchener, ON: Pandora, 1995), 89.

[44] Harold Bender, *The Anabaptist Vision* (Scottdale, PA: Herald, 1944), 20.

[45] William R. Estep, *The Anabaptist Story*, rev. ed. (Grand Rapids: Eerdmans, 1975), 157.

[46] Durnbaugh, *The Believers' Church*, 209–25.

ment to communal discipleship among all the free churches, including Baptists, Brethren, Quakers, Methodists, and Disciples.[47]

Dietrich Bonhoeffer's *The Cost of Discipleship* displays a similar intensity regarding the commitment expected of a follower of Christ.[48] In the German original, Bonhoeffer's classic work required only one word, *Nachfolge*. Among the many famous sayings that have come from this book are two propositions that encapsulate the believers' church mentality: "*Only the believer is obedient*, and *only the obedient one believes*."[49] In teaching that the falsehood of "cheap grace" should not be confused with the truth of "costly grace," Bonhoeffer mirrored, in some important ways, the theological legacy of the Anabaptists. The person who is justified by faith alone in Jesus Christ will obey alone Jesus Christ.

Martin Luther confined himself primarily to the beginning aspect of salvation, correctly stressing the importance of faith as a gift of grace resulting in the declaration of righteousness. This declared righteousness is properly not of the Christian but of Christ. And yet the Anabaptists—and four centuries later, Bonhoeffer—recognized that Christ's righteousness must characterize the Christian's actions. Christ, the righteous One, is not only *donum*, a gift to the Christian, but *exemplum*, an example for the Christian.[50] For Lutherans, the idea that "a true Christian must follow in Christ's steps" was "the first article of the Anabaptist heresy."[51] Luther, of course, was correctly arguing against the legacy of works-righteousness inherited from the Middle Ages, but he was always fearful of the reintroduction of works.[52] The Anabaptists agreed with Luther's doctrine of justification by grace alone, but they went beyond Luther to reclaim the totality of Christian salvation.

In the doctrine of salvation believers' churches began their journey away from Protestant theology. Discipleship to Christ alone led the first Anabaptists to disagree with Ulrich Zwingli, the first Reformed theologian, and the same doctrine led the Anabaptists to disagree with Luther. "Doctrinally [the Anabaptists] held to the fundamental tenets of Christian orthodoxy: God, Christ, man, sin, faith, salvation, Scripture, and eschatology. But they differed in the degree to which the fruit of faith must come to visible expression in the life of those who claim to be disciples."[53] The Anabaptists believed biblical salvation starts in justification but continues in sanctification and ends in glorification. The entire process of salvation

[47] J. Denny Weaver, *Becoming Anabaptist: The Origin and Significance of Sixteenth-Century Anabaptism*, 2nd ed. (Scottdale, PA: Herald, 2005), 161–65.

[48] Abram John Klassen, "Discipleship in Anabaptism and Bonhoeffer" (PhD diss., Claremont Graduate School, 1970).

[49] Italics are in the original. "*Nur der Glaubende ist gehorsam*, und *nur der Gehorsame glaubt*." Dietrich Bonhoeffer, *Nachfolge* (Munich: Chr. Kaiser, 1964), 35. Cp. "*Only he who believes is obedient, and only he who is obedient believes*." Idem, *The Cost of Discipleship*, trans. R. H. Fuller, 2nd ed. (New York: Macmillan, 1963), 69.

[50] Klassen, "Discipleship in Anabaptism and Bonhoeffer," 130, 144–45.

[51] The Nürnberg Rat, *Gründtliche Vnterrichtung* (1527), cited in Klassen, "Discipleship in Anabaptism and Bonhoeffer," 146.

[52] Egil Grislis, "The Meaning of Good Works: Luther and the Anabaptists," *Word & World* 6 (1986): 170–80.

[53] Klassen, "Discipleship in Anabaptism and Bonhoeffer," 137.

can be described as *Nachfolge*, discipleship, in which a disciple unswervingly displays the attitude of *Gelassenheit*, or yieldedness, to Christ. Through its doctrine of discipleship, Anabaptist soteriology proved itself more holistic and arguably more biblical than the alternative soteriologies of the Lutherans and the Reformed.

Bonhoeffer recognized that Lutheranism had become bankrupt among the German Christians, for they had forsaken *Nachfolge Christi*, and thus, Christ Himself. Bonhoeffer's call to discipleship included a rejection of the "cheap grace" evident among those who compromised with Adolf Hitler. "Cheap grace is the preaching of forgiveness without requiring repentance, baptism without church discipline, communion without confession, absolution without personal confession. Cheap grace is grace without discipleship, grace without the cross, grace without Jesus Christ, living and incarnate." On the other hand, there is "costly grace." "Such grace is costly because it calls us to follow, and it is grace because it calls us to follow Jesus Christ. It is costly because it costs a man his life, and it is grace because it gives a man the only true life."[54]

Bonhoeffer's call to radical Christian discipleship culminated in his own murder at the hands of the Nazi state only days before the liberation of his prison camp. Bonhoeffer's courageous denunciation of the Nazi tyranny has justly been celebrated in the broader Christian world.[55] Perhaps martyrdom seemed to be the only possible option after his prescient declaration that "the call of Christ leads every man to death."[56] Less well-known is the fact that an Anabaptist church, arising independently of any Anabaptist or Baptist influence, was apparently the first Christian church to proclaim that Christ, not Hitler, was their only leader (*einzig Führer*). Before the bold Declaration of the Confessing Church of Protestants meeting in Barmen on May 31, 1934,[57] or the first courageous sermon by the Catholic Bishop of Münster, Clemens August Cardinal Von Galen, against the Nazis on February 9, 1936,[58] an Anabaptist church founded by Eberhard Arnold sent a humble but profound rebuke to the chief of the Secret State Police in Berlin on December 6, 1933. These Anabaptists, who sprang up without contact with other Baptist groups while reading the Bible, argued that the Nazi apparatus jeopardized the Christian way of life and the church's freedom of conscience. "This freedom demands nothing else than the right to put into practice the utter goodness and purity of Jesus Christ in obedience to him. He is the only leader, master and liberator of his disciples."[59]

---

[54] Bonhoeffer, *The Cost of Discipleship*, 47. Cp. idem, *Nachfolge*, 14–15.

[55] A statue of Bonhoeffer is dedicated to him as a twentieth-century martyr above the main entrance of Westminister Abbey, London.

[56] "Jeder Ruf Christi führt in den Tod." Bonhoeffer, *Nachfolge*, 65. Cp., "When Christ calls a man, he bids him come and die." Idem, *The Cost of Discipleship*, 99.

[57] "The Barmen Synod: German Church Rivalries," *Times* (London), June 4, 1934, 13.

[58] Clemens August Kardinal Von Galen, *Predigten in Dunkler Zeit: Nec Laudibus, Nec Timore* (Münster: Bischöfliche Generalvikariat, 2005), 23–30.

[59] Marjorie Hindley, "'Unerwünscht': One of the Lesser Known Confrontations with the National Socialist State, 1933–1937," *GH* 11 (1993): 214–15.

Discipleship to Christ is not a distinctive confined to Anabaptists or to their theological brothers, the Baptists. One may also consider the medieval Catholic, Thomas à Kempis, whose classic work, *The Imitation of Christ*, represents the more mystical side of personal discipleship. Bonhoeffer's vision of discipleship as inclusive of ethics is much clearer than that derived from à Kempis, whose version is focused primarily on inner spirituality. E. Brandt noted a number of historical distortions of the doctrine of *Nachfolge*. Besides the mysticism of the *imitatio* tradition, he points to the imbalances of individualistic pietism and ethical rigorism.[60] Modern Roman Catholics also have a doctrine of *Nachfolge*, but the term is unfortunately used in the elitist sense of papal succession.[61]

Brandt agreed with the pietists that in the New Testament, "Discipleship means 'to work behind Jesus,' making the way of Jesus one's own way."[62] But he feared the communal side of the doctrine had been forgotten. Brandt, a German evangelical, wishes that discipleship would "be discovered again as faith taking concrete form in the Christian church."[63] Brandt's desires were the same as Bonhoeffer's. Both of these Lutheran theologians pined for the loss of genuine Christian community, a community of committed followers of Christ. Bonhoeffer spelled out his ideal of Christian fellowship in a number of places, but he never made the connection between the proper institution of the ordinances of Christ and the maintenance of Christian community. Even when given the opportunity to address the error of infant baptism, his critique would not take him as far as that offered by Karl Barth.[64]

Where other Christians have a doctrine of personal discipleship, the Anabaptists courageously applied the same doctrine to the community. Indeed, this indicates the singular contribution of the Anabaptists to Christian history. They exhibited "a highly integrated theology" that would not allow for the unfortunate division between doctrine and practice evident among other Christians.[65] Anabaptists assumed the basic Christian doctrines of the Apostles' Creed and the Reformation doctrines regarding Scripture, justification, and the communion of saints. But they

[60] E. Brandt, "Nachfolge," in *Evangelisches Lexikon für Theologie und Gemeinde: Studienausgabe*, ed. Helmut Burkhardt and Uwe Swarat (Wuppertal: Brockhaus, 1998), 2:1392–96.

[61] Joseph Ratzinger Benedict XVI, *Wort Gottes, Schrift—Tradition—Amt*, ed. Peter Hünermann and Thomas Söding (Basel: Herder, 2005), 10–11.

[62] "Nachfolge meint 'hinter Jesus hergehen,' den Weg Jesu zu seinem eigenen Weg machen." Brandt, "Nachfolge," 1392.

[63] "Angesichts eines verengten Verstandnisses von Nachfolge Christi aufgrund frommigkeitgeschichtliche Entwicklungen, die Nachfolge Christi vollig individualisieren oder in mystischem Sinn als Nachahmung deuten oder as ethischen Rigorismus intepretieren, ist Nachfolge Christi neu als dies konkrete Gestaltwerdung des Glaubens der christliche Gemeinde zu entdecken, die in dieser Welt den Zuspruch und Anspruch des Evangeliums Jesu Christi bezeugt." (ET: "In view of a narrowed understanding of the discipleship of Christ due to historical developments in pietism, which individualized or completely interpreted discipleship to Christ in a mystical sense as imitation or as ethical rigorism, discipleship to Christ should be discovered again as faith taking concrete form in the Christian church, which testifies to this world concerning the privilege and requirement of the gospel of Jesus Christ.") Ibid.

[64] Bonhoeffer, *Life Together*, trans. John W. Doberstein (New York: HarperCollins, 1954); Eberhard Bethge, *Dietrich Bonhoeffer: A Biography*, rev. ed. (Minneapolis, MN: Fortress, 2000), 707–8.

[65] Estep, *The Anabaptist Story*, 175.

went further and developed a tight correlation between the Spirit and the Word, the inner witness of personal regeneration and the outer witness of obedience to Scripture. They refused to confine their soteriology merely to Lutheran justification or to the rationalist formulation of the Reformed *ordo salutis*.

For the Anabaptists, true Christianity involved the essence of *Nachfolge* and an attitude of *Gelassenheit*. This played itself out in an ecclesiology preserving the regenerate church through believers' baptism, church discipline, and a memorial communion. It also manifested itself in the desire to be a visible witness to a hostile world of the saving grace available through faith in Christ. Sadly but gloriously, many Anabaptists were driven to pay the ultimate price for their Christian faith: martyrdom. They not only believed in Christ with their minds; they followed Him with their bodies.[66] In the words of Hans Denck: "Woe to him who looks elsewhere than to this goal. For whoever thinks he belongs to Christ must walk the way that Christ walked."[67]

The English Baptist Commitment to Yield to Christ Alone

Personal and communal discipleship is a truth that, if not directly inherited from the Anabaptists, was at least mimicked by the Baptists, who providentially read from the same Bible in the same way. The commonly held truths composing their shared theological foundation can be seen in two telling quotes from the early days of the earliest English Baptist movements. The English General Baptists, formed in the first decade of the seventeenth century, were committed to a radical agenda of Christian discipleship, evidenced in baptism for believers only, which involved the full powers of the human will. The English Particular Baptists, formed in the third decade of the seventeenth century, were committed to a radical agenda of Christian discipleship, evidenced in baptism for believers only, as a result of the gracious call of God. Both communities were Christocentric, biblicist, Spirit led, and congregational.

First, the English General Baptists saw themselves as rooted in a personal and communal relationship of vital dependence upon the Spirit and obedience to Jesus Christ as revealed in the Bible. Baptism was, for the General Baptists, an "Action of Obedience."[68] These beliefs were an inheritance from their English Separatist days. When first organizing as an independent congregation, almost certainly in the Old Hall in Gainsborough, Lincolnshire, the Smyth congregation, "as the Lords free people joyned them selves (by a covenant of the Lord) into a Church estate, in the fellowship of the gospell, to walke in all his wayes, made known or to be made known unto them, according to their best endeavours, whatsoever it should cost them, the Lord assisting them."[69]

From their covenant, we learn that the English General Baptists were personally committed to a relationship with Jesus Christ. This relationship was divine,

---

[66] Snyder, *Anabaptist History and Theology*, 83–99.

[67] *Anabaptism in Outline: Selected Primary Sources*, ed. Walter Klaassen (Scottdale, PA: Herald, 1981), 87.

[68] The Faith and Practice of Thirty Congregations, art. 49, in Lumpkin, *Baptist Confessions of Faith*, 182.

[69] Champlin Burrage, *The Early English Dissenters* (New York: Russell & Russell, 1912), 1:230.

disobedience [to the magistrate] or polygamy," all of which were identified with the growing myth of Münster.[77] The Particular Baptist disclaimer regarding their Anabaptist roots should be read politically rather than historically.

The English Particular Baptists realized that they might never reach a complete understanding of God's Word. They trusted God's Word completely and demanded that every doctrine should come from that Word: "Shew us from the Word of God that we see not." But the Particular Baptists recognized a distinction between inspiration by the Holy Spirit and illumination by the same Spirit. On the one hand, they affirmed zealously the authority of the Bible as an inspired book. "The Rule of this Knowledge, Faith, and Obedience, concerning the worship and service of God, and all other Christian duties, is not mans inventions, opinions, devices, lawes, constitutions, or traditions unwritten whatsoever, but onely the word of God contained in the Canonicall Scriptures."[78] On the other hand, they refused to confuse their beliefs based on the Word of God with the Word of God itself. They understood that there might be a truth in the Word of God to which their eyes were not yet open.

Such an attitude of humble conviction may appear equally contradictory to both fundamentalists and modernists today. Unlike the fundamentalists, the early Particular Baptists recognized that they might not have theologically grasped the entirety of God's Word. Unlike the modernists, the Particular Baptists were unwilling to depart from God's Word, even momentarily. To the modernist, the Particular Baptists are open-minded fundamentalists who will hear "onely the word of God." To the fundamentalist, the Particular Baptists appear to be confused liberals for admitting that there may be some things "that we see not." The Particular Baptists would reject both the fundamentalist and the modernist tendencies. They were merely reflecting upon the dynamic relationship between the Word and the Spirit and the Christian's dependence upon both for orthodox theology and correct practice. It was as they read the Word of God under the guidance of the Holy Spirit in the church that they discerned the mind of Christ.

And it was to this Christ that they submitted everything. They wanted to garner their theology and their ethics directly from Jesus Christ through Scripture illumined by the same Holy Spirit who inspired it to glorify Christ. They were convinced that their theology must not depart from "the least tittle of the truth of God." And their practices must be according to whatever is "commanded by our Lord Jesus Christ." They realized that their commitment to an entire "obedience to Christ" might result in the loss of liberty and even life, but this is a price they were willing to pay, for Christ was everything. The early English Particular Baptists, like their General Baptist countrymen, and their Continental Anabaptist cousins, were submissive disciples of Jesus Christ.

---

[77] Mark R. Bell, *Apocalypse How? Baptist Movements during the English Revolution* (Macon, GA: Mercer University Press, 2000), 74–76.

[78] The Confession of Faith (1644), art. 7, in Lumpkin, *Baptist Confessions of Faith*, 158.

The Historiographical Comprehensiveness of Discipleship

The theological foundation of the believers' churches is located in their doctrine of discipleship, which calls for an attitude of submissive obedience to Christ in all things, personally and communally. Discipleship also explains the various emphases manifested in the history of the Baptists. Discipleship to Jesus Christ, understood according to the Great Commission, is the theological dynamo that produced the various theological concerns of Baptists in the five periods of Baptist theological development previously identified.

First, the communal form of discipleship was the focus of the earliest English and American Baptists. This is why they were concerned with constituting proper ecclesiology on the basis of a baptismal covenant.[79] As noted, covenant was the basis of the local church and consisted of both a vertical aspect, between God and man, and a horizontal aspect, between men. Baptism for those who had truly become disciples by grace through faith in Christ was the symbolic entrance into the covenant. The Lord's Supper was the continuing evidence of one's membership in the church, an indication of salvation in days when experiential Calvinism encouraged people to seek assurance of salvation. And church discipline was regularly practiced so as to maintain the purity of the regenerate church membership. A high concern for the doctrine of the church—including baptism, the Lord's Supper, and church discipline—has rarely been far from the Baptist mind although church discipline went into decline after the rise of liberalism in the twentieth century. The Baptist concern for ecclesiology is an outgrowth of the desire for total discipleship, especially with regard to the community.

Second, the theological orientation of discipleship was the primary concern of late seventeenth-century and early eighteenth-century Baptists. The question before the Baptist mind in this period focused on who the recipient of Christian discipleship was. Baptists are followers of the ways of the God who is Father, Son, and Holy Spirit. Some English General Baptists, following the reservations of Matthew Caffyn, actually denied the trinitarian nature of the God they followed, and their denomination subsequently went into decline.[80] In response to the theological heresy they perceived around them, some English General Baptists and most English Particular Baptists renewed their interest in classical orthodoxy. Thomas Monck led General Baptists to adopt an Orthodox Creed, which dwelt upon the Trinity and Christology, and advocated the Apostles' Creed, the Niceno-Constantinopolitan Creed, and the Quicunque Vult (Athanasian Creed).[81]

Particular Baptists such as John Gill wrote lengthy treatises on classical and systematic theology.[82] But some Particular Baptists took their Calvinistic orthodoxy further and stressed the sovereignty of God to such a point that hyper-

[79] Fiddes, *Tracks and Traces*, 21–47.

[80] Jim Spivey, "Matthew Caffyn," in *ODNB*.

[81] *An Orthodox Creed, or A Protestant Profession of Faith* (London, 1679), arts. 1–8, 38, in Lumpkin, *Baptist Confessions of Faith*, 298–301, 326–27. The Orthodox Creed is also available in a complete critical edition at www.BaptistTheology.org.

[82] John Gill, *A Body of Doctrinal Divinity; or, A System of Evangelical Truths, Deduced from the Sacred Scriptures* (London, 1769); idem, *The Doctrine of the Trinity, Stated and Vindicated* (London, 1731).

Calvinism resulted. The hyper-Calvinists argued for eternal justification and against the duty of man to believe.[83] The hyper-Calvinist John Martin emphasized "Christian prudence" over "promiscuous preaching." Martin freely criticized his evangelical brethren for their invitational practices but offered no viable alternative for reaching the lost.[84] Whatever one's personal position in these matters, Baptist debates over the proper doctrine of God and salvation are really attempts to answer the questions: Whose disciples are we? and, How did we become His disciples?

Third, the missionary practices that arose in the late eighteenth-century in reaction to hyper-Calvinism display the evangelistic mandate of discipleship. Rejecting the extreme predestinarian teachings of his Calvinistic teachers, Andrew Fuller reminded Baptists that faith in Christ was the duty of all men and that preaching to the lost was a duty for Christians.[85] In 1792 William Carey preached a sermon before the Northamptonshire Baptist Association on Isaiah 54:2–3. He had two equalized exhortations: "Expect great things," and "Attempt great things." The first proposition reflects his belief in divine sovereignty; the second proposition reflects his belief in human responsibility. Neither proposition was denied or downplayed. It is said that the effect of Carey's sermon was "considerable." Andrew Fuller subsequently became the leader of the Particular Baptist Society for Propagating the Gospel Among the Heathen. After the society's organization in the home of Widow Wallis in Kettering, Fuller led Baptists to support Carey as the first missionary to India.[86] Thus began the modern missions movement, which affected many Christian denominations, but for which the Baptists receive accolades for beginning.

While certainly a reason for denominational pride and indicative of a desire held by most Baptists, evangelism and missions are best understood as an outworking of the disciple's desire to fulfill Christ's command in Matthew 28. Carey desired that Christians should enter "heartily into the spirit of the divine command," specifically the Great Commission. "Pity therefore, humanity, and much more Christianity, call loudly for every possible exertion to introduce the gospel amongst them." Carey's form of discipleship required vigorous efforts to evangelize the entire world, and many churches, especially the Free Churches, were galvanized into action by his call.[87] Evangelism and missions are efforts undertaken by disciples of Christ who desire to make disciples of Christ. The Great Commis-

[83] John Brine, *A Defence of the Doctrine of Eternal Justification, From Some Exceptions made to it By Mr. Bragge, and others* (London, 1732); John Martin, *Thoughts on the Duty of Man Relative to Faith in Jesus Christ; In Which Mr. Andrew Fuller's leading Propositions on that Subject are considered* (London, 1788).

[84] Martin, *Christian Prudence Exemplified in the Character of St. Paul: A Sermon on I Cor ix.22* (London, 1791); Raymond Brown, *The English Baptists of the Eighteenth Century* (London: Baptist Historical Society, 1986), 89–90.

[85] Andrew Fuller, *The Gospel of Christ Worthy of All Acceptation: Or the Obligations of Men Fully to Credit, and Cordially to Approve, Whatever God Makes Known* (London, 1785).

[86] William Staughton, *The Baptist Mission in India: Containing a Narrative of Its Rise, Progress, and Present Condition* (Philadelphia, 1811), 15–17.

[87] Carey, *An Enquiry into the Obligations of Christians*, 5, 13.

sion given by Jesus Christ is a call to disciples to make disciples by teaching the world to submit to all of Christ's commands, beginning with baptism.

Fourth, we noted above the conceptual and historical problems with employing the terms of *liberty* and *freedom* to describe the theological foundation of the free churches. This is especially so with regard to the negative meanings usually affiliated with freedom. In popular philosophical theology, freedom is often considered in terms of the human free will, understood by many as arbitrary choice (*liberum arbitrium*). This almost universal starting point for the popular doctrine of freedom lacks an explicit scriptural basis. The longstanding debates over free will in salvation originate with the dispute between Augustine and Pelagius, the latter believing he was advocating an earlier Augustinian doctrine of free will.[88] Debates over *liberum arbitrium* continue to divide Christians in most churches. A second popular theological understanding of freedom was given by Luther, who played with the paradoxical state of a Christian's bodily existence.[89] A third popular theological understanding of freedom as religious liberty is historical in origin and political in import and is dealt with in chapter 5. Over against these alternatives the New Testament construal of freedom places the church in a relationship of submissive yieldedness to the Lord. "Freedom implies release into a fellowship of obedience to God's known will."[90]

Paul's doctrine of freedom (*eleutheria*) is paradoxically correlated with the condition of slaves (*douloi*). Every person is simultaneously free from some power and enslaved to an opposing power. Freedom and slavery denote a state of locatable relationships: freedom in Christ is slavery to God; freedom from Christ is slavery to sin. True Christian freedom is freedom "from," freedom "through" and "in," and freedom "to." It is freedom from sin (Rom 6:15–23), from law (7:6–7; 8:1–4), and from death (6:22–23), or compositely "from the law of sin and death" (8:2). It is freedom through the atoning death of Christ (Gal 5:1) and in obedience to the indwelling Spirit (2 Cor 3:17). It is freedom to service (1 Cor 8:9; 9:12; cp. 1 Thess 2:2) and to eternal life (Rom 6:22–23). Employing a similar set of locatable relationships, Jesus taught the Jews that freedom comes only in the context of discipleship to Him as Lord. The person who abides in Christ is a disciple of Christ, and that person knows the truth that makes him free (John 8:31–32). The person who is outside of total obedience to Christ, the truth in person, is a slave to sin (8:33–36; cp. 14:6). True freedom is available only to the one who is a disciple of Jesus Christ. True Christian freedom is Christian obedience.

Fifth, many free churches, including the Baptists, participated in the debates regarding biblical inerrancy in the last half of the twentieth century. These later debates reflect earlier unresolved tensions regarding the authority of the Word

---

[88] Augustine, *On Free Choice of the Will*, trans. Thomas Wiliams (Indianapolis: Hackett, 1993); Eleonore Stump, "Augustine on Free Will," in *The Cambridge Companion to Augustine*, ed. Eleonore Stump and Norman Kretzmann (New York: Cambridge University Press, 2001), 124–47.

[89] "A Christian is a perfectly free lord of all, subject to none [in his spirit]. A Christian is a perfectly dutiful servant of all, subject to all [in his body]." Luther, *The Freedom of a Christian* (1520), in *Luther's Works*, ed. Harold J. Grimm (Philadelphia: Muhlenberg Press, 1957), 31:344.

[90] P. D. Browne, "Freedom," in *ESB* (Nashville: Broadman, 1958–1982), 1:507.

of God. Most northern American denominations addressed the problems raised by the historical-critical method of Bible study early in the twentieth century. The fundamentalist-modernist debates created new fundamentalist denominations peopled by Christians disenfranchised by the widespread triumph of the liberals.[91] Southern Baptists were also roiled, but E. Y. Mullins led the SBC to adopt a confession that calmed the waters in the South. The Baptist Faith and Message of 1925 was a revision of the moderately Calvinistic New Hampshire Confession of Faith of 1833. Southern Baptists, believing the fundamentalist-modernist controversy had been put to rest, turned their attentions toward building a large denomination. But the controversy over biblical authority reappeared in the 1960s, with the publication of Ralph Elliott's *The Message of Genesis* and the Genesis essay in the Broadman Bible Commentary series.[92] Ultimately Southern Baptists fought a long-term battle for the Bible beginning in 1979, culminating with the departure of the strength of the moderate party in 1990 to form the Cooperative Baptist Fellowship.[93]

The later debates revolved around the question of the authority for Christian discipleship. How do we know this Jesus Christ whose disciples we are? Can we trust every word of the books that teach us about Him and His will? The debate over inerrancy was a watershed event for most Southern Baptists, pro or con. In constructing their theological case, denominational scholars turned in two directions, with major importance for the current shape of the SBC. First, scholars turned to Baptist history, asking what Baptists have believed. Conservatives discovered that biblical authority had always been a major concern, concluding inerrancy was usually assumed if not always explicitly affirmed.[94] Moderates, as mentioned before, recovered the legacy of freedom, many turning to E. Y. Mullins, the inventor of "soul competency" and advocate of solipsistic Christianity.[95]

The second direction in which scholars turned was outside the denomination, to academics of like mind. For conservative Baptists this meant modern American evangelicalism, a movement that issued forth from the fundamentalist denominations. Southern Baptists joined northern Baptists, other free churchmen, and classical evangelicals in affirming the Bible to be truth without any mixture of error through such institutions as the Evangelical Theological Society. Inerrancy is not a distinctive reserved for Baptists or the free churches, nor are all Baptists and free churchmen inerrantists. Thus, although inerrancy is an important doctrine for many free churches, especially Southern Baptists, it would be difficult to maintain that the doctrine of inerrancy is a theological foundation. Inerrancy ably preserves

---

[91] George M. Marsden, *Fundamentalism and American Culture: The Shaping of Twentieth-Century Evangelicalism, 1870–1925* (New York: Oxford University Press, 1980).

[92] Ralph H. Elliott, *The Message of Genesis* (Nashville: Broadman, 1961); G. Henton Davies, BBC 1 (Nashville: Broadman, 1969), 101–303.

[93] Jerry Sutton, *The Baptist Reformation: The Conservative Resurgence in the Southern Baptist Convention* (Nashville: B&H, 2000).

[94] L. Russ Bush and Tom J. Nettles, *Baptists and the Bible*, rev. ed. (Nashville: B&H, 1999).

[95] *The Struggle for the Soul of the SBC: Moderate Responses to the Fundamentalist Movement*, ed. Walter B. Shurden (Macon, GA: Mercer University Press, 1993).

the epistemological source of Christian discipleship against the acids of modern criticism, but few Southern Baptists profess that they are disciples of the Bible. They are disciples of Jesus Christ, whom the Bible assuredly reveals. Scripture is the supreme epistemological authority for disciples.

Our two reviews of the five major theological emphases in Baptist history now indicate that neither ecclesiology, nor theology proper, nor evangelism, nor freedom, nor biblical inerrancy may alone maintain a proper theological foundation. While these doctrines shaped free church theology and indicate major aspects of their theological method, none of them is able to stand on its own. Ecclesiology, theology proper, evangelism, freedom, and biblical authority—doctrines that Baptists, the free churches, and all Christians would affirm in one form or another—point to a deeper reality. The free church response to Jesus Christ's call—"Whoever desires to come after Me, let him deny himself, and take up his cross, and follow me" (Mark 8:34)—is that deeper reality. At the center of everything stands the Master whom the free churches follow. It is Jesus Christ and His cross that they are most comfortable preaching, for He is their Savior and Lord (1 Cor 1:23; 2:2). Indeed, Jesus Christ is the church's only foundation (1 Cor 3:11). And a proper foundation for theology, temporal human reflection upon the eternal God, must derive from an eternal foundation. Christian theology arises from Christian discipleship to the one who reconciles rebellious creatures with the eternal Creator.

THE SOUTHERN BAPTIST WITNESS TO THE WORD OF GOD

Alongside the churches of the Southern Baptist Convention, the author understands the Word of God to be transmitted by Scripture under the illumination of the Holy Spirit as the supreme authority for theological formation. In 2000 Southern Baptists revised the first article of their common confession, the Baptist Faith and Message, in order to make it even clearer that the Bible is "totally true and trustworthy" and that "all Scripture is a testimony to Christ, who is Himself the focus of divine revelation."[96] We believe that the Bible is the Word of God, that it infallibly points to Jesus Christ, and that it is the inerrant standard by which all human beliefs and actions are to be measured. Because the Bible is the Word of God and not merely the record of the Word of God, we may ascribe to it a dynamic quality endowed by God Himself. The Bible is thus a living, active subject that addresses man as its object, indicating his sin, impending judgment, and potential salvation. Man, in turn, is called upon to respond with his own answering word to the written and proclaimed Word by confessing faith in the living Word, Jesus Christ. Southern Baptists arrived at their beliefs concerning the Bible through their reading of the Bible, which they consider a theological authority that speaks with clarity. Southern Baptist beliefs concerning the Bible may be summarized under two major doctrines: the inspiration of Scripture

[96] The 1925, 1963, and 2000 versions of the Baptist Faith and Message are conveniently aligned on the Web site of the Executive Committee of the Southern Baptist Convention. See http://www.sbc.net/bfm/bfmcomparison.asp; accessed 23 October 2006.

and the sufficiency of Scripture.[97] The doctrine of inspiration considers the origin of the Bible, while the doctrine of sufficiency considers its application.

Southern Baptists construct a doctrine of inspiration on Scripture's witness to itself as the divinely inspired revelation of God (2 Tim 3:16). Holy men were moved by the Holy Spirit to speak the Word of God and write the Bible (2 Pet 1:19–21). According to the first article of the Southern Baptist confession, the "Holy Bible was written by men divinely inspired and is God's revelation of Himself to man." As the doctrine of inspiration has been developed extensively elsewhere, the reader is referred for a fuller doctrine of the inspiration of Scripture and its attendant infallibility and inerrancy. *Infallibility* is a term applied either to describe the lack of falseness in the manuscript tradition or the doctrinal and soteriological efficacy of that tradition. "Inerrancy" indicates the Spirit's guarantee of perfection in the original manuscripts, with regard to history and science as well as doctrine.[98]

The Sufficiency of Scripture

The second doctrine under which Southern Baptist beliefs regarding the Bible may be classified, the sufficiency of Scripture, has, however, yet to be substantially considered by many theologians. Because the bulk of the Southern Baptist confession concerns the sufficiency of Scripture for the totality of the Christian life, a preliminary outline of the biblical basis for that confession is offered here. The Southern Baptist doctrine of the sufficiency of Scripture may be considered according to five aspects: Scripture as a treasure, Scripture as a dynamic entity, Scripture as a soteriological instrument, Scripture as a doctrinal deposit, and Scripture as applicable to the entire Christian life.

The Southern Baptist confession begins its doctrine of sufficiency by appealing to the truthfulness, beauty, and goodness of the Word of God. The Word of God describes itself as being able to convert souls, make wise, rejoice hearts, and enlighten eyes (Ps 19:7–8). It also endures forever, is altogether true and righteous, and is to be desired above all things (Ps 19:9–10). Psalm 119 is an extended litany of praise to God for the entire sufficiency of Scripture. The Bible is truly the pristine source of knowledge for man concerning all that is true, good, and beautiful. The Baptist Faith and Message thus describes the Bible as "a perfect treasure of divine instruction."

Second, any doctrine of the sufficiency of the Word of God must account for its dynamic nature. Admittedly, the Southern Baptist confession does not explicitly proclaim this aspect of the sufficiency of Scripture; however, the seeds for developing a doctrine of the dynamic sufficiency of Scripture are explicitly affirmed in Scripture and may be tangentially discerned within the Southern

[97] In a full systematic theology, these two foci might be expanded to include, for instance, biblical clarity.

[98] E.g. David S. Dockery, *The Doctrine of the Bible* (Nashville: Convention, 1991); Carl F. H. Henry, *God, Revelation and Authority* (1976–1983; repr., Wheaton, IL: Crossway, 1999). On Henry's theology, see R. Albert Mohler, "Carl F. H. Henry," in *Theologians of the Baptist Tradition*, ed. Timothy George and David S. Dockery (Nashville: Broadman, 2001); and, Yarnell, "Whose Jesus? Which Revelation?" *MidJT* 1–2 (2003): 33–53.

Baptist confession. The prophet Isaiah teaches that the Word of God accomplishes the purposes for which the all-wise God sends it (Isa 55:8–11). Interacting with the Old Testament witness, the author of the book of Hebrews concluded that the Word of God is a living, active, searching, and judging instrument of God (Heb 4:11–13). In apparent opposition to the critical approach, Scripture pictures the Word not as an object that is examined but as the subject who examines. The Word may be said to read the human being as the human being hears the Word.

Because of the Holy Spirit's dynamic involvement in the authorship, preservation, canonization, transmission, and proclamation of this dynamic Word in the Bible, Southern Baptists have learned to affirm the Bible's entire dependability. According to the Baptist confession's engaging phraseology of Lockean provenance, the Bible "has God for its author, salvation for its end, and truth, without any mixture of error, for its matter."[99] The confession's phraseology may reflect earlier Baptist attraction to empiricist epistemology. Although John Locke's theory of knowledge is imbalanced on its own, it does reflect one aspect of the human mind that the Bible also affirms, for the soul is a receptive entity in addition to being an active entity. Though the sanctified mind is not an empty slate (*tabula rasa*), it is worked upon and deeply transformed by the Word of God.

Herman Bavinck's thesis that the truth lies in the co-option both of rationalism and of empiricism provides complementary parallels for the relation of divine Word and human word. Roughly paralleling empiricist epistemology, the book of Hebrews pictures the Word of God as actively penetrating and judging the human soul (Heb 4:12). Roughly paralleling idealist epistemology, the book of Romans pictures the human heart and mouth as actively engaging with the Word of God that has come near it through preaching (Rom 10:8).[100] The German language may be used to suggest a similar dynamic understanding of God's Word in intimate dialogue with mankind by its terminology of *Wort und Antwort* (Word and answering word).[101] The call of God must be answered by the confession of man for a man to become a Christian. "A Christian who simply acknowledges and recognizes without confessing is not a Christian."[102]

Third, Baptists have also discovered within the biblical witness the soteriological sufficiency of the Word of God. Scripture effectively brings salvation by warning against human sin and revealing eternal reward (Ps 19:11–12). The Word has the ability to make one wise unto salvation (2 Tim 3:15) through the instrument of preaching, but it must be received by faith (Rom 10:14,17). The Word of God is first and foremost the subject that speaks to man as its object; but for salvation to occur, the Word must in turn become the object of internal faith by the

[99] Myron C. Noonkaster, "'God for Its Author': John Locke as a Possible Source for the New Hampshire Confession," *NEQ* 66 (1993): 448–50.

[100] For an introduction to the mutual necessity of the mainly British empiricist and mainly Continental idealist epistemologies, see Herman Bavinck, *Reformed Dogmatics: Prolegomena*, ed. John Bolt, trans. John Vriend (Grand Rapids: Baker, 2003), 214–22.

[101] Cp. Joseph Ratzinger, *Principles of Catholic Theology: Building Stones for a Fundamental Theology*, trans. Mary Frances McCarthy (San Francisco: Ignatius, 1987), 147: "The word is greater than any response."

[102] Karl Barth, *Church Dogmatics*, trans. Geoffrey Bromiley (Edinburgh: T&T Clark, 1958–1977), IV/1: 776.

human subject. The Word of God approaches the human heart and mouth through the preaching of the Word (Rom 10:8). Then the human object cum subject must respond with his own external word of confession in the objective message of the Word, most importantly in the death and resurrection of Jesus Christ (Rom 10:9–10). Baptists thus affirm that the Bible has "salvation for its end." The early church fathers also recognized the centrality of salvation in the construction of theology from Scripture. "Even in the most technically philosophical and dogmatic debates, issues of soteriological concern were always of paramount importance." The Word of God is sufficient to save human beings from sin.[103]

Fourth, growing out of its dynamic and soteriological sufficiency, Baptists affirm the doctrinal sufficiency of the Bible. The Bible uses objective and propositional terms to describe its content. The church is the pillar and ground of "the truth" that it teaches (1 Tim 3:15). Where the Word of God is received, people also become obedient to "the faith" (Acts 6:7). "The faith" is something that can be put in words and proclaimed (Gal 1:23). It is a form of knowledge concerning God that can serve as part of the foundation for the church and as a basis of unity among Christians (Eph 4:13; Col 1:23; 2:7). Christians may err concerning "the faith," and should therefore show concern for its content (2 Tim 2:18). Paul instructed Titus to exhort his people to become "sound in the faith" (Titus 1:13). This propositional faith is also the subject of tradition, being proclaimed from one generation to the next: Jude encouraged his readers "that you should earnestly contend for the faith which was once for all delivered (*hapax paradotheisē*) unto the saints" (Jude 3). According to the Southern Baptist confession, the Bible reveals "principles by which God judges us" and is "the supreme standard by which all human conduct, creeds, and religious opinions should be tried." The Bible conveys propositionally the deposit of the faith (*depositum fidei*). Revelation, of course, is both personal and propositional; neither may be denied.[104]

Finally, Southern Baptists teach the entire applicability of the Bible by noting that the Word of God is the only source of wisdom and knowledge that is eternal (Isa 40:6–8). The Bible is profitable for teaching, reproving, correcting, and instructing in righteousness (2 Tim 3:16) and is able to bring completion to pious people, thoroughly equipping them for every work that is good (2 Tim 3:17). Before the Word of God, all other forms of human knowledge pale in comparison. All human forms of wisdom and knowledge are temporary and thus ultimately lack relevance (Isa 40:6–7); they are corrupted by sin and thus utterly lack righteousness (Isa 55:6–7); and they are severely limited and thus are unable to redeem (Isa 55:8–9). This is why this convention of local churches speaks not only of Christian confessions as being judged by the standard of Scripture, but "all human conduct [and] creeds" come under its scrutiny. Therefore, Scripture may

[103] Maurice Wiles, *The Making of Christian Doctrine: A Study in the Principles of Early Doctrinal Development* (London: Cambridge University Press, 1967), 95.

[104] "An evangelical dogmatics is based on the supposition that God's Word is at the same time God's act. This Word is both conceptual and personal, propositional and existential." Donald G. Bloesch, *A Theology of Word & Spirit: Authority & Method in Theology*, Christian Foundations, vol. 1 (Downers Grove, IL: InterVarsity Press, 1992), 20. Colin E. Gunton, *A Brief Theology of Revelation* (London: T&T Clark, 1995), 1–19.

be considered sufficient for knowledge concerning, for instance, counseling the needs of the human psyche.

Theological Authority

Based on the theological authority of the Word of God according to a Southern Baptist understanding of the Bible as inspired (thus infallible and inerrant) and sufficient (thus beautiful, dynamic, saving, propositional, and applicable), this monograph elaborates an account of the true development of dogma. This particular theological authority does not deny a place for tradition, experience, or reason—the other three components of the Wesleyan Quadrilateral of authoritative theological sources—alongside and informative of Scripture. Indeed, it is impossible to deny the concurrent need to address and use the other three components. The Baptist theological method, however, does identify the active and overwhelming supremacy of Scripture as the authority in orthodox theology. Open to subsidiary considerations of tradition and reason and experience, Southern Baptist theologian James Leo Garrett Jr. proposed the nuanced category of the supremacy of Scripture (*suprema scriptura*), in contradistinction to the simplistic Reformation category of Scripture alone (*sola scriptura*). Garrett's proposal is linguistically and pneumatically preferable to the Reformed suggestion concerning the adoption of the alternative category of unaccompanied Scripture (*nuda scriptura*).[105] Evangelical theologian Donald Bloesch affirms a similar theory: "Reason, experience and church tradition have a servant role in explicating and proclaiming the truth of God's self-revelation in Jesus Christ given in Holy Scripture."[106]

The Word of God as theological authority has a preservative impact on Christian proclamation and personal faith. Apart from the gracious revelation of God in Scripture, Christian preaching, focusing on the Son, and Christian faith, applied by the Spirit, are fundamentally impossible.[107] In light of this fundamental axiom, the failure to refer theological reflection to the same Word of God that is proclaimed and believed appears not only irrelevant; but because of the limitations and depravity of humanity, including human thought, it also appears disastrous for Christian proclamation and faith. In other words, where tradition or reason or experience or any combination is elevated to the level of or above the Word of God, the introduction of heresy and error becomes far more likely. The introduction of human mediatorial agency in tradition, reason, and experience between the Word of God and the hearer of that Word increases the opportunity for distortion and perversion. And yet the Word of God itself identifies human instruments as neces-

---

[105] James Leo Garrett Jr., *Systematic Theology: Biblical, Historical, and Evangelical*, 2nd ed. (North Richland Hills, TX: BIBAL, 2000–2001), 1: 206–9.

[106] Bloesch, *A Theology of Word & Spirit*, 210.

[107] Barth, *Church Dogmatics*, I/1, passim. Although Barth's dialectical doctrine of revelation is attractive in many ways, his account of divine revelation as only potentially contained within Scripture, requiring existential encounter to actually become the Word of God, confuses soteriology with revelation. Cp. Erickson, *Christian Theology*, 209–11. Colin Gunton provides a similar critique but finds an additional problem in Barth's inadequate doctrine of the mediation of revelation. This is a problem not confined to Barth, however, for it also afflicts much evangelical theology. Gunton, *A Brief Theology of Revelation*, 18–19.

sary for the proclamation of the Word (Rom 10:14). The difficulty for Christians is in distinguishing the human mediatorial instrument from the Word of God itself. This book is in some ways an effort to identify the biblically sanctioned means of steering through the jungle of what should be complementary but often are competing theological authorities.

The opposition of Scripture to tradition is an uncontroversial proposition in classical evangelicalism. However, the claim that the Word of God is to be identified with the words of the Bible is problematic for liberal and neoorthodox evangelicals. The free-church position outlined here should not, however, be identified as fundamentalism, for it will become evident that the divide with the Reformed fundamentalism of a Charles Hodge is as insurmountable as the divide with the romantic liberalism of a Friedrich Schleiermacher. Recently, Paul McGlasson identified both the liberalism of Schleiermacher and the fundamentalism of Hodge as heresies.[108] Although we might categorize the problems differently and perhaps less stridently on the right, McGlasson expresses the rudiments of a mutual dissatisfaction. One conservative Southern Baptist seminary president has confided that he despises Calvinism as much as he does liberalism. If liberalism is unwelcome in many Southern Baptist churches on account of its deceptive use of language, a problem previously detailed by J. Gresham Machen in his magisterial *Christianity and Liberalism*,[109] Reformed fundamentalism is unwelcome in most Southern Baptist churches on account of its apparent disregard for biblical discipleship, a problem previously detailed in the voluminous polemical literature of the Anabaptist and Baptist traditions concerning believers-only baptism and the regenerate church.[110]

This is not to deny that there have been and will be Southern Baptists enamored with the theologies of either Reformed fundamentalism or Protestant liberalism. The movements of E. Y. Mullins on the left and of the Founders Fellowship on the right indicate the attraction of significant minorities to certain forms of those theologies. However, these movements remain marginal, fortunately evidencing an adept skill for adapting the external extremes represented by their theological infatuations to traditional free-church emphases, emphases difficult to dismiss due to a mutual belief in the clarity of Scripture. The free-church theological method advocated in this book deliberately seeks identification with traditional free church, especially Southern Baptist, thought away from the fringes, while maintaining a deep appreciation for the continuing contributions to free-church life represented in the fringe movements. In Southern Baptist life some of the most innovative and stimulating theological contributions have come from movements located at the margins, whether culture-chasing, Calvinist, or charismatic.

[108] Paul C. McGlasson, *Invitation to Dogmatic Theology: A Canonical Approach* (Grand Rapids: Brazos, 2006), 23–24.

[109] J. Gresham Machen, *Christianity and Liberalism* (Grand Rapids: Eerdmans, 1923).

[110] Cp. B. H. Carroll, *Baptists and Their Doctrines*, ed. J. B. Cranfill (New York: Revell, 1913); transcript available through www.BaptistTheology.org.

GOD'S CALL AND THE AUTHOR'S RESPONSE

Jesus loves me, this I know;
For the Bible tells me so;
Little ones to him belong;
They are weak, but he is strong.

Yes, Jesus loves me;
Yes, Jesus loves me;
Yes, Jesus loves me;
For the Bible tells me so.

"For God so loved the world that he gave his only begotten Son,
that whosoever believeth in him should not perish,
but have everlasting life" (John 3:16 KJV).

The Christian life began for the author as a result of attending a Vacation Bible School (VBS) class at Barksdale Baptist Church in Bossier City, Louisiana. A popular young man in the church was our teacher, and he made sure we knew the song "Jesus Loves Me" and that we could quote John 3:16 from memory. Everything else we did was fun and games, but this was the gift of the church to the children gathered for VBS, and it had to be taken seriously. I have long since forgotten what games we played and what snacks we ate, but this song and this Bible verse have remained close to my heart. During the difficult times in life, this simple liturgy and that simple Scripture have remained the ultimate comfort in this human life. Indeed, I have since taught the same song and the same Bible verse to all of my children, rehearsed at bedtime at tender, young ages.

After VBS, during the Sunday morning worship hour, my older brother, Scott, walked the aisle during the invitation and gave his heart to Jesus Christ as his personal Lord and Savior. The pastor presented my brother to the church and the church, accepted him as a candidate for baptism, which entailed membership in the church. The pastor visited with my brother and my parents, settling on the date for his baptism. It was an emotional time for my brother, and there was a palpable change in his attitude and demeanor. Indeed, he no longer fought with me, and he refrained from getting in trouble with my parents. Our entire extended family—mother, father, grandmother, and grandfather—expressed thanks and wonder for the change in Scott's life. They were proud of him and plainly said so.

Sensing this excitement and desiring the same attention, I too came down the aisle during the invitation on a Sunday soon afterwards. The pastor queried me concerning my need, and I explained to him that I wanted to be baptized. He presented me to the church, and the church accepted me as a candidate for baptism. The pastor also arranged the customary visit with me and my parents, presumably to settle on the date for my baptism. But the visit did not go nearly as smoothly as expected, for the pastor queried me as to whether I really understood what sin was and whether I sincerely understood who Jesus was and what He had accomplished for me. I understood the narrative of the gospel—the atoning death and life-giving resurrection of Jesus Christ, Son of man and Son of God—well enough to repeat what I thought the pastor wanted to hear from me, and he seemed satisfied in that regard.

And yet he questioned further, exactly what kind of sin had I committed that required repentance? Casting about for an answer, I responded—sheepishly, for my parents were present—that I had lied to my parents. Surely, I thought, they will all see through my facade, for I had just made that up. My parents and my pastor seemed satisfied that I did understand sin and that I had been born again by believing in Jesus Christ. I breathed a sigh of temporary relief and joined my brother in having the family's attention lavished on this recent supposedly Christian convert.

Yet the approach to the day of baptism was anything but joyous. My heart was unsettled, and I could not ignore a sense of dread that was clouding my young mind. I joined my brother in the line of baptismal candidates one Sunday morning at the church. Everybody in the queue seemed so happy, but I was not. It finally dawned on me that I now knew what sin really was. Yes, I had lied, but not only to my parents. I had deceived the pastor, the whole church, indeed the whole world; but most importantly, I had lied to God. As I watched my brother being baptized, I wept out of sorrow and asked God to forgive me for the deception concerning my readiness for baptism. It was only then that the pastor turned and extended his hand in order to guide me into the baptismal waters. With tears in my eyes, the pastor led me in my first public confession, baptizing me in the name of the Father and of the Son and of the Holy Spirit before everyone. The pastor explained that I had been buried with Jesus Christ in baptism and raised with Christ to walk in a newness of life.

At the end of the service, my hair was still wet, and I stood in the now empty church in the back, looking forward. Light poured in through the stained-glass windows, and my heart was filled with indescribable joy. Simultaneously, my enlightened mind and chastened heart were flooded with discernment. Now I understood why the pastor had questioned me about my sense of sinfulness and my beliefs in Jesus Christ. Now I understood why the church and my family had been so happy for my brother and me. The world and my part in it suddenly made sense. Before this I had often wondered about the purpose of the world in which I lived. Everything had been dull and gray and meaningless. Now I knew the purpose of the world and of my role in the world, and Jesus Christ was at the beginning, center, and end of it all. I can still remember the sense of wonder that overpowered me. That which had been dull and gray and meaningless was now sharp and colorful and meaningful. There was literally an explosion of color and meaning in my life. Again I wept but this time out of joy.

Reflecting back on this profound and seminal experience, I knew that I had been brought back alive, born again. God had called me through the teaching and preaching ministries of His church, and I had in turn called out to Him for forgiveness. The Father sent His only begotten Son to die on a cross for me so that

I would not have to perish but could enjoy an eternal and joyful life. The Son died on the cross for my sin and the sin of the entire world, and He had risen from the dead. He did these things in order to provide the way to life for all who would believe in Him, and I had believed and still do believe in Him. The Father and the Son sent the Holy Spirit to convict me of my sin, to grant me the faith by which I believed, and to regenerate me. My sense of sin was awakened by His Word and Spirit concerning a sin against an ordinance of Christ for the church, and of this I repented.

My sense of forgiveness had been awakened through a church—and a family ensconced in that church—that offered Jesus Christ to me as the only way of life, and Him I accepted. I know this Jesus Christ as the Son of God, fully God, who became a man, fully human, so that He could effectively atone for all of human sin. Those who will believe in Him alone for their salvation are justified before the Father by reason of their union with Christ and regeneration by the Spirit. A Spirit-led church proclaimed the Word of God to me through a Spirit-led pastor and a Spirit-led teacher. The church gave me John 3:16 and Matt 28:19, and would later give me John 10:10 during a crisis of rededication, and the rest of Scripture. Through the church the Holy Spirit showed me how to interpret John 3:16 and Rom 10:9–10 for my personal benefit with the liturgy of a simple hymn and introduced me to the mystery of the three-in-one God from Matt 28:19 with the liturgy of baptism. My experience of the Trinity's justifying love in spite of my sin occurred in the midst of His chosen community and the Word of God was the central focus of that community's life.

One task of a Christian church is to provide its members with an effective theological foundation and an understanding of the true development of doctrine from which to grow. From this confession of a spiritual and visible fellowship with the church, in justifying relationship with the God who is Father, Son, and Holy Spirit, this justified sinner approaches the task of theology. God called me to salvation, and I responded with a personal confession in an ecclesial context, and must continue confessing with the church. Because God is the beginning, center, and end of my life, as well as of all of history, I am compelled to proclaim the Word of God. Theology is the thinking aspect of such preaching. Arising out of the experience of faith, theology is the name for the Christian effort to understand the meaning of God, creation, humanity, and redemption that the church through its preachers and teachers proclaims. With this background of faith in mind, you are offered a believers' church account of theological formation in this book.

Chapter Two

THE FOUNDATION OF DOCTRINE: *Three Christian Alternatives*

In order to begin locating a believers' church theological method within the broader arena of Christian thought, let us begin by evaluating the theological foundations offered by three superb theologians representing other church traditions. These three theologians were chosen because of their extensive contributions to their respective churches and academies. Each theologian is a widely recognized, subtle, and appealing theologian whose career evidences sustained concern for the foundation, development, and continuing relevancy of Christian theology. These three theologians are Joseph Ratzinger, Maurice Wiles, and Herman Bavinck. Ratzinger, Wiles, and Bavinck present detailed theological foundations according to, respectively, the conservative Roman Catholic, liberal Anglican, and Reformed theological and ecclesiological traditions.

The decision to interact with these alternative Christian traditions reflects not only a concern to learn from the critical thought of other Christians but also an attempt to interact with various tendencies evident among the free churches as exemplified within the Southern Baptist Convention. It has been sporadically claimed, more often by opponents than proponents, that the Reformed, Roman Catholic, and liberal theological traditions outside the Southern Baptist fold have their counterparts, respectively, in the Founders, Landmarkist, and Moderate movements within that tradition. First, the connection between the Southern Baptist Founders movement and Reformed theology is not difficult to establish, as a visit to their sponsored Web site will show multiple links to Reformed and Presbyterian Web sites.[1] Thomas K. Ascol, editor of *The Founders Journal*, roots his movement in the Reformation generally and the Dutch Reformed Synod of Dort specifically.[2] Second, the connection between liberalism and the moderate movement is politically controversial; but the deep appreciation of E. Y. Mullins, who stands at the head of the moderate movement, for the introspective theological method of Friedrich Schleiermacher, the father of theological liberalism, indicates some convergence.[3]

---

[1] There are as many links on the site to Reformed and Presbyterian churches as there are to Baptist churches. Both Westminster Theological Seminary and Reformed Theological Seminary are linked, but no Baptist seminaries are represented. See http://geneva.founders.org/listing.html; accessed 27 December 2006.

[2] Thomas K. Ascol, *From the Protestant Reformation to the Southern Baptist Convention: What Hath Geneva to Do with Nashville?* (Cape Coral, FL: Founders, 1996), 4–6.

[3] Malcolm Yarnell, "Mullins, Edgar Young," in *Biographical Dictionary of Evangelicals*, ed. Timothy Larsen (Downers Grove, IL: InterVarsity, 2003), 458–60.

Third, Mullins said that the Landmarkists were "a Roman Catholic Party among the Baptists," but the claim is misleading.[4] Although Landmarkism has a high regard for the church, its Baptist ecclesiology significantly differs from Roman Catholicism by defining the nature of the church as visible, with which Catholics would agree, and strictly local, with which Catholics would adamantly disagree. Landmarkist ecclesiology is as contrary to Roman Catholicism as it is to Protestantism.[5] Despite the imprecise nature of relationship between internal Southern Baptist movements and their external exemplars, reflection upon the external movements may prove profitable. The internal movements—Founders, Landmarkist, and moderate—are important for understanding the theological history and heritage of Southern Baptists today. The external Christian traditions do not perfectly mirror the internal free-church tendencies in every case, as will become more evident, but they provide a means of analysis and comparison instructive for Southern Baptists, fellow believers' churches, and the broader Christian movement.

The choice of a Roman Catholic, an Anglican, and a Calvinist reflect an attempt to engage with the broader Christian tradition rather than only with an internal free-church tradition, for theology is best conducted in conversation with many rather than few. The choice of a German, an Englishman, and a Dutchman is also no accident. On his deathbed, the Dutch Reformed theologian, Herman Bavinck, remarked to a friend, "Henk, our theological thinking is too closely associated with the Germans. It's high time we turned our eyes towards England."[6] In order to avoid an approach to theological method that is too American and perhaps too English, reflecting my own background, it seems prudent from the standpoint of diversity to engage with a German and a Dutchman, too. We begin with a German Roman Catholic, a former professor of *Fundamentaltheologie*, who is now the bishop of Rome.

JOSEPH RATZINGER, CONSERVATIVE ROMAN CHURCHMAN

Ratzinger grew up in a Catholic home in the shadow of the Third Reich. Forced into military service as a teenager and imprisoned after World War II, he subsequently referred to his Nazi military trainers as "fanatical ideologues who tyrannized us without respite" and described postwar Europe as "disfigured by ideology and hatred."[7] He saw the Roman church as "the locus of all our hopes . . . the alternative to the destructive ideology of the brown shirts."[8] Trained in the

[4] Mullins wrote a number of articles against the Landmarkists in the *Religious Herald* defending William Heth Whitsitt. W. E. Ellis, *"A Man of Books and a Man of the People": E. Y. Mullins and the Crisis of Moderate Southern Baptist Leadership* (Macon, GA: Mercer University Press, 1985), 34.

[5] James E. Tull, *High-Church Baptists in the South* (Macon, GA: Mercer University Press, 2000), 14–16.

[6] Gerard Rothuizen, *Apologetics in Oxford: The Theology of Maurice F. Wiles*, trans. Vikas Sonak (Kampen: Uitgeversmaatschappij J. H. Kok, 1987), 20–21.

[7] Joseph Ratzinger, *Milestones: Memoirs 1927–1977*, trans. Erasmo Leiva-Merikakis (San Francisco: Ignatius, 1998), 33–34. For a general introduction to Ratzinger's theology, see Aidan Nichols, *The Thought of Benedict XVI: An Introduction to the Theology of Joseph Ratzinger* (New York: Burns & Oates, 2005).

[8] Ibid., 42.

best German Catholic scholarship, with some exposure to evangelical hermeneutics and theology, he taught theology, including *Fundamentaltheologie*, at Freising, Bonn, Münster, Tübingen, and Regensburg, serving the last as dean of the Theological Faculty. In his early career he considered biblical exegesis as central for his theological development. He also took interest in liturgical and pastoral theology. His doctoral thesis concerned the theology of history in Bonaventure, who adapted Joachim of Fiore's revolutionary trinitarian scheme for orthodox Franciscans.[9]

Ratzinger was a theological advisor (*peritus*) at Vatican II, playing a critical role, attending all its sessions, and rejoicing with others in the springtime that council introduced to the Roman church. While initially in favor of the program of modernization (*aggorniamento*) many perceived as the proper legacy of Vatican II, he eventually opted for a conservative assessment of the council. The shift in his thought climaxed with his negative reaction to the Marxist inroads among Christians that he witnessed during his tenure at Tübingen.[10] In 1975 he claimed Vatican II should not be interpreted as a rejection of the councils of Trent and Vatican I but as in continuity with them. Thus, while receiving Vatican II, he retained the earlier councils, in spite of their rejection by Protestants and difficulties for liberal Catholics.[11] This shift toward conservatism raised concerns among former colleagues such as Hans Küng, who would soon be disciplined by the Vatican for challenging papal infallibility.

After a Vatican appointment as archbishop of Munich and Freising in 1977, four years later he became the prefect of the Vatican's Congregation for the Doctrine of the Faith (CDF), popularly known as the "Inquisition." In these roles he garnered international respect from traditional Roman Catholics yet was loathed by liberals. His decisions regarding liberation theology, ecumenism, and liberalism proved unpopular in Latin America, Europe, and North America. In 2002 he was named dean of the College of Cardinals. And, in 2005, upon the demise of Pope John Paul II, Ratzinger was elected bishop of Rome, adopting the name Benedict XVI. Ratzinger's life project regards the definition and fostering of respect for the fundamentals of the Christian faith understood as both a personal response and a deposit of doctrine. Among his more important works in this regard are *Principles of Catholic Theology* and *The Nature and Mission of Theology*.[12] Also significant are some of the congregation's official documents during his prefecture, including "Instruction on the Ecclesial Vocation of the Theologian," which addresses

[9] Joseph Ratzinger, *Die Geschichtstheologie des Heiligen Bonaventura* (Munich: Schnell & Steiner, 1959).

[10] Stephen Mansfield, *Pope Benedict XVI: His Life and Mission* (New York: Penguin, 2005), 71; Ratzinger, *Milestones*, 134.

[11] Avery Cardinal Dulles, "From Ratzinger to Benedict," *First Things* 160 (February 2006): 24–29.

[12] Joseph Ratzinger, *Principles of Catholic Theology: Building Stones for a Fundamental Theology*, trans. Mary Frances McCarthy (San Francisco: Ignatius, 1987); idem, *The Nature and Mission of Theology: Approaches to Understanding Its Role in the Light of Present Controversy*, trans. Adrian Walker (San Francisco: Ignatius, 1995).

the differences yet correlation of the often conflicting roles of theologian and magisterium.[13]

Logos and Logic

Three aspects of Ratzinger's thought in regard to theological foundations should be considered. First, Ratzinger is no mere obscurantist. His concern for "certainty in religious knowledge" began with his reading of John Henry Cardinal Newman's *Grammar of Assent* under "my true teacher in theology," the fundamental theologian, Gottlieb Söhngen. Ratzinger believes that philosophy and theology must remain conversant with each other because both must keep ontology central. Ratzinger's prioritization of ontology is manifested in his desire for "the objectivity of dogma."[14] The ontological and seemingly abstract nature of Ratzinger's thought, especially with regard to the church, has been the subject of both scholarly and pastoral criticism.[15] He realizes that philosophy and theology are distinct disciplines. Philosophy is "the search of unaided reason for answers to the ultimate questions about reality." Theology, in contradistinction, is "rational reflection upon God's revelation; it is faith seeking understanding." Even so, the very core of biblical Christology invites interaction with philosophical inquiry.[16] Indeed, theology is "linked to philosophical inquiry as its basic methodology."[17]

In a recent papal address to the University of Regensburg, Benedict received international complaints regarding his positive allusion to the condemnatory comments against Islam by the late Byzantine emperor Manuel II Paleologus. Most, however, missed the primary intent of Benedict's speech. While taking swipes at Islam as well as Protestant Liberalism and cultural relativism, Benedict was advocating his belief that the Logos of the Johannine prologue, who is Jesus Christ, is simultaneously the source of the reasonableness upon which all the sciences, including theology, depend. The Logos as Word of God, the second person of the Trinity, is the creative source of the reason (*logos*) which science discovers. This is a theme repeatedly alluded to in Ratzinger's works but put forward most recently and firmly in his now infamous 2006 Regensburg lecture.[18]

The reasonable nature of reality is not, however, Ratzinger's primary concern. Rather, the logical nature of reality and the sciences that examine it are the result of their creation by the Logos. And it is the Logos who is at the center of the current pope's theological system. In his early book *Introduction to Christianity*, the young Ratzinger affirmed that the concept of Logos was the core of Christology,

[13] CDF, "Instruction on the Ecclesial Vocation of the Theologian" (Rome, 24 May 1990); see www.vatican.va/roman_curia/congregations/cfaith/documents; accessed 8 November 2006.

[14] Joseph Ratzinger, "Presentation by his Eminence Card. Joseph Ratzinger on the Occasion of the First Centenary of the Death of Card. John Henry Newman" (Rome, 28 April 1990); see www.vatican.va/roman_curia/congregations/cfaith/documents; accessed 8 November 2006.

[15] Ibid.; Richard P. McBrien, book review, *TS* 49 (June 1988): 347–49; Kilian McDonnell, "The Ratzinger/Kasper Debate: The Universal Church and the Local Churches," *TS* 63 (June 2002): 247.

[16] Ratzinger, *The Nature and Mission of Theology*, 16, 25.

[17] Ratzinger, *Principles of Catholic Theology*, 316.

[18] Benedict, "Faith, Reason and the University: Memories and Reflections" (Regensburg, 12 September 2006); see www.vatican.va/holy_father/benedict_xvi/speeches/2006; accessed 8 November 2006.

that Christology should be the fundamental approach to theology, and that ethics must be founded on theology. His entire system of thought, whether theological or philosophical or ethical, was constructed upon the Logos, the God who became incarnate. Nearly forty years later he reaffirmed in no uncertain terms that he still believed that Logos Christology was and is the correct approach to all doctrine, theological and moral.[19] In this way Joseph Ratzinger shares a common outlook with Carl F. H. Henry, a father of modern American evangelicalism and a Baptist theologian whose lifelong work in the doctrine of revelation also makes the Logos the fulcrum of rationality and Christology.[20] Of course, Henry too has received criticism for his intense rationalism.[21]

Faith in Christ

Second, Ratzinger is neither an analytical philosopher nor an uncaring bureaucrat. He habitually returns to his personal faith in the biblical Christ. One of the earliest influences upon him, a theological professor by the name of Alfred Läpple, wrote a dissertation on the concept of conscience in John Henry Cardinal Newman. Ratzinger's exposure to Newman's views of conscience was liberating after his experience with the Nazis, who "negated the conscience of the individual."[22] Thus, he discovered the philosophy of personalism, which he describes as "a spiritual experience that left an essential mark, especially since I spontaneously associated such personalism with the thought of Augustine, who in his *Confessions* had struck me with power of all his human passion and depth." He considered Thomas Aquinas's immaculate logic, in contrast, to be "too closed in on itself, too impersonal and ready-made."[23] Personalism remained and remains an important theme for Ratzinger. He begins his collected essays on the foundations of theology not with a discussion of church structures but with an extended discussion of salvation and faith.[24] Personal conversion is so important that to say "becoming and being a Christian rest upon conversion" may not adequately reflect the Pauline understanding. Conversion is "something much more radical than, say, the revision of a few opinions and attitudes. It is a death-event." The old subject must die, and Christ must become the new subject (Gal 2:20).[25]

Personal conversion to Jesus Christ is a necessity not only for the Christian but also for the theologian and the minister. "Since the object of theology is the Truth which is the living God and His plan for salvation revealed in Jesus Christ, the theologian is called to deepen his own life of faith and continuously unite his

---

[19] Joseph Ratzinger, "*Introduction to Christianity*: Yesterday, Today, and Tomorrow," *Communio* 31 (Fall 2004): 481–95.

[20] Carl F. H. Henry, *God, Revelation and Authority* (1976–1983; reprint, Wheaton, IL: Crossway, 1999), 1:181–201.

[21] Donald G. Bloesch, *A Theology of Word & Spirit: Authority and Method in Theology*, Christian Foundations, vol. 1 (Downers Grove, IL: InterVarsity, 58, 252–54.

[22] Ratzinger, "The First Centenary of the Death of Card. John Henry Newman."

[23] Ratzinger, *Milestones*, 44.

[24] Ratzinger, *Principles of Catholic Theology*, 15–83.

[25] Ratzinger, *The Nature and Mission of Theology*, 50–51.

scientific research with prayer."[26] "Theology is a specifically Christian phenomenon" and cannot be adequately accomplished apart from the church.[27] Moreover, Christian clergy, whom he describes with the extrabiblical name of "priests," must first be spiritual. "The priest himself should be a 'pneumatic,' a *homo spiritualis*, a man awakened and driven by the Holy Spirit."[28] The "essential foundation" of any Christian ministry is "a deep personal bond to Jesus Christ." "The priest must be a man who knows Jesus intimately, who has encountered him and has learned to love him." Out of this personal relationship with Christ, a man has the means to minister God's grace to others.[29]

This dynamic Christian personalism must be intimately bound with a strong ecclesial commitment. The personal conscience may not be set over against the church but must seek to be formed by her. "Conscience is not an independent and infallible faculty."[30] Ratzinger arrives at his conclusion regarding the fallibility of conscience through biblical interpretation. Psalm 19:12–13 asks, "Who can discern his errors?" And the psalmist prays, "Clear thou me from my unknown faults." According to Rom 2:14, the human conscience reflects the memory of divine law. Yet, according to Rom 14:23, nobody can act against personal conviction. These passages, viewed canonically, teach that the conscience, though a general guide, may be perverted. Liberalism's idea of conscience as an infallible and unquestionable authority thus lacks a firm biblical basis.[31]

Ratzinger concludes that consciences may err and must be formed. So far biblicists could agree with his theological exegesis. Most Protestants, however, demur with the next step. According to the inquisitor, for a theologian's conscience to be formed correctly, he must presume three things: "faith in the Word of God," "love for the Church," and "respect for her divinely assisted Magisterium."[32] The first two presumptions are without controversy, but the third presents significant difficulties from a strictly canonical perspective, a perspective Ratzinger dismisses as the reducing of the church to Scripture (*reductio ecclesiae ad Scripturam*).[33]

Architectonic Ecclesiology

This brings us to the third and most distinctive aspect of Ratzinger's theological foundations: his architectonic ecclesiology. Theology is ultimately dependent upon the church, for the church is "the ground of theology's existence and the condition which makes it possible."[34] Ratzinger recognizes three levels in the church:

[26] CDF, "Instruction on the Ecclesial Vocation of the Theologian," art. 8.

[27] Ratzinger, *The Nature and Mission of Theology*, 103.

[28] Joseph Ratzinger, "The Theological Locus of Ecclesial Movements," *Communio* 25 (Fall 1998): 484.

[29] Joseph Ratzinger, *Called to Communion: Understanding the Church Today*, trans. Adrian Walker (San Francisco: Ignatius, 1996), 128–30.

[30] CDF, "Instruction on the Ecclesial Vocation of the Theologian," art. 38.

[31] Joseph Ratzinger, "Conscience and Truth" (Dallas, February 1991); see www.ewtn.com/library/curia/ratzcons.htm; accessed 16 October 2006.

[32] CDF, "Instruction on the Ecclesial Vocation of the Theologian," art. 38.

[33] Ratzinger, *Principles of Catholic Theology*, 223.

[34] Ratzinger, *The Nature and Mission of Theology*, 61.

ecclesia universalis (universal church), *ecclesia localis* (patriarchal church), and *ecclesia particularis* (diocesan church).[35] His ecclesiology thus begins with the universal church as opposed to the particular church: the universal church is "a reality ontologically and temporally prior to every individual particular church."[36] This ontological claim brought him into conflict with leading ecumenists on both sides of the Protestant/Roman Catholic divide. Walter Kasper, a Roman Catholic bishop, feared a rejection of Vatican II's more local ecclesiology and a return to Roman centralism. In Kasper's eyes, Ratzinger seemed to be equating the Roman church with the universal church. Although Ratzinger denied an exact identity in that debate,[37] he nevertheless claimed the Petrine ministry is "a foundation and unity of the Episcopate and of the universal Church."[38] (Later, moreover, he alludes to "the full identity between the Church of Jesus Christ and the Roman Catholic Church."[39])

The debate between Kasper and Ratzinger demonstrates that Vatican II's statement that the universal church "subsists" (*subsistit*) in the Roman Catholic Church allows for a variety of claims, and Ratzinger takes the most traditional position possible, while still retaining Vatican II.[40] Johannes Hanselmann, a Lutheran provincial bishop, repeatedly challenged Ratzinger to provide a biblical basis for the ontological priority of the universal church and for Petrine primacy. In response to the first issue, Ratzinger referred Hanselmann to the temporal priority of the Jerusalem church and to Paul's allegory in Galatians, equating "theological"—which is generally understood as inclusive of both history and ontology—purely with "ontological." He did not respond to Hanselmann's request for a biblical foundation of the Roman claim to Petrine succession.[41]

Ratzinger is as hostile to the contemporary Roman Catholic concept of the "base community" (popularized by liberation theologians) as he is to the primary Protestant mark of the church. Both of the latter concepts of the church start "from below." According to the primary Protestant mark, the church is where the people gather to hear the Word proclaimed. In substantive agreement with Luther, the free churches have traditionally discerned the constitution of the local church in the word of Christ of Matt 18:20. Summarily dismissing all such ecclesiologies from below, Ratzinger asserts that, "as a constitutive principle of the church," the congregational doctrines drawn from Matt 18:20 "are not sufficient."[42] Nowhere does Ratzinger explain exactly why Matthew 18 is an insufficient theological

[35] Ratzinger, *Principles of Catholic Theology*, 289–90.

[36] CDF, "Letter to the Bishops of the Catholic Church on Some Aspects of the Church Understood as Communion" (Rome, 28 May 1992), art. 9.

[37] McDonnell, "The Ratzinger/Kasper Debate," 236.

[38] CDF, "Some Aspects of the Church Understood as Communion," art. 11.

[39] Ratzinger, *Principles of Catholic Theology*, 230.

[40] Joseph Ratzinger, *Pilgrim Fellowship of Faith: The Church as Communion*, trans. Henry Taylor (San Francisco: Ignatius, 2005), 145–49; *Lumen Gentium*, art. 8, in *Vatican Council II: The Conciliar and Post Conciliar Documents*, study ed., ed. Austin Flannery (Northport, NY: Costello, 1987), 357.

[41] Johannes Hanselmann to Joseph Ratzinger (5 February 1993), arts. 4, 7, and 9; and Joseph Ratzinger to Johannes Hanselmann (9 March 1993), arts. 4, 7, and 9; in Ratzinger, *Pilgrim Fellowship of Faith*, 242–52.

[42] Ratzinger, *Called to Communion*, 82.

foundation for the local church. He simply makes the dark assertion that those who appeal to congregationalism are anthropologically "self-sufficient" and driven by social utopianism.[43]

After dismissing the legitimacy of an exegetical ecclesiology constructed on Matthew 18, Ratzinger turns to a peculiarly Roman exegesis of Scripture that is heavily dependent on postapostolic developments. The New Testament accords a preeminent status to the apostle Peter, as affirmed, even if primarily through implication, by Paul (1 Cor 15:3–7; Gal 1:8; 2:11–14) and John (John 21:15–19) as well as the synoptic writers (Matt 10:2–4; 14:28ff; 18:21; Mark 1:36; 3:16–19; 5:37; 9:2ff; 14:33ff; Luke 5:1–11; 6:14–16; 9:32; 22:32; Acts 1:13). The classic Roman prooftext is Matt 16:17–19, where the disciple Simon is renamed *Petros* and granted the keys of binding and loosing. Ratzinger dismisses the historical-critical objections to the early nature of the text quite well but assumes the Protestant identification of *Petra* with Peter's confession is also forced. In a novel identification of the second-person and third-person objects under discussion in Matt 16:18, Ratzinger conflates the church with Peter. In a second allegory he also sees Peter as receiving the promise for the gathering of the universal church.

And in a third innovation, along with the "time-transcendent gathering" of the universal church to Peter comes the power of the keys, which Ratzinger says represents Peter's authority over both the doctrine and the discipline of the universal church. Yet Ratzinger cannot stop with the innovative and allegorical nature of his interpretation of Matthew 16. His ecclesiology demands not only a doctrinal and juridical primacy for Peter among the apostles and over the universal church, but it also requires Peter's primacy be (1) transmitted to the bishop of Rome, and (2) continually transmitted to the succeeding bishops of Rome. Ratzinger admits immediately "that there is no explicit statement regarding the Petrine succession in the New Testament."[44] At this point he turns to a reading of early church tradition that is generally rejected not only by Protestants but also by Eastern Orthodox theologians.

Ratzinger's ecclesiology, the primary foundation for his theology, may be described as "architectonic" due to its structurally directive and systematic nature. As noted above, he has been criticized within his own tradition for an abstract and idealized ecclesiology. Ratzinger's ideal church begins with the universal church, over which the Roman bishop has pastoral oversight, and is held together by the college of bishops. The college of bishops succeeds the body of the apostles as the bishop of Rome succeeds Peter. The college of bishops exercises a conciliar magistracy but always in communion with and under the bishop of Rome. The churches in the localities are united with the universal church through the Eucharistic presidency of their bishop. In this way the bishop is the "central element of the Church's constitution."[45]

---

[43] CDF, "Some Aspects of the Church Understood as Communion," art. 8; Ratzinger, *Principles of Catholic Theology*, 290–94.

[44] Ratzinger, *Called to Communion*, 48–65.

[45] Ibid., 94.

Yet the bishop of Rome is not dependent upon the local bishop in his relationship with the local church: "The ministry of the Successor of Peter is something interior to each particular church."[46] As for the churches that do not recognize papal primacy, "non-Catholic Churches and Christian communities" have been "wounded" in different ways. The Eastern Orthodox churches remain united to the Catholic Church by "the apostolic succession and a valid Eucharist." "The wound is even deeper in those ecclesial communities which have not retained the apostolic succession and a valid Eucharist."[47] The "ecclesial communities" include the Protestant churches. The Eastern Orthodox attained a level of restored communion in the twentieth century, even if it is not yet Eucharistic.[48]

This third aspect of Ratzinger's foundational theology, ecclesiology, has been treated at length because the church is not only architectonic but periodically conflated with God. Catholic theologians, including Ratzinger, speak in a way that Protestants find baffling. Often, where a Protestant might refer to God, a Catholic speaks of the church. This should not be taken as a universal confusion of the divine with the ecclesial but as a much stronger correlation than is biblically conceived. In Roman Catholic parlance, "To speak of the Church is to speak of God."[49] This conflation is evident throughout Ratzinger's writings in nominal exchanges between the church and all three persons of the Trinity. While discussing Augustine's psychological doctrine of the Trinity, Ratzinger notes that the Father is *memoria*. Without explanation he concludes, "The seat of faith is, then, the *memoria Ecclesiae*, the memory of the Church, the Church as memory."[50] Christology, too, becomes a means to ecclesiology. Because the church is the body of Christ, it also may claim to be a mediator.[51]

In his discussions both Christ and the Spirit are treated secondarily in reference to the church. As for the third person of the Trinity in particular, the church provides the structure of the faith in which the Spirit forms the content.[52] Ratzinger assumes that the church and the priesthood are automatically "pneumatic" and that the Holy Spirit speaks in the church councils. Where the Reformers spoke of the Word requiring the Spirit, Ratzinger speaks of the Word requiring the church and its priesthood.[53] The necessity of going through the church to come to God explains why he affirms that the sacraments of baptism and the Eucharist create access to the Trinity.[54] Ratzinger not only conflates God and the church but proceeds similarly to equate the apostolate, the episcopate, and the presbyterate with the particular priesthood. In this way the papacy, episcopacy, and the priesthood take center stage in the life of the church.[55]

[46] CDF, "Some Aspects of the Church Understood as Communion," art. 13.
[47] Ibid., art. 17.
[48] Ratzinger, *Principles of Catholic Theology*, 193–227.
[49] Kilian, "The Ratzinger/Kasper Debate," 237.
[50] Ratzinger, *Principles of Catholic Theology*, 23.
[51] Ibid., 272.
[52] Ratzinger, *Called to Communion*, 87.
[53] Ratzinger, *Principles of Catholic Theology*, 230, 263, 268.
[54] Ratzinger, *Called to Communion*, 33.
[55] Ratzinger, *Principles of Catholic Theology*, 273–84; idem, *Called to Communion*, 121–22.

According to this phenomenological review of Joseph Ratzinger's writings, Roman Catholic foundational theology is based on three pillars: the rational nature of faith provided by the Logos as Creator and Redeemer, a deeply personal relationship with Jesus Christ, and, above all, an architectonic and conflating doctrine of the church. The ecclesiastical focus of Ratzinger is his strongest characteristic. Indeed, his love for the church compels him to work against the acids of modern culture and modern theology. Indeed, he sees the two as connected with each other. "Ratzinger believes the empty churches of the West are at least in part the fault of progressive theologians who have reinterpreted Christianity to such an extent that it is virtually indistinguishable from culture."[56] To one of those progressive Western theologians we now turn.

MAURICE WILES, HOSPITABLE LIBERAL

Maurice F. Wiles, born in 1923 as the son of a prominent civil servant, had two grandfathers who were, on the one hand, a reserved Anglican, and, on the other, a conservative Baptist. Wiles was ordained in 1951 as an Anglican priest and held a series of prestigious posts in Cambridge, London, and Oxford during his academic career. He wrote fifteen books and numerous scholarly articles. Most famously Wiles collaborated with John Hick and John A. T. Robinson, among others, in a programmatic challenge spanning the theological disciplines to orthodox theology, especially the doctrine of the incarnation.[57] If Hick may be taken as the principal representative of philosophical theology within the liberal tradition[58] and Robinson as the foremost representative of liberal biblical theology,[59] Wiles is the most prestigious representative of historical and systematic theology within English Liberalism. According to Hick, his colleague's effort to reconstruct Christian doctrine so that it "can be credible today" makes Wiles "a light to liberals within the church and a pain to conservatives."[60] Without receiving challenge, Hick proclaimed Wiles to be "Britain's leading 'liberal' or 'radical' theologian."[61]

Wiles's historical expertise lay in patristic theology, but he displayed an enduring interest in reinterpreting the Christian faith for modern culture, especially in relation to the modern sciences. *The Spiritual Gospel* and *Archetypal Heresy* mark the beginning and end points of his lifelong program to refashion Christian understanding of the meaning and importance of the early fathers and orthodoxy.[62]

---

[56] John L. Allen Jr., *Cardinal Ratzinger: The Vatican's Enforcer of the Faith* (New York: Continuum, 2000), 265.

[57] Maurice F. Wiles, "Does Christology Rest on a Mistake?" in *Christ, Faith and History: Cambridge Studies in Christology*, ed. S. W. Sykes and J. P. Clayton (New York: Cambridge University Press, 1972), 3–12; John A. T. Robinson, "Need Jesus Have Been Perfect?" in ibid., 39–52. Wiles, "Christianity without Incarnation?" in *The Myth of God Incarnate*, ed. John Hick (London: SCM, 1977), 1–11.

[58] John Hick, *Philosophy of Religion* (Englewood Cliffs, NJ: Prentice-Hall, 1963).

[59] Robinson, *Honest to God* (London: SCM, 1963).

[60] John Hick, "Preface to Reissue," *The Myth of God Incarnate* (London: SCM, 1993), xiii.

[61] John Hick, "Interpretation and Reinterpretation in Religion," in *The Making and Remaking of Christian Doctrine: Essays in Honour of Maurice Wiles*, ed. Sarah Coakley and David A. Pailin (New York: Oxford University Press, 1993), 57.

[62] Maurice Wiles, *The Spiritual Gospel: The Interpretation of the Fourth Gospel in the Early Church* (New York: Cambridge University Press, 1960; new ed., 2006); idem, *Archetypal Heresy: Arianism through the*

In his 1967 volume *The Making of Christian Doctrine*, Wiles stimulated extensive and vigorous discussion regarding the propriety of developing new doctrine to address contemporary concerns through the rejection of older formulae.[63] *Working Papers in Doctrine* collected some of his most provocative earlier essays, including his inaugural lectures as professor of Christian Doctrine in the University of London and Regius Professor of Divinity at the University of Oxford.[64] His positive proposals were deepened in the *Remaking of Christian Doctrine*, subsequently incorporated in a prolegomena, *What is Theology?* and systematically popularized in *Reason to Believe*.[65]

Oxonian Hospitableness

Wiles somewhat reflects what Ben Quash describes as "Anglican habits of mind," by which Quash means openness rather than systematization and engaging in theology as a community rather than as an individual. Anglican theology is "provisional in its judgments" on the one hand and seeks to establish "forms of common life, common responsibility, [and] common prayer" on the other. These peculiar characteristics of Anglican theology are rooted in the historical vagaries of the Reformation, when a change in monarch required a change in religion, and theology was often performed by committee.[66] Quash's first habit of mind, provision in judgment, contributes to a perception of Anglican theology, at least within modern American evangelicalism, as fostering theological liberalism. Although this is manifestly not always the case (cp. J. I. Packer, John Stott, and Gerald Bray), it is true with regard to Maurice Wiles. Although Anglican in commitment, the "habits of mind" particularly evident in Wiles may be more properly characterized as an Oxonian discretion to be both hospitable and reasonable.

At his death in 2005, Wiles was appreciated by his colleagues and students for "his passion for truth, his integrity, and his transparent goodness."[67] These endearing personal characteristics were noted even by his theological opponents, one of whom sought "the honour of remaining his 'dearest enemy.'" According to Gerard Rothuizen, a Dutch Reformed critic, Wiles displayed a hospitableness that is characteristic

Centuries (New York: Oxford University Press, 1996).

[63] Maurice Wiles, *The Making of Christian Doctrine: A Study in the Principles of Early Doctrinal Development* (New York: Cambridge University Press, 1967). Cp. E. L. Mascall, book review, *Journal of Theological Studies* 19 (1968): 399–420; Robert Wilken, book review, *JR* 49 (1969): 313; Robert Evans, book review, *JAAR* 38 (1970): 111–12; J. C. M. van Winden, book review, *VC* 25 (1971): 225–26.

[64] Wiles, *Working Papers in Doctrine* (London: SCM, 1976).

[65] Maurice Wiles, *The Remaking of Christian Doctrine: The Hulsean Lectures 1973* (London: SCM, 1974); idem, *What Is Theology?* (New York: Oxford University Press, 1976); idem, *Reason to Believe* (Harrisburg, PA: Trinity Press International, 1999).

[66] Quash oddly attributes the Anglican habit of mind to common-law tradition rather than to any religious tradition, so we have taken the liberty to refocus his comments. The English Reformer Thomas Cranmer reflects the two habits of mind identified by Quash: he was instrumental in the theological formulations of many sixteenth-century committees (reflecting Anglican provision) and authored the *Book of Common Prayer* (reflecting Anglican community). Ben Quash, *Theology and the Drama of History*, CSCD (Cambridge: Cambridge University Press, 2005), 8–9.

[67] Obituary, "The Rev Professor Maurice Wiles: Liberal Church of England Theologian Who Constantly Urged the Need to Question the Conservative Aspects of Doctrine," *Times* (London, 7 June 2005).

of Anglican theology in general but especially of Anglicanism in Oxford. Drawing upon numerous sources, Rothuizen describes the Oxford theological tradition as one of "common sense and reason." The Oxford tradition is tolerant, moderate, and open, while simultaneously engaging in "rigorous theological inquiry." With regard to Scripture, twentieth-century Oxford theology is "markedly unauthoritarian"; with regard to theological method, it is partially detached; and yet, with regard to the church, it is deeply respectful of "personal piety and parish life."[68] Wiles superbly embodied this Oxonian theological hospitableness throughout his career.

Modern Reasonableness

Wiles has been noted less for a rigid theological method than for his openness to new thought. The hospitable nature of Wiles's theology might appear to diminish any theological foundation, yet there is a nonnegotiable foundation in his method. Above all, Wiles sought to be reasonable in a modern mood. His definition of theology—arrived at etymologically by defining *logos* as reason and *theos* as God—is "reasoned discourse about God" or "to speak rationally about God."[69] A consistent thinker, Wiles followed this definition throughout his career and sought to make theology reasonable, especially in conversation with other disciplines, including the natural sciences, the human sciences, and history. Above all, his goal was apologetic: "It is my hope [to lead others] to see Christian belief as something that can reasonably be affirmed without having simply to shut our eyes to difficulties of which we cannot help but be aware."[70] For Wiles, a reasonable apologetic served as both a theological foundation and a means of doctrinal development. On the basis of a reasonable presentation, he sought to develop doctrine that might speak to the contemporary skeptic. Although Wiles's goal was certainly laudable, to conservatives his method appeared to endanger essential Christian doctrines.

Wiles seemed to be unaware, or at least silently disapproving, of Karl Barth's critique of Friedrich Schleiermacher, who first pioneered the Liberal theological method, a method whose goal was primarily apologetic. According to Barth, the theologian who acts as an apologist may no longer claim to be a theologian.

> This white flag, which the theologian must carry as an apologist, means of course for the theologian himself that in so far as he is an apologist he must, as Schleiermacher once more expressly states, take his point of departure (standpoint) above Christianity (in the logical sense of the word) in the general concept of the community of pious people or believers. As an apologist, he is not a Christian theologian but a moral philosopher and philosopher of religion. He suspends to that extent his attitude to Christianity, and his judgment of the truth or even absoluteness of the Christian revelation."[71]

---

[68] Rothuizen, *Apologetics in Oxford*, 21–26.

[69] Wiles, *What Is Theology?* 1, 57; idem, "Looking into the Sun," in *Working Papers in Doctrine*, 149.

[70] Wiles, *What Is Theology?* pt. 3; idem, x.

[71] Karl Barth, *Protestant Theology in the Nineteenth Century: Its Background and History*, new ed., trans. Brian Cozens and John Bowden (Grand Rapids: Eerdmans, 2002), 430.

In response to the liberalism of his teachers, whose project was rooted in the apologetic task, Barth firmly rejected natural theology and promoted special revelation through the existential appropriation of Scripture. Barth's project captured the theological world's attention with his commentary on Romans and was fully fleshed out in his aptly named *Church Dogmatics* (*Die Kirchliche Dogmatik*).[72]

Due to the scathing critique of Carl Henry, Barth's reaction to liberalism was rather coolly received among twentieth-century American evangelicals. Barth's doctrine of revelation affirmed the Word of God as contained within Scripture, or more properly that Scripture becomes the Word, rather than allowing for a direct identification of the Word with Scripture.[73] Yet, alongside their rejection of Barth's neoorthodox doctrine of revelation, evangelicals also neglected his chosen theological context, which was to develop doctrine primarily in conversation with the Christian church rather than the academy. Through their neglect to appreciate Barth's project, modern American evangelicals sometimes unwittingly mirror the liberal method of Schleiermacher and Wiles, a method which may lead to the academic captivity of theology in the name of reasonableness, or the cultural captivity of the church in the name of relevancy.

Historical Criticism, Then Doctrinal Criticism

There are two sides to Wiles's idea of reasonableness, a negative one and a positive one. Negatively, Wiles rejected ideas he considered incompatible with modern standards of rationality. This resulted in his firm denial of the inspiration and inerrancy of Scripture and encouraged him to question major tenets of the Christian faith, especially as defined by the early church's councils. In his inaugural lecture at the University of London, "Looking into the Sun," Wiles acknowledged the historical critical method, in its most "thoroughgoing critical treatment of the Scriptures," as a necessary development in the academy. Since looking at Scripture critically had not hurt Christian eyes, in spite of fears otherwise, Wiles called for a similar critical approach to Christian doctrine. Wiles proceeded to advocate the new method of "doctrinal criticism," the second necessary step following biblical criticism in the Enlightenment challenge to Christian orthodoxy.[74]

In this inaugural lecture, he specifically considered the exclusivity of Christ. He said that Jesus did not view himself as unique; rather, uniqueness was assigned to him by the later church. According to Wiles, this change is unremarkable. With the transition from a Semitic to a Hellenistic context, the church was required to translate the ultimacy of Christ from a temporal dimension to an eternal or ontological dimension. This led finally to the unworkable definition of Chalcedon that Christ possessed two natures, the divine and the human. Now,

[72] Karl Barth, *The Epistle to the Romans*, 6th ed., trans. Edwyn C. Hoskyns (New York: Oxford University Press, 1933); idem, *Church Dogmatics*, trans. G. W. Bromiley, T. F. Torrance, et al. (Edinburgh: T&T Clark, 1958–77).

[73] Henry, *God, Revelation and Authority*, passim.

[74] Cp. Wiles, *The Remaking of Christian Doctrine*, 48.

however, we live in a worldview of "historical relativism," and it is difficult to privilege the events of Christ's life above the lives of others. Thus, the radical sense of Christ's uniqueness is historically conditioned, not eternally true. Similarly, just as the transition of a worldview from the Semitic to the Hellenistic contexts required the development of Chalcedonian doctrine, so the further transition to the modern context requires a contemporary restatement of the doctrine of Christ.[75] Preparatory to the restatement of Christian doctrine in contemporary terms, one must critique the ancient creeds of Nicaea, Chalcedon, and Athanasius.

Rejecting Scripture's inerrancy in the name of historical criticism and rejecting traditional authority in the name of doctrinal criticism, Wiles engaged in a systematic deconstruction, to borrow a later philosophical term, of Christian doctrine. The philosophical foundation of this deconstruction was "the modern understanding of reality." Contemporary philosophy must be privileged over both the authority of Scripture and the authority of tradition. The fathers' reading of Scripture cannot be authoritative because the canon seems arbitrary, the hermeneutical method they employed is indirect from modern standards, and Scripture may simply not teach true doctrine. The modern worldview of "historical consciousness" is helpful in letting us know where we have been and aids in the plotting of a course for the future.

According to Wiles, modern Christians must simply correct the early church and abandon the old doctrine in favor of a more relevant doctrine for modern culture.[76] The proper test of doctrinal development is not fidelity to the past. Doctrines must be constructed according to their creative potential for the future. Dogma is simply not "unchangeable," although it must "be seen in a continuity of fundamental aims" with prior Christians. Although Wiles accepts what he defines as the three appeals of the early fathers to Scripture, worship, and salvation, he rejects the way the fathers reasoned from them. He specifically rejected the patristic tendency to "objectification" and the very early practice of "incorporating new ideas into an existing body of doctrine." What is required is a "Copernican revolution" in theology that moves beyond the old formulae.[77]

On this foundation of reasonableness according to modern standards, Wiles went on to challenge nearly every major doctrine of the Christian faith. His most famous challenge occurred in his contribution to *The Myth of God Incarnate*, wherein he downplayed the idea that Christianity would be lost if it denied the historical truthfulness of the incarnation of the second person of the Trinity in Jesus of Nazareth. Just as a change in the understanding of the Lord's Supper from transubstantiation to other views during the Reformation did not result in the loss of Christianity, so a rejection of the historicity of the incarnation is not to be

[75] Wiles, "Looking into the Sun," in *Working Papers in Doctrine*, 148–63. Cp. idem, *What Is Theology?* 28–30, 39–41.

[76] Wiles, "The Consequences of Modern Understanding of Reality for the Relevance and Authority of the Tradition of the Early Church in Our Time," in *Working Papers in Doctrine*, 89–107.

[77] Wiles, *The Making of Christian Doctrine*, 159–81.

feared. Defining the incarnation as myth would not endanger Christian teaching regarding the holistic nature of humanity, Christ as a pattern for Christian living, nor the Christian understanding of salvation.[78]

Wiles defended at some length the liberal use of the word *myth* to describe the incarnation. He appreciated the very imprecision of the term, which some took to indicate deceit but others took to indicate religious truth without regard to historicity. He believed the application of *myth* to the incarnation allowed for a truer understanding of the possibility of human union with the divine in "every man." The particularity of Christ might be lost in the process, but the major positive affirmations of Christianity (what Harnack referred to earlier as the "kernel" of Christianity)—openness to God and love toward humans—would be retained. He answered the objections of more orthodox theologians by stating that the danger of identifying the incarnation as a myth was not overly great, that the term was valuable for theological analysis, and that the loss of literal meaning did not entail a loss of Christianity's power.[79] Moreover, Wiles was not content to question only the doctrine of the incarnation. Among other provocative moves, he also defended the heresiarch Arius,[80] questioned the orthodox doctrine of the immanent Trinity,[81] and queried whether Christology rested on a mistake.[82]

Remaking the Christian Faith

Wiles was not merely engaged negatively in a project of deconstruction. He also set about positively to offer a system of Christian doctrine that would help the world to see that Christianity provides, as mentioned above, *a* legitimate way of thinking and living. For Wiles, understanding "the making of Christian doctrine" yesterday was purely preparatory to "the remaking of Christian doctrine" for tomorrow. His colleagues and students honored the creative potential of Wiles's theological project, combining the titles of his two most famous books, *The Making of Christian Doctrine* and *The Remaking of Christian Doctrine*, for a 1993 festschrift, *The Making and Remaking of Christian Doctrine*.[83] Wiles remade Christian doctrine according to the objectives of "coherence," "economy," and "imaginative expansiveness."[84] He refused to say anything more than modern reason would allow in his interaction with Scripture and church tradition, and his

[78] Wiles, "Christianity without Incarnation?" in *The Myth of God Incarnate*, 1–10.

[79] Wiles, "Myth in Theology," in ibid., 148–65.

[80] Wiles, "In Defence of Arius," in *Working Papers in Doctrine*, 18–27. Even toward the end of his career, Wiles remained unsatisfied with the Nicene answers to the question raised by Arius. Wiles continued to consider Arianism a viable alternative to Nicene doctrine in spite of his careful reconstruction of its periodic disappearance in Christian history. A system that has garnered so little respect historically might be easily dismissed by others as unworthy of serious theological consideration, but Wiles was never satisfied with the majority answer and favored careful and hospitable reasoning above all. Wiles, *Archetypal Heresy*, 181.

[81] Wiles, "Some Reflections on the Origins of the Doctrine of the Trinity," in *Working Papers in Doctrine*, 1–17.

[82] Wiles, "Does Christology Rest on a Mistake?" in *Christ, Faith and History*, 3–12; idem, "A Reply to Mr. Baelz," in ibid., 35–38.

[83] *The Making and Remaking of Christian Doctrine: Essays in Honour of Maurice Wiles.*

[84] Wiles, *The Remaking of Christian Doctrine*, 17–18.

goal was to speak in a way succinctly helpful to modern humanity. The means of remaking Christian doctrine began with the flexible but provocative language of "myth" as applied to doctrines traditionally garnered from Scripture but transitioned over time to the more subtle yet suggestive language of "metaphor," "symbol," "legend," and "tale." Yet he was as clear as ever that the stories in Scripture are "patently not straightforward historical events." Events that are legendary "can have no claim to be treated as accurate accounts of what happened."[85]

His later systematic ruminations indicate how profoundly his method of remaking Christian doctrine resulted in a radical departure from traditional dogma. Regarding the doctrine of God, Wiles was willing to say, "There is a reality other than the human experiencing, but we are only able to speak of it indirectly by speaking of those experiences within which we are aware of its effective presence."[86] There is a transcendent cause who prompts in us a sense of wonder and of whom we may speak only analogically. God has some providential relation to the world dependent upon Him, but beyond this we cannot say much.[87] Regarding the doctrine of the Trinity, speaking of the Father is a symbolic way of saying there exists anything at all. Speaking of the Son is symbolic of "the transformative power of the historical figure of Jesus," an affirmation which should not be taken as approval of the historicity of Jesus Himself but as recognition of the church's construction of the historical figure of Jesus. And speaking of the Spirit symbolizes "the inwardness of profound human, and particularly Christian existence."[88]

Especially with regard to his doctrine of the Holy Spirit and divine grace as "characteristics of religious experience," it is apparent that Wiles conceives the Trinity from an almost exclusively anthropocentric perspective.[89] Similarly, atonement and salvation should not be understood in the traditional terms of sacrificial substitution and justification but as the possibility of individual attitudes and lives being transformed.[90] The church has a "Janus-like" or "Jekyll and Hyde-like" history that does not allow it to speak with any authority.[91] Finally, the Bible's eschatological statements are "not to be treated as specific predictions of the future, but rather as deep-seated human hopes finding expression in forms shaped by the Christian story and by the faith in God that stems from it."[92] In numerous ways Wiles profoundly reconstructed the Christian faith, offering simple, provisional, and ethical alternatives to traditionally complex, eternal, and ontological dogmas.

---

[85] Wiles, "Myth in Theology," in *The Myth of God Incarnate*, 148–166; idem, *Reason to Believe*, 10, 30–31, 34, 36–37, 40.

[86] Wiles, *The Remaking of Christian Doctrine*, 27.

[87] Wiles, *Reason to Believe*, 1–18.

[88] Ibid., 70.

[89] Wiles, *The Remaking of Christian Doctrine*, 101.

[90] Wiles, *Reason to Believe*, 77–78.

[91] Ibid., 84–88.

[92] Ibid., 76.

HERMAN BAVINCK, REASONABLY REFORMED

Herman Bavinck was a Calvinist theologian affiliated with the Dutch Christian Reformed Church, the ecclesiastical heir of a pietistic movement seceding from the state church. His choice to attend the modernist school at Leiden revealed an ongoing tension in his attraction to both orthodoxy and modernity. He taught theology at Kampen (1883–1902) and succeeded Abraham Kuyper at the Free University of Amsterdam as professor of dogmatics (1902–1920). He was noted for his broad vision of the universal church, in a distinctly Reformed note, and firmly denounced separatist Christianity for its distrust of public life. Like Kuyper he was active in the state as in the church, serving as a member of the Royal Academy of Sciences and as an elected member of the upper house in the States General of the Netherlands. Bavinck's experience of a tension between church and world found a Reformed theological center in Calvinism's doctrine of "common grace." Bavinck's system encompasses both church and society through the theme that "grace restores nature."[93] Bavinck visited North America to deliver lectures in Toronto and Princeton, but his most extensive influence in the twentieth century occurred through the heavy dependence of Louis Berkhof's popular *Systematic Theology* upon Bavinck.[94] Bavinck and Kuyper are the leading representatives of the Dutch Neo-Calvinist theological school.

Indicative of his growing importance in American Reformed theological circles is the fact that his magnum opus, *Gereformeerde Dogmatiek*, is currently undergoing a translation project overseen by a broad cross-section of Reformed theologians from multiple denominations that includes, among others, Joel Beeke, John Bolt, I. John Hesselink, Richard Muller, and M. Eugene Osterhaven.[95] The first volume of that project, *Prolegomena*, is a premiere source for any evaluation of Reformed theological foundations.[96] Bavinck's essays on common grace[97] and catholicity,[98] and his less technical systematic theology, *Our Reasonable Faith*,[99] are also helpful. Bavinck has been accused of being more philosopher than theologian, but Reformed theologians are generally susceptible to this criticism.[100] Bavinck's startling and intimate mixture of philosophy and theology is evident in his choice of subject for the Stone Lectures at Princeton: *The Philosophy of Revelation*. In these lectures Bavinck recognized the Reformed churches construction upon the same foundation as Roman Catholicism, noting that the Reformation was, after all, a re-forming that did not entail an entire destruction.[101]

---

[93] John Bolt, "Bavinck, Herman," in *BDCT* 58–59. Johan D. Tangelder, "Dr. Herman Bavinck, 1854–1921: Theologian of the Word" *CR* (29 January 2001); see www.banneroftruth.org; accessed 11 November 2006.

[94] Louis Berkhof, *Systematic Theology* (1932, 1938; repr., Grand Rapids: Eerdmans, 1996).

[95] John Bolt, "Grand Rapids between Kampen and Amsterdam: Herman Bavinck's Reception and Influence in North America," *CTJ* 38 (2003): 263–64.

[96] Herman Bavinck, *Reformed Dogmatics*, vol. 1, *Prolegomena*, ed. John Bolt, trans. John Vriend (Grand Rapids: Baker, 2003).

[97] Herman Bavinck, "Common Grace," trans. Raymond C. Van Leeuwen, *CTJ* 24 (1989): 35–65.

[98] Herman Bavinck, "The Catholicity of Christianity and the Church," trans. John Bolt, *CTJ* 27 (1992): 220–51.

[99] Herman Bavinck, *Our Reasonable Faith*, trans. Henry Zylstra (Grand Rapids: Eerdmans, 1956).

[100] Henry Zylstra, "Preface," in Bavinck, *Our Reasonable Faith*, 6.

[101] Herman Bavinck, *The Philosophy of Revelation: The Stone Lectures for 1908–1909, Princeton Theological Seminary*, trans. Geerhardus Vos and others (Grand Rapids: Eerdmans, 1953), 3.

Philosophy of Revelation

Bavinck's theological foundation (*principium*) is ostensibly Scripture, but his writings reflect a thoroughgoing rationalism that is prior to and formative for his treatment of Scripture. Indeed, there are two major aspects in his theological foundation: philosophy and Scripture. These two aspects of his theological foundation have a practical effect through his doctrine of the invisible, universal church. Bavinck's enigmatic, shifting, and often contradictory treatment of these two aspects of his theological foundation, or "two poles," has resulted in the conjecture that there were "two Bavincks." The "first Bavinck" is a Reformed and theological churchman, while the "second Bavinck" is a modern and progressive academic.[102] Bavinck has been criticized by Reformed scholars, including Cornelius Van Til and R. H. Bremmer, for his Neo-Thomist scholasticism. Van Til warned the Reformed to "go beyond Bavinck" to a more Christological and biblical theology, yet Bavinck's appeal continues, indicating the general rationalism that characterizes Reformed theology.[103] In spite of the inconsistency and "ambiguity" in his work,[104] Bavinck's theological philosophy provided the grounds for a Dutch school of Calvinist philosophy—the "philosophy of the cosmonomic idea"—that is still active. Bavinck's philosophical theology, drawing upon the Reformed invention of "common grace," continues to inspire Reformed theologians in North America as well as the Netherlands.[105]

Bavinck recognizes God as the essential foundation (*principium essendi*) and the existential foundation (*principium existendi*) of all creation. And yet God is known through mediated channels of revelation, the foundation of knowledge (*principium cognoscendi*). This *principium cognoscendi* has two aspects, the external (*externum*) and the internal (*internum*). The external foundation of our knowledge of God is His Word. The internal foundation of our knowledge of God is His Spirit, who illumines us.[106] With this definition, which has a biblical basis, one would assume that Bavinck could launch into a theology derived from Scripture. However, over three hundred pages lapse in his *Prolegomena* before he begins to construct the rudiments of a biblical theology. The first half of Bavinck's theological method is almost entirely an engagement in philosophical and historical discourse, and the latter half is still largely engaged with philosophical issues. This is especially interesting in light of his critique of the medieval scholastic method for its philosophical prolegomena, particularly its neglect of the original sources and dependence on Aristotle.[107] On the one hand Bavinck firmly rejects the scholastic method of building theology on top of natural theology, a

---

[102] Bolt, "Grand Rapids between Kampen and Amsterdam," 264–69, 265n.

[103] Even Van Til equivocated over whether the Reformed should allow for some form of scholasticism. For Van Til it seems the critical issue turns on whether scholasticism's influence is "dominant." Cornelius Van Til, "Bavinck the Theologian: A Review Article," *WTJ* 24 (1961): 50, 61.

[104] Van Til, "Common Grace—II," *WTJ* 8 (1946): 193–94, 200.

[105] Albert M. Wolters, "Translator's Preface," in Jan Veenhof, *Nature and Grace in Herman Bavinck* (Sioux Center, IA: Dordt College Press, 2006), 1–3; Bolt, "Grand Rapids between Kampen and Amsterdam," 270–79.

[106] Bavinck, *Prolegomena*, 211–13.

[107] Ibid., 104–5, 144–45.

method he admits was pioneered among Roman Catholics and furthered among the Reformed. On the other hand he constructs his theology in almost exactly the same manner that he criticizes.

This is why John Bolt has referred to two Bavincks. In the same work, *Prolegomena*, the first Bavinck writes in a way that prefigures Barth's declamation of natural theology, "The method that arose already with scholasticism and later found acceptance also among Protestants, viz., of first treating the natural knowledge of God (the preamble of faith) and then all the historical and rational proofs (*motiva credibilitatis*) supporting revelation, must be rejected. At the very outset and in principle it abandons the viewpoint of faith, denies the positive character of dogmatics, moves onto the opponent's ground, and is therefore in fact rationalistic, and makes dogmatics dependent on philosophy."[108]

In the same work, *Prolegomena*, the second Bavinck writes two chapters directly on theological foundations, but both chapters interact with philosophy more than with Scripture. The first chapter, on scientific foundations, is mostly concerned with solving the epistemological argument between rationalism and empiricism. The second chapter, on religious foundations, considers at length Aquinas's definition of religion according to the cardinal virtues, Schleiermacher's definition of piety as the absolute feeling of dependence, Hegel's idealism, Kant's voluntarism, and the historical study of religions.[109] The same man who believes dogmatics should not begin with natural theology also believes "general revelation is the foundation on which special revelation builds itself up."[110]

The contradictions in Bavinck with regard to the priority of Scripture and reason form an almost schizophrenic picture. He says that the Socinians have Roman tendencies that lead them to downplay special revelation, while the Anabaptists have medieval tendencies that lead them to downplay common grace.[111] The Socinians and the Anabaptists are thus tarred and feathered with the Roman Catholic brush, yet he subtly cites a high medieval scholastic theologian, Thomas Aquinas, as if he were a Reformed theologian and proceeds to emulate him.[112] Luther and the Anabaptists are criticized for too starkly distinguishing nature from grace, yet Calvin's common grace, which grants human reason great authority, flowed historically into Deism, Idealism, and acidic biblical criticism, movements Bavinck reviews without pausing to give warning.[113]

On the one hand he appreciated those who "were on their guard against philosophical terminology, scholastic distinctions, and futile academic questions and presented the truth in a simpler form."[114] On the other hand he used philosophical terminology and scholastic distinctions quite regularly. "His criticism of Scho-

[108] Ibid., 108–9.
[109] Ibid., chaps. 8, 9.
[110] Ibid., 322.
[111] Bavinck, "Common Grace," 52–53.
[112] Bavinck, *Prolegomena*, 224–25, 224n.
[113] Ibid., 305–6.
[114] Ibid., 181.

lasticism is at points little more than a matter of degree."[115] Indeed, it is "difficult to distinguish the position of Bavinck from that of [Etienne] Gilson [a Roman Catholic Thomist philosopher]. . . . For all his effort to the contrary, Bavinck seems to offer us a natural theology of a kind similar to that offered by the church of Rome."[116] Again and again, the first Bavinck's declamation of Roman rationalism is countered by the second Bavinck's dependence on Roman ways of reasoning.

Even in *Our Reasonable Faith*, his popular and more scriptural theology (an intentional distillation of his larger four-volume work), although Bavinck does not dwell long on philosophy, he still feels compelled to start there. This is telling in light of the importance he elsewhere places on the "theological starting point."[117] Man is incurably ontological because, although he lives in a temporal context, he possesses a "yearning for an eternal order" (*desiderium aeternitatis*). "Man's highest good" is admittedly "God, and God alone," but that good must be philosophically considered. There are two types of philosophy: good philosophy and false philosophy. His preference is to write about good philosophy, and he bypasses the Pauline warnings against speculation rather quickly: "When Paul calls the wisdom of the world foolishness with God, and when he elsewhere warns against philosophy, he has in mind that false and vainly imagined wisdom which has not acknowledged the wisdom of God in His general and special revelation and has become vain in all its imaginations. But for the rest Paul and the Holy Scriptures in their entirety raise knowledge and wisdom to a very high plane of importance." The Bible is a book that puts a high estimate on wisdom, which Bavinck takes to mean an exaltation of philosophy.[118]

How did Bavinck arrive at his high regard for human reason? The cause appears to be located in his decision to begin with general revelation and his elevation of the Calvinist doctrine of common grace. Revelation overcomes the limits of human knowledge that hides God from man's knowledge. God actively makes knowledge of Himself available to man in revelation, both generally and specially. General revelation is available universally and is epistemologically "first" by reason of being "directed to all men."[119] Although general revelation is limited, in that it cannot redeem, it "has been of great value" and "has borne rich fruits," especially in the arenas of religion, ethics, science, and art.[120] In addition to the rich contributions of general revelation, the special revelation of God is necessary "for a right understanding of His general revelation in nature and history and in heart and conscience."[121] This is where the Calvinist doctrine of common grace arises. Bavinck sought to ground his doctrine of common grace in the Bible by following the Reformed narrative of the covenant of works (*foedus operum*) and

[115] Van Til, "Common Grace—II," 188.
[116] Ibid., 192.
[117] Bavinck, *Prolegomena*, 209.
[118] Bavinck, *Our Reasonable Faith*, 17–23.
[119] Ibid., 37.
[120] Ibid., 59.
[121] Ibid., 62.

the covenant of grace (*foedus gratiae*). The grace that upholds those who live under the covenant of works is common grace (*gratia communis*). The grace that upholds those who live under the covenant of grace is special grace (*gratia specialis*). Common grace was operative in the life of the nations while special grace was operative in Israel. Ultimately, in Jesus Christ, common grace and special grace merged.[122]

As we shall see below, Bavinck's doctrine of covenants seems only loosely based in Scripture. Nevertheless, his doctrine of common grace fosters a greater appreciation for the things of the world. Similar to his treatment of the word *philosophy*, he also finds two strands in Scripture concerning "the world." The first strand considers the world as fallen and sinful, and it is this strand that was stressed from the earliest days of the church. The second strand considers the world as loved by God, and it is this strand that Bavinck wishes to stress.[123] Indeed, he saw God as working in wondrous ways in the world at large. The Spirit of God operates through common grace "not only in science and art, morality and law, but also in the religions."[124] According to the Roman Catholic conception of common grace, the natural man is true, good, and complete. Man is fallen and in need of redemption, but in his natural state he is capable of much.[125]

The Roman view is deficient because it views salvation as supplementary. Bavinck sees salvation as more than Roman Catholic supplement but as much less than the Anabaptist doctrine of the new creation. Bavinck's common grace focuses on the renewal of creation, the restoration of nature, the reformation of man and society. There is nothing revolutionary here. Bavinck is able to affirm the genuine good in natural man, a good that will become better as the gospel reforms not only man's spirituality but his society. Societies and states, wealth and welfare, arts and sciences, nature and history: all aspects of human existence are subject to reformation. The world can be rescued as it is by Calvinism without the need for the introduction of a new cosmos.[126] Calvinism is "the Reformation of the natural."[127]

The goodness of the natural man comes from a high view of the image of God in man, especially with regard to human reason. Even after the fall, the human ability to reason remained intact.[128] Bavinck's implicit trust in reason may be detected in his basic assumptions about authority. The Wesleyan Quadrilateral identifies four sources of authority in Christianity—Scripture, tradition, experience, and reason. Anglicanism identifies a threefold source—Scripture, tradition, and reason. Over against both of these models, which identify human rationality as influencing theological construction, Bavinck identifies three sources of theological certainty—Scripture, church, and Christian consciousness. Each of these

[122] Bavinck, "Common Grace," 39–44.
[123] Veenhof, *Nature and Grace in Herman Bavinck*, 10.
[124] Bavinck, *Prolegomena*, 319.
[125] Bavinck, "Common Grace," 46.
[126] Ibid., 52–53, 60–61.
[127] Ibid., 63.
[128] Ibid., 50–51.

three sources is examined by Bavinck, and he warns against overemphasizing any one, including Scripture, but he blindly disregards the rational process itself as able to influence theology.[129]

Bavinck admits that philosophy on its own will fail, but there is much truth in philosophy in spite of its errors.[130] He makes the bold claim that human reason is capable of perfection. Just as grace restores nature, human reason can also be perfected. "Nature precedes grace; grace perfects nature. Reason is perfected by faith, faith presupposes nature."[131] If Protestants may accuse Roman Catholics of having an unrealistic doctrine of the infallibility of the magisterium, Roman Catholics may accuse Protestants of having an unrealistic doctrine of the infallibility of the individual theologian.[132] Theology is thus a product of the common grace available to all men.[133]

The Invisible Catholic Church

Alongside and informing Bavinck's scholastic rationalism and inundated biblicism is an extrabiblical view of the universal church as invisible. Rather than reviewing the entire New Testament usage of *ekklesia*, Bavinck turns to the patristic combination of "catholicity" with the church. "Catholicity," notes Bavinck, considers "the church as a unified whole in contrast to the dispersed local congregations," "as inclusive of all believers from every nation, in all times and places," and "embraces the whole of human experience."[134] In his review of Scripture, he clearly cites only one passage in direct support for such a definition of the universal church, and here he relies on a disputed interpretation. The critical text, Acts 9:31, refers to "the church throughout all Judea, Galilee, and Samaria," while the textus receptus uses the plural. Following the typical Reformed interpretation, Bavinck conflates the two renderings so that the universal church requires the unification of the local churches. "In fact, the churches of Judea, Galilee, and Samaria considered themselves so unified that (assuming Tischendorf's reading of Acts 9:31 is, as I believe it is, correct) they were referred to in the singular as *ha ekklesia*."[135]

Bavinck fails to consider the lack of any reference to any church other than the Jerusalem church in the book of Acts until the Antioch church is introduced in 11:26. Christians outside Jerusalem in the twilight period between the persecution of the Jerusalem church and the establishment of the Antioch church are referred to as "disciples" or "saints" located elsewhere (9:10,19,32), and, most tellingly, the ones who had been "scattered" (8:1,4; 11:19). Indeed, the Jerusalem church functioned as if the scattered disciples and their converts—baptized into the church by apostle or evangelist or prophet (8:38; 9:18; 10:47–48)—were thereby subject to

[129] Bavinck, *Prolegomena*, 78–86.
[130] Ibid., 313–14.
[131] Ibid., 322.
[132] Ratzinger, *Principles of Catholic Theology*, 223.
[133] Bavinck, "Common Grace," 64–65.
[134] Bavinck, "The Catholicity of Christianity and the Church," 220–21.
[135] Ibid., 226.

the disciplinary authority of the Jerusalem church (11:1–2,18). Until well after the events of Acts 9:31, there is no reference to a specific gathering [*ekklesia*] other than in Jerusalem. In spite of his appeal to Scripture as *principium* of his theology, Bavinck's view of the universal church lacks a tangible biblical basis.

The Reformed definition of the church as universal and invisible allows Reformed theologians to take their eyes off the local church and focus them upon the culture. Bavinck's conceptions of "common grace" and of "catholicity," both of which lack a firm biblical basis, reflect his turn to the culture. Bavinck's philosophical focus on the culture in his theological method impacted his practices in profound and enduring ways. First, Bavinck encouraged elitism in theology. At the beginning of his popular systematic, he says that philosophy has "a special character" in that it is reserved for "only the few," the "select ones." Not everyone can devote time to the sciences, including the science of theology, so theology is reserved for the select few.[136] The Erasmian and Anabaptist ideal that all believers should be theologians is not paralleled in Bavinck's thought.[137]

Second, Bavinck's outlook focused more on a lower-level restoration or reformation than it did on the dramatic sense of spiritual conversion followed by discipleship. He scorned the Anabaptists, as well as the pietists, the Baptists, and the Methodists, for their piety. These "pious circles" are too dependent upon the Spirit, too sectarian, too distrustful of culture, and take the Sermon on the Mount literally.[138] Bavinck evidences an attitude that has been called "anti-spiritualism." Sin is an "accidental" matter that is not "substantial." Grace is related to nature, therefore, in the sense of reformation rather than revolution.[139] The doctrines of the invisible church and baptismal regeneration led the Magisterial Reformers to affirm that salvation is located in the universal church.[140] Baptists may wonder whether baptismal regeneration has also led to a reduced sense of the radicality of Christian conversion. In retort, Bavinck would claim that the Baptists and the Anabaptists unfortunately shifted the focus "from baptism itself to the believer's acceptance."[141]

The third practical impact of Bavinck's rationalism was encouraging the Reformed to be more interested in rescuing the sciences, the arts, and politics than in engaging in witness and catechesis. He elevated the Reformed idea that the kingdom is in and for the world rather than that the world is doomed. He rejected otherworldly emphases of Luther and the Anabaptists in order to restore the world. He identified the person who is concerned for evangelism as emulating Roman monasticism. He encouraged people to remain in their vocations, to follow their common callings, and to look at the evangelistic mandate as "the

[136] Bavinck, *Our Reasonable Faith*, 20.

[137] Desiderius Erasmus, *Paraclesis* (1516), in John C. Olin, *Christian Humanism and the Reformation: Selected Writings of Erasmus*, 3rd ed. (New York: Fordham University Press, 1987), 100–4.

[138] Bavinck, "Common Grace," 52–54.

[139] Veenhof, *Nature and Grace in Herman Bavinck*, 21–24.

[140] Bavinck, "The Catholicity of Christianity and the Church," 240.

[141] Ibid., 247.

exception rather than the rule."[142] After all, the gospel is not merely spiritual but cultural. Man needs to be converted twice: "first from the natural to the spiritual life, and thereafter from the spiritual to the natural life."[143]

Fourth, Bavinck distinguishes the Reformed theological movement over against not only the Roman Catholics but also Luther and the Anabaptists. Whereas Luther was concerned first and foremost with the Word of God and man's personal justification by faith alone, Zwingli and Calvin proceeded beyond this to other things. Like Luther, Zwingli and Calvin reformed the preaching of the Word, church worship, and church discipline. But proceeding beyond Luther, "they reformed not merely the religious life of Sunday but also the civic and social life of the days of the week."[144] Neo-Calvinism had a very public face in the Netherlands with Bavinck serving in the upper house and Kuyper actually leading the government at one point. The free-church conception of the separation of church and state does not fit easily with Calvinism. Bavinck lauds the Reformers for having founded a "worldly Christianity" and has little difficulty with theocracy in the state.[145] Bavinck's focus on this world is also evident in his antichiliastic eschatology. Concerning the destruction of the old heaven and earth, he remarks: "Nevertheless, we are not in this connection to think of an absolutely new creation."[146]

Fifth, Bavinck consistently berated "separatism" among Christians. Biographers assume that Bavinck was reacting against the separatist Reformed movement in which he was reared. His strongest denunciations, however, occur with reference to the Anabaptists and the Baptists. Bavinck believed that the invisible universal church was more glorious than even "the most wonderful church order." He laments those who become "enclosed in the narrow circle of a small church." "Such a person shortchanges the love of the Father, the grace of the Son, and the fellowship of the Spirit and incurs a loss of spiritual treasures that cannot be made good by meditation and devotion. Such a person will have an impoverished soul."[147] He reveres the church after Constantine for having avoided separatism, in spite of its increasing worldliness.[148] He despises the "perpetuation of division" and "rise of sectarianism," affiliated historically with English and American Christianity, and is confused by the idea that a church could be a "voluntary association."[149] Bavinck concludes with the telling statement that "in the Protestant principle there is indeed a church-dissolving element as well as a church-reforming one."[150]

Finally, discipleship in the Christian life is replaced by rationalism. Where the Anabaptists encourage Christians to glorify God with the entirety of life in

[142] Bavinck, "Common Grace," 62–63.
[143] Veenhof, *Nature and Grace in Herman Bavinck*, 28–29.
[144] Bavinck, *Our Reasonable Faith*, 125–26.
[145] Bavinck, "The Catholicity of Christianity and the Church," 236, 238.
[146] Bavinck, *Our Reasonable Faith*, 566.
[147] Bavinck, "The Catholicity of Christianity and the Church," 226–27.
[148] Ibid., 228–29.
[149] Ibid., 247.
[150] Ibid., 249.

the carrying of the cross and witness, Bavinck focuses on being reasonable. "And the whole intent of believers is to take the thoughts of God laid down in Scripture into their consciousness and to understand them rationally."[151] Bavinck had a high view of even fallen man's ability to reason. Although he recognized that the traditional proofs for the existence of God are weak as proofs, they are "strong as testimonies." His book *The Certainty of Faith* was written to enable Christians to strengthen their faith against attack in the realm of science, precisely because he believed science was the primary means and venue of Reformed theology.[152] In these six ways Bavinck's conflation of reason and Scripture in his theological method, as evidenced in his doctrines of common grace and the invisible universal church, issued forth in a theology that was more cultural than ecclesial.

Bavinck warned that the Protestant resort to rationalism might emancipate reason from faith. Moreover, it might involuntarily place "the dogmas of natural theology and of Holy Scripture outside of saving faith." Bavinck recognizes the problems with basing theology on apologetics. But he does not offer a way out of that dilemma, except to assert that faith must precede apologetics. Bavinck's own theological method—grounding theology in common grace and general revelation—follows the very method he regards as dangerous.[153] This dilemma arises ultimately because he cannot allow personal voluntary faith to be part of the foundation of theology. To do so would involve him in the errors of the Lutherans and the Anabaptists.

The Demotion of Faith

In his theological foundation Bavinck defined a place for revelation, especially general revelation understood in terms of common grace. He also made a place for the church, understood as the invisible universal church. The question arises as to what place he makes for faith. Faith, understood as *principium internum*, is considered in the fifth and last part of his *Prolegomena*. Faith has a role in theological method because revelation must be received, but Bavinck's doctrine of faith is never directly tied to a person's voluntary reception of revelation. Rather, the internal principle is entirely the external movement of the divine Spirit. Faith, moreover, is treated in terms of "religion" rather than personal response. Returning to his principle theme of common grace, he defines religion as "a natural human capacity for perceiving the divine," a capacity located primarily "in the mind (*nous*)."[154]

Bavinck recognizes that faith is more than intellectual, but he is dissatisfied with any definition of faith as experiential. Faith is a category of revelation, which is entirely a divine movement, and a benefit of grace, a second order doctrine. People cannot come to the revelation; they can only be the recipients of it. Properly speaking, the principle of internal knowledge is the Holy Spirit rather than

[151] Bavinck, *Prolegomena*, 93.
[152] Van Til, "Common Grace—II," 190–91.
[153] Bavinck, *Prolegomena*, 512–15.
[154] Ibid., 501.

personal faith. Bavinck's reminder to us that the internal principle of Christianity is a movement of the Spirit is not coupled with the biblical call for a voluntary reception of the Spirit's movement.[155]

In Bavinck's world, "The rule is that people die in the religion in which they are born" and "conversions are rare." Conversions come only at the beginnings of religious movements. Phenomenologically, faith is normally the result of the geographic location of one's physical birth.[156] Faith possesses "a most marvelous and mysterious power," so mysterious that it remains incommunicable.[157] The human being in Bavinck's system is dependent, even inactive. "But in every respect he remains a dependent creature. He cannot do as he pleases. . . . Man cannot think as he pleases, but is bound to laws. . . . Nor can man will and act as he pleases." Although Bavinck recognizes that man can act against his conscience, he is more comfortable with stressing that the human being is entirely dependent on the world around.[158] Perhaps due to these assumptions about faith, its incommunicability, and man's entire dependency, the missionary mandate to share the Christian faith does not loom large in Bavinck's system. His discussion of the missionary mandate is tangential and reserved for the apostles alone.[159] This is not to say that Bavinck denies that salvation comes by faith. He certainly affirms this, but faith appears to be almost entirely devoid of human involvement.

This appearance takes on substance when we turn to the systematic portion of his dogmatics. After reviewing the beginnings of the church's faith in Scripture, he transitions from a discussion of New Testament faith to the historical conversation surrounding grace. Bavinck's transition from considering faith according to the New Testament to considering grace according to historical debates is subtle but profound. This allows him to treat the doctrine of faith according to the framework of the Augustinian-Pelagian debate on grace and law.[160] Augustine's necessary defense of grace against Pelagius's dependence on law and weakening of grace becomes, in Bavinck's hands, the paradigm through which to consider the doctrine of salvation. In this way faith becomes a secondary, even tertiary doctrine. Grace and election become the lynchpins of Reformed theology.

Bavinck recognizes that, in reaction to the Roman focus on the sacramental transmission of grace, Luther returned to a biblical outlook by making repentance and faith coordinates of conversion. Repentance is a disposition created by the preaching of the law, and the law must condemn before the gospel can free. Faith alone is that which justifies the sinner: God's declaration of the righteousness of Christ is granted to the sinner by faith. As a result of his reorientation of soteriology around faith and repentance, Luther treated the doctrine of salvation under

---

155 Ibid., 506.

156 The modern editors have inserted the word *general* before *rule*. Ibid., 502.

157 Ibid., 504.

158 Bavinck, *Our Reasonable Faith*, 198; idem, *Prolegomena*, 501.

159 Bavinck, *Our Reasonable Faith*, 516–20.

160 Herman Bavinck, *Reformed Dogmatics*, vol. 3, *Sin and Salvation in Christ*, ed. John Bolt, trans. John Vriend (Grand Rapids: Baker, 2006), 506–8.

three components: contrition (repentance), faith, and good works. Reformed theologians, however, were unhappy with this presentation and constructed a detailed order of salvation (*ordo salutis*). The Reformed focused their attention on election and the divine decrees. Faith was driven back in the order where it was treated as part of the assurance of salvation, and repentance was removed to the doctrine of the Christian life.[161] Grace was brought forward as the central theme, and faith became one of the subsequent "benefits" of predetermined grace.

The Reformed chose to rearrange Luther's simplified *ordo salutis* because they were forced to do so in debates with the Anabaptists. "Following Luther's experience, many theologians spoke first of repentance and then about faith and good works. But soon they noted that not everyone went through such an experience, and, further, that such an experience could not be required of all, especially not of the children of the covenant." The Reformed believed the Anabaptists were wrong to demand proof of the personal reception of grace before baptism. The Anabaptists denied the benefits of grace to children. The major benefit of grace in baptism was, of course, regeneration. Without solving the dilemma, Bavinck noted that the Reformed never could decide whether regeneration occurred before, during, or after baptism. The question of the relationship between faith and regeneration was solved by placing regeneration before faith. Faith became an evidence of regeneration, which was received in baptism. The irrationality of the Reformed position is accepted without note.[162]

Bavinck perceives a continual dilemma for the Christian doctrine of faith. "The Christian religion seems to hold two irreconcilable positions, the heterosoterical and the autosoterical, when it attributes the acquisition of salvation completely to Christ and still exhorts us to work out our own salvation in fear and trembling" (cp. Phil 2:12–13). This dilemma forces Christian movements to one pole or the other. The first pole, the heterosoterical, salvation by the other, may lead to antinomianism, but it is the lesser problem and receives its strength from its likeness to the greater problem. The second pole, the autosoterical, salvation by the self, leads to a Pelagian *ordo salutis*, which is also evident in pietism and Methodism.[163] However, he also recognizes that the pietists and the Methodists protested legitimately against "dead orthodoxy." The only way out of this dilemma is through a trinitarian soteriology that makes salvation entirely the work of the Father who elects, the Son who redeems, and the Spirit who applies the benefits of grace already determined for the elect.[164] Thus, the Reformed system defines salvation, often in opposition to the free-church movements, according to the divine decrees, calling, election, and even eternal justification, which he recognizes may lead to antinomianism.

[161] Bavinck, *Sin and Salvation in Christ*, 517–28.
[162] Ibid., 580–83.
[163] Ibid., 566–68.
[164] Ibid., 590–93.

LOCATING THE FREE-CHURCH THEOLOGICAL FOUNDATION

Each of these three representative theologians contributes to a fuller understanding of theological foundations, concerning both its importance and limitations. Their various convictions also throw into relief the uniqueness of the free-church theological foundation. (For the sake of expediency, the author will deign to speak on behalf of the free churches, noting that other free-church theologians might wish to express themselves differently on some of the following matters.) The free churches have a focus on Christian discipleship, which is uncomfortable with emphases found in each of these writers. Yet Ratzinger, Wiles, and Bavinck variously strike numerous harmonious notes with a free church perspective. The logic of each representative seems fundamentally Christian, allowing the pious mind to hear echoes of the symphonic movement of the creative and redeeming Logos. And yet the free churches are ultimately uncomfortable with certain ways in which each theologian's voice sings the song of Christ.

Before attempting to define a believers' church theological foundation, it may be helpful to provide a short critique of these alternative theological foundations. In his massive contribution to foundational theology, Heinrich Fries discerns three major problems to be addressed by any foundation: faith, revelation, and the church. First, revelation must be considered because this is the way human beings are able to know God and of God. Second, faith must be considered because this is the way human beings receive the revelation of God. Third, the church must be considered "insofar as it is the bearer and traditor of revelation."[165] Fries's division of the problem provides an adequate format to critique our representative theologians, except that we must also address the problem of reason's role in theological formation.

The Unrivalled Supremacy of Scripture

The Roman Catholic model of *Fundamentaltheologie* spends much time considering the doctrine of revelation. In the debates over theological authority, the Reformers offered the doctrine of *sola scriptura* as the means of judging the church's tradition. At the Council of Trent, the Roman Catholic Church reconnected tradition with Scripture. The gospel, according to the council, "clearly perceives that these truths and rules are contained in the written books and in the unwritten traditions, which, received by the Apostles from the mouth of Christ Himself, or from the Apostles themselves, the Holy Ghost dictating, have come down to us, transmitted as it were from hand to hand." As a result of the gospel being revealed in both ways, Christians must revere "the books" and "the traditions." Moreover, individual Christians may not rely on their own judgment to interpret the Bible but must submit to "holy mother Church," who possesses the authority "to judge of their true sense and interpretation."[166]

[165] Heinrich Fries, *Fundamental Theology*, trans. Robert J. Daly (Washington, DC: Catholic University of America Press, 1985), 3–5.

[166] Fourth Session, in *Canons and Decrees of the Council of Trent*, trans. H. J. Schroeder (St. Louis: Herder, 1941), 17–20.

Martin Chemnitz took it upon himself to refute the doctrines of Trent, and his evangelical critique correlates with what free churchmen might say. Chemnitz began with the teachings of the fourth session. The Roman church tried to verify its dogma not according to Scripture alone but also according to tradition. This is the root of their problem: "They seek other proofs outside of and beyond the Scripture." Anybody who moves beyond Scripture runs the risk of moving "against" the Scripture. Chemnitz identifies three chief papal doctrines: "Concerning the insufficiency, the obscurity, and the uncertainty of Scripture; concerning traditions; and concerning the supreme authority of interpretation."[167] The first 307 pages of Chemnitz's treatise address the problems of Rome's doctrines of Scripture, tradition, and interpretative authority.

First, against Rome, Chemnitz affirms the sufficiency, the clarity, and the certainty of Scripture. There seems to be no middle ground whatsoever between the early Tridentine assertion of the insufficiency of Scripture and the early evangelical assertion of its sufficiency. Second, Chemnitz agrees to some extent with the Romans regarding the authority of interpretation. The gift of interpretation "is not found outside of the church in the unregenerate, for the light of the Holy Spirit is kindled in the hearts of the godly." Moreover, according to 2 Peter 1:20, individual interpreters may not follow their own wisdom. The ecclesiastical context for interpretation is not at issue. Rather, the issue is that the Romans have bound interpretation to a succession of bishops and turned it into a dictatorial authority. "For the church has the right and privilege of judging. But the papalists take this right of interpretation to themselves, so that by one and the same stroke they both exempt themselves from the labor of proving and take away from the church the privilege of judging."[168]

Chemnitz solved the third problem, regarding traditions, by distinguishing between eight types of tradition. The first and second kinds of tradition are beyond all doubt valid, while the remaining types introduce increasing problems. The first level of tradition concerns the ordinances commanded by Christ, particularly the Lord's Supper and baptism. These traditions are related by Scripture itself. The second level of tradition, concerning the early church's reception of the biblical books into a canon, must also be received. It is with subsequent traditions, which move beyond the Bible, that there is an increasing amount of disagreement. The eighth type of tradition, papal customs that lack any biblical basis whatsoever, are what the Council of Trent has required all Christians to accept. Chemnitz, along with most Protestants and the free churches, disagrees.[169] The evangelical doctrine of revelation is by and large accepted by the free churches.

Christianity is a religion entirely based on divine revelation. In his little book on the Bible, John Webster, a British evangelical, defines revelation thus: "Revelation is the self-presentation of the triune God, the free work of sovereign mercy in

[167] Martin Chemnitz, *Examination of the Council of Trent*, trans. Fred Kramer (St. Louis: Concordia, 1971), 1:39–41.

[168] Ibid., 1:211.

[169] Ibid., 1:223–307.

which God wills, establishes and perfects saving fellowship with himself in which humankind comes to know, love and fear him above all things."[170] The first part of Webster's definition is especially useful, even if the second part seems somewhat Barthian. Revelation involves the manifestation of the triune God. While one might perceive the revelation of God in history or nature or humanity, as most theologians have, it is difficult to argue that God has revealed Himself fully as the trinitarian God through general revelation.[171] The birth, life, ministry, death, and resurrection of Jesus Christ, the second person of the Trinity, also known as the Word, is sufficiently revealed to us today only through the New Testament. The salvation that comes to the hearer of the Word of God is brought this grace by the Holy Spirit, the third person of the Trinity. The revelation of Christianity, understood as a trinitarian revelation, stands or falls with the biblical revelation, inclusive of the Old and New Testaments.

The free churches follow the Protestants in rejecting the Roman Catholic elevation of tradition to the level of revelation. The free churches, however, are wary about the efforts of evangelical theologians to construct a theological method based on philosophical speculation. Yet alongside both the Roman Catholics and the evangelicals, the free churches find the categorical dismissal of Scripture as the unique and perfect revelation of God, often made by liberal evangelicals, who argue from the dictates of modern reason, to be entirely unacceptable. Echoing the confessions of earlier evangelicals and other free churches, the Methodist Articles of Religion drawn up by John Wesley state, "The Holy Scriptures contain all things necessary to salvation; so that whatsoever is not read therein, nor may be proved thereby, is not to be required of any man that it should be believed as an article of faith, or be thought requisite or necessary to salvation."[172] The free churches accept the Bible as the sufficient revelation of God that brings salvation, and they know nowhere else from whence to derive true saving faith.

Liberation from the Captivity of Philosophy

Martin Luther understood the need to affirm Scripture's sufficiency too well, so much so that he reacted violently against Christians theologizing on any basis other than Scripture. Two months before his famous posting of the Ninety-five Theses on the practice of indulgences, Luther wrote ninety-seven theses concerning the relationship between philosophy and theology. His *Disputation against Scholastic Theology* rejected the philosophical foundation for the medieval theological project of the schoolmen. He summarily discarded the work of John Duns Scotus, Gabriel Biel, Pierre d'Ailly, William of Ockham, and any other theologian who depended on Aristotle. The 43rd through 52nd theses are the most forceful: "44. Indeed, no one can become a theologian unless he becomes one without Aristotle. . . . 46. In vain does one fashion a logic of faith, a substitution brought

[170] Webster placed his definition in italics. John Webster, *Holy Scripture: A Dogmatic Sketch* (New York: Cambridge University Press, 2003), 13.
[171] E.g. Millard J. Erickson, *Christian Theology*, 2nd ed. (Grand Rapids: Baker, 1998), 180–223.
[172] Methodist Articles of Religion (1784), in *CC*, 6th ed., 808.

about without regard for limit and measure. . . . 47. No syllogistic form is valid when applied to divine terms. . . . 50. Briefly, the whole Aristotle is to theology as darkness is to light. This is in opposition to the scholastics."[173] Luther was driven to such a position because he saw the medieval schoolmen as obfuscating the Christian gospel with their speculations. His theological breakthrough in justification was predicated upon his return to Scripture alone.

The early Protestant Reformers rejected philosophy and sought to return to an austerely biblical form of theology. Indeed, the freshness of early evangelical theology is perceptible in the numerous commentaries of the Reformers. Unfortunately the biblical purity of this situation did not maintain itself. There were hints of a return to philosophy in the writings of Calvin, although he was a superb biblical expositor. It should be noted that Calvin's first book was a commentary on *De Clementia*, a Stoic treatise by Seneca. Calvin, the leading theologian of the first generation of the Reformed, shared a basic humanistic outlook with Ulrich Zwingli, the first Reformed theologian, whose book on providence also borrows heavily from Seneca. Protecting Reformed theology, Calvin found it necessary to defend himself against the idea that he imported the Stoic doctrine of fate into his doctrine of divine providence. "Indeed, we are falsely and maliciously charged with this very dogma." Unfortunately Calvin made the distinction between Stoicism and his doctrine of providence with regard to its origin, in nature or in God, rather than making any distinction with regard to their similar operation.[174]

If Luther rejected, while Calvin carefully appropriated, the speculations of the philosophers, the next generation was less constrained. On the Lutheran side of Protestantism, Philip Melanchthon, Luther's successor at Wittenberg, introduced scholastic categories into successive editions of his *Loci Communes*. John Dorsch, a seventeenth-century Lutheran divine, wrote a long book to try to prove that the "Doctor Angelicus," Thomas Aquinas, who subtly integrated Aristotle with Augustine, taught in agreement with the Lutheran Augsburg Confession. On the Reformed side, Peter Martyr Vermigli, who was schooled in Aristotle and Aquinas at the University of Padua, introduced the Thomist method to those Calvinists involved in debates with the Roman Catholics. One of Vermigli's students, Jerome Zanchi, whose work on predestination is still influential among Calvinists, is the supreme example of what has been called "Calvinist Thomism." Among other indications of a structural correspondence between Calvinism and Thomism, a comparison between the *Summa Theologia* of Aquinas and the *Opera Theologica* of Zanchi, shows the heavy dependence of Zanchi on Aquinas. This is especially interesting in light of Zanchi's appropriation of the Catholic Aquinas's doctrine of grace.[175]

---

[173] *Disputation against Scholastic Theology* (1517), in *LW*, 31:12–13.

[174] John Calvin, *Institutes of the Christian Religion*, ed. John T. McNeill, trans. Ford Lewis Battles, LCC (Philadelphia: Westminster, 1960), 1.16.8; François Wendel, *Calvin: Origins and Development of His Religious Thought*, trans. Philip Mairet (1963; repr. Grand Rapids: Baker, 1997), 27–37.

[175] John Patrick Donnelly, "Calvinist Thomism," *Viator* 7 (1976): 441–55.

The evangelical pastors ejected Zanchi from Strasbourg precisely because his theology departed from the Word of God to teach a highly speculative doctrine of predestination. Zanchi's claim that academic freedom allowed him such "orthodox" speculation did not sit well with those motivated by pastoral and practical concerns.[176] But the predestinarianism of Vermigli and Zanchi prevailed at the Synod of Dort, reflecting the Reformed penchant for rationalism. One of the most influential theologians to arise from Vermigli's circle was Francis Turretin, who provided the major theological textbook used in the American South during the antebellum period.[177] Alongside such Thomism, the categorical methods of Pierre Ramus were adopted by Reformed scholastics. Ramus treated reality in spatial rather than dialogical terms. Walter Ong has shown how, under Ramus, truth moved from being both personal and cognitive to being primarily cognitive. Christian discourse was suppressed and the text became a boxlike container of facts. Ramism encouraged a view of theology as the orderly arrangement of items without great concern for overlapping shades of meaning.[178]

Bavinck's narrative of the covenants, although an intriguing way to organize revelation and not entirely antithetical to the scriptural narrative, is subject to the same critique that Luther applied to Roman Catholic Scholasticism: it is a foreign imposition on Scripture rather than a paradigm derived from Scripture. The Reformed grid requires one to read Scripture in a manner derived from a relatively late scholastic tradition rather than in a manner widely regarded as illuminated by the Holy Spirit. Moreover, the Reformed narrative or grid need not be recognized by those who employ the rule of faith. The theological language and philosophical distinctions of Calvinism are admittedly interesting, characteristically subtle, and sometimes brilliant, but the language and definitions are too often only tangentially derived from Scripture. Where Paul called upon Christians to rightly divide the Word of truth, the Reformed have kept on dividing.

Just as there is no clear biblical precedent for adopting the Reformed discussion regarding the decrees, nor for Calvin's doctrine of double predestination,[179] so there seems to be no strictly biblical precedent for adopting Bavinck's paradigm of common grace, much less for building an entire theological system upon it. The Reformed fascination with philosophy yet sincere attempt to be biblical brings Bavinck, in a discussion on epistemology, to claim one moment, "A theologian, after all, is not a philosopher." But soon after, theological epistemology is made "dependent on a philosophy."[180] The schizophrenic nature of Bavinck's foundation—a schizophrenia caused by his inability to choose between a philo-

---

[176] James M. Kittelson, "Marbach vs. Zanchi: The Resolution of Controversy in Late Reformation Strasbourg," *SCJ* 8 (1977): 31–44.

[177] John H. Leith, "Calvinism," in *The New Encyclopedia of Southern Culture*, vol. 1, *Religion*, ed. Charles Reagan Wilson (Chapel Hill, NC: University of North Carolina Press, 2006), 47.

[178] Walter J. Ong, *Ramus, Method, and the Decay of Dialogue: From the Art of Discourse to the Art of Reason* (Chicago: University of Chicago Press, 2004).

[179] James Leo Garrett Jr., *Systematic Theology: Biblical, Historical, and Evangelical*, 2nd ed. (North Richland Hills, TX: BIBAL Press, 2000–2001), 2:483–88.

[180] Bavinck, *Prolegomena*, 503.

sophical or a biblical foundation—makes for interesting philosophy and unstable theology.

The theologies of the free churches often appear shallow to Catholic and Reformed theologians, perhaps because the free churches generally shun speculation. Free church naïvety regarding philosophy is sometimes accidental but often quite intentional. As we shall see in the next chapter, the most prolific theologian of the South German Anabaptists was an engineer steeped in Scripture with only a modicum of education in Latin. One may also point to the Pietists, who intentionally turned their backs on the philosophical sophistication of the Protestant scholastics in order to embrace once again "a living faith." Spener lamented about "how the scholastic theology which Luther had thrown out the front door had been introduced again by others through the back door."[181] To the early free-church theologians, human speculation, no matter how grand and brilliant the system, appeared vain and deceptive. The apostle equated the deceptive systems that enslave this world and oppose our Lord with *philosophias*. Such is "according to the tradition of men" (Col 2:8) and, like Rome's extrascriptural tradition, must be denied a leading role in theological formation. The Protestant energies previously directed toward reading philosophy were redirected by the free churches toward Bible study, evangelism, and social action.

While the free churches were unchained to pursue biblical piety, missionary fervor, and social change by their rejection of philosophy, they could become susceptible to following "every wind of doctrine" as a result of their ignorance of the winds (Eph 4:14). The search for a living faith among the sectarian movements issuing forth from historic evangelicalism makes for both exhilarating and depressing reading. It should be little surprise to see periodic calls for a return to scholastic Protestantism by some later free-church theologians. A careful reading of Benjamin B. Warfield's two volumes on the history of "perfectionism" in Germany and America could frighten any sensitive Christian back into the scholastic fold.[182]

Dead orthodoxy may appear to be a lesser danger than living chaos. Perhaps the key to the free-church dilemma regarding philosophy is an educated naïveté with regard to philosophy, avoiding the extremes of modernism's rationalist overconfidence and postmodernism's rationalist despair, coupled with a fervent biblicism. Free-church academies should be supremely aware of the historical and philosophical currents that pull theology hither, thither, and yon; historical and philosophical currents, however, should never be allowed to set the agenda for the free churches' theology. That should be reserved for Scripture as illumined by the Spirit, who works in the community of Christ's disciples.

This seems to be an appropriate warning in light of a recent paradigm shift advocated by some prominent free-church theologians. Rejecting the traditional

[181] Philip Jacob Spener, "Conspectus of Corrupt Conditions in the Church," in *Pia Desideria*, trans. Theodore G. Tappert (Philadelphia: Fortress, 1964), 54, 58.

[182] *The Works of Benjamin B. Warfield*, ed. Ethelbert D. Warfield and others (New York: Oxford University Press, 1932), 6–7.

foundationalism in modern Protestantism, Stanley Grenz and Nancey Murphy have advocated a nonfoundationalist or postfoundationalist conception of theology. This movement seems little more than a trading of modern philosophy for postmodern and postliberal philosophies. Stanley Grenz, an American Baptist with a great respect for pietism, sought to recapture community in theology. Grenz was a proponent of postmodernism and prior to his untimely death began reconstructing theology on a postfoundationalist basis.[183] Nancey Murphy, an ordained Brethren minister and the widow of James McClendon, a "baptist" theologian, demonstrated the common philosophical roots of competing fundamentalist and liberal theological methods. Fundamentalism treats Scripture as filled with facts that demand reconstruction, while liberalism considers experience authoritative. Murphy proposes that theologians reorient themselves to postmodern or postliberal theology in order to overcome the foundationalist divide.[184]

Yet the attempt to adjust theology to philosophy is always fraught with unforeseen difficulties, especially when a culture's worldview changes. The Copernican revolution in science, for instance, severely handicapped Roman Catholicism in the eyes of the European intelligentsia for centuries, precisely because the hierarchy wedded itself to Aristotelian philosophy, specifically Ptolemaic cosmology. Moreover, it should not be forgotten that the initial opposition to the Copernican worldview came from Protestants, who followed an overly literalist reading of Scripture, for Copernicus was a Roman cathedral canon.[185] The free church philosophers have pointed to a similar difficulty for Protestant theologians wedded to Enlightenment philosophy, which came to dominate the post-Copernican West, as a result of an apparent transition to a third worldview in the twentieth century.[186] Would it not be wise for the free churches to avoid repeating the errors propagated in the unholy marriage of theology to philosophy? Classically, theology was considered the queen of the sciences and philosophy was its handmaid. Theology abdicates its sovereignty whenever it allows the handmaid a place on the throne. Would it not be as gross an error to adopt the postmodern worldview as it was to adopt the modern worldview or the classical worldview?

Postmodernism is founded on the impossibility of the metanarrative, for every community's language becomes the final judge of truth and that community's language is incontestable from the vantage of another community. This elevation of every localism throws into doubt any possibility of an overarching ontology. Without an ontology that is true for all men in all times, the traditional view of God as Creator and Providence is severely undermined. Indeed, the postmodern

---

[183] Stanley J. Grenz, *Theology for the Community of God* (Nashville: Broadman and Holman, 1994); idem, *A Primer on Postmodernism* (Grand Rapids: Eerdmans, 1996); Grenz and John R. Franke, *Beyond Foundationalism: Shaping Theology in a Postmodern Context* (Louisville: Westminster John Knox, 2001).

[184] Nancey Murphy, *Beyond Liberalism and Fundamentalism* (Harrisburg, PA: Trinity Press International, 1996).

[185] Richard Tarnas, *The Passion of the Western Mind: Understanding the Ideas That Have Shaped Our World* (New York: Ballantine, 1991), 248–71.

[186] Grenz and Franke, *Beyond Foundationalism*, 28–38; Murphy, *Beyond Liberalism and Fundamentalism*, 11–34.

or postliberal worldview ultimately has room only for a number of competing gods over competing communities whose languages are authoritative only for those communities.[187] Against this the Bible teaches that there is only one true God, who has invaded time and established His revelation in a comprehensive community, the people of God composed of Israel and the church, to which all must come for salvation.

Ultimately the free churches would do well to reject any philosophical paradigm for theology, foundationalist or nonfoundationalist, scholastic or postmodern. But the free churches would also do well to reach a largely hitherto unrealized level of rational sophistication, for the sake of polemics as much as apologetics. Philosophy should be a playground, even a classroom, but never a temple for the free-church theologian. This is not to say that reason must be rejected in favor of faith, for an illogical theology (*logos* concerning God) is a contradiction in terms. Faith is supremely reasonable but reasonable according to a definite set of religious and moral presuppositions. Indeed, to be truly reasonable, human rationality must become a captive of faith and taught obedience to Jesus Christ (2 Cor 10:3–6). Faith must perfect reason, which has been limited by creation and perverted by the fall, through bringing it to submit to Jesus Christ. Reason, in turn, must serve faith, and the God whom Christians worship.

A Living Faith in Jesus Christ

Of our three representative writers, Wiles and Ratzinger focus on the personal appropriation of faith more than Bavinck. Following his apologetic program for a reasonable faith, Wiles rejected the idea of a biblical deposit of faith handed on within the church, preferring a chastened faith that draws upon the past only as reconstructed for the future. Wiles appeared interested in the propagation of the faith but the traditional foundations of Scripture and church were rejected in favor of reliance upon modern reason. Due to their appealing hospitableness, Wiles and like-minded liberal evangelicals attracted numerous followers to a symbolic faith that conservative evangelicals feared was a deceptive substitution for the faith once for all delivered to the saints. A free-church theologian would join the conservative evangelical in wondering whether Wiles was replacing a divinely revealed religion with a man-shaped faith.

From the free-church perspective, the goal of connecting with one's culture, though necessary in some sense to fulfill the missionary mandate, should never provide the basis for theological construction. Martin Luther's cry before the imperial culture—"my conscience is captive to the Word of God"—is too loud in the free churches' ear for them to loosen their mind's utter dependence on Scripture

[187] "It follows that the only rational way for the adherents of any tradition to approach intellectually, culturally, and linguistically alien rivals is one that allows for the possibility that in one or more areas the other may be rationally superior to it in respect precisely of that in the alien tradition which it cannot as yet comprehend." Alasdair MacIntyre, *Whose Justice? Which Rationality?* (Notre Dame, IN: University of Notre Dame Press, 1988), 388. Cp. idem, *Three Rival Versions of Moral Enquiry: Encyclopaedia, Genealogy, and Tradition* (Notre Dame, IN: University of Notre Dame Press, 1990).

for the definition of the faith. The free churches are ill-advised to allow culture, rather than the Word of God, to set their theological form in the mold of Wiles or Schleiermacher. This critique may also be applied to the recent culturally attuned goals of the seeker-sensitive and emergent movements.[188] A church should indeed engage the culture and its way of reasoning, but a church must transform the culture rather than being transformed by it. The churches are commissioned by Christ to lead people in every culture to worship the true God that humanity recognizes vaguely through the haze of sin and clearly recognizes only by the grace of the Holy Spirit shining upon the Word. Alongside his deep concern about the integrity of the Christian faith as remade by Wiles, a free-church theologian would fully agree with Rothuizen in affirming Wiles for his "intellectual integrity and honesty."[189]

As we have seen, Joseph Ratzinger's personal idea of faith is dynamically personal and grounded in Jesus Christ. In his basic catechetical lectures, Ratzinger follows the format of the Apostles' Creed, a propitious choice since it begins with "I believe" (*credo*). Ratzinger warns against a merely formal faith, laments the medieval mass of people, who were "nominal believers," and applauds those who "really entered into the inner movement of belief." He affirms the biblical conception of conversion as a complete "turning back." Ratzinger also denied the idea that truth and faith are something that human beings can craft. Against the modern paradigm of "know-make," he offers the paradigm of "stand-understand": meaning cannot be made, only received as a gift from the Logos. Although Ratzinger recognized the mysterious aspect of faith, he also considered faith to be utterly rational. Finally he noted that faith is not "in something," but faith says to Jesus Christ, "I believe in you." Ratzinger's doctrine of faith is internal, converting, rational, personal, and received by grace.[190] There is much in Ratzinger's doctrine of faith to applaud. Many free churches would, however, retain Luther's stress upon justification by faith alone.

Where Wiles allows apologetics, the defense of faith to unbelievers, to drive his theology, and Ratzinger places personal faith in Jesus Christ, the Logos, front and center, Bavinck considers faith only after he establishes a rational basis for theology. Moreover, Bavinck's treatment of faith is subsumed under the category of apologetics in his *Prolegomena* and is secondary to the doctrine of grace in the main body of his systematic theologies. Faith, seminal in the understanding of salvation taught by Luther and the free churches, is demoted by the Reformed tradition. Ultimately each of the three alternative foundations will be deemed unacceptable for a free-church understanding of faith's role in theological method. Liberalism disjoins faith from Scripture; Catholicism joins faith too tightly to the church; and the Reformed tradition rationalizes and demotes faith's importance.

---

[188] Cp. Carl Raschke, *The Next Reformation: Why Evangelicals Must Embrace Postmodernity* (Grand Rapids: Baker, 2004).

[189] Rothuizen, *Apologetics in Oxford*, 65.

[190] Ratzinger, *Introduction to Christianity*, new ed., trans. J. R. Foster (San Francisco: Ignatius Press, 2000), 39–81.

The free churches demand a personal, living, and rational faith in Jesus Christ. Theology should never be carried out without being grounded in a disciple's faith in Jesus Christ.

John Dagg, "the first Southern Baptist systematic theologian,"[191] may (and will) be criticized for many things, but he approached the task of theology with faith. The first sentence in his *Manual of Theology* states, "The study of religious truth ought to be undertaken from a sense of duty, and with a view to the improvement of the heart." For Dagg, theology is an obligation intended to advance the greater goal of religious piety. His repeated usage of "duty," "obligation," "call," "ought," and "subjection" implies that theology is the responsibility of the disciple of Jesus. But "duty" is only the motivation; the goal of theology must be "making the best possible use of it." The person who engages in theology should feel the "sanctifying power" of knowing God. Theology must never be merely speculative: "To study theology, for the purpose of gratifying curiosity, or preparing for a profession, is an abuse and profanation of what ought to be regarded as most holy." Again, "Equally unprofitable will be that study of religious doctrine which is directed to the mere purpose of speculation."

If theology is motivated by faith and results in the "practical," the span bridging faith and practice is Jesus Christ. The content of theology is "the simple truth as it is in Jesus." Dagg is simultaneously Christocentric and biblicist. There is a close correlation between the Word incarnate and the Word inscripturate. Dagg affirmed the Bible as the only proper source for the truth about Jesus. Moreover, because he believed men should always turn to Scripture, Dagg refrained from citing "human authority." "Religion is an affair between every man and his God; and every man should seek to know the truth for himself, whatever may be the opinions of others respecting it. It has been my aim to lead the mind of the reader directly to the sources of religious knowledge, and incite him to investigate them for himself, without respect to human authority." As a result of this commitment, Dagg's systematic theology is largely void of citations to any source but Scripture. Although Dagg was influenced by Reformed theology, there was enough of a free churchman in him to establish his theological foundation upon a living faith in the Jesus Christ revealed only in the Bible.

But human knowledge of "the simple truth as it is in Jesus" as revealed in Scripture must grow. The transition from theological foundation to development of doctrine is seamless for Dagg, and the fulcrum is found in the human mind and heart obeying Jesus. Rather than a building metaphor, so characteristic of scholastic and modernist foundations, Dagg opts for botanical and biological metaphors. Just as a seed grows and an animal adapts, so the human mind and heart is created to grow. "The high intellectual powers of man, call for appropriate exercise." "The human mind is fitted for continued progress in knowledge; and, therefore, for a state of immortality." The heart is the place where the Spirit of God works, "infusing light and life where darkness and death had previously reigned." The

[191] Mark E. Dever, "John L. Dagg," in *Theologians of the Baptist Tradition*, ed. Timothy George and David S. Dockery (Nashville: B&H, 2001), 52–72.

renewing power of such a theology must be "ever operative in our hearts." The correlation of mind and heart reflect a deeper holism in the theology of Dagg. He moves seamlessly from discussing "the progress of the human mind" to the Christian's "moral faculties" becoming adapted "to a state of subjection to moral government." Moreover, such "divinity of Christian truth" is "leveled to the capacity of all." Dagg's theological foundation and developmental doctrine reflect a free church holism arising from a living faith in Jesus Christ.[192]

The Biblical Church

Ratzinger's ecclesiology begins with the universal church as opposed to the particular church. For the current pope, the universal church is "a reality ontologically and temporally prior to every individual particular church."[193] This seems to be a fundamental error from a strictly biblical perspective where the universal church is not the primary concern and has an entirely eschatological existence and where there is no distinction between the local church and the particular church. Moreover, Ratzinger dismissed the covenantal basis of the church without adequately considering Matthew 18. Ratzinger does not deal with the believers' church claim that the local church's ability to participate in a covenant that has both temporal and eternal aspects is due to its dominical institution. The free churches believe that the right of the two or more to form a local church is not mere anthropological assertion. The gathering of the local church on a covenantal basis is a divine gift granted in relationship with Christ as Lord, not a claim for human self-sufficiency.

While many free church theologians would disagree with Ratzinger's visible universal church because of its lack of respect for the priority of the local churches, they would also disagree with Bavinck's invisible universal church. It should be noted that this is an increasingly controversial issue among free church theologians today. Some free-church theologians have in recent years moved toward a "thick ecumenism" that emphasizes "the One, Holy, Catholic, and Apostolic church," that is "the universal church, invisible and indivisible, the one Body of Christ scattered throughout time as well as space." The movement toward ecumenism and an emphasis on the invisible church is especially noticeable among both Reformed Baptists[194] and "catholic Baptists."[195]

As for the evangelical side of this phenomenon, Bavinck's movement toward Catholicism through his emphasis on the invisible church allowed him to de-emphasize the visible local church and excoriate separatism. The ecumenical, invisible church tendency of the Reformed without indicates a similar

[192] John L. Dagg, *Manual of Theology* (1857; repr., Harrisonburg, VA: Gano, 1990), v, 13–18, 361.

[193] CDF, "Letter to the Bishops of the Catholic Church on Some Aspects of the Church Understood as Communion" (Rome, 28 May 1992), art. 9.

[194] Timothy George, "Southern Baptist Ghosts," *FT* 93 (May 1999): 17–24.

[195] Steven R. Harmon delineates seven marks of the catholic Baptists: tradition as source of authority, place for creeds in liturgy and catechesis, liturgy as context for formation by tradition, community as locus of authority, sacramental theology, constructive retrieval of tradition, and thick ecumenism. Harmon, *Towards Baptist Catholicity: Essays on Tradition and the Baptist Vision*, SBHT 27 (Waynesboro, GA: Paternoster, 2006), 6–17.

ecumenical, invisible church tendency among evangelical theologians within the free churches. Perhaps this tendency is endemic to the academic context of theology, for academics prefer ideas to practice. Since evangelicals "tend to define the church more as an ideology than as an institution," professional theologians within the free churches are swayed by a similar tendency.[196] Timothy George, a leading free-church theologian, wrote his dissertation on John Robinson, an early English separatist. George has since become identified with the Reformed wing of Southern Baptist life. The predestinarian theology of Robinson, a partisan of the Synod of Dort, afforded George an opportunity to transition from the local church to emphasizing the invisible church.[197] George also discovered that the invisible church was a convenient means of ecumenical dialogue. His focus on the invisible church has not eliminated his concern for the local churches, but it certainly has eclipsed it. The invisible, spiritual, catholic church is now George's primary definition of the church, bringing him dissatisfaction with visible disunity and the "sectarian" Christ.[198] Robinson's Reformed convictions led his son and his congregation to unite with the Dutch Reformed Church. Whether George's Reformed convictions will lead his followers to do the same is yet undetermined.

As for the "catholic" side of this phenomenon, comparisons may be made between evangelical liberalism and free-church liberalism. There is a definite ecumenical, invisible church tendency among some who are more comfortable with the moderate party in the Southern Baptist Convention. This can be seen, for instance, among the advocates of "Re-Envisioning Baptist Identity: A Manifesto for Baptist Communities in North America."[199] Although the Manifesto theologians rightly call for a return to community and a biblical understanding of freedom among the free churches, their concept of "community" appears formless.[200] For instance, on the positive side, the Re-Envisioning Manifesto advocates the study of the Bible "in reading communities"; emphasizes "shared discipleship"; affirms baptism, preaching, and the Lord's Supper as meaningful signs; and, maintains the separation of church and state. Unfortunately, the group also denounces separatism as "withdrawn, self-chosen, or authoritarian"; emphasizes the "church catholic"; fails to mention church discipline; encourages a revisitation of sacramentalism; and

[196] Robert M. Kingdon, "The Church: Ideology or Institution," *CH* 50 (1981): 83.

[197] Timothy George, "Predestination in a Separatist Context: The Case of John Robinson," *SCJ* 15 (1984): 73–85. The correlation between predestination and the invisible church can be traced to Augustine, John Wyclif, and John Calvin.

[198] George, "What I'd Like to Tell the Pope about the Church," *CT* 26 (1998): 41–44; idem, "Is Christ Divided? and Two More Apostolic Questions Today's Church Must Answer," *CT* 33 (2005): 31–33.

[199] "Appendix: Re-Envisioning Baptist Identity: A Manifesto for Baptist Communities in North America," *PRS* 24 (1997): 303–10; Harmon, *Towards Baptist Catholicity*, 215–23.

[200] Jim McClendon, a native of Shreveport, Louisiana, and graduate of Southwestern Baptist Theological Seminary, was the leading theologian among the original signatories of the Re-Envisioning Manifesto. He spoke in vague terms of "the sphere of the communal." James William McClendon Jr., *Systematic Theology*, vol. 1, *Ethics* (Nashville: Abingdon, 1986), 158–86. Miroslav Volf, a Yugoslavian Baptist with loose connections to the Manifesto theologians, also returned to the historic source of the Baptist movement to construct his ecclesiology. Unfortunately the caricature of John Smyth that Volf presents parallels the individualist democratic politics imbedded in the social Trinitarianism of Jürgen Moltmann, Volf's mentor, more than Smyth himself. Miroslav Volf, *After Our Likeness: The Church as the Image of the Trinity* (Grand Rapids: Eerdmans, 1998).

fosters postmodern nonfoundationalism. Since the 1997 publication of their manifesto, these American free-church theologians have established relationships with a similar group of British Baptist theologians. These transcontinental partners share a concern for ecumenism and a revisitation of sacramentalism.[201] Although most of their energies have been directed toward the exploration of baptismal sacramentalism, John Colwell has proposed a reexamination of all seven of the traditional sacraments of Roman Catholicism in the name of postdenominationalism.[202]

Roland Bainton detected a significant divergence between the ecclesiologies of the evangelicals and the Radical Reformers in the sixteenth century. While Catholics and evangelicals (Lutheran, Calvinist, and Anglican) stressed "the church catholic," the Radical Reformers stressed "the church holy." Bainton also notes that "left wing" ecclesiology was characterized by longings for "primitivism"—a return to the church of the apostles—and for the separation of the church from the state.[203] Similarly, some Southern Baptists maintain that evangelical ecclesiological concepts contradict the traditional Southern Baptist understanding of the biblical church as primarily local and Christonomous, the ordinances as two and symbolic, discipline as beneficial to the church, supralocal Christian unity as primarily a spiritual concern, and the universal church as a purely eschatological gathering.[204] Whether modern trends among the free churches, characterized by the ecumenical desire to define the church primarily as universal or invisible, run counter to the ecclesiology of all the free churches is a matter best left to continuing conversations among the free churches. In the meantime we turn to the exemplary free-church theological foundation offered by a sixteenth-century Anabaptist layman. Pilgram Marpeck's theological foundation agrees substantially with the common Anabaptist idea of the essence of the church as "at the heart . . . discipleship."[205]

---

[201] Stanley K. Fowler, *More Than a Symbol: The British Baptist Recovery of Baptismal Sacramentalism*, SBHT 2 (Waynesboro, GA: Paternoster, 2002); *Baptist Sacramentalism*, ed. Anthony R. Cross and Philip E. Thompson, SBHT 5 (Waynesboro, GA: Paternoster, 2003).

[202] John E. Colwell, *Promise & Presence: An Exploration of Sacramental Theology* (Waynesboro, GA: Paternoster, 2005).

[203] Roland H. Bainton, "The Left Wing of the Reformation," *JR* 21 (1941): 124–34.

[204] Jimmy A. Millikin, "The Nature of the Church: Local or Universal?" *TM* 1 (2006): 59–74; Yarnell, "Article VI, The Church" in *The Baptist Faith and Message 2000: Critical Issues in America's Largest Protestant Denomination*, ed. Douglas Blount and Joseph Wooddell (Lanham, MD: Rowman & Littlefield, 2007).

[205] Robert Friedmann, "Recent Interpretations of Anabaptism," *CH* 24 (1955): 139–40.

Chapter Three

THE FOUNDATION OF DOCTRINE:
A Believers' Church Proposal

Because of his insightful contributions and location near the historical headwaters of the modern believers' church movement, the writings of Pilgram Marpeck, a sixteenth-century South German Anabaptist leader, provide a fit source for detailing the foundation of doctrine in the believers' church tradition. Because of his insightful responses to challenges from the Roman Catholic, Reformed, and Spiritualist-Rationalist traditions, he also serves as a fit source for a believers' church critique of alternative foundations.

PILGRAM MARPECK, DISCIPLE OF JESUS CHRIST

Pilgram Marpeck grew up in the Austrian Tyrol in a family of wealth and influence, receiving a coveted education in Latin. Building on his father's legacy, he rose within the economic and political life of the city of Rattenberg. He became a director of mines (*Bergrichter*) in 1525, a position with considerable political authority and of some military importance to the emperor. According to court records of his disputation with Martin Bucer, Marpeck began his religious pilgrimage as a Roman Catholic. Indeed, he evidences a deep familiarity with the classical doctrines of the Trinity and Christology. His doctrine of the Trinity takes seriously the distinctions yet coinherence of the three Persons. His Christology reflects the influence of Chalcedon, and his writings always expressed these basic Christian orthodoxies in biblical terms. Marpeck did not draw explicitly upon the early fathers or the councils because he sought to speak primarily in biblical terms.[1] But his fundamental orthodoxy with regard to the Trinity and Christology were integral to his understanding of discipleship as a theological foundation. Indeed, Marpeck used extensively the doctrines of the Nicene Creed, the Formula of Chalcedon, and the Apostles' Creed, and a copy of the Athanasian Creed is found in his works.[2]

---

[1] Williams's assessment of Marpeck's orthodox terminology is colored by his own Unitarian commitments. Marpeck's desire to speak from Scripture rather than earlier theologians may be misinterpreted. George Huntston Williams, *The Radical Reformation*, 3rd ed. (Kirksville, MO: Sixteenth Century Journal Publishers, 1992), 683.

[2] On the Athanasian creed in the *Kuntsbuch* of the Marpeck community, see Heinold Fast, "Pilgram Marbeck und das oberdeutsche Täufertum: Ein neuer Handschriftenfund," *AR* 47 (1956): 235. John Roth kindly informs me that the *Kuntsbuch* is being prepared for publication; unfortunately, it was not available for use in this book.

In the early 1520s, Marpeck came under the influence of "the Lutheran way."[3] The catalyst may have been Stephen Agricola, an imprisoned Lutheran preacher for whom the city of Rattenberg interceded with Marpeck as their representative.[4] "I give them testimony," Marpeck shared in 1531, "that I came to the truth partly through their writing, teaching, and preaching, for I was deeply possessed and imprisoned by the human laws of the papacy." On the basis of Lutheran freedom, Marpeck turned against the human accretions to the gospel that he came to perceive in Roman Catholicism. The freedom he learned from the Lutherans was both "new" and "of the flesh." To be sure, he was thankful for this "new" gift, as it helped him to discern the problem with "confession and other papist rules." He became convinced that the Roman Catholic system was composed of "human inventions" that enslaved a person.

Marpeck was always appreciative of his Lutheran heritage. He had learned of justification by faith and freedom from the Protestant Reformers. Moreover, his doctrine of law and gospel was Lutheran in outlook and enabled him to distinguish the Old Testament from the New Testament. Thus, the Lutheran teachings "in and of themselves were not wrong," but they composed only part of the total truth. Marpeck was disappointed with the lifestyle of "fleshly freedom" he saw among some Protestants. The problem with the "evangelical teachers" was that they "said nothing about the mystery of the cross of Christ, and the narrow gate." In other words, evangelicalism freed him from "Babylonian captivity" but failed to lead him "into the liberty of Jerusalem."[5]

Marpeck's first theological writings, from his Anabaptist period, reflect in part the mystical theologies of the cross of suffering characteristic of the *Theologia Deutsch* and the writings of two Anabaptist preachers in Austria, Leonhart Schiemer and Hans Schlaffer.[6] The *Theologia Deutsch* counseled poverty of spirit and abandonment (*Gelassenheit*) to God as the means of transformation by love

Das "Kunstbuch" des Jörg Probst Rotenfelder gen. Maler (Burgerbibliothek Bern, Cod. 464), transcr. Heinold Fast and Martin Rothkegel; ed. Heinold Fast and Gottfried Seebaß, Quellen zur Geschichte der Täufer XVII (Gütersloh: Gütersloher Verlagshaus, forthcoming 2007).

[3] *Täuferakten Elsass, Part 1: Stadt Strassburg, 1522–1532*, ed. Manfred Krebs and Hans Georg Rott, 352; cited in Stephen B. Boyd, *Pilgram Marpeck: His Life and Social Theology* (Durham: Duke University Press, 1992), 13.

[4] William Klassen, *Covenant and Community: The Life, Writings, and Hermeneutics of Pilgram Marpeck* (Grand Rapids: Eerdmans, 1968), 23.

[5] *Aufdeckung der Babylonischen Hurn* [*Exposé of the Babylonian Whore*] (1531), in *Later Writings by Pilgram Marpeck and His Circle*, vol. 1, trans. Walter Klaassen, Werner Packull, and John Rempel (Scottdale, PA: Herald Press, 1999), 28. Cp. Hans J. Hillerbrand, "An Early Anabaptist Treatise on the Christian and the State," *MQR* 32 (1958): 28–47; William R. Estep, "An Anonymous Anabaptist Pamphlet—(circa 1530)." This includes a partial translation in *Anabaptist Beginnings (1523–1533): A Source Book*, ed. William R. Estep Jr. (Nieuwkoop: B. De Graaf, 1976), 155–64; Walter Klaassen, "Investigation into the Authorship and the Historical Background of the Anabaptist Tract *Aufdeckung der Babylonischen Hurn*," *MQR* 61 (1987): 251–61; Werner O. Packull, "Pilgram Marpeck: Uncovering of the Babylonian Whore and Other Anonymous Anabaptist Tracts," *MQR* 67 (1993): 351–52.

[6] The author of *Theologia Deutsch* (or *Theologia Germanica*) was an anonymous mystic in the late fourteenth century from Frankfurt. Luther issued several editions of this work. *The Theologia Germanica of Martin Luther*, ed. Bengt Hoffman (New York: Paulist, 1980), 24–34. Harold Bender, "Pilgram Marpeck, Anabaptist Theologian and Civil Engineer," *MQR* 38 (1964): 235–239, and Boyd, *Pilgram Marpeck*, 25–42, give compelling evidence of the importance of all three of these writers to Marpeck.

into fellowship with the divine nature, which is the source of all good. Furthermore, when the human self yields to God, it is the beginning of a life characterized by obedience. Although accepting the medieval sacraments as a means of grace, the *Theologia Deutsch* downplayed their importance and stressed the inner working of Christ through successive experiences of suffering, enlightenment, and union. Schiemer and Schlaffer were influential in helping Marpeck himself to embrace the life of *Gelassenheit* to God, although Marpeck focused on the humanity of Christ rather than divine participation and was suspicious of the inward concentration of mystics and rationalists.

The meaning of true yieldedness to God as the carrying of the cross (Mark 8:34–38) and its relationship to disciples' baptism (Matt 28:18–20) came to him in a poignant way. He was most likely baptized sometime between the introduction of Anabaptist preaching in the Inn Valley in early 1527 and his exile in 1528. In November 1527, Archduke Ferdinand, disturbed by the growth of "the strange and annoying sects" in which "a new baptism has arisen," ordered the *Bergrichter* to assist in their apprehension and punishment. Marpeck at first protested this was not his responsibility but promised to uphold the mandate as part of his office. Two days after the archduke's administration acknowledged Marpeck's acquiescence, Leonhart Schiemer, the Anabaptist preacher, was beheaded and burned two hundred yards from Marpeck's residence. Five days later the archduke acknowledged Marpeck's request to be discharged from his duty. Three weeks later two other Anabaptist preachers, Hans Schlaffer and Leonhard Frick, were executed in nearby Schwaz. More executions followed.[7]

Knowing full well the hazards of covenantal discipleship with Jesus Christ but ready to embrace the danger-filled call to a visible witness to the cross of Christ, Marpeck soon left Rattenberg and his worldly positions and possessions. With the martyrs Schiemer and Schlaffer, Marpeck affirmed that the one who repents and believes in Christ "submits to the fellowship of suffering under God's hand and discipline."[8] His wife, Anna, accompanied him into exile. Their children, originally adopted as miner's orphans, remained in Rattenberg with portions of his estate. Marpeck was subsequently hounded from one city to the next. The civil societies of Strasbourg, St. Gall, and Augsburg benefited from his engineering expertise, but persecution by Catholic and evangelical theologians kept him on the move. In the meantime, thousands of Anabaptists, many of whose tragic deaths and heroic witnesses are recorded in *The Martyrs Mirror*, were put to death, often following excruciating and inhuman torture because they entered a disciples' covenant through believers' baptism.[9] Amazingly, in spite of his readiness to pay the final price for Christian discipleship, Marpeck himself was one of the few Anabaptist leaders to die a natural death.

[7] Boyd, *Pilgram Marpeck*, 21–24.

[8] *Clare Verantwurtung* (*A Clear Refutation*) (1531), in *Writings of Pilgram Marpeck*, 61.

[9] Thieleman J. van Braght, *The Bloody Theater or Martyrs Mirror of the Defenseless Christians Who Baptized Only upon Confession of Faith, and Who Suffered and Died for the Testimony of Jesus, Their Savior, from the Time of Christ to the Year A.D. 1660*, trans. Joseph F. Sohm (Scottdale, PA: Herald, 2004), pt. 2.

A HOLISTIC THEOLOGICAL FOUNDATION FOR THE CHURCH

In the preface to his *Vermanung* (*Admonition*) of 1542, Marpeck lamented the false theological methods that have resulted in the awful oppression of the people of God. "Through such methods, the insidious serpent, a true enemy of human salvation, has worn out and brutally oppressed the zealous and sincere people."[10] Although such language may appear unduly provocative, today's readers should consider the culture of persecution under which peaceable believers like Marpeck suffered and the gracious spirit evidenced within his entire corpus before easily dismissing this sincere theologian's witness. Marpeck was a polemicist, but he fought only with words from the Word of God and refused to "run ahead" of God by persecuting others physically, as early modern Catholics and evangelicals were more than ready to do. Marpeck was a patient man driven by the love of the Spirit to help build the true church on a true theological foundation rather than repeating the mistakes of the past. According to Marpeck, the true theological foundation is affiliated with a covenant of mutual belief in Jesus Christ: "We hope that each member of the covenant of the pure conscience with God will discriminate on the basis of unity of faith in Jesus Christ."[11]

A word about expectations may be appropriate at this point. To the average systematic theologian, the identification of *Gelassenheit*, *Nachfolge*, or covenantal commitment to Christ, as a theological foundation may appear less than "theological," especially if one is accustomed to making a sharp distinction between theology and praxis. But the South German Anabaptists believed that such a distinction was exactly what was wrong with the normal approach, as represented especially in the Protestant movement. As the *Täufer* (Baptist) told the evangelical *Predikant* (preacher), who was involved in his persecution in Augsburg, "Not the listeners but the doers are blessed (Jas 1[:22]). It bothers my conscience to talk too much about it with you, because you only want to hear about it but not act on it. Better to be silent than to talk uselessly into the wind."[12]

In this way Marpeck's theological foundation cannot be confined to a rational exercise. Indeed, this is one of the difficulties with reading and interpreting Marpeck's theology. Unlike the rationalist theological guild of modern evangelicalism (in which the present writer may, with reservation, be included), Marpeck was not so much concerned with precise theological definitions as he was with sincere and entire obedience to God, whose will was revealed in Scripture. His writings are thus filled with biblical references and passionate calls to obey Christ and be a visible witness for Christ, but he is almost entirely unsystematic.

Similarly, the believers' churches have never really been noted for their contributions to the scholastic artistry of *summa theologia*. This is not so much a failure as a continual rebuke to the aridity to which academic theology is too commonly

[10] *Admonition* (1542), in *The Writings of Pilgram Marpeck*, ed. William Klassen and Walter Klaassen (Scottdale, PA: Herald, 1978), 163.

[11] Ibid., 167.

[12] *A New Dialogue* (ca. 1531–1532), in *Later Writings of Pilgram Marpeck and His Circle*, 1:55.

subject. The Baptist's advice to the Protestant academic is that, if he wants to truly do things "properly" in the church:

> Completely surrender to God under his cross; look only to his will and command. Accept the suffering, persecution, and cross, inward and outward, which will result and will not fail to come to you. Such is the school of Christ into which he calls all who want to become his disciples. As one is instructed in this school and submits to God's discipline, one receives the key of David [the true hermeneutical principle], that is, the Holy Spirit. . . . But if you do not want to go to the proper school, you will never find Christ about whom you are now divided.[13]

In other words, the focus of the believers' church theologian is upon the church rather than the academy. And the church is busy about reading the Bible and living from it. Indeed, the undisciplined evangelical academy is recognized for what it has imported into the church, an unbiblical order (*Ordnung*). As the Baptist responded to the evangelical preacher, the problem with the Protestant churches is their unbiblical elitism. "Individual members are not permitted to exercise their gifts for the edification of the congregation; as if you alone had all the gifts."[14] Reacting against the Roman Catholic dualism between clergy and laity, and after Luther's modification of his earlier principle of the priesthood of all believers following the Peasants' Revolt of 1525, and considering the inherent elitism of Reformed ecclesiology, it fell to the believers' churches to reify the congregational principle. While Erasmus may have employed the principle of every believer as a theologian in his argument for the vernacular Bible, it was the believers' churches that made his theology concrete.[15] In the believers' churches the idea that constructing a biblical theology is the responsibility of every believer is accompanied by the idea that theological judgment is best carried out by the church.

Due to the unsystematic nature of Marpeck's works, describing his theological foundation in a systematic way may appear somewhat arbitrary. The vibrant nature of his theology cannot be entirely contained in words because words were simply a way, though a necessary means, to discuss his vital relationship with God and his community. Yet in our post-Enlightenment world the theologian must necessarily "translate" Marpeck for today. This venture has been in part tried before but not as an attempt to let Marpeck's own emphases discern his theological method. John C. Wenger attempted to pour Marpeck's writings into a Reformed mold, but such an effort unwittingly allows the Protestant paradigm for systematic theology to misrepresent Marpeck's actual foundation.[16] The implantation of a hostile theological system is especially problematic in light of the critique made by Marpeck. Recently Thomas N. Finger sought to construct a systematic theology from an Anabaptist perspective. Though intriguing, Finger's method is focused upon the

[13] Ibid., 60.

[14] Ibid., 57.

[15] Desiderius Erasmus, *Paraclesis* (1516), in *Christian Humanism and the Reformation: Selected Writings of Erasmus*, 3rd ed., ed. John C. Olin (New York: Fordham University Press, 1987), 97–108.

[16] John C. Wenger, "The Theology of Pilgram Marpeck," *MQR* 12 (1938): 205–56.

Anabaptists in particular rather than the Anabaptists as one strand of the believers' church tradition. Moreover, there is little in the way of theological formation in his book. What might be regarded as Finger's theological foundation is primarily narrative.[17]

In constructing a paradigm for approaching Marpeck's thought, it seems more appropriate to take Marpeck's words and allow his own emphases to form the paradigm. In the following section selected writings of Marpeck and inductive studies of his corpus provide a picture of the foundation of Marpeck's theology. It will be seen that covenantal discipleship is the foundation of a believers' church theology. As a major biographer of Marpeck commented, "The entire thought and effort of the [Ana]baptists focused on Christ and his church, or better yet on discipleship to Christ and brotherhood."[18]

Marpeck's personal confession of salvation by Christ and commitment to covenantal discipleship through the Holy Spirit exemplifies the holistic nature of the theological foundation of the believers' churches. Marpeck, who stands near the headwaters of the modern free churches, focuses on *Nachfolge Christi* within the church:

> My salvation depends alone on Christ's, the Lord's, dying and the shedding of His blood. In Him alone have I received the remission and forgiveness of sins from the Holy Spirit in the fellowship of His saints. Into this fellowship I have also been baptized, according to the witness and truth of my heart in the Holy Spirit, on my own testimony and confession of the truth. I also reject all ignorant baptism which happens without true, revealed, personal faith whether in children or adults. For this reason, I also was baptized with external water and external word, in confession of my faith. I was gladly baptized into this fellowship of the Holy Spirit, visibly gathered, for the remission and forgiveness of sins. In it I sincerely desire to remain until my end. Amen to all who desire this with me. That is briefly the testimony of my heart in Christ Jesus.[19]

THE GROUND PRINCIPLES OF A BELIEVERS' CHURCH THEOLOGY

In a 1968 article, Franklin H. Littell, a Methodist historical theologian interested in the ecclesiology of the Anabaptists, whom he considered to be at the origins of "sectarian Protestantism,"[20] set out what he believed were *Die Grundprinzipien* (the basic principles) of the free churches. Among the free churches or believers' churches, he included such diverse denominations as Waldensians, Mennonites,

---

[17] Thomas N. Finger, *A Contemporary Anabaptist Theology: Biblical, Historical, Constructive* (Downers Grove, IL: InterVarsity Press, 2004), pt. 1.

[18] "Das ganze Denken und Streben der Täufer konzentriert sich auf Christus und Seine Gemeinde, oder besser auf Nachfolge Christi und der Bruderliebe." Jan J. Kiwiet, *Pilgram Marbeck: Ein Führer in der Täuferbewegung der Reformationszeit* (Kassel: J. G. Oncken, 1958), 16.

[19] Marpeck, *Judgment and Decision* [Letter of Marpeck to the Swiss Brethren] (1541?), in *The Writings of Pilgram Marpeck*, 332–33.

[20] Franklin H. Littell, *The Anabaptist View of the Church: A Study in the Origins of Sectarian Protestantism*, 2nd ed. (Boston, MA: Starr King, 1958).

Baptists, Quakers, Moravians, Methodists, and Brethren. The basic principles of these churches, he was convinced, were the leadership of Jesus Christ in the church, voluntary church membership, the church's separation from the world, missions and evangelism, the integrity and discipline of the church, and the church's interaction with the world. Although these principles are certainly integral to the believers' churches, Littell largely limited his concerns to ecclesiology. Moreover Littell failed to integrate his principles with the theological foundation that most free-church scholars have recognized in some way as central to the believers' churches: discipleship. Littell, did, however, begin correctly with Jesus Christ.[21]

The following *Grundprinzipien*—Jesus Christ, the Word and the Spirit, biblical order, and the believers' church—are garnered from an inductive study of the Marpeckian corpus and the inductive studies of others. We allow Marpeck's own method to provide the paradigm rather than forcing it into an alien paradigm, as Wenger did. The inductive research methods advocated and used by William Klassen and Jan J. Kiwiet provide a more satisfactory approach to discern Pilgram Marpeck's own theological method.[22] Marpeck must be understood on his own terms, if we are to approach a theological method drawn from a free churchman. Thus, Marpeck's *Grundprinzipien* are presented as he himself might have presented them if asked the modern question regarding theological method. Marpeck's ground principles exemplify what the free churches have advocated as integral to their theological foundation. His contribution is a superb representation of "a theology of the free church."[23] The free churches begin their theology of discipleship with a personal relationship with Jesus Christ, seek to understand His ordinances through His Word illuminated by the Spirit, and institute those ordinances within the church, according to the biblical order.

1. Jesus Christ

Many theological systems begin with either philosophy, revelation, theology proper, or some mixture of the above; but Marpeck was far more interested in a personal relationship with our Savior and Lord, Jesus Christ. For Marpeck, the Christian's essential nature was, as seen in his personal confession, utterly dependent upon being united "in Christ Jesus." The reason that Jesus could take the human sinner into a loving relationship with God through the Holy Spirit was that Jesus is fully God and fully man. The writings of Marpeck have numerous parallels with the formula of the Council of Chalcedon, and the biblical conclusions won in the fifth century are fundamental to the thought of this sixteenth-century churchman.[24]

[21] Franklin H. Littell, "Der Beitrag der Freikirchen zur modernen Kirchengeschichte," *Zeitschrift für Religions- und Geiestesgeschichte* 20 (1968): 223–39.

[22] Cp. Klassen's glowing comments on the inductive research method of Kiwiet, as well as his own exemplary approach in *Covenant and Community*. William Klassen, "Pilgram Marpeck in Recent Research," *MQR* 32 (1958): 222–23.

[23] Kiwiet, *Pilgram Marbeck*, 149.

[24] *Decrees of the Ecumenical Councils*, trans. Norman P. Tanner (Washington, DC: Georgetown University Press, 1990), 1:86–87.

Person. In *Concerning the Humanity of Christ* (1555), Marpeck succinctly discusses the central aspects of his doctrine of Jesus Christ.[25] Notice in what follows the seamless transition from classical theology to the Christian life embodied in what Neal Blough calls the "typical Anabaptist *Nachfolge Christi* ethic."[26] The problem with Blough's description is that discipleship in Marpeck, as in all of the believers' churches, is more than an "ethic" understood as distinct from theology. Discipleship is the theological basis that grants the Anabaptists the principles for theology as a way of life. Yet Blough correctly notes, "Christology is the central concern of this Tyrolean lay theologian."[27] Christian discipleship is inseparable from the One to whom submission is granted. Marpeck's theology of discipleship originates in the Master of the disciples.

Marpeck begins this letter with the essential participation of Christ in the Trinity as the source of the church's participation by grace in the Trinity.[28] He addresses the persecuted church in Langnau as "beloved, loved in God the Father." They should thank God for all of His graces, which He works in them. These graces from God are Christ's graces in entirety, from beginning to end. They belong to the church "through Jesus Christ," "for the sake of Christ," and because Christ Himself is "working in us." The graces are worked in us "through His Holy Spirit."

Jesus Christ is God. "In Him alone the fullness of Godhead dwells bodily." Such honor must be ascribed to Him because the Father has ascribed such to Him. The Christian must "reasonably honor Him as much as the Father." He is "the Son of God" and, to state it in Nicene terms, He is "one essence with the Father." Jesus Christ is also a man. Marpeck speaks more of the humanity of Christ than the deity of Christ. This seems to be because the greater problem in his day was the effective undermining of the humanity of Christ, especially by those enamored with a theology of glory. On the one hand, he warns against those who "consider Him (the Lord) as purely human." On the other hand, he warns against those who "confess Him as purely the Son of God also according to the flesh, thereby failing to ascribe to him the honor of being a Son of Man, of the race of men, flesh, blood, and human."

Work. The work of Christ on the cross is elsewhere considered by Marpeck as the source of our redemption.[29] As Wenger details at length, Marpeck stressed the order of the life of Christ. Christ existed before His incarnation, and all things were created through Christ. The preexistence of Christ, however, did not yet involve his humanity. He was born of the virgin Mary by the Holy Spirit, and once He became a human being, Christ is always a human being. The human nature

[25] *The Writings of Pilgram Marpeck*, 507–15.

[26] Neal Blough, "Pilgram Marpeck, Martin Luther and the Humanity of Christ," *MQR* 60 (1987): 208.

[27] Ibid., 203.

[28] Cp. Blough, "The Church as Sign or Sacrament: Trinitarian Ecclesiology, Pilgram Marpeck, Vatican II and John Milbank," *MQR* 78 (2004): 29–52; Wenger, "The Theology of Pilgram Marpeck," 214–17.

[29] "Without sin, He bore our sin and our weakness, and fastened it to the cross. . . . And because the Son Himself had to become subject and innocently bear our guilt, all the others have had to wait in their guilt for the redemption." *Confession* (1532), in *The Writings of Pilgram Marpeck*, 124.

of Christ was brought up into relationship with the divine nature. Henceforth, we cannot separate the deity and humanity of Christ.[30] This is important, as we shall see, for his understanding of the relation of the covenants. It was impossible for the Old Testament saints to have been regenerated by the Holy Spirit, for the human nature of Christ, which worked the atonement, was not yet joined to the divine nature.

Because of Christ's work on our behalf, Marpeck specifically ascribes "all the honors which the Father has ascribed to Him" directly "to the flesh, body, and blood." This is an intentional reference to "the humanity of Christ" as the object of Christian worship. With the early church fathers, he seems to agree wholeheartedly in the *communicatio idiomatum*. One may worship the man as one would worship God because Jesus Christ is one person composed of two natures, the divine and the human. The Father has honored the man, Christ, and we must honor Him in the same way.

Externally the Father has made Jesus "Lord, Ruler, Leader, and Director of His saints." More intimately, "Christ lives in them and does and accomplishes the good pleasure of the Father." A submissive relationship to Christ is necessary for the disciple: "Nothing else shall impel, lead, and guide the believers than Christ, the Word of truth." The impetus for yieldedness does not begin with us but with Christ. "Therefore, it does not depend on our willing or running, but rather on the mercy of God and on His grace in and with Christ." And yet a person must not resist or run ahead of Christ as a result of his own nature: "We must simply in all of our actions stand idle ourselves, as dead in ourselves, if Christ is to live in us."

Christ is the final authority in the Christian's life because "all judgment" has been committed to Him by the Father. His life and death provide the pattern for our lives and deaths. We must expend effort to walk according to His walk and be especially careful not to confuse our natural impulses with His desires: "Ah, my brethren, how diligently and carefully we have to take heed that we do not consider our own impulse the impulse of the Holy Spirit, our own course the course and walk of Christ."

Marpeck makes a stark distinction between "natural piety" and "the compulsion of the Holy Spirit." A person with natural piety may have a "servile compulsion" to zealously pursue the good and hinder evil, but this is a residual of fallen creation. Unfortunately those who only have natural piety are often involved in the persecution of the church, like Paul before his conversion. The Christian who is truly compelled by the Holy Spirit may know of the Spirit's guidance by four measures:

1. "Love for God and granting my neighbor that which God has granted and given to me for His praise, and the salvation of my soul." Elsewhere, Marpeck is clear that this means practicing the patience of God towards others that God showed the Christian disciple before his conversion.

[30] Wenger, "The Theology of Pilgram Marpeck," 217–23.

2. "A devaluation and giving up of life unto death to suffer for the sake of Christ and the gospel in all patience." The life of Christ is elsewhere described by Marpeck as being "the pattern" and "example" for the life of the Christian.[31] This includes the readiness to follow Christ in the carrying of the cross.
3. "To realize when God unlocks or opens a door that one enter the same with the teaching of the gospel." The bold proclamation of God's Word by the visible church was central to Marpeck's program. There was not to be timidity in evangelism. Yet Marpeck realized that sometimes God closes the door in one area and opens it in another.
4. "That one be free and sound in teaching and judgments and in truth, in order that none speak unless Christ work through His Holy Spirit." Marpeck's understanding of biblical hermeneutics is indicated here. As we shall see below, the outer Word is the absolutely necessary means of God's grace, but the inner Spirit must also give faith in order for the Word to be properly interpreted.

Marpeck's fifteenth letter ends with particular items requiring his advice, especially concerning the problem of persecution for the Anabaptists in their Swiss canton. He counseled "the brethren from Langnau" to "exercise moderation and discretion" in their public interactions, especially with the government. They should not needlessly provoke the government to "wrongly" persecute the brethren. "However, if God's honor and truth are at stake, then we are obligated to give up all and to endure all persecution unto death." Marpeck never countenanced the idea that Christians should hide their beliefs when threatened with persecution. After all, being put to death because of witnessing for Jesus Christ may be what carrying the cross means for some Christians. A Christian disciple must follow Jesus Christ.

2. Word and Spirit

Coinherence. Marpeck's theology was founded upon faith in Jesus Christ, but according to his personal confession, he received Christ "of the Holy Spirit." The faith of Marpeck was substantiated in the Word and enlivened by the Spirit. Marpeck was clear that the external witness of the Word must be accompanied by the internal witness of the Spirit. In his time of leadership as a *Vorsteher* (leader) among the South German Anabaptists, he defended the church against two extremes: spiritualism and legalism. His personality was providentially strong enough to remain patient and biblical in the midst of being unjustly accused of legalism by the spiritualists, of spiritualism by the legalists, and of being a "stiff-necked heretic" by the evangelicals. Because of his personal stability and graciousness, even his opponents recognized that Marpeck "had received much from the Lord" and exhibited a "fine, blameless behavior." Because of his thorough

[31] *Concerning the Lowliness of Christ* [Letter of Marpeck to the Swiss Brethren] (1547), in *The Writings of Pilgram Marpeck*, 438.

biblicism and deep respect for the congregation, it should be little wonder that the Anabaptists were sarcastically said to have "worshiped him as a god."[32]

The unique balance of doctrinal stability and spiritual dynamism that made Marpeck's disciplined personality so appealing derived from the balance required by his classical doctrine of the Trinity. The coinherence of the Word and the Spirit within the Trinity became a model for him of the coinherence of spirit and letter (2 Cor 3:6),[33] the internal and the external, baptism by the Spirit and baptism by water, the visible sign and the sovereign activity of God, and the individual believer and the church. The coinherence of the distinct Persons of the Word and the Spirit is a classical theological doctrine that reaches back to the Cappadocians in the East and Augustine in the West. Due to his emphasis on the Holy Spirit as the love of God, Marpeck's doctrine of the Trinity could be described as Augustinian; but the descriptions of the dynamic interactions of the three Persons of the Godhead that permeate Marpeck's writings harmonize with the thought of the Eastern fathers too.

The willingness of Marpeck to use both the Western and the Eastern forms of Trinitarian thought can be seen in his *Vindication*, which has been described as similar to "the first draft of a systematic theology."[34] In that work the Trinity proceeds from the Father alone before the incarnation but through the Son afterwards. The procession that Marpeck describes is economic rather than essential, indicating his primary concern with God's outer work. "God's Word and Spirit work together. They proceed from the undivided, the one Jesus Christ—as they proceeded from the Father before the incarnation of the Word to things in need. Today the Spirit and the Word proceed from the Son Jesus Christ to the actions which need doing today."[35] Marpeck's contribution concerning the economic procession of the Trinity is unique, but it is orthodox, nonetheless, if one counts both the Eastern and Western doctrines of procession orthodox. Ultimately, however, Marpeck's doctrine of the Trinity is orthodox because it is strictly "biblical."[36]

Marpeck understood the coinherence of the Father, the Son, and the Holy Spirit as a subsidiary doctrine of the distinctions between the three persons of the one Godhead. The Marpeckian church's doctrine of the Trinity indicates his

---

[32] These comments were made by his Reformed opponent, Martin Bucer. Harold S. Bender, "Pilgram Marpeck, Anabaptist Theologian and Civil Engineer," *MQR* 38 (1964): 234.

[33] On the Reformation debates over 2 Cor 3:6, see Klassen, "Anabaptist Hermeneutics," 85–87.

[34] John Rempel, "Introduction," *Verantwortung* (*Vindication*), in *Later Writings by Pilgram Marpeck and His Circle*, 68.

[35] Marpeck uses Word [*Wort*] here to describe the inscripturated extension of the revelation of God in Christ. *Quellen und Forschungen zur Geschichte der oberdeutschen Taufgesinnten im 16. Jahrhundert: Pilgram Marbecks Antwort auf Kaspar Schwenckfelds Beurteilung des Buches der Bundesbezeugung von 1542*, ed. J. Loserth (Vienna: Carl Fromme, 1929), 516–17; *Response*, 120. (When citing Rempel's abridgement, his translation of *Verantwortung* as *Response* will be used. Translations by this author are indicated with the title of *Verantwortung* or *Vindication*.)

[36] Williams unfortunately sought to present Marpeck as a forerunner of Faustus Socinus. Marpeck's peculiar presentation of Christ as the "Third Person of the divine unity" is immaterial, as the *taxis* introduced by the Cappadocians is largely concerned with the monarchy of the Father rather than the order between the Son and the Spirit. Marpeck understands well the coinherence of the Father, the Son, and the Spirit, a commitment that may have been undetected due to Williams' Unitarianism. Williams, *The Radical Reformation*, 684–85.

fundamental orthodoxy. It is from this commitment to classical orthodoxy, especially understood according to the doctrine of coinherence (Gk., *perichoresis*) that Marpeck developed his view of hermeneutics.

> Namely, therefore, we believe that there is one God and one divine nature, but in the same divine nature three independent persons, the Father, the Son and the Holy Spirit; that all three are one God; and that the divine nature to each person is his own and entire and yet in itself undivided, which is common to all three persons. It is our Christian faith that there are not three Gods, but only one God in three persons and that each holy Person in the Godhead, the Son as well as the Father, and the Holy Spirit as well as the Son, are truly God in nature; and are of like authority, might, honor, glory and magnificence.[37]

Verbum Dei. Marpeck's belief in Jesus Christ as the incarnate Word of God was intimately bound with his belief that the Bible is the inscripturated Word of God. Against an attempt to drastically separate the Word into two, his community affirmed, "We say again that there are not two but only one Word of God; and the Word of divine, evangelical preaching (which Schwenckfeld calls the word of the letter) is truly the Word of the Holy Spirit and of God."[38] Klassen wrote that Marpeck refused to radically separate the oral Word from the written Word "because the Holy Spirit has written the Gospels and apostolic writings through the hands of the evangelists and apostles."[39] He did not worship the letter of Scripture, but he understood the letter as the means that the divine Word had chosen as his instrument. "It is not the ink and paper, not the perishable, creaturely parts of books or human speech which is God's Word, but rather that which it contains, its spoken and written sense."[40]

Although Marpeck did not define his doctrine of Scripture's inspiration by the Spirit in answer to the questions raised in the modernist-fundamentalist controversy, he may be described as a "biblicist" in the positive sense of that term.[41] The Bible is a divine production through the apostles. "Their script was God's script engraved. . . . Therefore, they are the writing of God or the Holy Spirit." The Bible may be legitimately called "Word," just as Christ is "Word" and the proclamation of the gospel is also "Word." Marpeck had a dynamic and integrative understanding of the Word of God. "Namely, we mean that there is only the

---

[37] "Nemlich also glauben wir, das ain gott und ainig göttlich wesen ist, aber in demselben ainigen, göttlichen wesen drey selbständige personen, der vatter, der sun und der h. geist sein, das alle drey ain gott und das göttlich wesen ainer yeden person aigen und gantz und doch in im selbs unzertailt, das is allen drey personen auch gemain sey. Das ist unser christlicher glaub, das nicht drey götter, sonder nur ain gott in dreyen personen und das ain yede heylige person in der gottheit, der sun sowol als der vatter und der h. geist sowol als der sun warhaftiger gott ains wesens, gleichs gewalts, macht, ehre, glorj und herrlicheit sey." *Verantwortung*, 551; cp. Wenger, "The Theology of Pilgram Marpeck," 217.

[38] Wenger, "The Biblicism of the Anabaptists," in *The Recovery of the Anabaptist Vision*, ed. Guy F. Hershberger (Scottdale: Herald, 1957), 173.

[39] Klassen, *Covenant and Community*, 59.

[40] William Klassen, "Anabaptist Hermeneutics: The Letter and the Spirit," *MQR* 40 (1966): 90.

[41] Wenger, "The Biblicism of the Anabaptists," 167–79.

unique word of the Father, which that comes to us from the human Word, the Lord Jesus Christ. . . . Through himself and his apostles this word was brought to us through the gospel, and now it still speaks in believers' hearts by the Holy Spirit, as a living word or speech of God."[42] The Word of God is revelation Himself written by the Spirit into Scripture, and this Word is spoken by the Spirit through the outward proclamation of the Bible. The Holy Spirit cannot be received apart from the Word's proclamation because the incarnate Word revealed in the inscripturated Word works now through the proclaimed Word.[43]

Marpeck was utterly respectful of the teachings of the Bible and sought to base his entire belief system from them. He believed that the Word is perfect and accomplishes God's will. "We would sincerely admonish every Christian to study the Scriptures, and have a care lest he permit himself to be easily moved and led away from Scripture and apostolic doctrine by strange teaching and understanding. But let every one, according to Scripture and apostolic teaching, strive with great diligence to do God's will, seeing that the Word of Truth could not fail us nor mislead us." It should be noted that Marpeck's biblicism was not for doctrine as definition alone but also doctrine as deed: the Word was given for us "to do God's will."[44]

Kiwiet distinguishes Marpeck's approach to Scripture from modern approaches. Marpeck's primary interest was not critical-exegetical or biblical-theological in the modern senses but strictly biblical. "As a genuine Baptist, he was interested only in holy Scripture, which he frequently cites and to which he frequently refers. Theology is, for Marpeck, a systematic hermeneutic of Scripture [*Schriftauslegung*]."[45] (This author chose not to repeat all of the references to Scripture in Marpeck's work, only the particularly relevant ones. A biblical apparatus to Marpeck's writings, including direct references and allusions, would make this chapter grossly large. The author hopes that the echoes of Scripture will be convincing enough to the discerning reader.)

Marpeck was concerned that others were not diligent to return constantly to the Word as their judge. On the one hand, he warned the spiritualists that they should "not go beyond the evidence of Holy Scripture."[46] On the other hand, he corrected the evangelicals for not consistently instituting their common belief in *sola scriptura*. He detected the evangelical error as arising from their dependence

[42] "Das wir nemlich nur ein ainigs wort des vatters mainen, welches uns von dem vermenschten wort, dem herren Jesu Christo . . . durch sich selbs und seine apostel zubracht ist durchs evangelium, und noch heut durch seinen h. geist in der glaubigen menschen herzen redet, als ein lebendig wort oder red gottes." *Verantwortung*, 298.

[43] *Verantwortung*, 516, 529; *Response*, 120, 123. Since the Spirit who saves cannot be received apart from the proclamation of the Christian Bible, Marpeck would probably condemn outright the "Camel Method" as unchristian. The Camel Method is a missiological methodology that seeks to use the Koran and Muslim conceptions to lead people to faith in "Jesus." Kevin Greeson, *Camel Training Manual* (Bangalore, India: WIGTake Resources, 2004).

[44] *Admonition*, cited in Wenger, "The Biblicism of the Anabaptists," 168.

[45] "Als echten Täufer interessiert ihn nur die Heilige Schrift, die er häufig zitiert und auf die er häufig hinweist. Theologie ist für Marbeck systematische Schriftauslegung." Kiwiet, *Pilgram Marbeck*, 84.

[46] *Verantwortung*, 373–74; Klassen, *Covenant and Community*, 58.

on the heathen culture, in its sophistic learning and in its resort to coercion. "The Word of the Lord is the only judge and sword of Christians. True Christians will use no other judge, nor sword."[47] For Marpeck, the Bible was in reality the ultimate theological authority, unlike those who only feigned *sola scriptura*.[48]

Verbum cum Spiritu. Marpeck's conviction that the Holy Spirit is the one who necessarily illuminates, to the inner heart, the meaning of the external Word, which is the necessary means of revelation, was fleshed out during his controversies with the *Geister* (spiritualists). Marpeck would not allow legalists among the Swiss Brethren or the Hutterites to separate the Word from the Spirit; neither would he allow the spiritualists to separate the Spirit from the Word. For Marpeck, theological truth is always found in the Word with the Spirit (*Verbum cum Spiritu*) and the Spirit with the Word (*Spiritus cum Verbo*). Against the errors to his left among the spiritualists and to his right among the legalists, Marpeck maintained a finely balanced theology of Word and Spirit.

Marpeck originally encountered the spiritualists during his Strasbourg period, first in their unstable Anabaptist form[49] but ultimately in their pure spiritualist form in Caspar Schwenckfeld von Ossig in Silesia.[50] Schwenckfeld was an intellectual spiritualist whom Marpeck had probably first met in Strasbourg and with whom he long struggled. The public debate between the two leaders began with the Marpeckian community's advocacy of a visible disciple's church in the *Admonition* of 1542, to which Schwenckfeld responded negatively in his *Judicium*. It was long carried out through surrogates—Helen Streicher, a shopkeepers' widow, representing Schwenckfeld, and Magdalene von Pappenheim, an aristocratic former nun, representing Marpeck.[51] Ultimately the debate resulted in a massive manuscript written by the Marpeckian community, the *Verantwortung* (*Vindication*). The *Vindication*, "the finest single source of the theology of the

---

[47] *Exposé of the Babylonian Whore*, 35–36.

[48] "Against such testimony of the New Testament all of your arguments are like snowballs [thrown] against the wall." *A New Dialogue*, 56.

[49] For Marpeck's earlier arguments against spiritualism among the Anabaptists in Strasbourg, see the 1531 pamphlets, *Clare Verantwurtung* (*A Clear Refuation*) and *Ain Klarer Vast Nützlicher Unterricht* (*A Clear and Useful Instruction*), in *The Writings of Pilgram Marpeck*, 44–67, 70–106. The latter work was written to keep Anabaptists from embracing Schwenckfeld's theory of a *Stillstand*, suspension of the sacraments. Persecution had recently brought many Anabaptists to consider suppressing their visible witness. These rare writings were rediscovered in the twentieth century. Cp. John C. Wenger, "The Life and Work of Pilgram Marpeck," *MQR* 12 (1938): 148–49; idem, "Additional Note on the Life and Work of Pilgram Marpeck," *MQR* 12 (1938): 269–70; Klassen, *Covenant and Community*, 36–43.

[50] Williams develops a helpful paradigm of Anabaptists, Spiritualists, and Rationalists to explain distinctions within the Radical Reformation, but his placement of various theologians is sometimes arbitrary. George H. Williams, "Introduction," in *Spiritual and Anabaptist Writers*, ed. George H. Williams and Angel M. Mergal (Philadelphia: Westminster, 1957), 19–38. For instance, he mislabels Marpeck as a "Spiritualist Anabaptist" but correctly identifies Caspar Schwenckfeld as an "Evangelical Spiritualist." Williams, *The Radical Reformation*, 685. David C. Steinmetz, "Caspar Schwenckfeld (1489–1561): The Renunciation of Structure," in idem, *Reformers in the Wings: From Geiler von Kaysersberg to Theodore Beza*, 2nd ed. (New York: Oxford University Press, 2001), 131–37.

[51] Williams's first edition called it a *Damenkrieg* [ladies' war]. There are various treatments of this debate in Williams, *Radical Reformation*, 3rd ed., 703–21, 1213–20; Franklin Hamlin Littell, "Spiritualizers, Anabaptists, and the Church," *MQR* 29 (1955): 34–43; and, *Sixteenth Century Anabaptism and the Radical Reformation*, ed. Jean-George Rott and Simon L. Verheus (Baden-Baden: Koerner, 1987), 131–47, 370–80, 381–99.

South German Anabaptists," was written between 1542 and 1556 and disseminated in two installments.[52]

With the appearance of the first installment of the *Vindication*, probably in early 1544, Caspar Schwenckfeld and Pilgram Marpeck exchanged a series of letters through their patronesses and personally. Schwenckfeld "always maintained that the Anabaptists lacked the requisite degree of intellectual fitness to prove their proposition."[53] This prompted a spirited defense of Anabaptist theology from Marpeck. In a letter of 1544, Marpeck argued that the true church is simple because Christ was "an uneducated carpenter's son" and God traps the wise within their own wisdom.[54] Echoing a common theme of Luther, Marpeck claimed the gospel is hidden in simplicity.[55]

Marpeck's letter to Schwenckfeld begins with a claim that self-understanding must precede all other understanding.[56] The understanding of self, however, is impossible without divine intervention. One may have great cultural learning, even the knowledge of Latin, Greek, Hebrew, or other languages, and still lack wisdom. One may even study Scripture with good reasoning skills, but apart from the movement of God, he will remain ignorant of the first truth. The problem with pride in human learning is that it does not understand that divine truth is closed to traditional methods. Marpeck was not arguing against learning in itself, for he considered intellectual skills to be "gifts of God." Neither was he arguing for the facile reading of Scripture. He believed it was necessary for a man to come to Scripture "in the true humility of Christ." Unless one comes under the judgment of God's Word, the Bible proclaimed by his humble church, one will not understand it.

Scripture came by the Spirit's inspiration, and the humility to understand it is also a gift of the Spirit. Marpeck stresses two related truths in his letter to Schwenckfeld. First, true faith in God, saving faith, is available only through the Word of God. Second, the hidden and simple message of the Word of God is opened only by the Spirit. The first truth, regarding the Scripture as the necessary means of salvation, is inseparable from the second truth, regarding the Spirit as the necessary illuminator of the Word. These two doctrines indicate the inability of man apart from the concurrent work of the Word and the Spirit. The two persons of the Trinity coinhere economically in how they work at the behest of the Father, just as they coinhere ontologically in who they are.[57]

These two doctrines, the necessity of the Word and the necessity of the Spirit, form one principle in Marpeck's holistic hermeneutics. The two doctrines that form one hermeneutical principle are expressed by Marpeck thus:

---

[52] Klassen, *Covenant and Community*, 47.

[53] Selina Gerhard Schulz, *Caspar Schwenckfeld von Ossig (1489–1561)* (Norristown, PA, 1946), cited in Littell, "Spiritualizers, Anabaptists, and the Church," 40.

[54] Letter of Marpeck to Caspar Schwenckfeld (1544), in *The Writings of Pilgram Marpeck*, 370.

[55] On the concept that God is hidden, see Blough, "Pilgram Marpeck, Martin Luther and the Humanity of Christ."

[56] Letter of Marpeck to Caspar Schwenckfeld (1544), in *The Writings of Pilgram Marpeck*, 369–75.

[57] Or to express it in inappropriate grammar by violating subject-verb agreement yet appropriate theologically: "in who they is," or, "in who God are."

> [First doctrine, on the necessity of the Word:] Only by the means of the Word of truth does the Holy Spirit generate faith, even in all truly believing hearts, no matter how foolish and contemptible they may often seem to man.
>
> [Second doctrine, on the necessity of the Spirit:] Indeed, even today, God will reveal His art and wisdom only through the Holy Spirit.

Marpeck ended his letter, appropriately enough, on the humble note that he would change his view of the matter if Schwenckfeld or anybody else could show him how he might be wrong, "because we are all fallible and deficient persons." In other responses to spiritualism, Marpeck bound these two doctrines even more tightly together with the language of outer (*eusserlich*) and inner [*innerlich*]. The work of Christ is an outer work accomplished today through His Word visibly proclaimed by His church. The work of the Spirit is an inner work accomplished sovereignly by God Himself in granting faith. The outward proclamation of the Word is thus a cowitness [*mitzeugnis*] to the inner work of the Spirit willingly received by the human heart.

Similarly, the inner baptism by the Spirit is witnessed to by the outer baptism in water. Baptism and the Lord's Supper are never referred to as symbol or sign in Scripture. Rather, the external act is a cowitness to internal faith previously granted by the Holy Spirit. Defining the ordinances as *ex opere operato* sacraments or forcing baptism upon infants is thereby rendered superfluous.[58] Against the spiritualists, the free churches of the sixteenth century found it necessary to emphasize the proclamation of the biblical Word by the visible church exercising Christ's visible ordinances as they followed the human Christ.

With regard to a distinction between the inner and the outer, the spiritualists could agree. However, the spiritualists' inherent dualism brought them to reject the outer entirely by suspending the visible witness of the church, while Marpeck's holism correlated the inner with the outer as a cowitness. The external work by the Son and the internal work by the Spirit are really one work by the one God. With regard to this general principle, Marpeck writes, "I would question whether the physical voice of Christ the Lord can be separated from the Spirit and life. . . . There are two doctrines: an outer and an inner one. There is, however, only one Spirit and life, and only one teaching, by the Lord Himself. . . . Far be it from us that we ourselves should divide the Lord in such a manner that the outer is separated from the inner, and the inner from the outer."[59]

Spiritus cum Verbo. "If it was necessary to begin with the Spiritualists on the primacy of the Word become flesh, with the legalists within Anabaptism it was necessary to emphasize the primacy of the Spirit, while asserting the empirical union of letter and spirit."[60] Marpeck expended much effort to unite the scattered and persecuted congregations of Anabaptists from the Melchiorites and

[58] *Verantwortung*, 112; *Response*, 75.
[59] Marpeck to Helena von Streicher (ca. 1544), in *The Writings of Pilgram Marpeck*, 378–79.
[60] Klassen, "Anabaptist Hermeneutics," 91.

Mennonites in the west and north to the Swiss Brethren in the south to the Moravians and Hutterites in the east. Marpeck's congregation continued this effort even after his death in 1556.[61] Stuart Murray detects a spectrum ranging from spiritualism to literalism among the Anabaptists, with Hans Denck and David Joris on the left to the Mennonites and the Swiss Brethren on the right. "Nearer the putative centre of Anabaptism on this issue was Marpeck."[62] His fine balance of Word and Spirit required him to correct the right almost as much as the left.

Marpeck initially directed his well-known statement, "The Word is dull without the thrust of its edge and the power of the Spirit," at the scholastic and persecuting evangelicals.[63] But he also directed the same truth to the legalists among the Anabaptists. Four letters by Marpeck to the Swiss Brethren are extant. In the lengthiest, entitled *Judgment and Decision* by Marpeck's editors, Marpeck encouraged the Swiss to suppress their habit of making hasty decisions when they excommunicated sinners.[64] Their basic problem is their misuse of Scripture. They wanted to be "masters of Scripture" by adding laws to it or by not waiting for the Spirit's illumination of it. On the one hand, Marpeck invited them to experience the freedom of Christ that comes with seeing God's only law as the law of love. From the vantage of love, they will learn to wait patiently upon God to reveal any known sinners and not proceed to "hasty judgments." On the other hand, he humbly invited them to correct him "through His Holy Spirit and the Scriptures" if he had erred. Marpeck opposed the freedom of the Spirit in the Word to the "human inventions" of the various sects of Christians.[65]

In the end he determined that the Swiss did not discern the apostles' three uses of Scripture—witnessing to the lost, warning the saved, and condemning the disobedient—and were thus misusing it. Indeed, they were legislating beyond what Scripture revealed[66] or determining sin was present when the fruit of sin was not yet evident.[67] In essence they were reading the letter without the Spirit. They were not allowing the Holy Spirit to judge those who should be banned. Christ and the apostles were reluctant to judge before a sin was revealed by the Spirit, who would make the sinner evident when it was time to judge. Just as Paul did not call for the fornicator's judgment until his sin was known, and Christ allowed Judas to remain among the disciples until He had actually been betrayed, the congregation

[61] Fast, "Pilgram Marbeck und das oberdeutsche Täufertum," 223–34; Kiwiet, *Pilgram Marbeck*, 65–68.

[62] Stuart Murray, *Biblical Interpretation in the Anabaptist Tradition* (Kitchener, ON: Pandora, 2000), 125–52 (esp. 147–49).

[63] *Admonition*, 299.

[64] Letter of Marpeck to the Swiss Brethren (1531?), in *The Writings of Pilgram Marpeck*, 309–61.

[65] There are seven sects, in Marpeck's paradigm: "those who use the bodily sword contrary to the patience of Christ," "those who institute, command, and forbid," "those who deny the true divinity [of Christ]," "those who destroy and deny His natural, earthly humanity," "those who [live] in open sin and gross evil," "those who tolerate such a thing," and "all who oppose and fight against the words and truth of Christ."

[66] "Making sin where there is no sin, setting up laws, commandments, and prohibitions against the authority of the Lord Jesus Christ, who gave His own no law except the law of love."

[67] "Therefore, even if one is concerned about a lapse and sees the leaves and blossoms of evil appearance, one ought only to warn and admonish, but not judge, before the time of the fruit. The Lord does not say, 'By their blossoms or leaves,' but rather, 'By their fruits you shall know them.' For love also covers a multitude of sins, and judges all things in the best light."

should not judge until a gross sin was evident. Unfortunately the Swiss Brethren were "running ahead" of Christ. (Alternatively those who do not exclude known sinners are guilty of "running behind" Christ.) The key is to live in the love of God with one another, be patient, and judge only when the Spirit makes sin known. "Especially where the Holy Spirit, the true teacher, does not precede in all knowledge of Christ, everything will be misused."

3. Biblical Order versus Human Invention

Judgment and Decision. In the middle of his biblical and ethical discussions regarding excommunication in *Judgment and Decision*, Marpeck dropped a bombshell on the discussion of theological method.[68] He introduced the concept of a strictly biblical *Ordnung* (order) in the midst of a broader conversation regarding the divine will. "God is a God of order, and He has firmly united His own omnipotence to His will and order." Through an inductive reading of Marpeck, Kiwiet came to the conclusion that Marpeck's theology requires the deployment of the axiom of *Ordnung Gottes* (order of God). "Marpeck's theological axiom may be indicated with the terminology of 'order of God.' [Moreover,] it was the basic thought of the South German Baptists in general."[69] The free church conception of order is not understood in the sense of a Hellenistic ontological order of "this side" versus "that side," but a Hebrew religious order that unites God and man. Kiwiet's emphasis on order in Marpeck has been glowingly affirmed by Klassen and is readily discernible in Marpeck.

The divine will had and has continued to be a subject of debate among philosophical and systematic theologians. In the Middle Ages critical discussions occurred over the absolute power and ordained power of God relating to man.[70] During and after the Reformation, a critical debate continued over the extrabiblical distinction between the hidden will of God and the revealed will of God.[71] The distinction between the hidden and revealed will of God was and is a lynchpin of the evangelical predestinarian systems of theology, such as those emanating from the Synod of Dort. Marpeck dismisses their entire project not merely as useless but as indiscriminate, even "deceitful." Indeed, predestinarian appeals to philosophical discourse are "the greatest blasphemy against God and the word of his truth" precisely because they have proposed their own inventions as true. There is always a danger for readers of the Bible to impose their "human inventions" upon the church, thus declaring themselves "masters of Scripture." When men invent novel doctrines, they effectively depose Jesus Christ as Lord of the church.

Marpeck set carnal reason over against Christian reason. In light of the critical role of believers' baptism in distinguishing the free churches from the state

[68] *Judgment and Decision*, esp. 331, 337–38, 341–44.

[69] "Das Axiom der Theologie Marbecks kann man andeuten mit dem Stichwort 'Ordnung Gottes.' Es war der Grundgedanke des süddeutschen Täufertums überhaupt." Kiwiet, *Pilgram Marbeck*, 84.

[70] Heiko Augustinus Oberman, *The Harvest of Medieval Theology: Gabriel Biel and Late Medieval Nominalism* (Grand Rapids: Eerdmans, 1967), 30–56.

[71] Ken Keathley, "Salvation and the Sovereignty of God: The Great Commission as the Expression of the Divine Will," *JGES* 19 (2006): 15–34.

churches, it was necessary for Marpeck to bring baptism into the debate over reason. Carnal reason was rooted in the fall and preserved by the invention of infant baptism. "The adversary and prince of pride has invented the baptism of innocents in order that when the proud head of the serpent, which is reason, matures, she refuses to submit to the baptism of faith and to the crushing of her head by the feet of Christ." Reason is "taken captive under the obedience of Christ" whenever a man places his faith in Christ. Of course, faith is the inner work of God, which should be accompanied by outer baptism. Those who will not abandon the human invention of infant baptism remain enslaved to carnal reason.

Marpeck's critique is not limited to the error of infant baptism. He found that any time the evangelicals wanted to subvert God's order, they would resort to a blind appeal to divine sovereignty. "Wherever the omnipotence and might of God serves their purposes, they imperiously and indiscriminately use it, without the will of his Father, as Luther does with the sacrament, child baptism, infant faith, and such like. Whenever they find themselves at their wits' end, they save their theology by appealing to the omnipotence of God." Such appeals, though deceptive to men, are futile before God. God has, by His own will, "subordinated" His power to the order that he Himself established in His word. By resorting to God's power, the evangelicals are departing from God's Word. "The wisest order [is] in and through His Word. . . . Whoever manipulates the omnipotence of God outside of this order is a deceiver and seducer."

So harsh is he in his assessment of the evangelicals' departure from Scripture to construct their theology because he believed sin is rooted in disobedience to God's Word. "There is only one sin from which all the fruit of wickedness begins, namely, disobedience to God's Word. The works of wickedness are only the fruit and revelation of sin." The chief sin, which begins in disobedience to the Word, is "arrogance, presumption, pride, self-importance, boasting, and stubbornness about one's own self-will and vainglory." Against the disorderly and disobedient papists, evangelicals, and legalists, each of whom invented doctrines not based in the Bible,[72] Marpeck thus opposed the concept of a revealed order.

Martin Bucer. In the *Exposé* of 1531 and the *Confession* of 1532, the doctrine of biblical order was introduced by Marpeck in controversy with a leading Reformed theologian, Martin Bucer of Strasbourg. Bucer, a Dominican monk, was steeped in the Aristotelian philosophical tradition of his Roman order, according to the so-called *via antiqua* of Thomist realism. Flirting with the ethical reform program of Erasmus, he converted to the theological reformation advocated by Luther after hearing the latter debate at Heidelberg. Always enamored with secular power, Bucer became the leading reformer of Strasbourg but was expelled late in his life by imperial pressure. He ended his days in England where he had been invited by Thomas Cranmer to lead the academic reformation of Cambridge University as

[72] Note the identification of Luther and the papists in the text (341–42), but the identification of "papacy, newly called evangelicals and Anabaptists" in the margins (342–43), and "Papists, Lutherans, Zwinglians, and false Anabaptists" in a later margin (351).

Regius Professor of Divinity. Bucer's impact on the English Reformed tradition was eclipsed perhaps only by that of John Calvin.

Martin Bucer and Pilgram Marpeck shared a number of theological concerns. They both accepted fully and built upon Martin Luther's recovery of the doctrine of justification by faith. They both embraced the Scripture as their theological authority. They were both pietistic in the sense of their emphasis on divine love, which was to be lived fervently.[73] They were both concerned with a correct doctrine of the church that would inculcate disciplined Christian living. Indeed, Bucer's advocacy of church discipline as a necessary third mark of the true church—*contra* Luther's two marks of the correct preaching of the Word and the administration of the sacraments—resulted from his attempt to appropriate the communal discipleship of the Anabaptists for the state church.[74] Bucer subsequently carried this emphasis into the English Reformation, where discipline, understood as church governance, remained a major concern.

With regard to theological foundations, both Bucer and Marpeck were concerned with the correct doctrine of order; but they departed significantly from one another with regard to the discovery of that order. For Bucer, the primary order was a partly biblical and partly speculative *ordo salutis*, a logical ordering; for Marpeck, the primary order was provided by the biblical narrative itself, a historical ordering. Reflecting his medieval philosophical training, Bucer's order began with predestination and remained there.[75] Reflecting his deep reading of Scripture, Marpeck's order was comprehensively scriptural. As a result of his overarching commitment to the logical priority of election, Bucer's ecclesiology remained largely experimental and malleable.[76] Because Marpeck's order was established upon the scriptural covenant with Christ, his ecclesiology remained stable. Bucer's ecclesiology was not shaped by the biblical covenant but rather by "the historical situation in which he worked."[77]

Bucer's confusion of the covenants. The controversy between Bucer and Marpeck apparently began with the publication of Marpeck's *Exposé* in late 1531.[78] In December of that year, the two leaders debated before the city council of Strasbourg in closed session. Marpeck wrote his *Confession* for the sake of Bucer and the council. Bucer responded and Marpeck added a short addendum to the *Confession* in response.[79] The council met in closed session due to the high pro-

[73] Martin Bucer, *Instruction in Christian Love* (1523), trans. Paul Traugott Fuhrmann (Richmond, VA: John Knox Press, 1952).

[74] Kenneth R. Davis, "No Discipline, No Church: An Anabaptist Contribution to the Reformed Tradition," *SCJ* 13 (1982): 43–58.

[75] W. P. Stephens, *The Holy Spirit in the Theology of Martin Bucer* (Cambridge: Cambridge University Press, 1970), 23–41.

[76] Bucer experimented with elder rule, magisterial rule, and *ecclesiola-in-ecclesia* but ended with the royal supremacy. This ecclesiological malleability is finally expressed in his theological fusion of the kingdom of Edward VI with the Kingdom of Christ. Martin Bucer, *De Regno Christi* (1550), in *Melanchthon and Bucer*, ed. Wilhelm Pauck (Philadelphia: Westminster Press, 1969), 225–27.

[77] Stephens, *The Holy Spirit in the Theology of Martin Bucer*, 156.

[78] *Exposé of the Babylonian Whore* (1531), in *Later Writings by Pilgram Marpeck and his Circle*, 24–48.

[79] Klassen, *Covenant and Community*, 27–29.

files of Marpeck, the city's engineer, and Bucer, pastor of Strasbourg's church of St. Thomas.

Although the title and introduction of the *Exposé* suggest Marpeck planned to critique the Roman Catholic Church, he treated Rome only summarily. His audience had long correlated Rome with the prophecy of Revelation 17: she was "the red Roman whore now exposed." He reminded them that although Rome had the Bible, it twisted it through "artifice" and required the inventions of infant baptism and the Mass for salvation. Although standing in substantial agreement with Luther and "the so-called evangelicals" concerning the priority of Scripture, the author proceeded to attack them for their unwillingness to follow Jesus Christ completely. The Protestants had the Word of God, but they used it merely to "whitewash" unethical behavior. "They do in part speak the truth about Christ, but they don't want to go through the narrow gate." To be genuine, justification must be evidenced in discipleship.

Submitting to Scripture rather than prooftexting Scripture was the exegetical issue. Justification by Christ without discipleship to Christ was the soteriological issue. But persecution, especially of those who wanted to be consistent disciples of the biblical Christ, was the ethical issue. The ethical issue was caused by mixture: "Satan seeks to mix temporal power with Christendom." The Catholics and the evangelicals are taking the Christ who surrendered all for love of others and turning him into a persecutor of others. Marpeck simply could not reconcile the humble, loving, peaceful Christ revealed in Scripture with the violent churches. Whereas true Christians follow Christ, who received death, they dispense death. Both the Protestants and the Catholics confused the swords because they confused the covenants.

The confusion of the covenants was manifested in the confusion of the office (*Amt*) of Christ with the office (*Amt*) of Moses. The primary figures of the Old Testament and the New Testament possess different offices. Moses came to bring the law that accuses, dominates, coerces, and condemns. Christ came to free people from sin through the gospel. The work of Moses was preparatory to the work of Christ. The work of Moses, through the law, is to maintain the world by identifying evil, restraining it, and preparing sinners to receive Christ. The work of the law is still ordained by God but only for those who are not Christians. The state still has a role in preserving human order. But the state's role is different from the church's role. The work of Christ, through the gospel, is to free sinners from their sin and judgment by the law. The life and work of Jesus Christ thus becomes a "mirror" for Christians. Christians are to pattern their lives on Christ, not Moses.

Because the work of Christ was to be patient with human beings and suffer for them, out of love for them, so too is the church of Christ. "It is the body of patience and love." The churches of patience and love, like Christ in His humanity, serve the world rather than seeking to dominate it. The problem with the violent churches is that they confuse the law with the gospel. "They judge according to the law of Moses and pollute the Lord Jesus Christ with blood." Marpeck used the Gelasian distinction between the two swords, the physical sword of the state and the spiritual sword of the Word.[80] The Protestants and Catholics sought to place the physical sword in service of the Word of God. But Marpeck recognized that in the New Testament Christ never commanded such. "In Christ, through faith, the only sword is the Word; with this only Christians judge and are judged. They have not been commanded by Christ to use any other sword."

How then are people to be converted to Christ if not by coercion? Marpeck's ingenious reply was formed by the pattern of Christ's life. Just as in the parable of wheat and tares, Christ delayed judgment until the final judgment, so the church must wait for Christ to come again to judge those outside. The purpose of the church now, with regard to sinners, is simply to mirror Christ's life and proclaim the gospel. Indeed, patience with the wicked is the proper means of evangelism. "Christ told this parable only to ensure that the grace of God would not be cut off for human beings and that the wheat would not be pulled out with the weeds. For as long as a person remains in this mortal life, no matter how wicked he may be, he may be converted to a better life through the grace of Christ and the patience and love shown to him by those around him. For there are twelve hours in the day as the Lord Himself said, but if he is pulled up like a weed, he can never repent."[81]

Bucer's "outrage to the Holy Spirit." During the debate before the city council, Marpeck and Bucer developed their respective positions.[82] Marpeck was not advocating pacifism but taking a position compatible with modern teachings of religious liberty. He denied not that Christians may serve as magistrates (after all, he was one) but that they may use their magistracy to promote particular beliefs.[83] The last article of his *Confession* concluded, "No external power has the right to rule, benefit, nor govern in Christ's kingdom." In their argument over this conclusion, both Marpeck and Bucer appealed to Scripture, but Ziegler noted Bucer's failure to stay with Scripture. Bucer was "unable to establish clear New Testament authority that explicitly authorized governmental regulation of the kingdom of Christ on earth, just as he was unable to justify the practice of infant baptism on the same grounds." Bucer often resorted to a vague appeal to "context" but relied primarily upon the practical problems with allowing religious liberty.

The arguments of Bucer developed the earlier arguments put forward by Ulrich Zwingli, after he retracted his own criticism of infant baptism and began to persecute the Swiss Brethren. Just as Zwingli's covenantal theology reads as human invention imposed upon Scripture, so does Bucer's. The strange responses of

---

[80] Joseph Canning, *A History of Medieval Political Thought, 300–1450* (New York: Routledge, 1996), 35–36.

[81] Marpeck, *Exposé of the Babylonian Whore*, 40.

[82] Donald J. Ziegler, "Marpeck versus Butzer: A Sixteenth-Century Debate over the Uses and Limits of Political Authority," *SCES* 2 (1971): 95–107 (commentary, 95–101; minutes, 101–7).

[83] On Marpeck's complex political theology, see William Klassen, "The Limits of Political Authority as Seen by Pilgram Marpeck," *MQR* 56 (1982): 342–64; Boyd, "Anabaptism and Social Radicalism in Strasbourg, 1528–32: Pilgram Marpeck on Social Responsibility," *MQR* 63 (1989): 58–76; C. Arnold Snyder, "An Anabaptist Vision for Peace: Spirituality and Peace in Pilgram Marpeck," *CGR* 10 (1992): 187–203.

Bucer to Marpeck's clear biblicism would be comical if they had not encouraged continued persecution of other Christians. When Marpeck said that Christians must serve as Christ served, Bucer responded, "We are not to serve in this manner." When Marpeck asserted that Christ is the only authority in the church and men should not claim that their violent actions are mandated by Christ, Bucer responded with the incredible claim that "all are Christian." When Marpeck ascribed all honor to Christ in His own kingdom, Bucer responded that the office of the magistrate is the most honorable office in the church. The magistrate's office, "guided by Providence," glorifies God "by putting a stop to wicked, erroneous corrupting teachings."

In response to Bucer's unseemly habit of playing to the audience while selectively using Scripture, Marpeck bluntly responded, "he brings outrage to the Holy Spirit, whose power and dominion is not dependent on human assistance." When Bucer claimed, "The sword of the Christian ruler can only be a comfort to the pious," Marpeck responded that the only Christian sword is the Word of God. When Bucer claimed that the magistrate cannot bring forth evil, Marpeck responded that the Scripture teaches that true prophets were slain by magistrates. To Bucer's appeal to glorify God by shedding blood like Elijah, Marpeck responds, "It is at once sufficient that God has given enough blood to satisfy all who desire it . . . It is plain that Christ chooses to purify his bride by his cross and blood."

As the argument concluded, Bucer resorted to worldly concerns and historical precedent, while Marpeck continued to look to Christ. When Bucer said that Marpeck's ideas would result in multiple factions, Marpeck reminded him that the Pope said the same thing about the evangelicals. When Bucer claimed that we must live in the world and Marpeck's solution was unworkable, Marpeck reminded Bucer through a myriad of biblical allusions that our hope is in the resurrection, not in making this world workable. (This is a strange turn of events for an engineer to have to argue such to a preacher!) Bucer replied that Marpeck still needed to eat. Marpeck's final words reflected his commitment to follow Christ no matter what: "On these matters I am commanded by the judgment of Christ." Having the last word, Bucer appealed for the continuation of infant baptism on the basis of historical precedent. Ultimately, the council listened to Bucer's practical reasoning rather than to Marpeck's biblical theology, and Marpeck was expelled from the city.

Marpeck's biblical order.[84] In his *Confession* of 1532, after the twenty-nine articles, Marpeck defined the biblical order as he perceived it, paralleling the narrative of Scripture.[85] His general principle is "everything must remain in its order and time." His specific principle is, "Whatever is bound to Christ's Word and order, no one will be able to sever in all eternity."[86] This focus on the biblical

[84] This doctrine is now often called progressive revelation.

[85] *Rechenschaft seines Glaubens* (*Defense of His Faith* or *Confession*) (1532), in *The Writings of Pilgram Marpeck*, 108–57; German transcript in John C. Wenger, "Pilgram Marpeck's Confession of Faith Composed at Strasburg, December, 1531–January, 1532," *MQR* 12 (1938): 167–202.

[86] "Wz an crisstus wort vnd ordnung punden ist. Dz wirt in ewigkhait niemannt auf mögen lösen."

order begins with the relationship of the covenants but is applied to his doctrines of salvation, baptism, religious liberty, and the church. He is adamant that there is a distinction between the old and new covenants. Both of the covenants comprise the one Word of God, but there is a progression from the old covenant to the new covenant. The progression of the covenants is inviolable in spite of the confusion introduced by the philosophical theologians. Once he discerned the covenantal order, Marpeck applied it to salvation, baptism, and covenantal discipleship.

There are four primary spiritual events related to the old covenant. First, there is the creation of all by God through the Word as revealed by God in the Word. Second, the fall occurred, which brought sin and shame. The fall corrupted all men through man. Third, the law was given in order to give man the knowledge of his own sin. The law condemns him to death and hell, bringing fear. Personal condemnation does not occur until knowledge itself is present. Fourth, there was also a promise given. The promise brought hope of comfort but not the comfort itself. Abraham and the others had to wait patiently for Christ. There is no redemption apart from the atoning work of Jesus Christ who was merely promised in the old covenant.

There are four primary spiritual events related to the new covenant. First, the promise of atonement was fulfilled in the incarnation, life, death, and resurrection of Jesus Christ. Where the law brings fear and death, the gospel of Christ brings freedom and life. Second, with his descent into hell, Christ brought the redemption to the patriarchs for which they could hitherto only hope. Third, the Spirit, who is the only one that can bring "understanding and recognition of the truth," could not come until Christ ascended. The Spirit brings the sinner the potential of being born again when the Word is proclaimed. Fourth, Christ instituted baptism so that those who were born again would participate in a visible cowitness to their internal regeneration. In baptism, the believer enters "the covenant of a good conscience with God" (*Den punnt der guetten gewissen mit got*).

The proper location of these spiritual events was carried out on the basis of biblical precedent. For instance, with regard to the waiting of the Spirit for Christ's ascension, he cited John 16:13. Again, with regard to the priority of faith to baptism, he cited Matt 28:18–20. The proper location of the covenants that contained the spiritual events was carried out in biblical terms. The law must precede the gospel because God allowed it as "the right order of teaching" (*die recht ordnung der ler*). When speaking of the inability of the law to save, because its role is preparatory to the gospel that saves, Marpeck refers to Paul's extensive arguments on justification in the epistles to the Romans and the Galatians. The old covenant's deference to the new covenant was gleaned from Jeremiah 31.

"For all their good deeds and godliness, the ancients are figurative (*Figurliche*) witnesses who point to Christ as the shadow (*schatten*) points to the light (*liecht*) which, by its advent into this world, is to enlighten all men, old and new." "Figure" and "shadow" are obviously references to the language of Hebrews (cp. 8:5; 10:1), a theological epistle that makes a sharp distinction between the covenants. Indeed, Marpeck's manuscript refers to Hebrews 8 and 10 in the margin. The margin also cites Colossians 2, where Paul pits Christ against the elementary principles and vain philosophy of this world.[87] The text also alludes to the language of John (cp. 1:9), which stresses the incarnation of Christ as light coming into the world.

Thus, Marpeck's emphasis on order was an early development from Marpeck's thorough familiarity with Scripture. It was also an emphasis that deepened with time. While defending his biblical faith against Martin Bucer's efforts to have him expelled by the magistrates from Strasbourg in late 1531 and early 1532, Marpeck first addressed the issue of biblical order, applying it to the problems of baptism, religious persecution, personal faith, and the church. In his *Admonition* of 1542, Marpeck further clarified his understanding of biblical order with application to baptism.[88] These earlier works reached their fulfillment in his community's massive biblical concordance on the Old and New Testaments, *Explanation of the Testaments*, which substantiates their commitment to the doctrine of biblical order.[89]

In the preface to *Explanation of the Testaments*,[90] Marpeck furthered his argument regarding the difference between the two covenants. Paired terms were used to describe the relation: "figurative" and "actual," "prefigured" and "reality," "shadow" and "light," "temporal" and "eternal," and most prominently, "yesterday" and "today."[91] "Yesterday" refers to the old covenant and the Mosaic law; "today" refers to Christ's incarnation, death, and ascension; "tomorrow" refers to the second coming. Marpeck also listed four major errors resulting from the confusion of the biblical order, especially by those who use the sword on the basis of the Old Testament theocracy. First, the common Christian article of faith regarding the descent into hell would be denied. Marpeck's appeal to the Apostles' Creed was common among the early Anabaptists, who emphasized the simple faith of the apostles.[92] "Second, the suffering, death, resurrection, and ascension of Christ would be greatly slandered and insulted in this view." Third, "actual salvation" was not present for the Old Testament saints until Christ came. Fourth, the worldly power, which should be the "servant of God" wickedly interposes itself

[87] Wenger, "Pilgram Marpeck's Confession of Faith," 177.

[88] Marpeck is loosely accused by some scholars of "plagiarism" due to his large-scale appropriation of Bernard Rothmann's *Bekentnisse* (*Confession*) of 1533; however, the attribution is inappropriate by sixteenth-century standards and according to Marpeck's congregational theological method. In the preface Marpeck admitted that the following "witnesses" to the covenant were in part "published by others," but the words of these "other witnesses" were "tested by us and purged of all the errors which we have in part found among them." Moreover, the emphasis on baptismal order in Rothmann is largely an echo of earlier teachings by Marpeck (and Hubmaier, etc). The primary problem with Rothmann's group, who were "false messengers of Satan mixed with the members of the covenant of truth in Christ," was that they "do not agree with our faith, love, and patience in Christ." *Admonition*, 163, 166; Frank Wray, "The 'Vermanung' of 1542 and Rothmann's 'Bekentnisse,'" *AR* 47 (1956): 243–51; Klassen, "Pilgram Marpeck in Recent Research," 215. Rothmann was the leading theologian among the violent Anabaptists of Münster. James M. Stayer, "The Münsterite Rationalization of Bernhard Rothmann," *JHI* 28 (1967): 179–92.

[89] *Testamentserleutterung* (*Explanation of the Testaments*) (ca. 1544–1550), comprised of some 800 pages, resides in manuscript form in two extant copies in Zürich and Berlin. The concept of biblical order also appears in his community's response to Schwenckfeld in the two-part *Vindication*.

[90] Preface to the *Explanation of the Testaments*, in *The Writings of Pilgram Marpeck*, 555–66.

[91] Cp. Kiwiet, *Pilgram Marbeck*, 94–102.

[92] "Excursus II: Marpeck and the Descensus ad Infero," in Klassen, *Covenant and Community*, 183–85.

"into the holy place." It is perhaps the slander and insult to Christ that concerned him the most.

4. The Believers' Church

The biblical order concretized. According to Kiwiet, the covenant is where Marpeck's doctrine of biblical order became concrete.[93] Many of the Reformers, including Luther, detected the congregational ideal of Scripture but considered it unworkable and secondary to theology.[94] But there was never a severe distinction between theology proper and ecclesiology for Marpeck. His was a holistic theology that integrated Christology with ecclesiology and the community with the individual believer. The keystone to that integration was his doctrine of the covenant of a good conscience with God. Marpeck's ecclesiology extended from his Christocentrism through an epistemology of the Word understood according to the biblical order. In his *Confession* of 1532, Marpeck applied the concept of order to personal salvation, baptism, and the church in general.

Marpeck's correlation of Christology and ecclesiology, according to the biblical order, had a profound effect on his view of the church. Christ's humanity and the church's visibility must be maintained against those who would prefer to stress Christ's deity and the church's invisibility. One major problem that Marpeck had with Schwenckfeld was that Schwenckfeld wanted only a glorious Christ and ignored the order of Christ's life.[95] Against Schwenckfeld's glorious Christ, Marpeck posited the humble Christ. According to the biblical order, Christ had to suffer before he could be honored. Similarly, the body of Christ today, the church, must be visible and embrace the suffering that is potential in any life yielded to Jesus Christ. There are three bodies of Christ in Marpeck's Christology: the first was his human flesh before the resurrection; the second was his transfigured flesh after the resurrection; and the third is his untransfigured body, which is the church. "Oh, it annoys the fleshly to the highest degree that the Son of Man, in a physical way, should act and walk upon the earth by means of His members, His body, His flesh and bone."[96] The church, the untransfigured body of Christ, has, of course, not yet experienced the resurrection, and must embrace Christ's cross.

Personal salvation. Applying the biblical order to the doctrine of salvation, Marpeck showed how the Reformed theologians erred. Their philosophical doctrine of predestination led them away from the biblical witness regarding justification by faith alone. In response to Bucer's articles, Marpeck expressed agreement that "personal confession and carnal reason" avail nothing, but Bucer missed the point Marpeck made, for "personal faith in Christ does avail. If such is not the case,

[93] Kiwiet, *Pilgram Marbeck*, 85.

[94] For Luther's earlier view of congregationalism, see his treatise of 1523, *That a Christian Assembly or Congregation Has the Right and Power to Judge All Teaching and to Call, Appoint, and Dismiss Teachers, Established and Proven by Scripture*, and his description of a third liturgy in the 1526 preface to the German Mass. *LW*, 39:301–14., 53:63–64.

[95] Schwenckfeld also advocated the novel doctrine of the celestial flesh of Christ in order to protect Christ from material contamination. Steinmetz, *Reformers in the Wings*, 135–36.

[96] *A Clear and Useful Instruction*, 81.

Paul is a liar when he says: Faith justifies, and confession brings salvation, etc." The soteriological disagreement between Marpeck and Bucer concerns the instrument of the sinner's entrance into the covenant. For Marpeck, only those who have faith enter into the covenant, and "no one can have faith for anyone else." For Bucer, faith is indeed instrumental for adults, but infants enter the covenant by baptism. Although Marpeck was willing to countenance the church's prayer for infants, he rejected their baptism because the practice lacked what Scripture required: personal faith.[97]

Some reviewers have accused Marpeck, and the Anabaptists generally, of confusing sanctification with justification, as the Council of Trent did.[98] But Marpeck never confused the two. Recognizing the importance of a biblical order, he kept justification prior to sanctification; but also recognizing the importance of a biblical order, he required those who claimed to be justified actually to follow Jesus Christ. This is the genius of the biblical Anabaptists. They were "evangelical" with regard to justification but did not stop there. They continued to follow Jesus Christ into covenantal discipleship. Marpeck wanted to be a consistent disciple of Jesus Christ, even if that meant exile or death. Bucer, on the other hand, could only weakly confess to a friend after his debate with Marpeck, "our teaching is the true, authentic teaching of Christ, in spite of how poorly it is being followed."[99]

Baptism. Applying the biblical order to baptism, Marpeck brought Bucer back to New Testament practice. "There the order of God and man was observed: first teaching, then faith, and only then baptism."[100] Zwingli invented an analogy between the sign of circumcision of infants under the old covenant and water baptism of infants under the new covenant. Bucer taught that by baptism, infants are received into the covenant. Against this human invention, Marpeck offered the teaching of the New Testament. Water baptism is not a symbol (*zaichen*), nor is it a divine covenant (*punt gottes*) because Scripture never refers to water baptism as such. Rather, baptism is a witness (*zeug*) to the internal work of the Spirit with the Word.

The "baptism of the Spirit" is primary, but water baptism is not to be neglected. "Water baptism is to be an earthly and elemental witness" of personal rebirth by the Holy Spirit. People who seek to force baptism overturn the grace of Jesus Christ, for "God's covenant depends on God's assurance and not on man, for man has not been able to help himself." The eternal covenant is entered by the gift of faith in Christ. This covenant of a good conscience with God is cowitnessed by water baptism. Salvation is by grace through faith alone, and the doctrine of infant baptism makes baptism a presumptuous human work rather than a responsive

---

[97] Marpeck believed that children were going to be saved since they never came to the knowledge of their sin and thus were not held accountable. They are saved by grace apart from personal faith.

[98] Blough, "The Church as Sign or Sacrament."

[99] *Täuferakten Elsass, Part 1*, 526–27; cited in Martin Greschat, *Martin Bucer: A Reformer and His Times*, trans. Stephen E. Buckwalter (Louisville: Westminster John Knox Press, 2004), 120.

[100] "Da got es nach der ordnung gottes, vnd des mennschen, am ersten lernen, darnach glauben, vnd alsdann erst tauffen."

witness to divine grace. Man simply cannot force others into the divine covenant without the Spirit's sovereign inner work of faith.

Applying the biblical order to the church, Marpeck offered his personal confession. This was appropriate, for Marpeck's ecclesiology was deeply personal at the same time that it was Christological and communal. The theological keystone for the intimate triadic relationship between Christ, His church, and the believer was the covenant. Marpeck's confession begins, "First, whoever confesses faith in Christ, according to the witness of Christ, shall be baptized upon his own profession of faith, and whoever believes thus and is baptized shall be saved."[101] Personal confession is followed by ecclesiological commitment. And within the biblical order in the church, he discerns baptism, the Lord's Supper, church discipline, congregationalism, the separation of church and magistracy, and the headship of Jesus Christ.

The commemoration. After dismissing infant baptism on the basis of personal faith and allowing prayer for the child, he turned to the issue of the Lord's Supper. The Lord's Supper is "the commemoration of the body of the Lord, our testimony to His death."[102] Such a memorial practice was meaningful because it was reserved for the regenerate alone. The lost were thereby visibly reminded of their judgment and the saved of their dependence upon God's grace. Zwinglian memorialism is so often accused of being mere symbolism. In contrast Marpeckian commemoration was meaningful because of its reminder to the church of the Christological pattern of discipleship. The Lord's Supper was a continual witness to his human death and resurrection. It was a "proclamation of the death of the Lord until He comes." It was also a reminder that the church was a "bond of love," "unity of faith," and "fellowship of the saints." The elements were a "parable of the mystery of Christ's body and blood." The ceremony could even be described as "a spiritual food," but it was to be "eaten in faith" rather than becoming superstitious with the elements of the bread and wine.

Church discipline. In spite of his chiding the Swiss Brethren for their harsh use of church discipline, Marpeck was clear that church discipline preserved the integrity of the church. Moreover, the place for practicing church discipline is the Lord's Supper. The person who is uncircumcised of heart (i.e., unconverted) "shall be rooted out from among the people, that is to say, from the remembrance of the Supper." Marpeck argued against the idea of open communion as inviting divine judgment, likely an allusion to 1 Cor 11:31.[103] Perhaps drawing on the *Form of the Last Supper* by Balthasar Hubmaier,[104] Marpeck defined the commemoration as a place to "warn, admonish, teach, discipline, hear, and understand one another in integrity and truth, and live in obedience to the Word in faith." These three ordinances—baptism, commemoration, and church discipline—were

[101] "Zum ersten, wer den glauben in crissto Iehsu nach zeugkhnus crissti bekhennt, den sol man tauffen auf aignen furgehalltnen glauben, Vnnd wer also glaubt, vnd wirt taufft, der wirt selig."

[102] ". . . der gedäachtnus des leib des herrn, vnns durch seinn tod bezeugt. . . ."

[103] 1 Cor 11 is cited in the margin.

[104] Balthasar Hubmaier, *A Form for Christ's Supper* (1527), in *Balthasar Hubmaier: Theologian of Anabaptism*, ed. H. Wayne Pipkin and John H. Yoder (Scottdale, PA: Herald Press, 1989), 393–408.

the liturgical foci of the Anabaptists' effort to maintain the integrity of the church. This was no less true for Marpeck, perhaps because they were the three ecclesial events clearly ordered by Christ.[105]

Gemeindetheologie. As has been noted, Marpeck excoriated the state church theologians, the evangelicals, for their elitism. The Anabaptists took the doctrine of the priesthood of all believers that Luther rediscovered within Scripture and reified it. They took the doctrine of the theological responsibility of all believers that Erasmus advocated and put it into practice. The phenomena, which point toward a thoroughgoing congregationalism among the biblical Anabaptists, are numerous, especially with regard to Marpeck. Many of the extant writings were written directly by Marpeck, while others were written in cooperation with his church. For instance, *Vermanung*, *Verantwortung*, and *Testamentserleutterung*, the three largest works in the Marpeck corpus, were all written by Marpeck in conjunction with Leopold Scharnschlager among others. Noting this congregational effort, Klassen coined the term *Gemeindetheologie* (church theology) to describe the communal provenance of the Marpeckian corpus. "It is quite obvious that Marpeck felt it most important that individualism be tempered by the interaction of the Christian brotherhood." Klassen later identified the church as one of the hermeneutical principles in Marpeck's interpretation of Scripture.[106]

Stuart Murray applied the terms "the hermeneutic community" and "congregational hermeneutics" to the interpretative method he discovered among the early Anabaptists.[107] One of Marpeck's closest coworkers, Scharnschlager left a description of the Marpeck church's worship services. The elders did guide and facilitate worship, but multiple members read Scripture, discussed it, and proclaimed it. Williams uses a number of terms to describe this communal hermeneutical practice, including *lex sedentium* and *Sitzennrecht*, the Latin and the German, respectively, for "law of sitting." Biblically, the practice was based in the admonition of Paul to allow one "prophet"—"prophecy" in the Reformation was understood as "preaching"—to speak at a time while the others sit and judge (1 Cor 14:29–33). Historically, the Anabaptists seem to have radicalized the practice of the school of prophets instituted by Zwingli in Zürich.[108] There were cultural factors behind their congregationalism too.[109]

Marpeck affirmed a basic egalitarianism in the congregation in his *Confession*. "In this house of Christ, . . . there is no Christian magistrate except Christ himself. For men, the title lord is too great; it minimizes Christ, although that is perhaps

[105] Cp. Baptism in Matthew 28, the Lord's Supper in Matthew 26, and church discipline in Matthew 18; *Schleitheim Confession*, arts. 1–3; Hubmaier's "liturgical trilogy" of 1527: *On Fraternal Admonition, A Form for Water Baptism*, and *A Form for Christ's Supper*, in *Balthasar Hubmaier*, 372–408.

[106] Klassen, *Covenant and Community*, 56, 77–87.

[107] Murray, *Biblical Interpretation in the Anabaptist Tradition*, 157–85.

[108] A similar practice, obtained either through the itinerant ministry of Francis Lambert or from Protestant exiles in Zürich during Mary's reign, was practiced by Puritans in Elizabethan England under the title of "prophesyings." Williams, *The Radical Reformation*, 405, 415, 518–21, 1254–56, 1278–79.

[109] Werner O. Packull, "In Search of the 'Common Man' in Early German Anabaptist Ideology," *SCJ* 17 (1986): 51–67.

not the intention."[110] In *Clear and Useful Instruction*, he promoted the idea that all Christians receive spiritual gifts and are empowered by Christ to fulfill the Great Commission.[111] Their belief that the Spirit spoke to the entire community as it read the Scripture together encouraged the Anabaptists to seek conversation with other Christians. Theology, for them, was always done best in communal Bible study. This helps explain one of the most poignant facts of the Continental Reformation. The Anabaptists seemed more than willing to enter debates with the state church theologians, even when it led to persecution. What surprised their opponents repeatedly was the intricate knowledge of Scripture that even illiterate Anabaptists expressed, a knowledge learned in church.

The beautiful church. In three works from the mid-1540s, Marpeck described the ideal church of the New Testament. A theme common to each of these writings is his description of the church as the beautiful bride of Christ. He says the beauty of the church results from the love that flows to her from the Father through Christ and the Spirit.[112] Because of God's sovereign choice of her as His temple, "she will be the most beautiful of all." Her garments of God's love "are the virtues of the Holy Spirit." "Her Christ and King who is Himself thus dressed and adorned, has dressed her. Whoever, even once, truly sees this loveliest of all brides in her adornment and form will praise her in wonderment." Marpeck has a deep love for the church because his Lord has such a deep love for her.

The children of the Father are born again through the Holy Spirit "by the seed of the Word" and brought to the church for her to nurture. Drawing upon the allegory of Galatians 4, Marpeck distinguishes the true children of Sara from the false children of Hagar. Those who have not been regenerated are false children. Those who claim to be Christians apart from the church are false children. Those who will not separate from the world and gather with the church are false children. The true children are mediated the grace of the Trinity through the church's discipline. These children form "the everlasting royal priesthood" who reign eternally and offer spiritual sacrifices. Their royal priesthood is a gift through Christ, who is "the only High Priest and King."

In the second treatise Marpeck discusses "the inner church," by which he means the universal church that gathers at the end of time.[113] The inner church is composed of those in whom the Spirit resides as the result of the Father's dedication and the Son's intercession. The inner church will be revealed in her glory only when Christ comes again in His glory. The Holy Spirit, however, compels the inner church to bear witness through external works now. The inner church is made visible by separation from the world and witness to the world. In bearing witness, the church should not outrun the Holy Spirit through coercion but pray for the Spirit to work in the hearts of sinners.

[110] Marpeck, *Confession*, 149.

[111] Marpeck, *Clear and Useful Instruction*, 76–77.

[112] Marpeck, *The Churches of Christ and of Hagar* (1544), in *The Writings of Pilgram Marpeck*, 390–401.

[113] Marpeck, *On the Inner Church* (1545), in *The Writings of Pilgram Marpeck*, 418–26.

In the third and longest treatise, the subject is spiritual gifts, which are "treasures hidden and locked in the trunk of His body, the ark of the covenant."[114] In His death Christ bore our sin; in His resurrection He took life for us. In His descent He showed us the humility that we must practice now. In His ascent He promises us the glory that will be ours. Baptism is identification with the descent and ascent of Christ. Following the divine order, we should not expect to experience His glory yet, for we have not been bodily resurrected. Rather, we must wait patiently for the glory to come.

Spiritual gifts are given for two reasons only: to worship God and to serve others. Christ as the high priest has given gifts to Christians who are his priests. Every church member is gifted by Christ and is valuable. "The gifts in every single member must be heard and seen. There can be no unendowed member who has not been given something of the treasures of Christ, such as virtues and the fruits of the Holy Spirit in the body of Christ." With these the church should edify and sanctify one another with love. The royal priesthood has received gems, sacrifices of praise, holy utensils, and patience to use. Marpeck ends by returning to his hermeneutical principle of the Word and the Spirit, which can only be properly understood in the church.

> The Spirit takes the treasures and good things of the Father and the Son, and has poured into our hearts the love which is the mind of Christ and the true and only understanding. Only what Christ Himself has said and taught, and no other word, does the Spirit of wisdom bring to remembrance in His own. Therefore, no matter how holy they may appear, all those who take away and add to this word and teaching are false priests. Nor does God teach those who only hear the Word from the mouth of Christ, the apostles and other saintly people, nor does He teach those who read their writings only according to the letter, without the reminder of truth and teaching of the Holy Spirit. They are thieves and murderers who run before, and lag behind, Christ. With their own inventions and sophistries in Scripture, they either run ahead of the Holy Spirit of Christ, before they have been driven by Him, or else they lag behind Christ, and presume to teach those who are under God's judgment.

The humble church. As we noted in the last chapter, early English Baptists shared some common traits with Anabaptists. Among them is one also seen repeatedly in Marpeck: convictional theological humility. Marpeck's ideal of the humble church arose from his doctrine of the humble Christ. Many of his works end with an appeal for those who are more clearly illumined to offer him correction, which he will gladly receive. This humble appeal is common to the early believers' churches but uncommon to Roman Catholic and Protestant theologians. And any correction has to come from Scripture correctly interpreted. Perhaps a dual citation will help end this chapter on a solid note. The first quote comes from

[114] Marpeck, *Concerning the Lowliness of Christ* (1547), in *The Writings of Pilgram Marpeck*, 427–63.

his early personal confession; the second from what is probably his last communal writing. They both show willingness to be corrected but only by Scripture.

> In Christ we have a true God, and we must remain in His teaching and order. Whoever does not remain in the teaching of Christ has no God. Thus, the beginning of love is to believe in and hold to God and His Word. . . . I am prepared to show human love to everyone according to the word of Paul, to serve everyone from the heart, and not to hurt anyone's feelings. If I have unaware, not followed these strictures, I ask forgiveness from everyone.[115]
>
> Our side is also prepared in case it has missed the correct interpretation to yield its position without controversy, when a better understanding or exposition of Holy Scripture is offered. In such instances we will not cling to error in our view, for we know that the more thoroughly Holy Scriptures are interpreted the more clearly the meaning will agree with it, for the Holy Scriptures cannot contradict each other as long as they are correctly compared and interpreted. . . . Above all the text of the Holy Scriptures is innocent of errors.[116]

CONCLUSION

Marpeck's Holistic Theology in Action

Christocentrism, correlation of Word and Spirit, stress on the biblical order while opposing human theological invention, and covenant ecclesiology shaped Marpeck's entire religious outlook. These basic principles, which form his theological foundation of discipleship, were manifested in his pastoral writings. He believed conversion would not occur unless the external Word of God is publicly proclaimed; however, the Word may be proclaimed without result if the Spirit does not sovereignly move (moreover, the hearer must not resist the Spirit). Internal baptism by the Spirit, or personal regeneration, must occur first in order for the external baptism in water by the church to be a true baptism. The church must wait patiently for God to move inwardly in another person's heart and not seek wickedly to preempt God through infant baptism, or *ex opere operato* sacraments, or rigorous church discipline, or religious persecution. Yet, when God has moved inwardly, the new Christian will not fail to enter a visible church covenant through believers' baptism, seek continual communion with that church through the Lord's Supper, preserve the integrity of that church through redemptive discipline, and boldly proclaim the beautiful Word to the world.

The Contribution of the Free Churches to Modernity

Because Marpeck kept the sovereign inner work of the Spirit and the responsive outer work of Christ's church so finely balanced, these early believers'

[115] Marpeck, *Confession*, 156–57.
[116] Marpeck, Preface to *Explanation of the Testaments*, 565.

churches in southern Germany were able to avoid multiple doctrinal problems. Where the Schwenckfeldians stressed the invisible church so that they suspended the sacraments and kept Christ to themselves (and thus remain a tiny sect), the free churches survived even through horrific persecution and eventually grew in number and influence, especially in English-speaking countries. Where the Protestants retained the traditional confusion of church and state and thereby brought suffering to myriads of their fellow human beings, the free churches embraced the ideal of religious liberty, and it is their tolerant outlook the modern world largely approves. Where Roman Catholicism retained the visible church but often repressed their people's religious vigor through a sacerdotal hierarchy, the free church model of congregationalism was a basis for capitalist democracy, if a leading sociologist is to be believed.[117] Where modern evangelicals have experienced revival and growth, it is largely through the appropriation of a concern for the spread of true internal faith through visible witness. The Baptists, the Quakers, the Brethren, and the Methodists, among others, have often looked to the sixteenth-century Anabaptists for their theological roots.

Marpeck's Contributions to the Current Crisis in Theological Method

Marpeck contributes significantly to the modern discussion of theological method. First was the necessarily negative work of demarcating the free churches. His writings make clear that the free churches, especially believers-only baptism churches, possess a distinct theological method. This is generally recognized with regard to the Roman Catholic method but has been less recognized with regard to liberalism and Reformism. In setting his theology against the evangelicals and Reformed and the Spiritualist-Rationalists, Marpeck showed how the free-church proposal is sui generis. It may draw upon the theological contributions made by the Catholic churches, the Reformation churches, and spiritualist-rationalist circles, but the free churches are different because their theological method is different.

Kiwiet's detailed study brought him to a startling conclusion: "If we place the theology of the Reformers and the theology of the Baptists next to one another, then we get the impression that two worldviews (*Weltanschauungen*) collided with one another."[118] There is as much of a "difference in modes of thought" between the free churches and the evangelicals as there is between the evangelicals and the Catholics: theological conversations between them require the translation of language.[119] Kiwiet suggested that the Reformers' central doctrine of predestination indicates a Hellenistic philosophical worldview while the Baptists employ a Hebrew biblical worldview. Others have noted the difference between the Reformers and the Anabaptists regarding the church's history. The Reformers, building on

[117] Max Weber, *The Protestant Ethic and the Spirit of Capitalism*, trans. Talcott Parsons (New York: Scribner, 1958), 144–54.

[118] "Wenn wir die reformatorische und die Theologie der Täufer nebeneinander stellen, bekommt man den Eindruck, dass zwei Weltanschauungen aufeinander stossen." Kiwiet, *Pilgram Marbeck*, 149.

[119] Ebeling posited a difference between Catholicism as an "intellectualist type of idealist philosophy" and, following Julius Kaftan, Protestantism as "knowledge based on a personal relations to its object, i.e., to God." Gerhard Ebeling, *The Word of God and Tradition*, trans. S. H. Hooke (London: Collins, 1968), 98–99.

the late medieval councils, sought a re-formation of the church on the basis of their various views of the idealistic "form." But the Anabaptists saw the church as having utterly fallen with Constantine and sought not *reformatio* but *restitutio*.[120] Marpeck did not want to reform to a humanly invented ideal but to restore the divine order revealed in the New Testament. Restitution and reformation are ultimately incompatible agendas.

Klassen's work with regard to the hermeneutics of Marpeck, alongside Murray's survey of early Anabaptist hermeneutics, elucidates the division between the biblical Anabaptists on the one hand and the spiritualists and their rationalist kin on the other. Although Caspar Schwenckfeld was not a liberal in the modern sense of the term, his ways of thinking are echoed in modern liberalism. The spiritualists and rationalists ably described by George Huntston Williams find a comfortable home in that Harvard Divinity School dean's unmatched contribution to Reformation historiography because his own theological commitments were to the "evangelical rationalism" he made integral to *The Radical Reformation*.[121] Marpeck stood against the spiritualists because of their departure from Scripture and denial of the visible church. His theological descendants have taken a truth he discovered four centuries earlier—"Above all the text of the Holy Scriptures is innocent of errors"—and developed a doctrine embraced now by most modern evangelicals, biblical inerrancy. Some evangelicals are now rediscovering the importance of ecclesiological integrity, as well.

Marpeck's second major contribution to the current crisis among the free churches is his positive proposal for a theological foundation. At the theological headwaters of the believers' church movement stands his theological method. Its foundation is a complete yieldedness to Christ in covenantal discipleship. The ground principles are Christocentrism, the coinherent work of the Word and the Spirit, fidelity to the biblical order against human invention, and a covenantal community interpreting and living out the Word. On this foundation and from these principles are derived the free churches' understanding of the proper development of doctrine. It is from the problem of the foundation of theology to the problem of the correct development of doctrine on that foundation that we now turn.

[120] Franklin H. Littell, *The Anabaptist View of the Church* (Boston: Starr King, 1958), 79.

[121] On Williams, see William R. Hutchison, Peter J. Gomes, and C. Conrad Wright, "Memorial Minute for George H. Williams," *Harvard University Gazette*, March 20, 2003. On the impact of Williams's faith commitments to his historiography, see my review of *The Radical Reformation* in *FM* 14 (1996): 103–6.

Chapter Four

THE DEVELOPMENT OF DOCTRINE: *Biblical and Historical Considerations*

This chapter turns our attention from the foundation of doctrine to its development. Before offering a believers' church definition of the proper development of doctrine, it is appropriate to examine the historic alternatives. There are three major alternatives to the free-church definition: the classical thesis concretized in the councils of Trent and Vatican I, the liberal Protestant thesis that undermined the classical thesis, and the thesis of John Henry Newman. Evangelicalism has not offered a uniformly accepted doctrine of development. After reviewing the alternative theses offered by these Christian traditions, the scriptural doctrines of tradition and dogma must be considered, for it is upon Scripture that the free churches demand any doctrine be founded.

THE DEVELOPMENT OF DOCTRINE AS A HISTORICAL DOCTRINE

The Classical Thesis Defined

The classical theory of doctrinal development is that there is no real development in doctrine. In his famous *Commonitorium*, Vincent of Lérins laid down the principle, "All possible care must be taken, that we hold the faith which has been believed everywhere, always, by all [*quod ubique, quod semper, quod ad omnibus*]."[1] The three tests of universality, antiquity, and consent are ostensibly applicable to any and every doctrine. In the surviving portion of his treatise, Vincent focuses primarily on the test of antiquity, only cursorily treating universality and consent. He is especially concerned to show "how great a calamity the introduction of a novel doctrine causes."[2] The emphasis on antiquity had an especially chilling impact upon subsequent Christian discourse. Until the rise of the modern historical method demonstrated that doctrine was perennially variable, it was assumed that Christian doctrine must be immutable in order to be true. His fear of novelty brought Vincent to suggest that the key to proving one's orthodoxy faith is to, first, look to the canon, and second, to examine the tradition through the teachings of the councils and certain church fathers.[3] Subsequent proponents of

[1] Vincent of Lérins, *Commonitorium* 6, in NPNF^2, 11:131–56.

[2] Ibid., 11.

[3] Ibid., 76–77.

the classical theory, for instance among Anglican evangelicals, were thus led to give authoritative preference to select writings of the early church.[4]

The biblical passages that Vincent considered in order to arrive at his test of antiquity included Gal 1:8, Deut 13:1, Prov 22:28,[5] and 1 Tim 6:20. Vincent's exegesis of the last passage, which he treats in more depth than the others, demonstrates the limits imposed upon him by the Latin Vulgate.[6] Whereas the Greek text treats that which Timothy is to guard dynamically, the Latin text treats it in a static manner. The Greek *parakatatheke* is a verbal noun that indicates the activity of trust, only secondarily implying an object; the Latin *depositum* focuses upon the object itself rather than the activity of trust. Perhaps as a result of this subtle yet significant transposition in meaning, the deposit of faith (*depositum fidei*) that requires guardianship was conceived in the Western theological tradition as a fixed content more than a dynamic relationship of faith. In the mind of Vincent, "if novelty is profane, antiquity is sacred." While favoring prior interpretations, this static definition also brought the deposit of faith to be viewed as primarily, even exclusively, cognitively formulaic.

Vincent himself did not deny the idea of progress in the church, but he was concerned that such progress never involves the "alteration of faith."[7] There may be progress in doctrine, "yet only in its own kind; that is to say, in the same doctrine, in the same sense, and in the same meaning." Paradoxically, the organic metaphors Vincent chose were later used to undermine his penchant for fixity. A physical body may develop, but Vincent believed it remains substantially the same. A seed may grow, but Vincent was convinced that it may not yield anything substantially dissimilar. Doctrines must be "cared for, smoothed, polished," but they may not be changed. "They may receive proof, illustration, definiteness; but they must retain withal their completeness, their integrity, their characteristic properties." Vincent's idea of development may be characterized as a lack of substantial development that allows only a polishing in presentation:

> But the Church of Christ, the careful and watchful guardian of the doctrines deposited in her charge, never changes anything in them, never diminishes, never adds, does not cut off what is necessary, does not add what is superfluous, does not lose her own, does not appropriate what is another's, but while dealing faithfully and judiciously with ancient doctrine, keeps this one object in view: if there be anything which antiquity has left shapeless and rudimentary, to fashion and polish it, if anything already reduced to shape and developed, to consolidate and strengthen it, if any already ratified and defined to keep and guard it.

[4] Among modern American evangelicals, see Christopher A. Hall, "What Evangelicals and Liberals Can Learn from the Church Fathers," *JETS* 49 (2006): 94–95; idem, *Reading Scripture with the Church Fathers* (Downers Grove, IL: InterVarsity Press, 1998).

[5] Vincent, *Commonitorium* 21–22, 28, 51.

[6] Ibid., 51–53, 60–63.

[7] Ibid., 54–59.

Vincent, however, was no obscurantist. His theory of language recognized that words may change in order to preserve an old article of faith, but he preferred to avoid changes in language, for alterations in language may indicate alterations in meaning: "profane novelties of words" (cp. 1 Tim 6:20).[8] The issue of doctrinal stability amidst linguistic elasticity had arisen during the early controversies over the Trinity and Christology. For instance, Origen used *ousia* in various ways while Arius employed the term in only one sense. Arius maintained that the Father is alien in *ousia* to the Son. In response, the Council of Nicaea retained Arius's singular use but refuted Arius's conclusion by affirming that the Father and the Son are *homoousion* (of the same substance). Of course, the Nicene council also anathematized the idea that the Son possessed a distinct *hupostasis* from the Father, treating *hupostasis* as a synonym of *ousia*.[9] The Cappadocians used *hupostasis* to distinguish the persons of the Trinity while maintaining the unity of Christ. Moreover, Basil of Caesarea was initially suspicious of the terminology of *homoousios*.[10]

Athanasius, the champion of Nicene orthodoxy, was not as concerned with the exact words to be accepted, for he recognized that different words may be used to indicate the same meaning. Athanasius led the Council of Alexandria in 362 to recognize those who relied upon different terminology but nevertheless affirmed the substantial identity of the Father and the Son. He argued that the confessions of various Christians should be checked but for meaning rather than technical vocabulary: "not to enquire further into each other's opinions, not to fight about words to no useful purpose, nor to go on contending with the above phrases, but to agree in the mind of piety." Athanasius wanted no more than agreement concerning the essentials of the trinitarian faith, which in his day meant anathematizing the Arian dogmas that did violence to the persons of Christ and the Spirit while confessing the faith of the Nicene fathers.[11]

Only with the Cappadocians did the language of *mia ousia treis hupostaseis* (one essence, three persons) become regularized and theologically normative in Greek-speaking Christianity. In a letter of 375, Basil identified orthodoxy as residing between the extremes of the mechanistic monotheism of Sabellius and the pagan polytheism of Arius: "as he who fails to confess the community of the essence or substance falls into polytheism, so he who refuses to grant the distinction of the hupostases is carried away" into Sabellianism.[12] At the Council of Constantinople, the anathema against the use of *hupostasis* to describe a distinction within the Godhead was dropped from the creed.[13]

Not only was there an initial variation within orthodox Greek terminology; there was also confusion introduced by translations between Latin and Greek. Western theologians could become confused by the East's language such that they

[8] Ibid., 59, 61.

[9] *DEC*, 1:5.

[10] Anthony Meredith, *The Cappadocians* (Crestwood, NY: St. Vladimir's Seminary Press, 2000), 102–6.

[11] Athanasius, *Tomus ad Antiochenos*.

[12] Basil of Caesarea, Letter 210.5, trans. Blomfield Jackson, in *NPNF2*, 8:251.

[13] *Decrees of the Ecumenical Councils*, 1:24.

detected tritheism. Conversely, Eastern theologians could interpret the Latin formula *una substantia tres personae* (one essence, three persons) in modalist terms. As the conversation transitioned to Christology, there were similar difficulties in settling upon the language of *physis* (nature) and *hupostasis* (person). Only with time, explanation, and patience, and often only after numerous councils was a language crafted to describe Christian orthodoxy in terms generally acceptable to all.[14] Orthodox theologians might agree with one another over the basic meaning of truth, but an acceptable language was not always readily available.[15]

The classical theory of doctrinal development had, therefore, these two major aspects: static meaning and elastic (at least, initially) language. A third major characteristic of the classical theory was that it considered heresy to be a dangerous perversion of orthodoxy. Vincent appealed to 1 Cor 11:19 for this understanding: "There must also be factions [*haereseis*] among you, that those who are approved may be recognized among you." The heretic's purpose is to make apparent those who are "tenacious and faithful and steadfast" in their faith.[16] This interpretation was common in the early church: The church was originally pure and faithful. Heresy came out of orthodoxy as a perversion of it. Moreover, heretics are restless and unsettled, tend to be local, and follow the speculations of philosophers. Classical theologians tended to overlook diversity among the orthodox themselves by focusing on their common commitment to the rule of faith.[17] The positive statement of Paul—that factions are intended to reveal approved teachers—was eventually, however, replaced by a negative assumption that heresy must be violently suppressed.

The classical understanding of orthodoxy as fixed and heresy as innovation held general sway among Christians until the sixteenth-century Reformation. In the medieval period heresy was "defined by reference to orthodoxy. It does not exist alone. A doctrine or sect or an individual becomes heretical when condemned as such by the church. For this, there has to be a body of accepted beliefs to violate and a recognized authority to enforce it." The body of beliefs was defined in the medieval West by the clergy who made reference to creeds, councils, fathers, doctors, and popes in the context of canon law. Heretics were Christians who held tenaciously to their error and would not allow the church hierarchy to correct them. Heresy was not a denial of Christianity but "a deviation from accepted beliefs." Because of the clerical monopoly on doctrinal definition, "to be heretical was also to be anti-sacerdotal." Gordon Leff makes a distinction between orthodoxy, heterodoxy, and heresy in the Middle Ages. Orthodoxy was right belief;

---

[14] H. E. W. Turner, *The Pattern of Christian Truth: A Study of the Relations between Orthodoxy and Heresy in the Early Church* (1954; reprint, Eugene, OR: Wipf & Stock, 2004), 33–34.

[15] Gregory of Nazianzus warned that orthodoxy is not always guaranteed by the letter. "I should have been looking, not so much at the terms used, as at the thoughts they were meant to convey." Gregory of Nazianzus, *On the Holy Spirit*, The Fifth Theological Oration, 24, trans. Charles Gordon Browne and James Edward Swallow, in *NPNF*², 7: 325.

[16] Vincent, *Commonitorium* 48.

[17] Turner, *The Pattern of Christian Truth*, 3–10.

heterodoxy was error subject to censure; while heresy was pertinacious error to be anathematized.[18]

Because of their concern for the interwoven spiritual and social welfare of the people, medieval theologians supported the death penalty for heretics. Modern conceptions of religious toleration and religious freedom were inconceivable. Society and Christendom, politics and religion, were inextricably bound together. It was believed that social harmony must be preserved by the removal of religious dissenters. It was the bishop's role to suppress false teaching, first by discovery, then by correction. Some bishops saw their pastoral role as not allowing for violent response, but most feared the social ramifications of inaction. "Fear was part of the impulse to violence. Authority assumed that heresy and rebellion went together."[19] If the errant Christian refused repentance and remained recalcitrant, he was declared a heretic.

It was typically considered inappropriate for the church to kill a person, so although the heretic was tried by the church, he or she was delated to the state for execution. The state also considered heresy a novelty intended to subvert the divinely fixed order of church and society. According to *De Haeretico Comburendo*, the English parliament's act against the followers of John Wyclif, "divers false and perverse people of a certain new sect" have undermined the "hitherto" devoutly observed faith. In order to preserve the church and the realm, those who will not abjure when corrected by the church, or who have relapsed into heresy after abjuring, were "to be burnt" by the local magistrate.[20] The classical theory of the early church was thus transformed into religious tyranny in the Middle Ages.

The Classical Thesis Concretized

The classical thesis of a fixed doctrinal tradition, maintained by medieval tyranny, began to crack during the Reformation. One of the greatest polemical weapons used against the Reformers was "the perennial Romanist demand: 'Where was your church before Luther?'"[21] Of course, Luther responded with his own query: "Why, then, should we reject the word, and the understanding of good Christians, and follow the pope, who has neither faith nor the Spirit?"[22] The Roman claim to antiquity was countered by the Reformers' claim to consent, both of which had a place in the Vincentian dictum. Moreover, Luther pulled a trump card that was difficult to refute. Why believe the supposedly apostolic origin of oral tradition when we have the written apostolic tradition in the Bible? Luther spent a great

[18] Gordon Leff, *Heresy in the Later Middle Ages: The Relation of Heterodoxy to Dissent c.1250–c.1450* (1967; repr., Manchester, UK: Manchester University Press, 1999), 1–4.

[19] Malcolm Lambert, *Medieval Heresy: Popular Movements from the Gregorian Reform to the Reformation*, 3rd ed. (Oxford: Blackwell, 2002), 33.

[20] 2 Henry IV cap. 15 (1401), in *Documents Illustrative of English Church History*, ed. Henry Gee and William John Hardy (London: Macmillan, 1896), 133–37.

[21] Anthony Milton, *Catholic and Reformed: The Roman and Protestant Churches in English Protestant Thought, 1600–1640* (New York: Cambridge University Press, 1995), 270.

[22] Martin Luther, *To the Christian Nobility of the German Nation*, trans. Charles M. Jacob and James Atkinson, in *Three Treatises* (Philadelphia: Fortress Press, 1989), 21.

deal of time pointing out the abuses of the church that had accumulated to her over time. The cry of *sola scriptura* became an antidote to the mantra of tradition. During the Reformation, tradition lost its universal appeal. The Reformers criticized Rome because it placed tradition above Scripture and the church above tradition. Reformers claimed to be correcting a tradition gone astray; Romanists claimed to be preserving the faith once for all delivered to the saints.

The polemical questions raised in the early Reformation continue to haunt both sides of that debate. Did Luther rebuke corruption or introduce a corruption? Vatican II theologian Yves Congar recognized in the critique of Karl Barth an appeal for the Roman church to consider whether its elevation of tradition bypassed God in order to engage in a monologue with itself. "This reproach, this question thus addressed to us [Roman Catholics] by the Reformation is terribly important. It issues from the heart of its protest: the will to withdraw from the Church what belongs to God, in order to restore it to God, i.e. to reject the Church's claim to be a rule and to embody so adequately the work of God that to all practical purposes there is no longer either distance or tension between this Church and its Lord." Congar then turns the Catholic question back to Protestants, "Do they not misunderstand and ignore, as unworthy of attention, the permanent reality of the Spirit united to the Church by a covenant relationship, and the reality of the instituted and assisted apostolic ministry?"[23] The Reformation's dueling questions regarding fidelity to Scripture and the possibility of corruption in theology contributed to skepticism with the rise of historical consciousness in the modern period.

At the beginning of his superb study on John Henry Newman, Owen Chadwick peered into a 1623 debate in a London dining room between the Anglican Dr. Featley and the Roman Jesuits Sweet and Fisher. During this debate the Roman Catholics avoided the Anglican question of perpetuity: "Where was your church in the time of the gospels?" Conversely, the Anglican avoided the Roman question of continuity: "Where was your church a century ago?" In this way, in spite of the Protestant appeal to Scripture alone, history became the new battleground. "The centre of theological gravity was shifting from the Bible into the field of ecclesiastical history."[24] Chadwick traces the history of this shift in the conception of the development of doctrine.

Immediately after the Reformation, most theologians still believed that novelty indicated error. Jacques Bénigne Bossuet, bishop of Meaux and popular orator, wrote numerous works against Protestants. The title of one anti-Reformation treatise indicates his preference for theological continuity: *Histoire des variations des Églises protestantes* (History of the Variations of the Protestant Churches). Bossuet was characterized by certitude with regard to the continuity of Catholic doctrine. He recognized that God controlled history and that the history of em-

---

[23] Yves Congar, *Tradition and Traditions: The Biblical, Historical, and Theological Evidence for Catholic Teaching on Tradition*, trans. Michael Naseby and Thomas Rainborough (London: Burns & Oates, 1966; reprint, San Diego, CA: Basilica Press, 1996), 466–69.

[24] Owen Chadwick, *From Bossuet to Newman: The Idea of Doctrinal Development* (New York: Cambridge University Press, 1957), 3–4.

pires was variable, but history's pattern was ecclesiastical and Rome's doctrine was stable. "The Church's doctrine is always the same. . . . The Gospel is never different from what it was before."[25] Bossuet appears to have had no concept of the church's growth in knowledge. The gospel is church doctrine and vice versa.

Other Roman Catholic theologians were not as simplistic in their approach. They recognized, as they researched Christian history, that the church had defined new articles of faith. Medieval scholars argued that in defining doctrine, such as Nicaea did with the *homoousion*, Christians were simply making explicit that which was implicit. After the Reformation, this concept of "logical explication" was given serious treatment through various syllogisms. Some theologians, such as Francisco de Suarez, recognized that the divine gift of faith was certain but that human reason is fallible. As a result he was compelled to turn to the authority of the Roman church in order to provide certainty regarding any doubtful issues. Suarez even went so far as to posit some type of equivalence between the Roman church's definition of doctrine and divine revelation.

Suarez's successors taught that the Holy Spirit guides the church infallibly to new truth. The contributions of these scholars eventually led to the definition of papal infallibility at Vatican I, wherein it was declared that the "see of St. Peter always remains unblemished by any error." The council denied that there was any new revelation in papal proclamations; nevertheless, they affirmed that the pope speaks with infallibility when he speaks from the episcopal throne (*ex cathedra*).[26] Vatican I solidified the Vincentian dictum's doctrine of perpetuity for Roman Catholics, protecting it with an appeal to the bishop of Rome as the infallible source of doctrinal definition.

The Classical Thesis Cracked

While the Roman church hierarchy was defining itself in terms of an unchanging and unchallengable infallibility in doctrine, the world of historical scholarship was experiencing a revolution. Even Roman Catholic scholars began to admit that history provided indications that doctrines do change over time; they were, however, slow to develop a theory to explain how doctrine changed. In modern Europe the Enlightenment was swinging into full force. Historians moved away from a providential explanation of history and began to recount history according to scientific patterns, such as that of progress. Scientific historians were concerned to interpret events according to the data alone, so previous paradigms, especially religious ones, were thrown out, and new philosophies ventured.[27] Even Christian historians began to see that the data of history indicated changes in the way people had thought about God. Christian historians and theologians began to search about for an explanation to this phenomenon.

---

[25] Ibid., 17.

[26] *Decrees of the Ecumenical Councils*, 2:816; Chadwick, *From Bossuet to Newman*, 21–48.

[27] Ernst Breisach, *Historiography: Ancient, Medieval, and Modern*, 2nd ed. (Chicago: University of Chicago Press, 1994), 199–201, 268–71.

Among English Protestants, the eighteenth century saw the rise of theologians who regarded doctrine as mutable, even if they conceived revelation as stable. "For the revelation was the propositions enshrined in Scripture. Tradition consists in the passing of the same book from generation to generation. But Christian doctrine was not part of the revelation. Christian doctrine consisted in successive human attempts, from age to age, to express in modern terms and perhaps with the aid of modern philosophies, the nature of this scriptural revelation."[28] English Protestants, therefore, evinced a stark distinction between divine revelation and human doctrine, which entails second-level reflection upon that revelation. Soon England was overwhelmed by a skeptical theological wave emanating from the continent, especially from Germany. The concept of doctrinal development became an increasingly major problem, especially with regard to the New Testament period.

Among German Protestants the new historical consciousness that accompanied the Enlightenment and the Romantic response had serious ramifications not only for the understanding of the historical development of doctrine but for the historical development of Scripture itself. The various quests for "the Jesus of history," as supposedly opposed to "the Christ of faith," have been rehearsed before and need only abbreviation here. Suffice it to say that the modern period witnessed a growing skepticism toward the doctrine that Scripture is the inspired Word of God kept infallible by the Holy Spirit. Adopting a speculative paradigm for the history of the early church, Ferdinand Christian Baur sought to peer behind the words of Scripture and perceived warring parties of Jew and Gentile in the formation of the early Christian church.[29] Baur's student, David Friedrich Strauss, introduced the much-ballyhooed idea of "the mythical" into his interpretation of the New Testament. Form criticism, source criticism, and redaction criticism came into their own as the preferred methods of Bible study. The inspiration, infallibility, and inerrancy of Scripture became increasingly incredible to the academic.[30] The dominant view among New Testament critics was that the early church had developed the human Jesus into the divine Christ.[31] For some academics, especially among biblical theologians, theology became a means of disbelief.[32]

---

[28] Chadwick, *From Bossuet to Newman*, 81–82.

[29] Karl Barth claims that Baur's major flaw was that he confused the Spirit that rules history with the spirit of the historian. Church historians "have to observe the barriers which separate the men who understand history from God as the judge and guardian of history." Barth, *Protestant Theology in the Nineteenth Century: Its Background and History*, new ed., trans. Brian Cozens and John Bowden (Grand Rapids: Eerdmans, 2002), 492–93.

[30] Albert Schweitzer, *The Quest of the Historical Jesus: A Critical Study of Its Progress from Reimarus to Wrede* (Baltimore: Johns Hopkins University Press, 1998); Stephen Neill, *The Interpretation of the New Testament*, 1861–1961 (New York: Oxford University Press, 1964), 1–32; Luke Timothy Johnson, *The Real Jesus: The Misguided Quest for the Historical Jesus and the Truth of the Traditional Gospels* (San Francisco: HarperCollins, 1997).

[31] This paradigm of development has more recently been challenged by those advocating an "early high Christology." Fred Sanders, "The State of the Doctrine of the Trinity in Evangelical Theology," *SWJT* 47 (2005): 155–58.

[32] "Strauss offered to his time the sight of the theologian who has become an unbeliever, for all to behold and without denying it." Barth, *Protestant Theology in the Nineteenth Century*, 533.

Among church historians, the idea that the early church was innovative in its theology became an unquestionable presupposition. Adolf Harnack, a highly influential historical theologian, cast into doubt the basic dogmas of the Christian faith by arguing that the teaching of Jesus was originally quite simple. It consisted of three propositions: the kingdom of God is coming; God the Father has assigned infinite value to the human soul; and, love is the greatest commandment. While orthodox Christians would agree with these propositions and more, Harnack severely limited the teaching of Jesus to them. Harnack believed that the early church fathers began a process of the "Hellenization" of Christianity. "Christendom became more and more penetrated by the Greek and philosophical idea that true religion is first and foremost 'doctrine,' and doctrine, too, that is coextensive with the whole range of knowledge." As a result of Hellenization, the gospel of love was buried, Jesus was defined as divine, and Christianity became more Greek than Christian. According to Harnack, the premiere proponent of German liberalism at its height, Christianity must be shed of its desire for the immortal, and its Christological formulae must be rejected, in order to return to the essence of the gospel.[33] Unfortunately, one must destroy the biblical text in order to obtain the liberal view.[34]

If traditional Roman Catholics officially opted for a fixed understanding of doctrine (fixed according to papal definition), liberal Protestants opted for an endlessly variable understanding (variable according to the scholar's whims). Vatican I strongly suggested that Christian doctrine never developed but was only clarified by papal pronouncements ex cathedra. Harnack taught that Christian doctrine was a continual series of developments from the early church through the accretions of the Greek church and through the formal institutionalization of the Roman church. In Harnack's presentation all doctrinal developments were corruptions. The Reformation, a supremely German event, started the return to the kernel of the gospel that culminated in the liberal view of Jesus as merely a Palestinian teacher of ethics. Other liberals might quibble with his conclusions, but Harnack's basic method was accepted as sound, so doctrine was set free from its biblical and ecclesial moorings. The simultaneous existence of such a wide diversity of thought in the Christian world, from an uncompromising Roman fixation to unrestrained liberal variation, was ultimately unsustainable. It was the task of an academic historical theologian, devoted churchman, and lifelong opponent of theological liberalism to set out a theory of doctrinal development that attempted to respect both the fixity of the faith and the continuing development of doctrine.

A New Thesis Proposed

John Henry Newman's impact on modern theology has been profound. Indeed, a free-church response to his magisterial *An Essay on the Development*

---

[33] Adolf Harnack, *What Is Christianity?* trans. Thomas Bailey Saunders (New York: Harper, 1957), 51, 211, 236.

[34] Paul Tillich, *Perspectives on Nineteenth and Twentieth Century Protestant Theology* (New York: Harper, 1967), 219–23.

of Doctrine was the original impetus for this book.[35] Jaroslav Pelikan, the leading historical theologian, considered Newman's essay the seminal treatise for all theologians and historians considering issues of methodology. Pelikan went so far as to say that Newman is "the most important theological thinker of modern times."[36] This writer agrees with Pelikan's assessment and hopes perhaps to craft one day a suitable free-church answer to "the charismatic don,"[37] but such a response should properly come at the end of a theologian's career rather than at its relative beginning. This book is a first step in that direction but is still not an adequate answer to "the most influential mind of the past two hundred years."[38] Newman's contributions to the disciplines of history, theology, and philosophy, as well as the institutions of the university and the church, are so profound and so deep that a lesser treatment would be inappropriate and properly dismissed as immature. Nevertheless, we begin with a preliminary response to Newman's doctrine of development in the few pages allowed.

Newman was converted to Christianity under the tutelage of his mother, an avid Bible reader, and Walter Mayers, a Calvinist clergyman in the Church of England.[39] In other words, Newman began his Christian theological pilgrimage as a son of the loosely evangelical Church of England. The official theology of this church affirmed the sufficiency of Scripture regarding "all things necessary to salvation."[40] English theologians tended to see the Scripture as "the only sacred and infallible guide" to the fundamentals of the faith.[41] But the problem of interpretation of Scripture brought to light a "distinctively Anglican" approach to tradition: favoring patristic tradition as universal, allowing the church freedom to set its own forms, and qualifying the church's freedom only insofar as it conflicts with the freedom of the individual believer.[42]

By affirming Scripture's sufficiency, the Anglican formulary implied hostility to unwritten tradition and an infallible church, but these implications were

---

[35] The first edition of the essay was written in 1845, during the writing of which Newman submitted to Rome. There were a few changes in the second edition of 1846. The final edition of 1878, incorporating significant revisions, largely in ordering, is generally accepted as the authoritative edition by Newman scholars. Newman, *An Essay on the Development of Christian Doctrine: The Edition of 1845*, ed. J. M. Cameron (Baltimore: Penguin, 1974); idem, *An Essay on the Development of Christian Doctrine*, 6th ed. (1878; repr., Notre Dame, IN: University of Notre Dame Press, 1989).

[36] Jaroslav Pelikan, *The Melody of Theology: A Philosophical Dictionary* (Cambridge, MA: Harvard University Press, 1988), 181.

[37] Noel Annan, *The Dons: Mentors, Eccentrics and Geniuses* (Chicago: University of Chicago Press, 1999), 39–60.

[38] As noted on the occasion of Pelikan's death, Newman is unusual among the great theologians of modernity in that he sought to construct a positive and bearable theology for his church. Richard John Neuhaus, "The Public Square," *FT* 169 (2007): 71–72.

[39] A number of biographies of Newman are available. A recent popular treatment is Brian Martin, *John Henry Newman: His Life and Work* (New York: Continuum, 2000). For the scholar, there is Ian Ker, *John Henry Newman: A Biography* (New York: Oxford University Press, 1988).

[40] Thirty-Nine Articles, art. 6.

[41] J. Jortin, *Works*, 4:373, cited in Günter Biemer, *Newman on Tradition*, trans. Kevin Smyth (Freiburg: Herder, 1967), 8.

[42] Oliver O'Donovan, *On the Thirty-Nine Articles: A Conversation with Tudor Christianity* (Exeter: Paternoster, 1986), 52–53.

increasingly questioned by theologians in the early nineteenth century. The appreciation of Anglicans for the early councils and church fathers encouraged some to affirm tradition as a necessary guide for scriptural interpretation. Edward Hawkins, Newman's superior at Oriel College, Oxford, convinced his student that Scripture's unsystematic nature of presenting revelation required "universal tradition as our guide to Scripture." By "universal tradition," the early Newman understood the creed, essentially the Apostles' Creed, which comes to us "from the earliest times, so that there is no assignable origin to it short of the Apostles."[43]

The patristic principle of the Anglicans thus led Newman to grant authority to tradition as fixed by the orthodox creeds of the early church. In other words, the Vincentian dictum, especially applied to the doctrinal formulations of the early councils, became for Newman and his colleagues in the Oxford Movement the *sine qua non* of biblical interpretation. In effect, the first-century Bible must be interpreted through the formulae of the fourth and fifth centuries. This progression from a standpoint of full biblical sufficiency to the earliest tradition as a necessary supplement for biblical interpretation was the authoritative lynchpin for the famous middle way (*via media*) of the Oxford Movement.[44] Newman opined bluntly, "Reading the Bible is not (ordinarily) sufficient for salvation."[45]

Newman's doctrine of development may be properly understood only as an integral feature in his own personal religious development. Newman's personal religious commitments shifted by degrees, first from evangelicalism to a *via media* between Protestantism and Rome, and then to a fervent Roman Catholicism. The first key to perceiving Newman's own theological development is discerning his movement from a position of respecting tradition coupled with the full sufficiency of Scripture to a position of viewing tradition as a necessary supplement to Scripture. Once the entire sufficiency of Scripture was compromised, Newman's trajectory toward Rome appeared set and his conversion all but inevitable. The shift in his doctrine of revelation was accompanied by roughly contemporaneous shifts in his doctrines of the church and of faith. The components of *Fundamentaltheologie*—revelation, faith, and the church—proved themselves inextricably intertwined, at least in the case of Newman.

For Newman, conversion from the loosely Reformed Church of England to the post-Tridentine Roman Catholic Church occurred alongside an increasing stress on "the Notes of the Church Catholic."[46] Newman's pilgrimage indicates that

[43] Edward Hawkins, *A Dissertation upon the Use and Importance of Unauthoritative Tradition, as an Introduction to the Christian Doctrines* (1819), cited in Biemer, *Newman on Tradition*, 25, cp. 36–37. Cp. John Henry Newman, *Tract 85* (1835), reprinted in *Discussions and Arguments on Various Subjects* (New York: Longmans Green, 1907), 135–38.

[44] Biemer, *Newman on Tradition*, 36–43; Michael Peterburs, "Newman and the Doctrine of Development," in *By Whose Authority? Newman, Manning and the Magisterium*, ed. V. Alan McClelland (Bath: Downside Abbey, 1996), 49–60.

[45] Newman stated this upon his withdrawal from the evangelical Bible Society, in June 1829, well before his conversion to Rome. *The Letters and Diaries of John Henry Newman*, ed. Charles Stephen Dessain et al. (Oxford and London, 1961–1984), 2:264–65, cited in Ker, *John Henry Newman*, 37.

[46] Newman, "Private Judgment," *British Critic* (1841), reprinted in *Essays Critical and Historical* (New York: Longmans Green, 1919), 2:373.

religious conversion may occur for those moving from the definition of the church as primarily local and visible (a typical free-church definition) to the definition of the church as primarily universal and invisible (Reformed or spiritualist) to the definition of the church as universal and visible (Roman Catholic). Similarly, a transition from a full affirmation of justification by faith alone as imputation (the typical Reformation view) to justification as impartation (Roman Catholic) may indicate a tendency toward an ecclesial conversion. Newman's mediating doctrine of justification, formed in his Anglo-Catholic period, intentionally sought to rectify Lutheran solafideism with the Tridentine conflation of justification with sanctification: "The separate doctrines, justification by faith, and justification by obedience, thus simply stated, are not at all inconsistent with one another."[47] Thus, as in Newman's own theological pilgrimage, revelation, ecclesiology, and soteriology are integrally related. For the theologian, a shift in one fundamental doctrine indicates a foundational shift in the others.

The last sermon that Newman preached at St. Mary's in Oxford, lasting an hour and a half, was entitled, "The Theory of Development in Religious Doctrine." It was among the final statements he made as an Anglo-Catholic and created something of a stir.[48] Expounding on Luke 2:19 and drawing from his reading of Joseph Butler's philosophy of religion,[49] Newman construed the Christian religion as an "idea" that is revealed. This idea, through revelation, leaves an impression on "the mind," which Newman understood to be the mind of the church. The idea and its revelation, being divine, are always greater than the created human mind is able to comprehend. The church, like Mary, long mulls over this "impression," and expresses its perception of the revelation to others in the form of "dogma." Because of the lag time in its perception, the church's dogma may take centuries to develop. Yet the church's dogmatic statements, once made, are authoritative and thus true.[50]

Newman's rudimentary doctrine of development has several advantages: it is holistic and avoids a merely rationalist definition of dogma. It properly distinguishes the church's limited dogmatic reflections from divine revelation, recognizing the limits of human language and the unlimited nature of divine glory. Yet it affirms a verbal correspondence between the earthly dogma and its heavenly archetype, refuting the tendency toward a formless symbolism. Moreover, it al-

---

[47] Newman, *Lectures on Justification*, lecture 1, in *John Henry Newman: Selected Writings to 1845*, ed. Albert Radcliffe (Manchester: Carcanet, 2002), 157.

[48] Ker, *John Henry Newman*, 257.

[49] Joseph Butler (1692–1752), moral philosopher and theologian, during his studies as an evangelical in Tewkesbury, conformed to the Church of England and attended Oriel College, Oxford. Butler rose high within the church hierarchy, ending his career as bishop of Durham. Butler's doctrine of analogy, composed as an apology against the challenge of skeptical rationalism, considered revelation an overarching idea that cannot be fully comprehended, that proof derives normally from probability rather than certainty, and that faith precedes rather than follows reason. These were themes taken up by Newman. Butler, *The Analogy of Religion Natural and Revealed, to the Constitution and Course of Nature*, 7th ed. (Aberdeen, 1775), i–xii, 187–215. Newman's *Oxford University Sermons* were focused on the problems of faith and reason, and his *Essay on the Development of Doctrine* mentions Butler approvingly at several points. Ker, *John Henry Newman*, 257–64. Cp. Newman, *Apologia Pro Vita Sua*, ed. William Oddie (London: J. M. Dent, 1993), 94.

[50] Newman, *Sermons and Discourses, 1839–57* (New York: Longmans Green, 1949), 64–94.

lows for growth in the church's understanding of truth, a phenomenon that the serious historical theologian finds difficult to dismiss. Finally, Newman constantly dismisses the liberal Protestant thesis that Christian doctrine is always mutating and is thus unstable. Newman's disdain for liberalism characterizes every period of his theological development and, with qualifications, seems fundamentally correct to this writer.[51]

Yet Newman's doctrine of development suffers significantly in at least three ways, especially from the evangelical and free-church perspectives.[52] First and foremost, Newman's doctrine of development suffers from its preference for a misapplied biblical metaphor.[53] Newman's metaphors for doctrinal development are organic, both botanical and biological, and probably derive from his reading of the *Commonitorium*, in spite of his stated rejection of the Vincentian dictum early in his mature statement, *An Essay on the Development of Doctrine*.[54] For Newman, Vincent's thesis of antiquity cannot bear the load placed upon it by Anglican divines. It is an "intelligible" thesis but is insufficient on its own. For instance, it ultimately calls into question not only the papacy but all of episcopacy, for the earliest church did not attain the structure of the Church of England, much less the structure of Rome. Moreover, the ante-Nicene fathers may be read equally in an orthodox or a heterodox fashion. The appeal to a static antiquity undermines orthodoxy as conceived by Christians at large.

Newman's exposure of the weaknesses of the Vincentian appeal to antiquity is difficult to refute. For Anglicans, who tend to focus on developments in the first five centuries as authoritative, the appeal to antiquity creates as many problems as it solves. Although it preserves classical orthodoxy, especially regarding the Trinity and Christology, it also can normalize conflicting ecclesiologies. An appeal to patristic history in support of the Trinity may just as easily support the spiritual and juridical claims of the Roman papacy. Newman goes so far as to assert that among the ante-Nicene fathers there is more support for the doctrine of papal supremacy than there is for the doctrine of a real presence in the Eucharist. This

---

[51] Frank Turner's revisionary thesis regarding Newman's personal theological development requires a much longer response than can properly be afforded here, but it should be noted that whereas Turner makes a stark distinction between liberalism and evangelicalism, Newman recognized a much more subtle difference, faulting them both for a similar theological method. Frank M. Turner, *John Henry Newman: The Challenge to Evangelical Religion* (New Haven, CN: Yale University Press, 2002), 23. For Newman, liberalism was the supreme danger facing Christianity in his time, and evangelicalism lacked the intellectual capacity to address it properly. Evangelicalism, moreover, compromised with liberalism by advocating the right of private judgment. The transition from evangelicalism to liberalism is merely a matter of degree. Newman, *Apologia Pro Vita Sua*, 385–95.

[52] Significant and helpful evangelical critiques may be found in J. B. Mozley, *The Theory of Development: A Criticism of Dr. Newman's Essay on the Development of Christian Doctrine, Reprinted from 'The Christian Remembrancer,' January 1847* (New York: E. P. Dutton, 1879); William Cunningham, "Newman on Development," *NBR* 5 (1846): 418–53; Peter Toon, *The Development of Doctrine in the Church* (Grand Rapids: Eerdmans, 1979).

[53] Newman cites the parables of the growing seed, the mustard seed, and leaven (Mark 4:26–29, 30–34; Matt 13:33; and parallels), but those parables concern the growth of the kingdom of God rather than the growth of doctrine. *An Essay on the Development of Christian Doctrine* (1878), 73–74.

[54] Vincent, *Commonitorium* 55–57; Newman, *An Essay on the Development of Christian Doctrine* (1878), 10–29.

is especially troublesome for Anglo-Catholics who reject the former but advocate the latter. In general, those theologians who appeal to developments within the early centuries as ultimately authoritative "will be sanctioning and encouraging the religion of Rome." As a modern critic stated, "a notion of patristic consensus" is simply unworkable.[55] One can only say that some church fathers agreed with a certain position. To speak of a patristic consensus is to say more than the sporadic, diffuse, and often-conflicting evidence allows.

For Newman, the Vincentian test of antiquity, especially as used by Anglican divines, failed, but the organic analogy of biological or botanical growth succeeded.[56] Through the organic analogy, in the *Essay*, Newman considered the test of universality that Vincent mentioned but did not stress in the surviving portion of his *Commonitorium*. Newman's definition of doctrinal development in the *Essay* focused on the organic analogy of revelation as an idea: "The increase and expansion of the Christian Creed and Ritual, and the variations which have attended the process in the case of individual writers and Churches, are the necessary attendants on any philosophy or polity which takes possession of the intellect and heart, and has had any wide or extended dominion."[57] In other words, the Christian revelation interacts dynamically with the human mind and only over time, which allows for "deeper thought," will "the highest and most wonderful truths" become evident to it. This revelation was fixed in the sense that it was "communicated to the world once for all by inspired teachers" but developing in that "could not be comprehended all at once by the recipients."[58]

And yet, as Newman was fully aware, doctrine may develop in a positive direction or in a negative direction. To put it in a way that Newman did not use, the created limitations of the human mind, on the one hand, and the fallen nature of man, on the other hand, as often as not foster false "corruption" rather than true "development."[59] Newman offers seven "tests" (in the earlier edition) or "notes" (in the later edition) to help the church to discern proper developments from corruptions.[60] The transition to the term "notes" in the later edition indicates Newman's opinion that the earlier "tests" may not be used to make any type of final judgment

[55] Hugo A. Meynell, "Newman on Revelation and Doctrinal Development," *JTS* 30 (1979): 140.

[56] Newman employs the metaphors of "germination and maturation" regarding true development. Cp. *An Essay on the Development of Christian Doctrine* (1878), 38.

[57] Ibid., 29–30.

[58] According to Avery Dulles, Newman's doctrine of revelation as an idea has three attributes. It is "comprehensive," "living," and "real." Dulles, "From Images to Truth: Newman on Revelation and Faith," *TS* 51 (1990): 254; Dulles, *Newman* (New York: Continuum, 2002), 70.

[59] Newman does not consider the source of doctrinal corruption at any length. Rather, he merely states corruption as a possibility. *An Essay on the Development of Christian Doctrine* (1878), 41.

[60] The seven notes are "preservation of type," "continuity of principles," "power of assimilation," "logical sequence," "anticipation of its future," "conservative action upon its past," and "chronic vigour." *An Essay on the Development of Christian Doctrine* (1845), 116–47; *An Essay on the Development of Christian Doctrine* (1878), 169–206. For scholarly commentaries on the seven notes, see Chadwick, *From Bossuet to Newman*, 139–63; Meynell, "Newman on Revelation and Doctrinal Development," 141–45; John R. Griffin, *A Historical Commentary on the Major Catholic Works of Cardinal Newman* (New York: Peter Lang, 1993), 14–24; Dulles, *Newman*, 74–76; Biemer, *Newman on Tradition*, 55–57.

regarding proper development.[61] Moreover, as Chadwick discerned, the tests were ultimately unworkable because they may be taken out of their Roman Catholic context and used to support any tradition's theological development.[62]

For Newman, the tests indicate that "modern Catholicism is nothing else but simply the legitimate growth and complement, that is, the natural and necessary development, of the doctrine of the early church."[63] The biblical truth of the incarnation thus leads through "Mediation" to such doctrines as the Mass and the merits of martyrs and saints, and through the "Sacramental principle" to such doctrines as confirmation and the real presence and original sin. If one development is accepted, then all of the Catholic developments must be accepted.[64] But even Newman recognized that such tests were just as applicable to the Protestant movement as they were to Roman Catholicism. The only difference being that he saw Protestantism as inevitably leading through private judgment to liberalism and, ultimately, skepticism. One had a choice: he could either accept the Nicene dogma and, along with it, the medieval and Roman developments; or one could accept the Lutheran dogma of private judgment and along with it the developments of John Calvin and Faustus Socinus. Newman denied any middle grounds.[65]

Besides the inappropriate application of the growth metaphor to doctrinal development, the second major problem with Newman's theory was his expansive definition of revelation. Although Newman claimed that divine revelation was fixed, his treatment of revelation indicated a movement beyond Scripture. Newman's model of revelation presents several difficulties from the free-church perspective. First, it separates revelation from the biblical text: "Ideas are in the writer and the reader of the revelation, not the inspired text itself."[66] Against Newman, the free-church model of revelation, closely paralleling the evangelical model, considers the biblical text necessary for the transmission of revelation to Christians today. Originally, the Holy Spirit superintended the process of transmission from the writer to the text by inspiration (2 Tim 3:16). Today the Holy Spirit superintends the process of transmission from the text to the reader by illumination (2 Pet 1:20–21; 1 Cor 2:10–14).[67]

The second difficulty with Newman's model of revelation is that it lacks a clear distinction between progressive revelation within the scriptural canon and doctrinal development after the scriptural canon was closed. Newman could not precisely determine "an historical point at which the growth of doctrine ceased,

---

[61] *An Essay on the Development of Christian Doctrine* (1878), 78.

[62] "If you allow development at all, how shall you confine development to certain developments?" Chadwick, *From Bossuet to Newman*, 143. Cp. Meynell, "Newman on Revelation and Doctrinal Development," 138–39.

[63] *An Essay on the Development of Christian Doctrine* (1878), 169.

[64] Ibid., 94.

[65] Ibid., 96–98.

[66] Ibid., 56.

[67] The free-church model of revelation does not exactly fit with any of the five outlined by Avery Dulles but has similarities with several of them: "Revelation as Doctrine," "Revelation as History," "Revelation as Inner Experience," "Revelation as Dialectical Presence," "Revelation as New Awareness." Dulles, *Models of Revelation* (Garden City, NY: Doubleday, 1983), 27–28.

and the rule of faith was once for all settled."[68] In the next sentence Newman seamlessly transitioned from the apostolic to the postapostolic. The development of doctrine from Pentecost to the Pauline epistles is on a par with Ignatius's doctrine of episcopacy and the later determination of the canon. The Christian system of belief of the first centuries, "the creed," and the Christian New Testament, "the canon," and a postapostolic high ecclesiology, "the doctrine of episcopacy," are concurrent developments of doctrine. Newman had long affirmed that the canon and the creed were developed by the church in the postapostolic period. As a result, he believed the Christian cannot accept the canon without affirming the developments of doctrine in the early church. The canon and the creed, the latter of which is significantly broadened to include the sacraments and the priesthood, stand or fall together.[69]

This leads us to the third major problem with Newman's theory, after his misapplied metaphor and his expansive definition of revelation: dependence upon an "infallible developing authority." Because of the unsystematic and unclear nature of biblical truth, "an authority is necessary to impart decision to what is vague."[70] Newman defined the church's authority as "deciding whether this, that, and a third, and any number of theological or ethical statements are true." And he defined infallibility in personal terms: "When we say a person is infallible, we mean no more than that what he says is always true, always to be believed, always to be done." Newman, however, was not at first comfortable with the idea of papal infallibility.[71] He preferred to focus on the church's infallibility, although the papacy should always be obeyed. The idea of Roman infallibility was more acceptable than the "hollow uniformity" of the Anglicans, or the "interminable division" of the sects, or the "skepticism" of Germany and Geneva. Where the free church focuses on the Holy Spirit, Newman focused on the church as a "present informant and guide, and that an infallible one."[72] Newman could not conceive of the Bible as its own guide, and when he turned to the Holy Spirit, he pictured him as necessarily guiding through the church. In this way the church itself became "that living and present Guide."

In the *Essay*, Newman also mentioned Vincent's third test of development, that of consent. "A Church, or a Council, or a Pope, or a Consent of Doctors, or a Consent of Christendom, limits the inquiries of the individual in no other way than Scripture limits them."[73] Later in his career Newman returned to the third Vincentian test, consent, proposing that the laity had a consulting role in the development in doctrine. The discussion began with Newman's obscure editorial note in the May 1859 *Rambler*: "If even in the preparation of a dogmatic definition, as lately in the instance of the Immaculate Conception. . . . Bishops would like to know the sentiments of an influential portion of the laity before they took

[68] Newman, *An Essay on the Development of Christian Doctrine* (1878), 68.
[69] Newman, *Tract 85*, 196–98, 216–17.
[70] Newman, *An Essay on the Development of Christian Doctrine* (1878), 78–81.
[71] Ibid., 86, 90–91.
[72] Ibid., 87–89.
[73] Ibid., 83.

any step which perhaps they could not recall."[74] This prompted a response from conservative Romanists, one of whom accused Newman of implying "that the infallibility of the Church resides in the *Communitate fidelium* [community of the faithful], and not exclusively in the *Ecclesia docente* [teaching church]." In other words, conservatives considered the clergy infallible and the laity fallible, and could not see how Newman might advocate that consulting the laity was necessary. Shortly thereafter, Newman was referred by the bishop of Newport to the papal curia regarding his apparent error.[75]

Newman felt constrained to clarify his own position, and his treatise *On Consulting the Faithful in Matters of Doctrine* was the result. Newman began by noting two definitions of *consult*: "inquiring into a matter of fact" and "asking a judgment." Newman was clear that the consultation he advocated was of the former rather than the latter kind. Newman wanted the church hierarchy to consult "the *fideliumsensus* and *consensus*" as a "branch of evidence" prior to their formulation of doctrine.[76] He was not seeking to undermine the *ex cathedra* teaching authority of the hierarchy by referring them to the consensus of the faithful throughout history. Rather, he believed the "*consensus* through Christendom is the voice of the Infallible Church."[77] The lay consensus would surely reflect only what they had been taught by their pastors, so it was natural to consult their opinion before delivering doctrinal statements. Indeed, the failure of so many clergy during the Nicene-Arian debates only set into relief the relative stability of the laity.[78] The fact that Newman's rather measured statement was considered dangerous indicates the quiescent position commonly assumed for the laity of the Tridentine Roman Catholic Church.

In summary, we note that Newman's doctrine of development paralleled his own religious development. In its mature sense, Newman's understanding of development used an organic metaphor as part of his philosophy of mind, allowing him (and many others who followed him) to personally embrace doctrinal growth, especially as it exists in the Roman Catholic Church. From a free-church perspective, the fixity of divine revelation was undermined by Newman's organic analogy as well as his decoupling of revelation from the biblical text. Chadwick's question remains a haunting one for Newman's followers: "In what meaningful sense may it be asserted that these new doctrines are not 'new revelation'?"[79]

Because doctrine was decoupled from Scripture, Newman was compelled to find another anchor to provide doctrinal stability. The infallible church, ultimately as defined by the papal *magisterium*, preferably in an ecumenical council, hav-

[74] Reprinted in John Coulson, "Introduction," in Newman, *On Consulting the Faithful in Matters of Doctrine*, ed. Coulson (New York: Sheed & Ward, 1961), 13–14.

[75] Ibid., 30, 37.

[76] *On Consulting the Faithful in Matters of Doctrine*, 54–55.

[77] Ibid., 63–65. Newman laid out five ways that *consensus* may be regarded: "1. as a testimony to the fact of the apostolical dogma; 2. as a sort of instinct, or *phronema*, deep in the bosom of the mystical body of Christ; 3. as a direction of the Holy Ghost; 4. as an answer to its prayer; 5. as a jealousy of error, which it at once feels as a scandal." Ibid., 73.

[78] Ibid., 76–101.

[79] Chadwick, *From Bossuet to Newman*, 195.

ing consulted the laity before promulgating opinions, was Newman's basis for Roman Catholic doctrinal stability. Late in his career, in the period of the Vatican I, Newman's contemporaneous commitment to papal infallibility and personal conscience was tested. His ultimate solution was to prioritize the first but deny that the *magisterium* could ever truly violate the correctly formed conscience.[80] From a free-church perspective, Newman's thoughtful submission is still unacceptable, for it seems to place someone other than Christ in the seat of infallible rule over the church.

Modern Catholic theologians[81] and some evangelicals[82] tend to return to Newman's theory, or a similar theory offered by Johann Adam Möhler, as the starting point for their doctrine of development. Like Newman, Möhler turned to the problem of dogmatic development as a result of the challenge of modern historicism. Möhler and F. C. Baur, the liberal Protestant theologian, were colleagues in the separate Catholic and Protestant faculties at the University of Tübingen. Like Baur, Möhler adopted the chief characteristics of German Romanticism: "consciousness of historical continuity, of organic growth, and of life as something dynamic and ever active."[83] Unlike Baur, however, Möhler was unwilling to compromise the rudiments of the Christian faith, in his case, of a Roman Catholic persuasion.

Möhler's theory has many of the strengths of Newman's without some of Newman's weaknesses. He distinguishes between two aspects of tradition: the objective and the subjective. The objective tradition is composed of the rule of faith (*depositum fidei*), which serves as "the norm and standard of scriptural interpretation" kept immutable by the Holy Spirit.[84] The subjective tradition is the ecclesiastical consciousness of the faith, "the word of God living perpetually in the heart of the faithful."[85] This distinction preserves the stability of the faith, while allowing for the work of the Holy Spirit. Unfortunately Möhler also prefers the organic analogy invented by Vincent, offers a doctrine of "consciousness" similar to Newman's "idea," and maintains an even stronger doctrine of

[80] On Newman's thoughtful but agonized submission to the declaration of papal infallibility at Vatican I and his desire to see a second council trim the definition, see Dulles, *Newman*, 92–96; Griffin, *A Historical Commentary on the Major Catholic Works of Cardinal Newman*, 163–81; Stanley L. Jaki, *Newman's Challenge* (Grand Rapids: Eerdmans, 2000), 149–78.

[81] Cp. Karl Rahner, "The Development of Dogma," in *Theological Investigations*, vol. 1, *God, Christ, Mary and Grace*, trans. Cornelius Ernst (London: Darton, Longman & Todd, 1961), 39–77. In comparison with Newman, Rahner grants a larger role to the Holy Spirit and prefers dogmatic propositions to the organic analogy. He affirms ecclesial infallibility but as an afterthought.

[82] Jaroslav Pelikan used Newman's theory of development but preferred to focus on the process of developments rather than on their verification. Pelikan, "An Essay on the Development of Christian Doctrine," *CH* 35 (1966): 3–12; idem, *Development of Christian Doctrine: Some Historical Prolegomena* (New Haven, CN: Yale University Press, 1969). See the scathing critique of Pelikan's "vindication" of Newman's *Essay*, from a theological perspective, by Maurice Wiles in *JTS* 21 (1970): 255–57. For a critique of Pelikan's larger project, from a historical perspective, see Darrell Jodock, "Christian Doctrine and Modern Culture: Assessing its Limits," *JAAR* 61 (1993): 321–38.

[83] Gustav Voss, "Johann Adam Möhler and the Development of Dogma," *TS* 4 (1943): 424.

[84] Möhler, *Symbolik oder Darstellung der dogmatischen Gegensätze der Katholiken und Protestanten*, 9th ed. (Mainz: Kupferberg, 1884), 357–58, cited in ibid., 427.

[85] Möhler, *Symbolik*, 357, cited in ibid., 428.

infallibility for the *magisterium*. Moreover, Möhler follows Irenaeus of Lyons in confining the Spirit to the church, especially the hierarchy.[86] Like Newman and Ratzinger, Möhler conflates the church with God: "The visible Church is the Son of God."[87]

Evangelical Responses

The leading theories of development offered by Vincent and Newman used an organic analogy of the germinating seed or the growing body. Harnack, too, used an organic analogy, but any growth was deemed negative. For the liberal theologian, the historical husk must be peeled away in order to reveal the diminutive seed at the center. These three understandings of doctrinal development—the Vincentian, the liberal Protestant, and the modern Catholic—proved ultimately unacceptable to evangelicals.[88] The most important reason they are considered objectionable, for all their other advantages, is their explicit or implicit denial of the sufficiency of Scripture.

Vincent's theory assumes that Scripture must be supplemented by that which has been believed everywhere, at all times, by all. The early church fathers, such as Irenaeus of Lyons, only contributed to this problem by positing an episcopal succession to preserve the rule of faith by which Scripture must be interpreted.[89] Patristic theology presents the perennial problem of casting Scripture's sufficiency into doubt,[90] even though the fathers often referred to Scripture as their leading criterion.[91] O'Donovan appropriately reminds evangelicals, who might be persuaded otherwise, "The value of the fathers' contribution to our theology has always to be measured against Scripture itself."[92] The patristic theory of the development of doctrine is ultimately antithetical to a consistent evangelical theory, and especially to a free-church theory.

The need to preserve the sufficiency of Scripture also marginalizes the modern Catholic and liberal Protestant models. As will be remembered, Newman, the premiere modern Catholic, spent a great deal of effort trying to overcome the idea that Scripture's clarity allowed common discernment of its truths.[93] Scripture's

[86] Irenaeus *Adversus Haereses* 3.24.1; Möhler, *Die Einheit in der Kirche oder das Prinzip des Katholizismus* (1825; repr., Mainz: Matthias Grünewald, 1925), 8–9, cited in Voss, "Möhler and the Development of Dogma," 438.

[87] Möhler, *Symbolik*, 356, cited in ibid., 439.

[88] For contemporaneous Protestant critiques of Newman, see Mozley and Cunningham, cited in note 53.

[89] D. Jeffrey Bingham, "Evangelicals, Irenaeus, and the Bible," in *The Free Church and the Early Church: Bridging the Historical and Theological Divide* (Grand Rapids: Eerdmans, 2002), 39–40.

[90] Bingham, "Development and Diversity in Early Christianity," 64n.

[91] Wiles identifies three fundamental appeals of the fathers—to Scripture, to the liturgy, and to salvation—and two patristic ways of reasoning—objectifying and addition versus modification. Wiles, *The Making of Christian Doctrine: A Study in the Development of Early Doctrinal Development* (New York: Cambridge University Press, 1967), 159.

[92] O'Donovan, *On the Thirty Nine Articles*, 55.

[93] "The structure of Scripture is such, so irregular and immethodical, that either we must hold that the Gospel doctrine or message is not contained in Scripture (and if so, either that there is no message at all given, or that it is given elsewhere, external to Scripture), or, as the alternative, we must hold that it is but indirectly and covertly recorded there, that is, under the surface." Newman, *Tract 85*, 142.

insufficiency required Newman to posit an infallible teaching authority in the church. Representing the best of liberal Protestantism, Maurice Wiles also denied that the Bible could "provide a definition of theology as a whole."[94] Such a denial was part and parcel of Wiles's belief that Scripture was fallible, just as the church is fallible. As with his foundation of theology, for Wiles, the final criterion of dogmatic development is "the position of our contemporary world."[95] The major theological models for understanding the development of dogma, as offered by the church fathers, by liberal Protestants, and by modern Roman Catholics, are ultimately unacceptable because they each, though in separate ways and often in denial that they are doing so, undermine the sufficiency of Scripture.

In response, various models of the development of doctrine have been offered by modern evangelicals. Recent evangelical understandings of doctrinal development have been put forward by two prominent Anglican evangelicals, Peter Toon and Alister McGrath. Characteristic of these evangelical models is the assumption that rational tests may discern true developments from corruptions and/or that tradition necessarily supplements Scripture. Neither tendency is perceived by the evangelicals themselves to compromise the sufficiency of Scripture. Unfortunately, the evangelical rationalist criteria are just as susceptible to Chadwick's criticism as Newman's notes were. The evangelical "criteria" or "theses" may be used to justify almost any tradition.[96]

Toon is more careful to preserve the sufficiency of Scripture than is McGrath. The latter, reacting against Protestant liberalism, proposes a reappropriation of tradition as "an inherited manner of *interpreting* scripture and transmitting the kerygma which it contains, rather than a source of revelation in addition to scripture." McGrath does not explain how such a "mutual coinherence of scripture and tradition" does not compromise the sufficiency of Scripture. Rather, he simply pronounces that his proposal "poses no difficulties for theologians in the tradition of the magisterial Reformation, whether Lutheran or Reformed."[97] Positively,

---

[94] Wiles offered two fundamental reasons the Bible cannot define theology as a whole: "In the first instance it is clear that there is no such thing as 'a coherent account of the teaching of the Bible which does not draw its criteria of coherence from outside the Bible itself.'. . . And secondly, even in so far as there is a coherent unity of biblical teaching, that cannot simply be taken over as it stands and treated as the end product of the work of theology." Wiles, *What Is Theology?* (New York: Oxford University Press, 1976), 5.

[95] Wiles, *The Making of Christian Doctrine: A Study in the Development of Early Doctrinal Development* (New York: Cambridge University Press, 1967), 11–13, 17. "The test of a true development in doctrine is not whether it preserves all the distinctions of the old in their old form; it is whether it continues the objectives of the Church in her earlier doctrinal work in a way which is effective and creative in the contemporary world." Ibid., 177. John Macquarrie, after a solid critique of the older theories, including the Enlightenment, modifies Wiles's theory with greater concern for continuity superintended by the Holy Spirit. Macquarrie's theory, however, does not adequately recognize the problem of human sin, a common liberal lacuna. Macquarrie, "Doctrinal Development: Searching for Criteria," in *The Making and Remaking of Christian Doctrine*, ed. Sarah Coakley and David A. Pailen (New York: Oxford University Press, 1993), 161–76.

[96] Toon offers six "criteria by which we can decide whether any given doctrine is a valid statement." He then admits that his model does not allow for judgment between competing confessions, nor does it address ecclesiology. Toon, *The Development of Doctrine in the Church*, 116–19. McGrath offers four "theses" that he believes account "for the historical phenomena associated with doctrinal formulations." McGrath, *The Genesis of Doctrine*, 37.

[97] Ibid., 173.

Toon and McGrath allow places for both Christ and Scripture in their models, but both are weak with regard to pneumatology and ecclesiology. Indeed, McGrath ignores the Holy Spirit for rationalist criteria, while Toon actually denies the Spirit a continuing role beyond the patristic period in guiding the churches' doctrinal formulations.[98]

THE DEVELOPMENT OF DOCTRINE AS A SCRIPTURAL DOCTRINE

Fixed and Developing

Before proposing a doctrine of development from a free-church perspective, the free-church theological method requires an examination of Scripture's teaching regarding doctrinal development. The scriptural basis for the development of doctrine tests the hypothesis that doctrine is both fixed and continually developing. Most theologians typically affirm doctrine is fixed in the sense that revelation is "something unique, accomplished once and for all,"[99] but free-church theologians have also understood doctrine is developing in the sense that "the Lord hath yet more light and truth to break forth out of his holy Word."[100] The distinction between stable doctrine and developing doctrine, as we have seen, is a conclusion reached by most historical theologians. But does this distinction between doctrine as fixed and doctrine as developing have a scriptural basis?

The words used by Scripture to describe its message have both a substantive and dynamic aspect. In chapter 1, we noted both the fixed and dynamic natures of *logos theou* (Word of God) and *pistis* (faith). *Euangelion* (gospel) likewise has a fixed and developing sense. Mark prefers the substantive form of the word group, while Luke favors the verbal form. Although liberals quibble with whether the passage may be attributed directly to Christ, Mark's use of *euangelion* is "intended to supply a summary of the gospel preached by Jesus" that the remainder of his book exposits. The kingdom of God which the gospel of Jesus proclaims is a substantive reality with both present and future components, but it above all indicates a "*dynamic activity of God*."[101] Paul used the substantive *euangelion* as a *nomen actionis* (name of action) indicating the act of proclaiming "a specific content." The gospel witnesses to the historical event of the cross and resurrection in history, but it also transcends history. The gospel is a gift that comes from without and that may become "our" or "my" *euangelion*, a personal possession.[102] The gospel is objective and subjective, fixed and dynamic, historical and eternal; but above all, it actively saves through the believer's willing reception of the Spirit's application of the accomplished work of Christ.

---

[98] Toon, *The Development of Doctrine in the Church*, 120–23.

[99] Yves Congar, *The Meaning of Tradition*, trans. A. N. Woodrow (New York: Hawthorn, 1964), 48.

[100] John Robinson, "Parting Advice," in "Memoir of Rev. John Robinson," in *The Works of John Robinson, Pastor of the Pilgrim Fathers*, ed. Robert Ashton (London: Snow, 1851), 1:xliv.

[101] His emphasis. G. R. Beasley-Murray, *Jesus and the Kingdom of God* (Grand Rapids: Eerdmans, 1986), 71–75.

[102] Gerhard Friedrich, "*Euangelion*," in *TDNT*, 2:721–33.

The doctrine about Christ, which encounters the sinner from without and transforms the believer from within, is substantive and definable, and because of this, it is also transmittable. In the Gospels, Jesus Christ speaks of the *didache* (teaching, doctrine) (Luke 7:16) or *logos* (word) (John 15:20) or *marturion* (testimony or witness) (Matt 10:18), which has come from His Father, which He has in turn given to His disciples, which becomes their own, and which they must share with the world. In the various forms of the Great Commission, there is little doubt that there is a substantial and living truth that they must transmit to others, who will in turn transmit the same to yet others. Indeed, the goal of Christ is for this "word" or "faith" or "doctrine" or "witness" to be heard in all places by all people (John 20:21; Matt 28:18–20). Whoever receives this doctrine from a Christian is really receiving it from God the Father Himself; conversely, whoever rejects the Christian rejects the Christ (Luke 10:16). The truth taught by the church is both propositional, in that it can be communicated cognitively through language, and personal, in that God transforms the inner man. "To bear witness is to announce Jesus Christ, not only as an historical event which happened in the past, but as the meaning of the present, each day, today and tomorrow until the end of time."[103]

The dominical command to transmit the gospel that saves immediately raises the issue of transmission or "tradition" understood in a technical sense. How is the doctrine of Christ transmitted from the church to the world so that sinners may become believers? The doctrine of Christ is transmitted through a tradition. *Paradosis* is the Greek noun for "tradition"; *paradidomi* is the verb for "transmitting" or "handing over." Both terms are used in the New Testament to describe the process of making and growing disciples of Jesus Christ.[104] Jude encouraged his readers "that you should earnestly contend for the faith which was once for all delivered [*hapax paradotheise*] unto the saints" (Jude 3). Jude obviously understands this tradition of faith which he has also received as a permanent gift handed over to the holy ones of God. Moreover, he appeals to his readers to advance or defend this tradition. But this raises further questions: Whence did this tradition come? Whither does this tradition go? How is this tradition preserved from deformation in the process of communication? Is the tradition always perceived correctly by the various churches?

Fixing the Tradition

In a brilliant set of lectures, published in French and German but worthy of being summarized here in English, Oscar Cullmann discusses the biblical concept of "tradition."[105] As is generally recognized, Jesus Himself referred to tradition

[103] Congar, *The Meaning of Tradition*, 52.

[104] Friedrich Büchsel, "*Paradidomi*" and "*Paradosis*," *TDNT*, 2:169–73.

[105] Oscar Cullmann, *La Tradition: Problème Exégétique, Historique et Théologique* (Paris: Delachaux et Niestlé, 1953), 51–52. The following interacts with the three main chapters of this book, which concern the correlation of the ascended Lord with the apostolic tradition (*La tradition apostolique et le "Seigneur" élevé à la droite de Dieu* [Paradosis et Kyrios]), the uniqueness of the apostolate (*La portée de l'unicité de l'apostolat*), and the fixing of the biblical canon (*La portée de la fixation du Canon par l'Eglise du IIe siècle*). Cullmann's contribution, though profound, is colored by his neoorthodoxy. Although he views Scripture as the fixation of the apostolic tradition, he believes their writings are marred by imperfections. The imperfections of the text are only com-

only in a negative way. For Christ the "tradition of men" (*paradosis ton anthropon*) was used by the Pharisees to nullify, reject, replace, and lay aside the law of God (Mark 7:1–3; cp. Matt 15:1–9). In light of this negative review by the Lord, surprisingly, Paul repeatedly used tradition in a positive sense to refer to the gospel itself. In 1 Cor 11:23, Paul described his tradition of the Lord's Supper as coming "from the Lord" (*de la part du Kyrios*). Cullmann rejects the competing explanations that Paul's "tradition" was the result of direct revelation or that it presupposed a succession of human intermediaries. Rather, he favors the idea that the ascended Lord is the agent who guaranteed the truth of the tradition that developed in the apostolic church.[106] It was this tradition, the apostolic tradition, that Paul required the churches to maintain (2 Thess 2:15), even if he, an apostle himself, were to proclaim something else (Gal 1:8).

First Corinthians 11:23 and 15:3 simply invert the reciprocal actions of tradition: "to transmit" (Gk., *paralambanein*; Hb., *qibbel min*) and "to receive" (Gk., *paradidonai*; Hb., *maser le*), a pairing derived from the Hebrew rather than the Hellenistic world:

1 Cor 11.23: *(ego) parelabon (apo tou kyriou) ho kai paredoka humin.*
1 Cor 15.3: *paredoka humin (en protois) ho kai parelabon.*

The reversed pairing indicates an intended correlation of the two passages. Paul received the primitive tradition, "the 'kerygmatic' formula" (*la formule "kerygmatique"*) both directly from the Lord and from the other apostles. Some modern exegetes have opined that the facts of the life of Jesus came to Paul by human mediation while their theological interpretation came from God, but the kerygmatic formula of 1 Cor 15:1–11 treats the tradition as both coming from the other apostles and directly from the Lord. Apparently, Paul received the gospel directly from Christ but also partially through the apostles. He "received" the information regarding the various other resurrection appearances from those particular eyewitnesses but also from Christ Himself.

Yet Gal 1:12, where Paul denies that he received the gospel "from man" (*para anthropou*), requires an accounting. Cullmann notes that the reference to the tradition "of men" is consistently negative in the New Testament, even in Paul. In Col 2:6–8, Paul sets the tradition that the church received from Jesus Christ, "the Lord" (*ton kyrion*), over against the tradition "of men" (*ton anthropon*). This opposition between the tradition of the Lord (through the apostles) and the tradition of men (cp. 1 Thess 2:13) allows Paul to correlate the teaching of Jesus regarding false tradition with a necessary role for the transmission of the true tradition of Jesus Christ by the apostles. The apostolic community's testimony, which in its entirety constitutes the Christian tradition, is the only place in which the Lord

---

pounded by the imperfections of readers and the imperfections introduced by intermediaries. This is a common problem among modern biblical theologians.

[106] "Mais le Seigneur élevé à la droite de Dieu; ce serait lui le veritable agent de toute la tradition qui se développe sein de l'Eglise apostolique."

Himself is at work.[107] Paul was an apostle according to the classic definition of someone who had received a direct commission from the resurrected Christ (cp. Paul's Damascus road calling), yet he was apparently dependent upon the other apostles for his knowledge of the deeds and teachings of the preresurrection incarnate Christ. It was in the apostles corporately that the ascended Lord directly worked through His Holy Spirit to create the true Christian tradition.

The comprehensive promise of communication made by Christ regarding the Paraclete in John 14:26 and 16:13 was directed to the apostles. The Holy Spirit whom the Father would send in the name of Christ would teach them all things, specifically everything He had taught the apostles. By extension, this included Paul, an apostle who did not follow the preresurrection Christ. The apostolic tradition is created by Christ working directly upon the apostles through the Holy Spirit. "*The transmission by the apostles is not a transmission worked by men, but by Christ the Lord himself who communicates this revelation in this particular way*."[108] Cullmann is careful to define this tradition as involving the entire apostolic community rather than any individual apostle. The Holy Spirit works directly upon and through the apostles in such a way that there is no contrast between the Spirit and the apostles who transmit the gospel of Jesus Christ, but it must be remembered that the Spirit is not restricted to the apostles alone in the new covenant, though He restricted Himself to the prophets in the old covenant. The Spirit has come upon the entire church at Pentecost, not just upon the apostles (and we might extend Cullmann by noting the Spirit is certainly not restricted to the clerical and academic elites today).

In his second chapter Cullmann takes up the relationship between Scripture and tradition, "tradition" being understood in its modern theological sense as a distinct source of theological authority. He argues that the tradition embodied in Scripture is uniquely the tradition of the apostolate, which must not be confused with postapostolic developments. He begins by building on his magisterial work regarding Christ and time.[109] The history of salvation has a past, a present, and a future, but the center of all history is found in the direct revelation of God in Christ. From approximately the beginning of the common era to AD 70 or 80, or from the birth of Christ to the death of the last apostle, there was a direct revelation of God. The apostles commissioned by Christ continued His revelation through their oral and written testimony. The testimony of the apostles was fixed upon their passing. This period, "the years of revelation" (*les années de la revelation*), is "the center and norm of the totality of time" (*le centre et la norme de la totalité du Temps*) not just for sacred history but for profane history, too.

In the intermediate time between His first and second comings, the church prolongs the central time in which Christ is incarnate. Developing further an idea

[107] "C'est seulement le témoignage réuni de tous les apôtres qui constitue la paradosis chrétienne dan laquelle le Kyrios lui-même est à l'œuvre."

[108] His emphasis: "*La transmission par les apôtres n'est pas une transmission opérée par des hommes, mais par le Christ, le Seigneur lui-même qui communiqué cette revelation de cette manière-là*."

[109] Cullmann, *Christ and Time: The Primitive Christian Conception of Time and History*, trans. Floyd V. Filson (London: SCM, 1951).

already propounded by Marpeck, who considered the church to be the "unglorified body of Christ,"[110] Cullmann correlated yet distinguished between Christ and the church. "That is to say that the time of the church prolongs the central time, but it is not itself the central time: it prolongs the time of Christ incarnate, but it is not the time of Christ incarnate and of His apostolic eyewitnesses. The church is structured on the foundation of the apostles; [and] she continues to be structured on the foundation from which she exists; but she may not produce more apostles in the present time."[111] Because the New Testament teaches such, Cullmann is ready to identify the revelatory authority of the apostles with that of Christ, but he is unwilling to grant the same authority to the postapostolic church. The ministers of the church today follow the apostles in transmitting the tradition of Christ, but the apostles bear a "direct testimony" (*témoignage direct*) to Christ while the church bears a "*derived* testimony" (*témoignage* dérivé).[112]

Harking back to the previous chapter, he notes that the apostolic tradition is the only normative tradition because it is the tradition of Christ and not of men. In his high priestly prayer, Christ Himself distinguished three related entities involved in the future process of transmitting the Gospel: Christ, the apostles, and the postapostolic church. "I do not pray for these alone, but also for those who will believe in me through their word" (John 17:20). The church, "those who believe in me through [the apostles'] word," is built upon the foundation of Christ and the apostles, and that foundation as revelation is limited in time to the beginning of the church. Because the process of transmission is subject to the introduction of human error, the apostolic witness was necessarily put into writing. Putting the apostolic witness in writing is intended "to *reduce to the minimum* its deformation by the human element" (*pour* réduire au minimum *sa deformation par l'élément humain*).[113] Although we would disagree with Cullmann's ascription of error to the writings of the apostles, his point is well taken that the human element in postapostolic tradition may and has often led to the deformation of the Christian tradition.

Because of the human introduction of error, God assigned to the apostles the task of fixing the revelation (*la fixation de la revelation*) in writing. Because Christ reveals Himself directly to and through the apostles, and this revelation has been stabilized in their writings, we may say that Christ the Lord "*is present*"[114] in their writings. As a result, the believer can no longer look at the biblical writings as merely ancient historical documents. In these books the Holy Spirit enables them to look directly "in the face of Christ" (*en face du Christ*). As a result of the "real presence" (*la presence realle*) of the apostolic witness to the

[110] Marpeck, *A Clear and Useful Instruction*, 81.

[111] "C'est dire que le Temps de l'Eglise prolonge le temps central, mais qu'il n'est pas le temps central: il prolonge le temps du Christ incarné et de ses apôtres-témoins oculaires. L'Eglise est bâtie sur le fondement des apôtres, elle continuera à être bâtie sur ce fondement tant qu'elle existera, mais elle ne peut plus produire, dans le temps present, des apôtres."

[112] His emphasis.

[113] His emphasis.

[114] His emphasis: "*est present*."

church in the New Testament, the church must constantly "return to the sources" (*retour aux sources*) of its faith. This presence of Christ to the church through the presence of the apostolic witness in writing implies that "the theological method" (*la méthode théologique*) of the church is "the scriptural principle" (*la principe scripturaire*).[115]

Cullmann, not limiting inspiration by the Holy Spirit to the apostles, believes that the Holy Spirit continues to inspire the church because He is the Spirit of truth. He is also willing to say that revelation continues but categorizes such revelation as nonnormative. The language of "illumination" is an appropriate alternative to Cullmann's two distinct definitions of both "inspiration" and "revelation," which too easily create confusion. Cullmann sees Scripture as the superior norm, even the sufficient norm, which was designed to control the present action of the Holy Spirit in the church. "*God speaks to the church today through the testimony of the apostles* [which is] a *sufficient norm*."[116] The norm that is Scripture is an authoritative norm precisely because it may no longer grow. Unfortunately the Roman Catholic Church made their *magisterium* a norm in the place of Scripture. This enabled them to create a doctrine not on the basis of Scripture but of the consensus of the church.[117]

In response, Roman Catholics argue that the Scripture must necessarily be interpreted and offer the *magisterium* as the necessarily official interpreter. However Cullmann notes, neither the necessity of interpretation nor the errors of individual interpreters are sufficient theological justification for creating an extrabiblical *magisterium*. Rather, to be consistent with Scripture, only Scripture may interpret Scripture. Later, in his conclusion, Cullmann claims that God Himself interprets Scripture by being present in it. "The presence of the Lord in Scripture—the presence of the Holy Spirit in the reader who believes."[118] Certainly extrabiblical tradition may serve modern exegetes loosely as a guide, but it may never serve as a norm nor as a criterion. If the church were to require any norm other than Scripture, it would repeat the error of the rabbinic tradition, which is what Jesus condemned in the first place (Mark 7:9). Falling back on what we previously called "pneumatic exegesis," Cullmann ends the chapter thus: "*The Holy Spirit interprets Scripture, but at the same time he is controlled by it*."[119]

In chapter 1, Cullmann identified the apostolic tradition as the revelation of the ascended Lord. In chapter 2, he identified the writings of the apostles as a unique revelation. In chapter 3, he considers the theological meaning of the establishment of the canon. In recognizing the canon, the church simultaneously recognized a difference between apostolic tradition and ecclesiastical tradition. In the second

[115] Reflecting his humanist commitment, Cullmann connects the Scripture principle with the scientific method. Reflecting his Protestant commitment, he defends the idea that the sacraments are miraculous without assigning the Roman magistracy a similar extrabiblical authority.

[116] His emphasis: "*Dieu parle à l'Eglise d'aujourd'hui par le témoignage des apôtres* . . . une *norme suffisante*."

[117] Cullmann alludes to the 1950 promulgation regarding the heavenly assumption of Mary.

[118] "Présence du Kyrios dans l'Ecriture—presence du Saint-Esprit dan le lecteur qui croit."

[119] His emphasis: "*Le Saint-Esprit interprète l'Ecriture, mais en meme temps il est contrôle par elle*."

century, the church was challenged by Gnosticism, which claimed access to a secret tradition. In response, the church came to realize that the apostolic tradition had been fixed by the apostles in oral and written form, but the emphasis must be upon the written form. In recognizing the canon, the church also recognized that the *magisterium* of the church was insufficient on its own to preserve the purity of the gospel against subversive challenges.

The authority of the canon comes not by reason of the church's authority but because the books in the canon "imposed themselves on the church by their intrinsic apostolic authority."[120] In the same way Christ speaks through them today, indicating their canonical authority to every generation. Although the canon is an act of ecclesiastical tradition, it is merely a human recognition of the fact that the books are divinely authorized. Cullmann uses a number of related ideas to indicate the authority of the canon: "control," "superior norm," "superior criterion," "codified," "alone apostolic," and "sufficient norm." Cullmann notes that the second-century church engaged in an act of humility when it submitted itself to a norm, but the church was motivated to do so by God. "It was precisely at this moment that the grace to recognize the difference between the time of the incarnation and the time of the church was accorded to the church."[121] Moreover, by humbly recognizing the unique authority of the apostles of the New Testament (and of the Old Testament which prepared for Christ) when fixing the canon, the church abandoned all pretensions to infallibility.

Cullmann concludes that the apostolic "rule of faith" was definitively fixed at about the same time as the canon of the apostolic writings was fixed. The rule of faith seems roughly identifiable with the Old Roman Creed, the forerunner of the Apostles' Creed. The attribution of each phrase in that creed to one of the apostles is legendary, but the creed was formed from the New Testament itself. Cullmann develops this idea elsewhere, but he is not alone in such a contention. Ultimately Cullmann's little book is important because it takes the New Testament viewpoint regarding tradition as the basis for a historico-theological understanding of both apostolic tradition and ecclesiastical tradition. While Protestants have too often focused only on the negative words of Jesus regarding tradition, Roman Catholics have too often focused only on the positive words of Paul. Cullmann offers, instead of the Catholic perspective or the Protestant perspective, the New Testament's own subtle message regarding itself as the fixed aspect of tradition distinct from the church's developing understanding of it.

Developing the Tradition

Cullmann's thesis did not go unchallenged. Yves Congar, a subtle and highly influential Roman Catholic theologian, responded to Cullmann. A *peritus* at the Second Vatican Council, Congar understood the two-source theory of Trent in as scriptural a sense as possible. He disagreed with the *partim . . . partim* interpretation

[120] His emphasis: "*se sont imposes à l'Eglise leur autorité apostolique intrinsique*."

[121] "C'est à ce moment précis que Dieu a accordé à l'Eglise la grace de reconnaître la difference entre le temps de l'incarnation et le temps de l'Eglise."

of Trent that divided Scripture and tradition into two separate sources because it implied the insufficiency of Scripture. He preferred, rather, to say that "the saving Gospel is contained entirely in the Scriptures," while he affirmed it also resided in tradition.[122]

Subsequently, in his major work on tradition, Congar moved back toward the conservative Catholic position. "Scripture is the norm of our faith only when conjoined to the Church and her tradition." In other words, Scripture is "the supreme rule," but it may not be considered "sufficient" on its own. The apostolicity of the church is in the Scriptures, but it is also in "the succession of presbyters and bishops." In other words, Scripture is sufficient only insofar as it is interpreted with the Roman hierarchy. Displaying a typical lacuna in Roman apologetics, Congar offered no biblical support for his critique of Cullmann.[123] Congar, perhaps the most prominent lay-oriented theologian in the twentieth-century Roman church, in the end always returned to the "superiority" of the clerical priesthood.[124]

Even so, Congar did offer a biblical basis for his idea that tradition continues its development in the life of the church. His favorite texts were the Paraclete sayings of John 14–16, supported by the phenomenological evidence of the concurrency of Spirit and Christian witness in the book of Acts. From the perspective of a doctrine of development, the Johannine Paraclete texts must be considered.[125] This raises the issue of what Jesus meant by His promise regarding the Spirit of truth who would guide the church into all truth. Was this truth restricted to only a few? How would the church come to know this truth? And would there be more truth revealed to the church than that revealed to the apostles? The answer to these questions may come with a review of the Johannine Paraclete sayings with special attention given to his role as "the Spirit of truth" (*to pneuma tes aletheias*). The expression is probably best understood as "the Spirit who communicates truth."[126]

In the first Paraclete saying, John 14:16–17, Jesus promised the disciples that He would not leave them alone when He left. Answering Christ's prayer, the Father would send the Spirit to abide with them forever. The world will not know who the Spirit is, but the disciples will know Him "for He dwells with you and will be in you." The only criterion the disciples are here given for knowing the Spirit is the abiding and internal presence of the Spirit. Paul agrees with John that the epistemological evidence of the saving presence of the Spirit is the witness of the Holy Spirit with the human spirit (Rom 8:16). Moreover, according to Peter, in fulfillment of Joel's prophecy, the Spirit came upon the entire gathered church at Pentecost.

---

[122] Yves Congar, *The Meaning of Tradition*, 42–43.

[123] Congar, *Tradition and Traditions*, 38–42.

[124] Aidan Nichols, *Yves Congar* (London: Geoffrey Chapman, 1989), 63–95; Congar, "Respect for the Apostolate of the Laity among Priests and Religious," in *Christians Active in the World*, trans. P. J. Hepburne-Scott (New York: Herder & Herder, 1968), 3–28; idem, *Jalons pour une Théologie du Laïcat* (Paris: Éditions du Cerf, 1953).

[125] Congar, *The Meaning of Tradition*, 53; idem, *Tradition and Traditions*, 15–17.

[126] Leon Morris, *The Gospel according to John*, rev. ed., NICNT (Grand Rapids: Eerdmans, 1995), 577.

The Spirit came not only upon the select judge or prophet, as in the Old Testament, but upon every believer, male and female, young and old, and the servants (Acts 2:14–21). The indwelling presence of the Spirit is for all believers, who must receive external baptism as a cowitness to their repentance and internal reception of the Spirit (Acts 2:38). One cannot be counted among the redeemed without the Spirit's indwelling (Rom 8:9–11). The "Spirit of truth" then is for the entire church (cp. 1 Cor 12:13). Indeed, Paul would not countenance any claim that the Spirit or the Word was anything but the church's shared possession (1 Cor 14:36; 2 Cor 4:13; 12:18; 1 Thess 4:8).

The church's knowledge of the true faith was described in terms of a common mind of Christ brought about by the church's common possession of the Holy Spirit. Paul hoped that he might hear of the Philippian church, "that you stand fast in one spirit, with one mind striving together for the faith of the gospel" (Phil 1:27). He explained to the Corinthians that their knowledge of God was enabled by the Spirit's work, understood as a collective possession: "We have the mind of Christ" (1 Cor 2:16). The wisdom of God is not available to those who abide in this age. Rather, the wisdom of God in Christ is made available by the internal work of the Holy Spirit to those who abide in Christ (1 Cor 2:11–13). Christian epistemology is dependent on the work of the Holy Spirit and results in truly knowing Christ. The Spirit of truth must work within a man for him to understand the things of God. The unbeliever cannot understand the Word of God because he lacks the Spirit of God (1 Cor 2:14). While the apostles had the direct witness of Christ to open up the meaning of the Scriptures (Luke 24:27,32), the church must rely on the direct witness of the Spirit regarding the meaning of the Bible.

In the second Paraclete saying, John 14:26, Jesus gave more detail regarding how the Spirit guides the church into truth: "He will teach you all things and bring to your remembrance all things that I said to you." The first clause may be taken as a reference to the sufficiency of the Spirit's teaching. The second clause is obviously restricted to the preresurrection disciples. The apostles were to be led by the Spirit in their proclamation of the teaching of Jesus Christ. The Spirit led the apostles to remember what Jesus said, which after the resurrection took on its deepest meaning. Beasley-Murray refers to two specific illustrations of such memory in the Gospel of John (2:19; 12:16). In narrowing the Spirit's ministry of teaching to remembrance of Christ's words, "It is clear that the Spirit brings no new revelation."[127] The teachings of Christ renewed in the apostles' memories by the Holy Spirit were subsequently written down in the books contained in the New Testament.

The third Paraclete saying, John 15:26–27, has normally been discussed in connection with the debate between East and West over the *filioque* addition to the Nicene-Constantinopolitan Creed regarding the personal procession of the Holy Spirit. Although the ontological Trinity is a critical issue, and this text is vital for a proper understanding of the relation of the Holy Spirit therein, the focus of the

[127] George R. Beasley-Murray, *John*, WBC (Waco, TX: Word Books, 1987), 261.

passage is on the Spirit and the disciples as cowitnesses. The Spirit will testify of Christ, and the disciples are to bear witness, too. The fact that the apostles have been with Christ "from the beginning" again calls for a primary application of this passage to the establishment of the apostolic tradition. The confluent witnesses of the apostles and of the Spirit are mutually necessary. "At the same time it is *their* [the apostles'] witness. They cannot simply relax and leave it all to the Spirit. . . . But the really significant witness is that of the Holy Spirit, for he alone can bring home to people's hearts the truth and the significance of the truth."[128] Pilgram Marpeck's doctrine of *mitzeugnis* extends this primary application to the ecclesiastical tradition (cp. 1 John 5:6–9).

The final Paraclete saying(s), John 16:5–15 (or, 16:5–11 and 12–15), concerns the truth-revealing work of the Holy Spirit in the world and in believers. In verses 5–11, Jesus discusses how the Spirit will function as an advocate of truth to the world. He has a threefold ministry of conviction to the world: of sin as unbelief, of righteousness as belonging to Christ, and of judgment upon the world and the devil. If verses 5–11 concern the Spirit's work "in the world," Leon Morris says verses 12–13 concern the Spirit's work "in believers." Donald Carson, a Reformed theologian, however, is adamant that the passage primarily applies to the apostles: "The emphasis is so transparently on the first witnesses." Further betraying his evangelical presuppositions, Carson then immediately separates Christian discipleship from Christ Himself, making discipleship one of many "subsidiary themes."

Carson's transparent sight is not so apparent to other exegetes, perhaps because Carson is blinded by his presuppositions. Moreover, it is difficult to see how one can separate Christian consideration of Christ from Christian discipleship to Christ, except in the bifurcated world of evangelical rationalism.[129] Douglas Kennard, another modern evangelical, denies this text concerns the Spirit's illumination of the text. Kennard argues that interpretation is entirely a human work and categorically denies the Spirit's illumination of the biblical text. Kennard, however, fails to consider 2 Pet 1:20–21, which makes clear that interpretation is not a private human matter, just as the Spirit inspired the prophets.[130] In an interesting twist, believers' church commentators, alongside some evangelical commentators, do not severely limit this last Paraclete saying to the apostles. Carson's Reformed commitments have colored his commentary in such a way that the text's restrictive "transparency" is not recognizable by exegetes investigating the same text.

[128] Morris, *The Gospel according to John*, 607.

[129] Donald A. Carson, *The Gospel according to John*, PNTC (Grand Rapids: Eerdmans, 1991), 541–42 (cp. 505, 529–30). Carson is affiliated with the Evangelical Free Church of America, which embraces an ecumenical and evangelical theological paradigm in doctrine and polity. A recent proposal for the church's statement of faith removes their commitment to congregationalism. Evangelical Free Church of America, "Second Draft Revision of the Statement of Faith"; available from http://www.efca.org/about/media/sof_second_draft_revision.pdf ; accessed 24 January 2007.

[130] Kennard also fails to recognize the longer history of the doctrine of illumination, rooting it in Pietism rather than the Reformation. Douglas Kennard, "Evangelical Views on Illumination of Scripture and Critique," *JETS* 49 (2006): 797–806.

Morris, an Anglican, notes that the audience here is "believers" in general. "The Spirit is called 'the Spirit of truth,' for his work here is to guide the followers of Jesus into 'all truth.' As the days go by, the Spirit will lead them deeper and deeper." Beasley-Murray, a British Baptist, went further: "It was surely part of the Evangelist's intention to make it plain that the Paraclete who illumined the minds of those about Jesus continues the same ministry in the church, that the revelation in Christ may constantly be freshly perceived and powerfully expressed." Gerald L. Borchert, a Southern Baptist, retained but softened Carson's Reformed restriction. Summarizing all of the Paraclete passages, he concluded the message was "intended primarily for the anxiety filled disciples who knew Jesus firsthand and were troubled by his imminent departure. But John was not writing merely for the first group of disciples. His intention was that this fivefold message concerning the Paraclete would have continuing implication for his own readers and, therefore, derivatively for us today. The divine resource of the Spirit is the gift Jesus sent from the Father to Christian disciples."[131] E. Earle Ellis, a Southern Baptist biblical theologian with Reformed leanings, perceives the various Paraclete sayings as arguing against clerical elitism in favor of the Spirit's activity within the entire church. "No Christian is more 'in' Him than another. The Holy Spirit is given to all and is the disciple's true teacher. Therefore each Christian has the responsibility to judge or test any other Christian who exercises a ministry or place of leadership."[132]

Answering the division among commentators regarding the application of especially the last Paraclete saying is critical to the believers' church theological method, especially with regard to the development of doctrine. Modern Reformed commentators restrict the Spirit's guidance to the apostles. Believers' church and other exegetes recognize the continuing ministry of the Holy Spirit whom Jesus promised would "guide you into all truth" (16:13). If one downplays the Spirit's guidance of the church into a deeper understanding of the truth, the temptation will be to look to the rationalism of the academic elite for proper exegesis rather than praying for the Spirit to illumine the Scripture to the entire church. Although the doctrine of illumination may be conceptually affirmed, the Spirit's work of illumination is often ignored in the evangelical academy's practice of scientistic exegesis and is not consistently applied in Reformed systematics. For the believers' church exegetes, the Spirit's work of "insight" or "illumination" or "communication" is central, although they are careful to state that there is no further "revelation" distinct from Jesus Christ.[133]

It is also highly instructive that the Reformed commentators reflect negatively upon discipleship while the believers' church exegetes appeal to discipleship as integral to the Christian discernment of truth. Finally, it should be recognized

[131] Morris, *The Gospel according to John*, 621; Beasley-Murray, *John*, 290; Gerald L. Borchert, *John 12–21*, NAC (Nashville: Broadman & Holman, 2002), 171. Cp. George R. Beasley-Murray, *Gospel of Life: Theology in the Fourth Gospel* (Peabody, MA: Hendricksen, 1991), 78.

[132] E. Earle Ellis, *The World of St. John: The Gospel and Epistles* (Grand Rapids: Eerdmans, 1984), 44–45.

[133] Morris, *The Gospel according to John*, 620–22; Beasley-Murrary, *John*, 277, 284; Borchert, *John 12–21*, 132, 160, 168–69.

that the final Paraclete saying expands upon the truth of Christocentrism within a trinitarian framework. Morris says, "The work of the Spirit is Christocentric. He will draw attention not to himself but to Christ." And yet Christocentrism need not undermine the doctrine of the Trinity, for there may be "no division in the Godhead." Reflecting the Christocentric Trinitarianism of the Johannine text, Beasley-Murray remarks, "It is to be presumed *the one revelation of God in Christ* is the content of that which the Spirit is to convey to the disciples."[134]

In summary, the same central theme and four aspects found in the believers' church theological foundation are evident in the scriptural doctrine of development: The Christian disciple submits to the will of Jesus Christ revealed in the Scripture illuminated by the Holy Spirit as it is read with the entire church. Although the revelation is affixed to the Bible, its illumination by the Spirit is dynamic in that it is not limited to previous perceptions. And yet there should also be a deep respect for the work of the one Spirit in the entire history of the churches of the one Christ, a truth not always adequately accounted for among the free churches.

FROM APOSTOLIC PATTERN TO CHURCH DOGMA

To speak of an apostolic pattern of teaching is not to deny the personal nature of Christian faith; to speak of Christian faith and discipleship as the foundation of theology is not to deny the propositional nature of doctrine. The personal and the propositional, in spite of the modern (and postmodern or postliberal) tendency to separate the two, are best seen as united.[135] The etymological history of the New Testament word for "pattern" (*tupos*) may be helpful here. In nonbiblical Greek, a *tupos* was an impression created by a blow, a form created by a stamp, or a mold that creates an example. In the New Testament one of the word's more important uses is "teaching as a mold or norm," used in Rom 6:17—"the pattern of teaching [*tupon didaches*]"—and in a related form in 2 Tim 1:13—"the pattern of sound words [*hupotuposin echehugiainonton logon*]."[136]

It is noteworthy that this pattern of communicable concepts is received with salvation and continues to be vitally related to Christian discipleship. Paul orders Timothy to hold on to the pattern of the words "in the faith and love which are in Christ Jesus" (2 Tim 1:13). Paul reminds the Romans that their acceptance of the pattern occurred when they transitioned from slavery to sin and that they should

[134] Morris, *The Gospel according to John*, 622; Beasley-Murray, *John*, 283; Borchert, *John 12–21*, 171.

[135] The postliberal movement in theology drives an untenable wedge between the warring tendencies of modern theology, "cognitive-propositionalism" and "experiential-expressivism," in order to set up a particularist view of language communities, "cultural-linguistic," as the only viable alternative. Although the concept is subtle and perhaps fruitful, its basis in a straw man argument undermines its validity. George A. Lindbeck, *The Nature of Doctrine: Religion and Theology in a Postliberal Age* (Philadelphia: Westminster, 1984), 16.

[136] *Tupos* is also used to describe the wounds created in the body of Jesus put forward to the apostles as marks of identity (John 20:25). Paul and Peter used the word to describe the apostle or the church or the minister as an example or model of the obedience of faith (Phil 3:17; 1 Thess 1:7; 2 Thess 3:9; 1 Tim 4:12; Titus 2:7; 1 Pet 5:3). A third use of the word or its cognate is as a hermeneutical term for relating the Old and New Testaments (Rom 5:14; 1 Cor 10:6,11; 1 Pet 3:21). A fourth use is to describe the heavenly original of the tabernacle (Acts 7:44; Heb 8:5). Leonhard Goppelt, "*Tupos, antitupos*, [etc.]," *TDNT*, 8:246–59.

continue to be obedient to that pattern (Rom 6:17). The pattern of the gospel both creates an imprint and reflects an imprint. The making of a disciple includes the instrumentality of a definite teaching and results in a cognitive understanding of that teaching. The making of a disciple occurs when God, through a powerful blow by His Spirit, unites a believer with Christ. This divine movement in the human heart creates an impression in the human head that may be formed into words and disseminated. Those words were the very words used instrumentally to bring about the impression in the first place.

But what is the apostolic pattern of teaching? Where is it written down? How can it be encapsulated? Is the "pattern" of which Paul speaks identifiable in the New Testament? Does the pattern create examples in the New Testament writings that then allow us to reconstruct the original mold from which these examples came? The attempt to reconstruct the core or center or kernel of New Testament truth, the gospel itself, is filled with fruitful possibilities and fraught with grave difficulties.

A Perilous Necessity

On the one hand, it is necessary to distinguish between the central principle of biblical tradition and what is derived from it. A New Testament scholar can write, "The whole problem of Scriptural exposition depends on this distinction."[137] Words have meanings, but those words must be arranged into the proper sequence and given the proper emphasis in order to allow communication to occur properly. Every systematic theologian knows this to be true as well, for the system he adopts ultimately shapes the very truth he is seeking to communicate. The Bible preacher also realizes that he must emphasize one thing in order to communicate correctly, and that one thing must be clearly seen. Thus, the responsible Christian theologian may not forsake the task of identifying the center and pattern of the biblical message.

On the other hand, the attempt to identify the center of Christianity is filled with peril. The entire Word of God is without error and intentionally given; thus, every word must be accounted for in the attempt to identify the center and describe the circumference of Christian truth (2 Tim 3:16). This massive task is simply impossible for one theologian, for one church, for one seminary, and, I would argue, even for Christians throughout all time, past, present, and future. The Bible is a rich vein of gold that cannot be completely mined. The truth of God Himself, which we shall fully see only in eternity, is so great that Scripture uses the terminology of "light" to describe it (Rev 21:23–24). We will be engulfed by God's light, a light that cannot be contained in its totality by any concept of our own making. His thoughts are greater than our thoughts (Isa 55:8–9), and what He has already revealed is to be searched out and discovered (Acts 17:11), but we should be biblically humble enough to know that none of us individually, or even corporately, may claim to understand it all.

[137] Oscar Cullmann, *The Earliest Christian Confessions*, trans. J. K. S. Reid (London: Lutterworth, 1949), 11.

Historically, there have been attempts to reconstruct the center or core or essence of Christianity. In the seventeenth century Protestant Scholastics developed a movement that attempted to downplay distinctions and return to a minimal definition of the true faith. They distinguished between fundamental and nonfundamental articles of faith. The nonfundamental articles were marginal themes such as the reason for the fall of angels or whether the end of the world is essential or accidental. This resulted in the need for a further distinction between primary fundamental articles and secondary fundamental articles. The resulting division of theology into a tripartite hierarchy had a devastating impact, for it could lead close definitions into absurdity.[138]

The Enlightenment also encouraged Protestant theology to liquefy itself. As a result of the earlier ecumenical attempts, theological distinctions were played down in favor of an irreducible minimum of the Trinity and Christology as defined by the early councils. But after the classic doctrines became the irreducible minimum, the lowest common denominator, then the classical doctrines, too, came under assault. Finally, as previously noted, Adolf Harnack, in his search for the "kernel" of Christianity, dismissed classical orthodoxy as the mere "Hellenization" of Christianity. All doctrinal development was corruption in Harnack's view. Original sin, the devil, and the atonement, among other doctrines, were thus opened to critical revision. According to Nicholas Lash, "few programmes have proved more seductive during the last century and a half than the search for the 'essence' or 'leading idea' of christianity. When such a programme is announced in terms of organic analogies, the search is on for christianity's originating 'seed' or 'germ.'" In response, Newman correctly perceived that the divine nature of the center of Christianity meant that it was ultimately mysterious and must be treated with reverence at the same time that it received dogmatic definition.[139]

The transition from Protestant scholasticism to Protestant liberalism was a largely seamless affair. One key issue historically was that evangelical theologians came to understand the mediation of faith as merely "theoretical statement" (*satzhafter Aussagen*). Since doctrine was also separated from the average Christian's life through complex theoretical argumentation, theological differentiation contributed to "a pronounced academic, doctrinal understanding of the faith" (*einem ausgeprägt lehrhaften, doktrinalen Verständnis des Glaubens*). More recently, manifesting a new ecumenism, the Roman Catholic Church also toyed with the idea at Vatican II, under the rubric of a "hierarchy of truths." Some Southern Baptists have offered similar ideas under the rubric of "theological triage."[140]

[138] "Die Distinktion zwischen fundamentalen und nichtfundamentalen Glaubensartikeln führt sich durch die inhaltliche Näherbestimmung selbst ad absurdum." Honecker, *Glaube als Grund christlicher Theologie*, 131.
[139] Lash, *Newman on Development*, 137.
[140] Justo L. Gonzalez, *A History of Christian Thought*, rev. ed. (Nashville: Abingdon, 1987), 3:256–60; Honecker, *Glaube als Grund christlicher Theologie*, 130–32; "Decree on Ecumenism," 11, in *Vatican Council II*, 462; R. Albert Mohler Jr., "First-person: A Call for Theological Triage and Christian Maturity" (Nashville: Baptist Press, 23 August 2006); available from http://www.baptistpress.com/bpnews.asp?ID=23842 ; accessed 26 October 2006.

With the dangers of the irreducible minimum and the reduction to the absurd in mind, Christians still, however, have felt it necessary to define the simple pattern of the gospel. This pattern, or "impression" as Newman would call it, is the dogmatic reflection of divine revelation. It is from this pattern that the remainder of the scriptural witness might perhaps then be considered, but any "pattern" for Christian theology should be the pattern suggested in Scripture, not a pattern imposed upon Scripture. The pattern must come from Scripture, and it should also seek to reflect directly the pattern suggested by Scripture. It is insufficient to adopt just any Scripture teaching and claim that it provides the pattern for the entirety of Christian theological discourse.

The problem is that any particular doctrine chosen as central by human fiat (e.g., the doctrine of election) must often be supplemented by philosophical ruminations or traditional categories lacking a revelatory basis. Christian systematicians necessarily use categories or loci to organize their reflections on Scripture, but they should never do so without explicit self-criticism. The problem comes when the adopted pattern owes more to the Christian speculations of Peter Lombard or Philip Melanchthon or John Calvin or Francis Turretin or J. N. Darby or Charles Hodge or George Lindbeck than to the pattern suggested by Scripture. This becomes an even more severe problem when the humanly derived categories masquerade as divinely sanctioned tests of orthodoxy and fellowship.

The beauty of Pilgram Marpeck's thought is that he fought through to a theology which, although extremely unsatisfying according to the Aristotelian penchant for categorizing (whether medieval, Protestant scholastic, or Enlightenment in its manifestation), reflects the subtle and beguilingly simple patterns of Scripture itself. Marpeck's respect for the pattern of Scripture drove him toward radical discipleship to Jesus Christ, toward believers-only baptism, toward a New Testament understanding of the Old Testament, and toward the early creeds. As previously noted, Marpeck respected Scripture above all, but he also had a deep concern for the classic definitions provided by the early creeds. Why? Marpeck did not have the resources available to the modern scholar, nor did he even have the education available to the scholars of his day; Marpeck was, after all, a mere layman. But Marpeck's reading of Scripture was so consistent and so thorough that he recognized that the form of the creeds reflected the pattern of Scripture.

Christocentric *Kerygma*

A New Testament theologian, C. H. Dodd, set out to identify the *kerygma*, the preaching of the gospel by the apostles. What was it that Peter and Paul proclaimed? Is there a discernable pattern to their preaching, as recorded in the New Testament? Dodd was careful to note that the biblical record may not be treated as a mine from which to construct an arbitrary pattern. The kerygma is preserved by and conveyed in the New Testament records. The foundation of the kerygma is Jesus Christ Himself and His cross (1 Cor 3:10). The Christocentric nature of the apostolic preaching has long been recognized by scholars of many stripes, including Oscar Cullmann and J. N. D. Kelly, who, as we shall see, vigorously disagreed over the importance of the Trinity.

Important Pauline passages that conveyed the basic witness of the early church include 1 Cor 15:3–11, as well as Rom 1:1–4; 8:31–34; and 10:8–9. (Indeed, it would behoove every Christian preacher to memorize these passages and constantly refer to them in their preaching, for they summarize well the gospel!) Based upon his critical research into the Pauline corpus, although he unfortunately set aside the important Christological confessions in the Pastoral Epistles (cp. 1 Tim 2:5–7; 3:16; 6:13–14; 2 Tim 4:1) and strangely bypassed the ancient Christological hymn of Phil 2:5–11, Dodd summarized the Pauline kerygma as follows:

- The prophecies are fulfilled, and the new Age is inaugurated by the coming of Christ.
- He was born of the seed of David.
- He died according to the Scripture, to deliver us out of the present evil age.
- He was buried.
- He rose on the third day according to the Scriptures.
- He is exalted at the right hand of God, as Son of God and Lord of quick [living] and dead.
- He will come again as Judge and Saviour of men.[141]

In order to reconstruct the primitive preaching of the leading apostle, Dodd turned to Peter's sermons recorded in the first part of the book of Acts (2:14–36,38–39; 3:12–26; 4:8–12; cp. 5:17–40;10:34–43). Although Dodd noted some distinctions between the preaching of Paul and Peter, he concluded that Peter's preaching is substantially recorded in Paul as well. The search for and presentation of the kerygma have been criticized because the effort tends to result in a merely propositional understanding. This critique may be applied against Dodd; however, Rudolf Bultmann's existential understanding is just as problematic. "For the former [Dodd], the early Christian message consists of a formula of facts and doctrines about God's action in Christ; for the latter [Bultmann], the gospel is itself God's powerful act in which Christ is dynamically present calling men to a decision of faith."[142]

Characteristic of their differing emphases, Dodd interprets the personal way in which Paul presents the gospel in Gal 1:11–17 through the objective listing in 1 Cor 15:3–8, while Bultmann emphasizes the exact opposite. Again, the best solution is not choosing between either a propositional listing of kerygmatic facts or a personal encounter through the kerygma; rather, the kerygma requires both propositional communication and personal decision! According to Dodd, the kerygma of Peter may be summarized in six parts:

[141] Dodd's work, widely influential upon English-speaking theology, is weighted by historical-critical presuppositions. Moreover, he makes an insupportable distinction between *didache* (teaching) and *kerygma* (preaching). C. H. Dodd, *The Apostolic Preaching and Its Developments: Three Lectures with an Appendix on Eschatology and History*, new ed. (London: Hodder and Stoughton, 1963), 17.

[142] William Baird, "What Is the Kerygma? A Study of 1 Cor 15:3–8 and Gal 1:11–17," *JBL* 76 (1957): 183.

- First, the age of fulfillment has dawned.
- Second, this has taken place through the ministry, death, and resurrection of Jesus.
- Third, by virtue of the resurrection, Jesus has been exalted at the right hand of God.
- Fourth, the Holy Spirit in the Church is the sign of Christ's present power and glory.
- Fifth, the Messianic Age will shortly reach its consummation in the return of Christ.
- Finally, the kerygma always closes with an appeal for repentance, the offer of forgiveness and of the Holy Spirit, and the promise of "salvation," that is, of "the life of the Age to Come," to those who enter the elect community.[143]

When Dodd turned to a discussion of the kerygma within the Gospels, he noted the comments of the Muratorian Fragment, a work from the late second century sometimes attributed to Hippolytus. The Muratorian Fragment is mostly known for its early listing of what became known as the canon and the principles of canonical selection implied there.[144] However, the fragment also reflects how the early church viewed the importance of the four Gospels to the Holy Spirit's work of proclaiming the one basic Christological faith through the church. The fact that there were four Gospels that manifested some differences did not detract from the singular work of the Holy Spirit in all of them together. Note also the hints of a trinitarian structure in the fragment's summary of the Christological faith. "Although various principles are taught in the several Gospel-books, this makes no difference to the faith of believers, since by one governing Spirit in them all, the facts are declared concerning the Nativity, the Passion, the Resurrection, His converse with the disciples, and His two advents, the first which was in

[143] Dodd, *The Apostolic Preaching and Its Developments*, 21–24. Reviewing the twentieth-century conversation regarding the kerygma, Drummond outlined ten essential points of the gospel (*euangelion*), which he considered synonymous with the kerygma:

1. Jesus Christ of Nazareth is the fulfillment of Old Testament prophecies concerning the coming of God's salvation through His Messiah.
2. Jesus Christ was incarnated as the Son of God.
3. Jesus lived a sinless, revealing perfect life, doing many glorious miracles.
4. Jesus Christ was crucified on the cross for the sake of the sin of the world.
5. Jesus Christ was raised bodily from the dead, triumphing over sin, death, and hell.
6. Jesus Christ is coming again to usher in the fullness of the kingdom.
7. People are called to repent and believe and to commit their lives to following Christ, as symbolized in baptism.
8. Christians receive the promise of the forgiveness of sins.
9. Christians receive the gift of the Holy Spirit.
10. Christians experience a whole new life.

He also included the "bad news" of human sin and the judgment of hell in his subsequent discussion. Lewis A. Drummond, *The Canvas Cathedral: Billy Graham's Ministry Seen through the History of Evangelism* (Nashville: Thomas Nelson, 2003), 84–95, 105–25.

[144] Johannes Quasten, *Patrology* (1950; repr. Allen, TX: Christian Classics, 1989), 2:207–10.

humility of aspect, according to the power of His royal Father, and the glorious one which is yet to come."[145]

Dodd's focus on the cognitive content of the kerygma must not be taken as an endorsement of the modern separation of doctrinal speculation from the moral life. By means of a detailed study of the early Christian practice of communication, focusing on *propheteia* (prophecy), *paraclesis* (homily), *paraenesis* (moral teaching) and *catechesis* (doctrinal teaching), and *paradosis* (tradition), James McDonald concluded that preaching and teaching were intimately related. Reacting against the cognitive focus of Dodd, McDonald stressed that while the kerygma has content, its dynamic nature must not be denied. As a result, he refused to identify the kerygma with a "list of items" and preferred to stress its context of *koinonia* (fellowship).[146] McDonald also denies that the neat division between *catechesis* and *paraenesis* is a postapostolic development: "Thus *catechesis*, in so far as it represents basic instruction, is properly effective only when it is put to work in the applied area of *paraenesis* and of Christian living and discipleship."[147] The kerygma is personal in that it concerns Jesus Christ and disciplinary in that it concerns His cross (1 Cor 1:23; 2:2).

Trinitarian Identification

Oscar Cullmann, reflecting his evangelical academic perspective, took a curious stand with regard to the development of the earliest Christian confessions.[148] He could not agree with the longstanding scholarship regarding the importance of the New Testament's liturgical witness to the Trinity functioning as confessional terms. Worship and doctrine are sharply divided in his thought. The debate concerns the confessions of Matt 28:19—"baptizing them in the name of the Father and the Son and the Holy Spirit"—and 2 Cor 13:14—"the grace of the Lord Jesus Christ, and the love of God, and the fellowship of the Holy Spirit, be with you all."

Cullmann claimed that such trinitarian declarations in Scripture "have rather a liturgical character, and are not confessions of faith." Again, these Trinitarian declarations exist "independently of the confessions of faith" and, "properly speaking," are not confessions. The New Testament confessions contain only one article, "the dogmatic kernel," the Christological. The basic Christian confession is simply *Kyrios Christos*, "Christ is Lord" (cp. 1 Cor 12:3). The identification of the Christian confession as tripartite is "altogether lacking" in the New Testament and is "a falsification of the perspective" theologically. Bipartite (God and Christ) and tripartite (Father, Son, and Holy Spirit) confessions resulted from Gentiles struggling with paganism and heresy.[149]

[145] Dodd, *The Apostolic Preaching and Its Developments*, 55.

[146] James I. H. McDonald, *Kerygma and Didache: The Articulation and Structure of the Earliest Christian Message* (New York: Cambridge University Press, 1980), 126, 131.

[147] Ibid., 99–100.

[148] D. Lyle Dabney, "Cullmann, Oscar," in *BDCT*, 138–40.

[149] Cullmann, *The Earliest Christian Confessions*, 36n, 38–39, 43–44, 50.

In comparison with his careful work elsewhere, Cullmann's theological exegesis here is inexcusably immature. J. N. D. Kelly, the premiere twentieth-century Anglophone patristics scholar, described Cullmann's theory in uncharacteristically harsh terms as "dangerously misleading." Kelly listed three errors with Cullmann's theory. First, not all binitarian confessions in the New Testament are given in the context of battling paganism (cp. 1 Tim 6:13–14). Second, Cullmann's idea that "one baptism" in the sevenfold affirmation of Eph 4:4 was replaced by the traditional third article, concerning the Holy Spirit, is "farfetched in the extreme and depends upon an ingenious guess." Third, Cullmann, and the few other German scholars who agree with him, "have been mesmerized by the evolutionary axiom that the less complex must always precede the more complex, and that there must be a line of progressive development."[150]

Criticisms of Cullmann's theory could be multiplied. For instance, Cullmann never explains how liturgical formulae are not also confessional formulae. Again, he never explains how confession of faith in Christ is different from confession of faith in God.[151] Again, he summarily dismisses Paul's own claim for the origin of his confession in 1 Corinthians 15, a claim that, as we have seen, Cullmann himself considered in *La Tradition*.[152] Again, Cullmann inexplicably transitions from the basic confession as *Kyrios Iēsous*, a pairing of titles filled with important ramifications for a two-nature Christology as the early fathers recognized, to *Kyrios Christos*, a conflation that does not occur in his central text.[153] Again, he does not discuss the first creed, the *Shema*, that Jesus Himself affirms.[154] Finally, he simply ignores trinitarian passages where the Father and the Spirit appear first.[155] In summary, Cullmann's contribution to the debate over the "essence of Christianity" fails miserably. Although he is correct regarding the Christocentrism of the New Testament, Cullmann exceeds the New Testament in claiming the pattern is "wholly Christological."[156]

The baptism commanded by Jesus Christ was different from the baptism of John the Baptist, a difference not altogether insignificant to the apostles. When Paul encountered disciples who had never heard of the Holy Spirit, he queried

[150] J. N. D. Kelly, *Early Christian Creeds*, 3rd ed. (New York: Longman, 1972), 25–27.

[151] Cullmann, *The Earliest Christian Confessions*, 39.

[152] Ibid., 32.

[153] Cullmann states, "'Jesus Christ is the *Kyrios*' (1 Cor 12:3)." However, the Greek text does not mention *Christos* but simply *Kurios Iesous*. Neither the Aland critical edition nor Metzger's textual commentary mentions alternative readings. *The Greek New Testament*, 3rd ed., ed. Kurt Aland et al (Stuttgart: Biblia-Druck, 1983); Bruce M. Metzger, *A Textual Commentary on the Greek New Testament* (Stuttgart: Biblia-Druck, 1971); Cullmann, *The Earliest Christian Confessions*, 55.

[154] Cp. Deut 6:4; Mark 12:29. Jaroslav Pelikan, *Credo: Historical and Theological Guide to Creeds and Confessions of Faith in the Christian Tradition* (New Haven, CN: Yale University Press, 2003), 130.

[155] Ibid., 39. Of nine occurrences where the three persons appear together in the same New Testament text, the Father appears first twice, the Son appears first thrice, and the Spirit appears first five times. Using Cullmann's logic, we would have to affirm Pneumatocentrism. The argument itself is flawed, however, for the three always work together. Moreover, other texts make clear that the Father is the source of the Trinity. Although we may claim Christ is the focus of the New Testament witness, so that we may speak of "Christocentrism," each of the three persons is equally due Christian worship as the one God. James Leo Garrett Jr., *Systematic Theology: Biblical, Historical, and Evangelical*, 2nd ed. (North Richland Hills, TX: BIBAL, 2000–2001), 1:314.

[156] Cullmann, *The Earliest Christian Confessions*, 64.

them with regard to their baptism. John's baptism did not identify a "disciple" as a disciple of Jesus. True Christian baptism requires a prior personal commitment to Jesus Christ and prior genuine regeneration by the Holy Spirit (Acts 19:1–6). Although Luke often spoke of baptism "in the name of the Lord Jesus" (Acts 8:16; 19:5) or "in the name of Jesus Christ" (2:38; 10:48), baptism was always preceded by or accompanied the reception of the Holy Spirit (2:38; 8:16–17; 10:47; 19:6).

True Christian baptism, even in the book of Acts, is never apart from the person of the Holy Spirit. Luke's various names for baptism concern events subsequent to the preascension granting of the Great Commission by Jesus Christ in Matthew 28 and must therefore be seen as shorthand terms for distinguishing Christian baptism from non-Christian baptism (cp. 1 Cor 1:13). Such shorthand may not, however, stand alone, as shown in the encounter between Paul and the Ephesian disciples of John. Christian baptism requires knowledge of the Holy Spirit, and the Son never works where the Father does not also work (John 14:8–11). Proper Christian baptism is baptism in a threefold singular name because it entails identification with all three persons of the one Godhead (Matt 28:19).

A name in the ancient world was significant for identification and authorization. To be given a name was a sign of possession. Adam named the animals over which he was given dominion. Moses and Jacob desired to know the name of the powerful One they separately encountered. Jesus asked the demons for their names before casting them out of the Gerasene demoniac. To be given a name (*onoma*) is to be given an identity that indicates a relationship entailing authority. To be placed or to be gathered into the name of another means to come into an intimate relationship, a relationship of corporate identity, with that other person. Christ is present with those who are gathered in His name (Matt 18:20). New believers are baptized into the one name of the God who is yet three (Matt 28:19), and thereby become members of the body of Christ, the church (Acts 2:41).[157] The baptismal pattern that Jesus Christ ordained is just that: dominically ordered, not ecclesiastically optional. As a result, the Great Commission text of Matthew becomes absolutely critical for discerning the proper pattern with which the churches must approach the theological exegesis of Scripture. Our scope of interpretation is limited to Scripture's rule of faith.

The symbolic entrance into the covenant with God and His church that baptism represents is also the key to orthodox theological interpretation. Christ interpreted Scripture for the disciples and commissioned them to carry that message as witnesses to others (Luke 24:44–49). The Bible must thus be interpreted according to the rule He established, not freely according to the private whims of men (2 Pet 1:20). The interpretation given by Christ is recorded in the written tradition of the apostles, as we have seen, and which interpretation was encapsulated by Christ in the Great Commission itself. As I have elsewhere discussed, the Great Commission has four major points, and one of those is the command to baptize.

[157] Bryan D. Spinks, *Early and Medieval Rituals and Theologies of Baptism: From the New Testament to the Council of Trent* (Burlington, VT: Ashgate, 2006), 5–6; Hans Bietenhard, "*Onoma*," in *TDNT*, 5:274.

In that commandment to baptize are locked the words that became integral to the church's understanding of the doctrine of the Trinity.

In the early church, worship was inseparable from doctrine. The church's liturgy embodied the church's confession. This principle has been captured with the Latin rubric *lex orandi lex credendi* (the law of prayer is the law of belief). Among the church fathers the idea carried great theological weight. Athanasius argued for the full deity of Jesus Christ on the basis of the church's prayers to Him. Basil of Caesarea extended that argument with regard to the Holy Spirit in baptism. From a believers' church perspective, this is a sound principle. The liturgical practices established by Christ and the apostles are liturgical practices normative for Christians of all time. Indeed, this principle was implied in the recovery of believers' baptism among the Anabaptists, the Baptists, and the Brethren.[158] The disjunction of worship and doctrine (or, similarly, theology and morality) is a phenomenon peculiar to the evangelical tradition, in contradistinction to the Roman Catholic and believers' church traditions.[159]

Lex orandi lex credendi is shorthand for the theological normativity of the Christian practices of baptism, the Lord's Supper, and the model prayer. Theological teachings embodied in liturgy instituted by Christ—for instance, regarding the sinner's submissive prayer for forgiveness (Matt 6:9–13), or the doctrine of the Trinity as delivered in baptism (Matt 28:19), or the need to teach the entire counsel of Christ (Matt 28:20), or the Lord's Supper as the appropriate context for church discipline (1 Cor 11:23–32)—are also doctrinally normative. And yet *lex orandi lex credendi* must be limited to worship directly ordained in Scripture. Ascribing creedal authority to worship based only on tradition is unwarranted, although the argument from extrascriptural liturgical tradition is common in the Roman church and among some evangelicals.[160]

Healthy Church Dogma and Postbiblical Claims

When used in the New Testament, *dogma* may refer to the decrees of a state (Luke 2:1; Heb 11:23; Acts 17:7), the judgment decrees of God (Col 2:14; Eph 2:15), or man-made religious decrees (Col 2:20). In Acts 16:4, however, the word takes on an entirely new meaning. At a conference of the church of Jerusalem, recorded in Acts 15, the apostles and elders led the church to discuss and decide upon

[158] For instance, John Robinson reports that John Smyth's congregation "would not so much as pray together before they had" proper baptism after they had discovered the proper form of baptism. John Robinson, *Of Religious Communion* (Leyden, 1614), 48, cited by B. R. White, *The English Separatist Tradition: From the Marian Martyrs to the Pilgrim Fathers* (New York: Oxford University Press, 1971), 132. John Smyth, who had a deep interest in orthodox liturgy, was even more explicit. An orthodox liturgy of baptism is so important that infant baptism subverts the very constitution of the church. A false constitution in turn leads to "false ministery, worship, & government." *The Character of the Beast* (1609), in *The Works of John Smyth, Fellow of Christ's College, 1594–8*, ed. W. T. Whitley (Cambridge: Cambridge University Press, 1915), 2:565.

[159] Cp. Cullmann's separation of liturgy and confession, and Alister McGrath's separation of dogma and morality. Cullmann, *The Earliest Christian Confessions*, 36, 36n, 43–44; McGrath, *The Genesis of Doctrine: A Study in the Foundation of Doctrinal Criticism* (Grand Rapids: Eerdmans, 1990), 10, 205n42.

[160] Wainwright has a lengthy discussion regarding the principle. Geoffrey Wainwright, *Doxology: The Praise of God in Worship, Doctrine, and Life* (New York: Oxford University Press, 1980), 218–83.

a response to the arguments over grace and law in relation to Gentile converts. The decisions of the church are described in Acts 16:4 as *ta dogmata*.[161] These *dogmata* were then delivered to the other churches scattered throughout various Asian cities.

The dogmas were generated by a church itself under the leadership of the apostles. They severely limited the ethical rules to what was clearly demanded in Scripture, rebuked the false teaching of some Jewish legalists, and established grace as the basis of salvation.[162] The dogmas were thus both moral and theological in nature (Acts 15:22–29). The church at Antioch received their sister church's decrees with gladness because they recognized that they were intended for encouragement (15:31). The result of the transmission of these dogmas was that "the churches were being strengthened in the faith, and were increasing in number daily" (16:5). Against the modern myth that says evangelism unites but theology divides, the book of Acts shows that proper dogma unites. Moreover, orthodox dogmatic formation resulted in the deepening of Christian faith and encouraged evangelism and missions.

On the basis of the principles enumerated above regarding tradition within Scripture, we may claim infallibility for the decision of the first and only church dogmatic conference that was definitely led by the Holy Spirit (Acts 15:28). Biblical dogma is actually the only indisputable dogma ever promulgated by the church. The dogmas created by postapostolic church conferences and supralocal church bodies may not pretend to the same authority as that of the Jerusalem conference. Indeed, it should be noted that the leaders reached a fundamental agreement with the entire church. Neither Paul, nor Peter, nor James sought to impose his will on the assembly or promote their offices. Moreover, the Jerusalem conference was held by one church only and should not be confused with the concept of a council or synod or association, postbiblical gatherings involving persons from more than one local church. The respect with which the Jerusalem church addressed the Antioch church should be a warning against the concept that any church or council of churches has authority over any other.

Postapostolic church councils remain the subject of disagreement among those who call themselves Christian, even when the councils themselves have laid claim to inspiration by the Holy Spirit. For instance, the Council of Constance, infamous for burning the evangelical preacher John Hus at the stake, repeatedly declared that because it was "legitimately assembled in the Holy Spirit," it has immediate power from Christ. Therefore, every Christian is bound to obey its decrees, even the pope. This decree came on April 6, 1415. The condemnation of John Hus came exactly three months later after many similar pious claims. Hus was burnt at the stake on the same day that his "errors and heresies," as well as those of John Wycliffe, the reputed "Morning Star of the Reformation," were firmly denounced.[163]

---

[161] Gerhard Kittel, "*Dogma, dogmatizo*," in *TDNT*, 2:230–32.

[162] I. Howard Marshall, *The Acts of the Apostles: An Introduction and Commentary*, TNTC (Grand Rapids: Eerdmans, 1980), 242–47, 253–55.

[163] Officially, the council relinquished John to the secular arm for burning at the stake, but the distinction is merely one of convenience, for the state executed the man based on the judgment of the church. Council of

Martin Luther could not agree with Roman claims to conciliar infallibility. Luther, in his tome on the councils, remarked that councils may "overtake the Holy Spirit and outstrip him by far!" Moreover, Luther noted that when conciliar decrees have been gathered and compared, they simply do not stand together with one voice. He cited Augustine, the father of Western theology, as an authority who stood against the facile acceptance of human writings without comparing their statements to the Word of God.[164] Luther's doctrine of development was firmly set against the idea that the official church could make infallible pronouncements through its hierarchy and councils. The Spirit, rather, works with the true church at the level of local preaching and following Christ's ordinances. Sometimes the Spirit leaves the official church to its own devices.[165]

Augustine raised the distinction between apostolic and postapostolic writings in a letter to Jerome addressing the proper interpretation of the Jerusalem council. Augustine chided Jerome for treating Scripture as a playground for amusement and severely reminded him that the Scripture alone is our final authority. Augustine was clear that postapostolic writings are subject to error while God's Word alone is not. Although we would qualify Augustine's final clause (and Luther's similar statement at the Diet of Worms), his advice to Jerome is profound:

> I have learned to yield this respect and honour only to the canonical books of Scripture: of these alone do I most firmly believe that the authors were completely free from error. . . . As to all other writings, in reading them, however great the superiority of the authors to myself in sanctity and learning, I do not accept their teaching as true on the mere ground of the opinion being held by them; but only because they have succeeded in convincing my judgment of its truth either by means of these canonical writings themselves, or by arguments addressed to my reason.[166]

Recognizing that the Bible must remain the final authority, we nevertheless realize that our understanding of it develops and is sometimes corrupted. The discussion of the fixity and development of doctrine in Scripture may provide us with some general principles for making judgments about postapostolic developments, but it has primarily taught us that only Scripture is without error. Discerning subsequent Christian theological reflection requires patience, careful consideration, and hope mixed with skepticism. Christian history is a gold mine of orthodoxy and piety interspersed with minefields of error and corruption. Unfortunately the gold mine and the minefield are too often found in the same church, even the same person.

Constance, Sessions 5 and 15, in *DEC*, 1:409, 428–29. Cp. Norman P. Tanner, *The Councils of the Church: A Short History* (New York: Herder and Herder, 2001), 66, 118.

[164] Martin Luther, *On the Councils and the Church* (1539), in *Luther's Works*, ed. Helmut T. Lehmann (Philadelphia: Fortress, 1966), 41:10, 14, 25.

[165] Paul Althaus, *The Theology of Martin Luther*, trans. Robert C. Schultz (Philadelphia: Fortress, 1966), 341–44.

[166] Augustine to Jerome (405), in *NPNF*[1], 1:350, (letter 82).

Chapter Five

THE DEVELOPMENT OF DOCTRINE: *A Believers' Church Proposal*

The free-church model of doctrinal development is characterized by many things, but it begins with a trinitarian belief in the Word and the Spirit as the Father's way to reveal Himself to humanity. The first major characteristic, therefore, of a free-church doctrine of development is a fervent commitment to the person and work of Christ who is revealed in the written Word of God. The Bible is the epistemological anchor that keeps the free churches from becoming deceived by their own subjectivity. Jesus Christ is the ontological anchor who mediates between the eternal God and historically bound humanity. His atoning work on the cross is the source of salvation and the pattern for history. His commission is the source of the free church's missionary zeal and ecclesial form, as well as its doctrines of trinitarian revelation, personal salvation, and covenantal freedom. Christ's imminent return is the hope that gives Christians confidence in the end of history.

The second major characteristic of the free-church doctrine of development is the biblical analogy of illumination, which bonds the Spirit with the Word. This conviction derives ultimately from allegiance to the economic Trinity alongside the ontological Trinity. John Henry Newman recognized the illumination analogy, especially in his Anglican period, but did not treat it at length and largely ignored it in his Roman period.[1] As noted in chapter 4, evangelicals are not entirely committed to the illumination analogy. In the separate history of the free churches, the illumination analogy of doctrinal development is pivotal, precisely because it was considered scriptural. The free-church model of doctrinal development is characterized by a Christocentrism and biblicism coupled with pneumatological illumination.

The free-church model of doctrinal development correlates in many ways with models offered in other traditions, while it yet speaks with a distinctive voice. In comparison with the other models, the free churches prefer to give justice to the fideistic, anthropological, and hamartiological aspects of doctrinal development. Although the typical free-church model is plainly reasonable, it distrusts rationalism as a human contrivance and seeks spiritual discernment. Although the free-church model is deeply ecclesiological, it treasures the personal dimension of Christian faith, stressing absolute religious freedom as a necessary consequence

[1] "And much more can He shed upon our path supernatural light, if He so will, and give us an insight into the meaning of Scripture." This qualification was made while denying private judgment. Newman, "Private Judgment," *British Critic* (1841), reprinted in *Essays Critical and Historical* (New York: Longmans Green, 1919), 2:342.

of the personal nature of created humanity and the necessary basis of covenantal community. Although the free-church model is interested in the truths of history, it recognizes that all men, even the redeemed, are limited by creation and tainted by sin: the free churches are humble while convictional.

Since no prior free-church theologian has sought to formulate a doctrine of development, what follows is, by definition, a tentative proposal precisely because it is a particular theologian's creative exercise. From a historical perspective, theological creativity is fraught with danger. Therefore, it seems best to allay novelty by proceeding appropriately according to the dominant dissenting ecclesiology as a compilation. We begin with some important pre-twentieth-century precedents. We then examine the historiographical theories of such exemplary twentieth-century free-church historians as Herbert Butterfield and, in the next chapter, Robert Baker. We will offer a theology of history based on the lordship of Jesus Christ and a pattern of history based on the cross of Christ before considering a history of theology based on the Great Commission, which proclaims the cross of Christ. Like all historical theology, any history of theology is a cursory and partial outline of significant moments in church history presented from a particular perspective, in this case that of the believers' churches.

THE EARLY FREE-CHURCH DOCTRINE OF DEVELOPMENT

The sixteenth-century Anabaptist theologian, Balthasar Hubmaier, considered the Holy Spirit the Christian's necessary guide to truth. In his prayer form of the Apostles' Creed, he proclaims an orthodox pneumatology and holistic understanding of faith: "I also believe in the Holy Spirit, which proceeds from the Father and Son and yet is with them one true God, . . . that he will teach me all truth, increase my faith, and stir up the fire of his love in my heart."[2] And yet for Hubmaier, who wrote the previous words while imprisoned by Zwingli, the Bible was also the final authority. In an earlier appearance at Zürich, during that city's second disputation, called in order to introduce theological changes, Hubmaier extolled the ultimate authority of Scripture.

The humility and submissiveness to the church displayed by Hubmaier are exemplary:

> Dear pious Christians! These are my convictions, which I have been taught out of Scripture. . . . If they should not be right and Christian, I beg you all through Jesus Christ our only Savior, I plead and admonish you by reason of the last judgment, please correct me in a brotherly and Christian way with Scripture; for I may err, I am a human being; but a heretic I cannot be. I want—and desire from the heart—to be instructed.

[2] "The Twelve Articles of Christian Faith" (1527), in *Balthaser Hubmaier: Theologian of Anabaptism*, trans. and ed. H. Wayne Pipkin and John H. Yoder (Scottdale, PA: Herald, 1989), 238.

For the sixteenth-century Anabaptist theologian, the Spirit was the Christian's teacher, all belief must be "according to the Word of God," and the Christian must be willing to submit his beliefs to the church for their instruction.[3]

The English Separatist Doctrine of "Further Light"

While the Continental Anabaptists were severely persecuted and their theologians martyred, the English Separatists were granted more space to reflect on theological method, especially with regard to the development of doctrine. John Smyth, founding pastor of the first English Baptist congregation, began his journey into nonconformity at Gainsborough, Lincolnshire, together with Richard Clifton. Clifton subsequently formed a sister congregation in nearby Scrooby. As rehearsed in chapter 1, the covenant of the congregation, according to William Bradford, later governor of the Plymouth colony, was a commitment to join, in so many words, "into a church estate, in the fellowship of the Gospel, to walk in all his ways, made known, or to be made known unto them."[4] The latter clauses indicate a significant openness, not to further revelation, but to further understanding of the biblical revelation. The Gainsborough covenant's "further light" doctrine, as it became known, was bound to Scripture.

A fuller description of the separatist belief in further light is found in the works of John Robinson, who affiliated with Clifton, then became pastor of the Leyden separatist congregation from whom America's pilgrim fathers came forth. According to one of the *Mayflower* pilgrims, Edward Winslow, Robinson explained the Gainsborough covenant in his final sermon to them, as they departed Holland for New England in 1620. Robinson said that "he was very confident the Lord had more truth and light yet to break forth out of his holy word."[5] He did not separate this light from the written Word but exhorted the pilgrims "to take heed what we received for truth, and well to examine and compare it with other Scriptures of truth before we received it." For the English Separatists, spiritual illumination never occurred apart from the clear meaning of the biblical text.

Robinson explained that the reclamation of congregational governance was the direct result of God giving the Separatists light that others did not possess. Martin Luther saw much truth in God's Word, but the Lutherans erred because "they could not be drawn to go beyond what Luther saw" and refused to accept the truths discovered by Calvin. Similarly, the Calvinists were stuck where Calvin

---

[3] Statements made at the Second Zurich Disputation in 1523, cited in ibid., 28–29.

[4] Alexander Young, the early historian of the Pilgrim fathers, following the narrative of Bradford, considered the covenant to have occurred around 1602, but Stephen Wright places it more clearly in 1607. "Governor Bradford's History of Plymouth Colony," in *Chronicles of the Pilgrim Fathers of the Colony of Plymouth, from 1602 to 1625*, ed. Alexander Young (Boston: Little & Brown, 1841), 20; Stephen Wright, *The Early English Baptists, 1603–1649* (Woodbridge: Boydell, 2006), 18–19.

[5] Edward Winslow, *Hypocrisie Unmasked* (1646), in *Chronicles of the Pilgrim Fathers*, 396–97. Cp. Robert Ashton "Memoir of Rev. John Robinson," in *The Works of John Robinson, Pastor of the Pilgrim Fathers*, ed. Ashton (London: John Snow, 1851), 1: xliv–xlvi (cp. lxxi). Ashton's chronology places Robinson in Lincolnshire by 1604; if so, Robinson might have been involved in the formation of the covenant for the church led by Smyth and Clifton at Gainsborough. Cp. ibid., xix–xxv. Barry White believes, however, that Henry Barrow and Francis Johnson, Smyth's former tutor at Cambridge and later pastor of a Separatist church in Amsterdam, were the formative theological influences upon both Robinson and Smyth in their separatism. B. R. White, *The English Separatist Tradition: From the Marian Martyrs to the Pilgrim Fathers* (New York: Oxford University Press, 1971), 124.

had taken them, "a misery much to be lamented." Luther and Calvin "were shining lights in their times, yet God had not revealed his whole will to them." Thus, it is incumbent upon the church "to embrace further light" when it comes. Although this pregnant phrase was common to diverse English theological traditions, Separatists used it to reintroduce biblical ecclesiology.[6]

For John Smyth the concept of further light was useful in his transition from Separatist to Baptist convictions. Smyth recognized theological inconsistency was "folly or weaknes" but accounted it "a vertue to retract erroers." Smyth was ever ready to change his theology for the better, in spite of long-standing conventions and the opprobrium of traditionalists. "Well, let them thinke of mee as they please, I professe I have changed, and shall be readie still to change, for the better." Smyth was more concerned with obedience to the ordinances of God revealed in His Word than with the opinions of men.[7] At the end of his life, Smyth regretted the times he overstated his case with personal invective but did not repent of his doctrine of development.

Thomas Helwys, who brought the English Baptists back to England, created a historical paradigm for understanding the development of free-church ecclesiology as a progressive movement away from theological error toward the recovery of the New Testament church. The "first beast" of Rome and the "second beast" of English episcopacy were excoriated by Helwys in book 1 of his 1612 appeal for religious liberty. In turn he examined and dismissed the unbiblical innovation of the royal supremacy (book 2), the false profession of Puritanism (book 3), and the error of Brownism (book 4). For Helwys, movement toward a free-church model involved a Spirit-led return to Scripture from the historical errors of the papacy, culminating in the biblical churches that became known as Baptist.[8]

---

[6] The first use of "further light" in English theological literature probably occurred with regard to Scripture's interpretation of Scripture in Martin Luther's commentary on Psalm 130. "But why doth he adde moreouer: *That thou mayest be feared?* Forsoth to set forth vnto vs what they are against whome he fighteth, and to giue a further light to the former sentence by setting forth the contrary: As if he should say: I haue learned by experience O Lord, why there is mercie with thee, & why of right thou mayst chalenge this title vnto thy selfe, that thou art merciful and forgiuest sinnes." Luther, *A commentarie vpon the fiftene Psalmes, called Psalmi graduum, that is, Psalmes of degrees*, trans. Henry Bull (London, 1577), 225.

The imagery of further light encapsulated the Elizabethan insistence on the formation of the Christian conscience by the Word. Francis Johnson was the first Separatist to publish concerning the concept of "further light," but Henry Barrow apparently introduced it into the Separatist vocabulary. It was an image used by Elizabethan writers as diverse as Richard Hooker (conformist), Dudley Fenner (Puritan), and Robert Parsons (Roman Catholic).

"But you haue not alwayes been of this minde, that such livings ought not of right to apperteyne to the ministerie of the Gospell. Neverthelesse if you haue seene a further light by the opposers of Prelatisme abroade, then you had at home, it would be good to make your friends and countrey partakers therof." *Mr Henry Barrowes Platform Which may serve, as a Preparative to purge away Prelatisme: with some other parts of Poperie . . . Anno 1593* ([n.p], 1611), C2r.

"So long then as they [the underground Marian congregation in London] kept communion in this way, we deny not but they were a true visible Church: though (it may be) in some defects through want of further light and instruction. The like we think also of our countreymen that were then at Frankford, Geneva, and other where beyond seas." Francis Johnson, *A Treatise of the Ministery of the Church of England* ([n.p.], 1595), 125. Cp. idem, *An Inquirie and Answer of Thomas White his Discoverie of Brownisme* ([n.p.],1606), 34–36.

[7] "Epistle to the Reader," *The Differences of the Churches*, and *The Last Booke*, in *The Works of John Smyth, Fellow of Christ's College, 1594–8*, ed. W. T. Whitley (Cambridge: Cambridge University Press, 1915), 2:564, 1:271; 2:752; cited in Jason K. Lee, *The Theology of John Smyth: Puritan, Separatist, Baptist, Mennonite* (Macon, GA: Mercer University Press, 2003), 290–91.

[8] Thomas Helwys, *The Mistery of Iniquity* (repr., London: Baptist Historical Society, 1935).

Reflecting their Separatist credentials, Smyth and Helwys believed dogmatic development was necessary as the Word of God became better known. They arrived at Baptist convictions as the result of a spiritual outworking of their fundamental belief in the progressive appropriation of biblical knowledge. Such appropriation, or reappropriation, was the result of the Holy Spirit's work of illumination in the church's reading of Scripture. The gift of illumination required the concurrent rejection of merely historically derived doctrinal inventions.[9]

The Cross-Centered Prolegomena of Andrew Fuller

Andrew Fuller has perhaps had more impact upon the Baptist ethos than any other theologian. Although trained under the Calvinist system advocated by such Reformed Baptists as John Gill, his influence exceeds that of the greater systematician. Fuller's phenomenal impact did not come through his systematic theology. Rather, it resulted from his biblical response to the problem of an attenuated passion for evangelistic preaching brought about by the tendency of the healthier branch of eighteenth-century English Baptists toward scholastic Calvinism. Fuller's *The Gospel Worthy of All Acceptation* (1785), as previously mentioned, prompted Baptists to reaffirm universal human responsibility. In the last year of his life, Fuller began to develop a systematic theology, never completed. Fortunately, however, he began with a prolegomena that corrected Gill.

In 1796 Fuller struggled with the proper system for explaining the Word of God. At the time he could not discern a particular system explicitly advocated by the Bible, but he was convinced that God nonetheless proceeds on systematic principles: "There is a beautiful connexion and harmony in every thing which he has wrought."[10] The "best criterion" of a theological system is "its agreement with the Holy Scriptures." It proceeds from "first principles," which remain the fundamental ground. From this fundamental ground, one must then move to the deep things of God. Moreover, this system does not exclude practice, for Christian experience must itself "arise from the influence of truth upon the mind."

In 1814 Fuller addressed the best way of connecting the doctrines of Scripture. "A system, if I understand it, is a whole, composed of a number of parts, so combined and arranged as to show their proper connexions and dependencies, and to exhibit every truth and every duty to the best advantage."[11] Fuller's fundamental theology used a twofold paradigm: Christ and His cross. Christ provided the unity for all Christian teaching, and the cross provided the center. "Upon this principle, as foundation, Christianity rests." This emphasis accorded with his views expressed elsewhere, and also accords with the broader free-church emphasis on discipleship to Christ. The transformation of theology between Gill, who adopted

[9] On the problem of theological invention, as opposed to the proper appropriation of biblical *inventio* (discovery), see Yarnell, "Congregational Priesthood and the Invention or *Inventio* of Authority," *JBTM* 3 (2005): 110–23.

[10] Fuller, "The Nature and Importance of an Intimate Knowledge of Divine Truth," in *The Complete Works of the Rev. Andrew Fuller*, ed. Joseph Belcher (repr., Harrisonburg, VA: Sprinkle, 1988), 1:160–74.

[11] Fuller, "Plan Proposed to be Pursued," in ibid., 1:690–92.

the Reformed paradigm of election for his foundation, and Fuller, who returned the paradigm to Christ and the cross, instructs the free churches regarding the limits of human reason. Fuller also affirmed the Spirit's illumination of the Bible and the congregational context of dogma.

That there was a movement away, under Gill, from the Bible's explicit theme (the gospel as salvation through personal repentance and faith in the death and resurrection of Jesus Christ[12]) to a humanly derived theological framework (speculative philosophical determinism[13]) indicates the natural tendency of human reason toward sin. Fuller was reminded by Ps 94:11 that the human mind tends toward vanity. He concluded that the human intellect of even Christians may err. "Men who have the Bible in their hands, but who, instead of learning the mind of God in it, and there resting contented, are ever bent on curious speculations, prying into things beyond their reach, vainly puffed up with a fleshly mind; to what do their thoughts amount? Nothing!"[14] The minds of created men, including the regenerate, are fallible. Fuller's experience with hyper-Calvinists on the one hand and Socinians on the other reminded him that theological speculation detracts from the Word of God.[15] "The true knowledge of God," he concluded, "is less speculative than practical."[16]

Moreover, like earlier free churchmen, Fuller believed the Holy Spirit is necessary for our understanding of truth as well as our regeneration. The Holy Spirit guides us into truth but never apart from the Word. "In order to try whether that which we account light be the effect of Divine teaching, or only a figment of our

---

[12] Fuller, "The Common Salvation," in ibid., 1:409–13.

[13] Timothy George provides a veiled criticism of Gill in this regard. George, "John Gill," in *Theologians of the Baptist Tradition*, ed. Timothy George and David Dockery (Nashville: B&H, 2001), 31.

[14] Fuller, "The Vanity of the Human Mind," in *The Complete Works of Rev. Andrew Fuller*, 1:437.

[15] Charles Haddon Spurgeon similarly complained of some Calvinists: "They bring a system of divinity to the Bible to interpret it, instead of making every system, be its merits what they may, yield, and give place to the pure and unadulterated Word of God." Iain Murray, *The Forgotten Spurgeon*, 2nd ed. (Carlisle, PA: Banner of Truth Trust, 1973), 46.

B. H. Carroll considered the Reformed confusion of the covenants a significant dividing line between Baptists and paedobaptists. If one places the Reformed system upon the biblical text, one will "drift into ritualism, accept the doctrine of union of church and state and coercion of conscience by the magistrate." But if one properly reads the Old Testament through the New Testament, "he naturally rejects union of church and state, believes in liberty of conscience, opposes all hierarchies, advocates congregational form of church organizations and their independence of each other." Carroll, *An Interpretation of the English Bible: Genesis*, ed. J. B. Cranfill (repr., Grand Rapids: Baker, 1973), 253.

The baptizing free churches may also consider here numerous speculative doctrines that have little if any basis in Scripture yet function as major pillars of the Reformed system: the distinction between the hidden and revealed wills of God as the basis of particular redemption; the divine decree of reprobation as a corollary to the divine decree of election; the human attempt to define a logical/temporal ordering of the divine decrees established in eternity; preference for the distinction between the covenant of works and the covenant of grace over the biblical distinction regarding the old and new covenants; Israel as the "church" in the Old Testament; baptism as the seal of the covenant; infant baptism as introduction into the covenant; the "half-way covenant"; limited atonement; irresistible grace; eternal justification; the removal of faith as a condition of regeneration; the demotion of repentance as a component of the beginning of salvation; regeneration by the Holy Spirit in the Old Testament period; the invisible church; synodal, regional, or national churches; and elder rule's displacement of biblical congregationalism. Of course, Arminianism's infatuation with an extrabiblical doctrine of libertarian free will, and acceptance of many Calvinistic tenets, likewise leads to multiple extrabiblical speculations.

[16] Fuller, "The Being of God," in *The Complete Works of the Rev. Andrew Fuller*, 1:693.

own imagination, we must bring it to the written word. . . . The test of Divine illumination, therefore, is whether that in which we conceive ourselves to be enlightened be a part of Divine truth as revealed in the Scriptures."[17] Fuller recognized that the Spirit must illumine the human mind if it was correctly to perceive divine truth, but he never countenanced theological illumination apart from the Bible. The key to distinguishing a figment of the human imagination from the Spirit's illumination was the presence of the doctrine in the Bible.

Fuller also affirmed the importance of both the personal and the social aspects of Christianity, as grounded in salvation. "Social religion begins with individual, and individual religion with 'coming' to Christ."[18] Fuller favored the individual but ultimately began with Christ. Although Fuller prioritized the individual in relation to the church, he was reticent to allow "the right of private judgment" boundless liberty. Every person has such a right, but the church must exercise judgment with regard to discipline in doctrine and ethics.[19] Fuller placed the local churches squarely in the center of the divine plan: they are "the appointed means of establishing his kingdom among men."[20] These churches are known to have the presence of God by the three marks: "the word of truth be preached," "the worship of God preserved in its purity," and "the ordinances of Christ observed according to their primitive simplicity." Although he stressed the high calling of the minister, Fuller was a congregationalist: "Christianity knows of no priesthood, except what is common to all believers."

Fuller's understanding of history was that God created man for a personal relationship. This relationship, lost in the fall, was redeemed by Christ and appropriated by the gift of faith through the Holy Spirit. For Fuller, the church is the ordained instrument for extending the divine mission of redemption to all of humanity. The mission to proclaim the cross was the key to his thought. As a result, Fuller's system of theology was organized historically. As he stated repeatedly in the fragments of his systematic divinity, his plan was to show how everything in Christianity pertained to the cross. The cross is central to Christianity, showing it to be a historical faith.

Fuller's systematic proposal was for a historical arrangement centered in the cross of Christ; that is, the principles "*presupposed by it*, *included in it*, or *arose*

---

[17] Fuller, "Importance of a True System," in ibid., 1:688.

[18] Fuller, "Individual and Social Religion," in ibid., 1:432–34.

[19] The idea that the "right of private judgment" was a principle of Protestantism and subsequently of dissent originated with the debates over the repeal of the Test and Corporation Acts. Cp. Caleb Fleming, *Delays Dangerous* (London, 1739). Two Baptist associations listed the right of private judgment as one of the distinctive principles of both Protestantism and nonconformity, alongside the sufficiency of Scripture and the sole headship of Christ over the local church. *The Circular Letter of the Eastern Baptist Association* (Hemel Hempstead, 1776), 9; *The Circular Letter: The Elders and Messengers of the Several Baptist Churches* (Cirencester, 1779), 7.

Fuller was not entirely comfortable with the concept of private judgment. He recognized it as a principle of both Protestantism and dissent but granted this right to all human beings. Therefore, private judgment never excuses the church from protecting its doctrinal integrity. Furthermore, vigorous church discipline implies no claim to doctrinal infallibility. Fuller, *Expository Remarks on the Discipline of the Primitive Churches* (London, 1799), 17–18; idem, *Socinianism Indefensible* (London, 1797), 39–41.

[20] Fuller, "Individual and Social Religion," in *The Complete Works of the Rev. Andrew Fuller*, 1:433–34.

out of it."[21] The cross thus serves simultaneously as the touchstone for both theology and history. Fuller did not survive to complete his systematic theology or to write a history of the churches, but the fragments of *Fundamentaltheologie* we possess indicate the historical shape of his thought.[22] Fuller was painfully aware that existing historiography was unsatisfactory, for church history was written primarily by the persecutors, who woefully neglected the free churches in their writings.[23] Fuller left it to later free churchmen to flesh out the historiography of the dissenting churches and begin molding a believers' church doctrine of development.

FREE-CHURCH HISTORIOGRAPHY

The problem of historiography has confronted the free churches since at least the sixteenth century. The earliest attempt at a comprehensive believers' church historiography was compiled in the sixteenth century by an opponent, Heinrich Bullinger. Bullinger's *Origin of the Anabaptists* (*Widertäufer Ursprung*), published in 1560, traced the Anabaptists back to Münster, Thomas Müntzer, the Zwickau prophets, and ultimately Satan. This intemperate diatribe against the believers' churches of the sixteenth century, combining the biblical Anabaptists with the worst excesses of the radicals, "established the basic pattern for the interpretation of the radical Reformation by scholars in the traditions of the European state churches down to most recent times."[24] Bullinger crafted his historiographical pattern in order to discredit the Anabaptists and distance the Swiss Reformation from Lutheran claims that Anabaptism arose in Zürich. It was not until the twentieth century that this inadequate and heinous evangelical historiography was even seriously challenged among mainline historians.

The earliest attempt at a comprehensive believers' church history written by a free churchman came in the seventeenth century.[25] Thieleman J. van Braght believed church history should begin with Scripture and proceed to a consideration of two subjects. "As there are two different peoples, two different congregations and churches, the one of God and from heaven, the other of Satan and from the earth; so there is also a different succession and progress belonging to each of

---

21 Author's italics. "The Being of God," in ibid., 1:692. Cp. "Plan Proposed to be Pursued," in ibid., 1:690.

22 In the midst of his theology proper, Fuller introduces revelation and interposes a discussion of history centered on Christ. "The Uniform Bearing of the Scriptures on the Person and Work of Christ," in ibid., 1:702–4.

23 Thanks to Bart Barber for indicating the importance in this regard of a letter by Fuller in the archives of Southwestern Seminary, Fort Worth, Texas. Fuller expressed his disappointment with most church historiography as serving only the interests of the powerful. "However we could say Blessed be God pure & undefiled, Religion has been upheld tho' by an obscure people independent of these Church crawlers. So thought I, doubtless Pure Religion in every period has been carried tho' perhaps by a people so obscure as seemed unworthy the notice of Ancient Historians, from whom we know the Moderns must derive all their materials." Fuller to John Sutcliffe (28 January 1781).

24 George Huntston Williams, *The Radical Reformation*, 3rd ed. (Kirksville, MO: Sixteenth Century Journal Publishers, 1992), 1292–96.

25 The work of Sebastian Franck is not considered here because, although a radical reformer, Franck's rationalist program elevated the invisible church to the detriment of the visible congregations.

them."[26] Braght's *Martyrs Mirror* did not follow the Augustinian division of two cities but posited two churches, the true and the false. The fall of the church originated with the Constantinian synthesis of church and state. The true church is being renewed in spite of persecution by the state church.

The idea of the fall of the church was a maxim for the sixteenth-century Anabaptists and has since characterized most free-church historiography. Indeed, this historiography has not been confined to the free churches. Littell found three major elements in the idea of the fall of the church. First, the earliest church is glorified as the "Golden Age" of the faith when the church lived according to the pattern of the New Testament. Second, the church declined as a result of its association with the state under Constantine. The free churches subsequently coexisted alongside the state church but under a state of intense persecution. Third, the true churches must constantly seek the restitution of the primitive New Testament pattern.[27] For the first free-church historians, the true church is known by faithful submission to Christ's commands; the false church is known by its resort to wicked persecution. This compelling and interwoven tapestry of discipleship and persecution has become less polarizing with time, but the basic concerns for faithfulness to Christ and religious freedom remain hallmarks of modern free-church historiography.

In the nineteenth and twentieth centuries, a number of free churchmen, including such luminaries as Henry C. Sheldon, Kenneth Scott Latourette, Herbert Butterfield, and Robert A. Baker, approached free-church history, general church history, general history and/or historiography from a modern scientific perspective. (Particular debates within particular free-church traditions—for instance, regarding theological monogenesis and social polygenesis among Anabaptist historians[28]—are not detailed here in light of the wider concern for general free-church historiography.) Sheldon, a Methodist at Boston University in the late nineteenth century, downplayed his free-church convictions in his broad approach to church history yet retained his disapproval of the Constantinian synthesis.[29] Latourette, a Baptist at Yale University in the twentieth century, also took a broad even ecumenical approach to church history yet retained a focus upon the disciple-making mission of the church.[30] The significant contribution to a philosophy of history made by Butterfield and the exemplary free-church historiography of Baker may be more helpful in defining a free-church doctrine of development.

[26] Van Braght, *The Bloody Theater or Martyrs Mirror of the Defenseless Christians Who Baptized Only upon Confession of Faith, and Who Suffered and Died for the Testimony of Jesus, Their Savior, from the Time of Christ to the Year A.D. 1660*, trans. Joseph F. Sohm (repr., Scottdale, PA: Herald, 2004), 21.

[27] Franklin H. Littell, *The Anabaptist View of the Church: A Study in the Origins of Sectarian Protestantism* (Boston: Starr King, 1958), 57–78.

[28] For reviews of recent Anabaptist historiographies, see A. James Reimer, "From Denominational Apologetics to Social History and Systematic Theology: Recent Developments in Early Anabaptist Studies," *RSR* 29 (2003): 235–40; C. Arnold Snyder, "The Birth and Evolution of Swiss Anabaptism (1520–1530)," *MQR* 80 (2006): 501–645.

[29] Steven E. Woodworth, "Henry C. Sheldon," in *Historians of the Christian Tradition: Their Methodology and Influence on Western Thought*, ed. Michael Bauman and Martin I. Klauber (Nashville: B&H, 1995), 377–88.

[30] Richard W. Pointer, "Kenneth Scott Latourette," in ibid., 411–30.

The Herbert Butterfield Problem

Herbert Butterfield was a Methodist raised in a working class family, who came to Cambridge on a scholarship and successively received his doctorate; international acclaim for both a subtle historiography and deep Christian commitment; the mastership of Peterhouse and vice-chancellorship of Cambridge University; multiple honorary doctorates from German, American, and British universities; and was ultimately knighted by Queen Elizabeth II for his service to the university and the discipline of history.[31] For our purposes, among the most important of his more than twenty books are *The Whig Interpretation of History* (1931) and *Christianity and History* (1950). If there were a dissenter who might claim the intellectual capability of responding to Newman, it would have been Butterfield. Butterfield never attempted a response to Newman, perhaps because Butterfield was more the historian while Newman was more the theologian. Yet Butterfield's contributions to English-speaking historiography remain unsurpassed by any modern historian, much less any nonconformist historian. He was, according to his intellectual biographer, definitively "a seminal thinker."[32]

Butterfield's rise to the top of the academy in the discipline of history indicates profound commonalities between free-church historiography and scientific history. In his construction of a scientific philosophy of historiography, Butterfield himself was influenced by two leading historians of the nineteenth century, Leopold von Ranke (1795–1886) and John Lord Acton (1834–1902).[33] Tracing the contributions of Ranke and Acton outline the emphases of Butterfield himself. Both men are important, for they developed the earlier attempts at a history of historiography offered in the progressive school to which Acton belonged and the historicist school to which Ranke belonged. Moreover, it was Lord Acton who mediated the historical theory of Ranke and the German school to the English academy.[34] David Bebbington, a nonconformist historian and ardent admirer of Butterfield, believed the deficiencies of both the progressive school, which culminates in positivism, and the historicist school, which culminates in idealism, can be overcome in the Christian pattern of history.[35]

Ranke was a Lutheran pietist, who became the founding father of modern critical history. Ranke's advocacy of historicism (*Historismus*) was driven by his personal faith. Indeed, Ranke's significant contributions to the university study of

[31] For the life and work of Butterfield, see especially C. T. McIntire, *Herbert Butterfield: Historian as Dissenter* (New Haven, CN: Yale University Press, 2004). Cp. Denis Brogan, "Sir Herbert Butterfield as an Historian: An Appreciation," in *The Diversity of History: Essays in Honour of Sir Herbert Butterfield*, ed. J. H. Elliott and H. G. Koenigsberger (Ithaca, NY: Cornell University Press, 1970), 1–16; C. T. McIntire, "Introduction," in *Herbert Butterfield: Writings on Christianity and History*, ed. McIntire (New York: Oxford University Press, 1979), xi–lviii.

[32] McIntire, *Herbert Butterfield*, 403.

[33] To Butterfield, Ranke and Acton together represented "the richest kind of historical writing." Butterfield, "The Role of the Individual in History," in *Writings on Christianity and History*, 31.

[34] Acton, "German Schools of History," *EHR* 1 (1886): 12–17; Butterfield, *Man on His Past: The Study of the History of Historical Scholarship* (New York: Cambridge University Press, 1955).

[35] David Bebbington, *Patterns in History: A Christian Perspective on Historical Thought*, 2nd ed. (Vancouver, BC: Regent College Publishing, 1990), 88, 107–8, 151, 168–71.

history reflect his desire to discern God's movements in history for the purpose of worship.[36] Ranke began with the principle that God created human beings as individuals with free wills to act accordingly (*geistige Macht*). Divine providence may be discerned by examining individual actions. History thus properly follows only an inductive method if it wishes to be scientific. As the historian toils through historical archives, examining the facts deposited there, he may reach an apprehension (*Anschauung*) of how the facts connect. Induction—working from specific facts to general theory—contradicts the dogmatic deductiveness in Georg Hegel's idealism.

Ranke's focus on facts does not, as later historicists asserted, entail a denial that connections between facts may be examined for ideas that explain (*Ideenlehre*) how the world functions. Although Ranke considered the search for maxims of how the world functioned (*Lebenswelt*) legitimate, he was distrustful of the theory of inevitable progress because it sought to make men into gods. To the contrary, every generation is equally guided by divine providence.[37] Ranke also suspected that claims to universality veiled political absolutism. Any theory of development (*Entwicklung*) must be chastened, for the historian must be careful to state clearly his own presuppositions. The historian's goal is to present the facts as they are, to represent the past according to the past. According to Liebel-Weckowicz, the "scientific spirit" of the Rankean historian is to "seek knowledge honestly and rationally."[38]

Lord Acton was a liberal Roman Catholic schooled in the best of German historical and theological scholarship. Committed to Whig politics and a confidant of Prime Minister William Gladstone, Acton had been tutored by Ignaz von Döllinger, a prominent Munich theologian. Döllinger taught Acton a love for truth, the value of critical historiography, and the need for freedom of conscience, lessons Acton learned well. Surprisingly for a layman, Acton served as the nerve center for the episcopal opposition to the formulation of the doctrine of papal infallibility at Vatican I.[39] When Acton perceived his political opposition was failing, he employed history to convince Catholics not to receive papal infallibility as a legitimate doctrinal development. Acton sought to defend English Catholicism by publicly exposing Rome's historical faults. In his conflict with the ultramontane view, he appointed the historian as the final arbiter.

[36] Butterfield discusses Ranke in numerous places, but the following review draws upon Butterfield's *Man on His Past* and on three articles, one by Butterfield himself: H. Butterfield, "Review of George G. Iggers, *The German Conception of History*," *EHR* 86 (1971): 337–42; M. A. Fitzsimmons, "Ranke: History as Worship," *RP* 42 (1980): 533–55; Helen Liebel-Weckowicz, "Ranke's Theory of History and the German Modernist School," *CJH* 23 (1988): 73–93. Ranke made four contributions to the university study of history: (1) the use of manuscript sources; (2) the critical treatment of sources; (3) the professor's seminar as a historical laboratory; and, (4) the hand of providence may be seen only through accurate representation of the past. Fitzsimmons, "Ranke," 542–43.

[37] "I would maintain, on the contrary, that every epoch is immediate to God, and that its value in no way depends on what may have eventuated from it, but rather in its existence alone, its own unique particularity." Lectures to Maximilian of Bavaria (1854).

[38] "Ranke's Theory of History," 93.

[39] Owen Chadwick, "Lord Acton at the First Vatican Council," *JTS* 28 (1977): 465–97.

Indeed, for Acton, history necessitated the exercise of moral judgment. In a letter to Mandell Creighton, whom he had criticized for insufficiently condemning the medieval popes, Acton made his famous statement that "power tends to corrupt, and absolute power corrupts absolutely."[40] Acton's later work focused upon the development of freedom of conscience in history. He criticized Constantine, among others, for making "the Church serve as a gilded crutch of absolutism." He was no friendlier to Luther and Calvin, for the "Protestant theory of persecution" is different in approach rather than substance. Acton yearned for the principle of the early church "that men are free in matters of conscience."[41] Acton's historical work received academic honor with his appointment as Regius Professor of Modern History at Cambridge University.

Butterfield, Acton's successor at Cambridge, incorporated the thoughts of both Ranke and Acton into his historiography, but Butterfield did not receive them uncritically.[42] Butterfield's own theological convictions led him to denounce roundly Acton's use of history to make final moral judgments.[43] Owen Chadwick, a third notable occupant of the royal chair, defended Butterfield's fascination with Acton, which Geoffrey Elton had criticized.[44] Chadwick believes Butterfield was attracted to Acton in part because of common concerns for personal spirituality, as evidenced in Acton's appreciation for Thomas à Kempis and for personal liberty. Yet in spite of Acton's poetic defense of liberty, Butterfield detected absolutism in Acton just as pernicious as the papal absolutism Acton opposed. Acton, according to Butterfield, wanted the historian to be "the real Pope," and Butterfield's doctrine of universal sin would never countenance that claim.[45] Similarly Butterfield criticized Ranke, again from a theological perspective, for treating providence as mechanical, lacking the intimacy of personal relationship that God desires.[46]

Butterfield, the historiographer, seamlessly correlated scientific history with personal faith. Even his sympathetic biographer is sometimes taken aback by

[40] Acton to Creighton, 3 April 1887, cited in Josef L. Altholz, "Acton, John Emerich Edward Dalberg, first Baron Action (1834–1902), *historian and moralist*," *ODNB*. Lionel Kochan, *Acton on History* (London: Andre Deutsch, 1954).

[41] Acton, *The History of Freedom and Other Essays*, ed. John Neville Figgis and Reginald Vere Laurence (London: Macmillan, 1907), 31, 186.

[42] For instance, Butterfield overturned Acton's theory that the Catholic massacre of French Protestants on St. Bartholomew's Day was premeditated. In a series of interesting shifts fostered by the advance of scientific historiography, earlier Protestants claimed that Roman Catholics had planned the massacre with Rome's forbearance, which Roman historians hotly denied, but the Roman Catholic Acton sided with the earlier Protestants while the Protestant Ranke and the Dissenter Butterfield sided with the earlier Roman Catholics. Ranke and Butterfield were more interested in fitting the facts than in condemning Rome while Acton was pursuing his argument against Rome. Cp. H. Butterfield, "Acton and the Massacre of St. Bartholomew," *CHJ* 11 (1953): 27–47.

[43] Butterfield, *The Whig Interpretation of History* (1931; reprint, New York: Norton, 1965), 64–89.

[44] G. R. Elton, "Herbert Butterfield and the Study of History," [First Sir Herbert Butterfield Memorial Lecture, Queen's University, Belfast] *HJ* 27 (1984): 731–32. Elton, however, praised Butterfield as a historian for fighting against two prominent errors: studying the past for the sake of the present rather than the past and punishing past misdeeds by present censure.

[45] Owen Chadwick, "Acton and Butterfield," [Second Sir Herbert Butterfield Memorial Lecture, Queen's University, Belfast] *JEH* 38 (1987): 402.

[46] Nevertheless, Butterfield quoted Ranke on the importance of faith to the historical task: "It was this and this alone, which drove me to historical research." Butterfield, *Man on His Past*, 138, 140.

the way in which Butterfield, the proponent of the scientific method, correlated history and religion. J. G. A. Pocock, noted historian of early modern political philosophy, referred to this as *das Herbert Butterfieldproblem*, by which Pocock meant the seeming disjunction between the hammer of the Whigs in *The Whig Interpretation of History* and the historian of liberty's progress in *The Englishman and His History*. In his famous *Whig Interpretation*, Butterfield blasted the historian who "studies the past with reference to the present" and offers "the last word in a controversy."[47] However, in the second work, written during World War II, Butterfield lauded the very Whigs who taught personal liberty was a historical phenomenon that progressed especially in England. According to Butterfield, England learned with the Whigs that the best way to live is through "co-operation with Providence."[48] Keith Sewell denied there was a recantation between 1931 and 1944, positing a distinction between Butterfield's historical ruminations and political commitments.[49] Although helpful, this is still an awkward distinction, for Butterfield's political commitments are difficult to pigeonhole.[50]

Perhaps the better way to understand Butterfield's correlation of scientific history and personal religion is through his own distinction between three levels of historical thinking that require three different methods of analysis. Butterfield begins with a discussion of "technical history," which encompasses the first two levels. The first level concerns the free actions of persons and requires biographical analysis. The second level concerns the laws of history and requires narrative analysis, or "the scientific examination of the deep forces and tendencies in history." At both of these levels, Butterfield consistently reflected the scientific severity of Ranke, excoriating those who read the past for the sake of the present and import their own judgments.

The third level, providence, establishes and encompasses both human free will and the historical laws; its analysis requires personal moral commitment. Butterfield believes a historian may function at the levels of technical history without proceeding to providential history. But the third level is impossible for the historian, "if you have not found God in your daily life."[51] To those objecting to the complexity of three-level thinking, Butterfield appeals to adulthood. A culture must accept the "necessity" of complex historical thinking "as the consequence of growing up."[52]

From a scientific historian's perspective, Michael Hobart registers a certain discomfort with Butterfield's paradigm, but admits, "In making his abstractions, the scientist is forced to make metaphysical assumptions about the natural world." These include the uniformity of nature and the universality of scientific principles, especially assumptions regarding cause and effect. Moreover, while the scientist examines man from the outside, the artist examines man from the inside. Thus, at

[47] Butterfield, *The Whig Interpretation of History*, 11, 65.

[48] Butterfield, *The Englishman and His History* (New York: Cambridge University Press, 1944), 83.

[49] Keith C. Sewell, "The 'Herbert Butterfield Problem' and Its Resolution," *JHI* 64 (2003): 599–618.

[50] McIntire, *Herbert Butterfield*, 373. McIntire affirms the Sewell thesis. Ibid., 115–32.

[51] Butterfield, "God in History," in *Writings on Christianity and History*, 5–7, 10–12.

[52] Butterfield, *Man on His Past*, 139–41.

both levels—that of the scientist and that of the artist—the historian, who is actually both artist and scientist (again, a Rankean dictum), engages in metaphysical abstractions.

The solution for the modern historian is not to deny engagement at the third level but humbly and clearly to confess one's presuppositions. In this way, the historian functions much as a theologian. "Both will make metaphysical assumptions which express values—religious, broadly, in character; historical in conditioning—and they should deal with those assumptions as consciously as possible."[53] Even Elton, a historian notoriously uninterested in religious meaning, noted both Butterfield's humility and realism, advocating every historian deal with the presuppositions Butterfield so honestly exposed.[54]

Butterfield took scientific history seriously. He required his research students to spend long periods in the archives before allowing themselves opportunity to construct maxims explaining the historical data encountered. One must read the past for the sake of the past rather than the present. One must not impose a present model upon the events of the past and read a nonhistorical ideal into it. The historian may not set herself up as final judge of past individuals.

However, the historian is also an artist who must employ "imaginative sympathy" with regard to the "significances" of the past. Human decisions and actions are not merely mathematical "facts." The historical task is scientific and artistic, involving the inner life of the individual personality. The historian receives an almost impossible calling—abridging the past without altering its fabric. This means that "apprehending the whole pattern upon which the historical process is working" is really a "gift."[55] Again Butterfield's scientific historiography depends upon theological assumptions.

Free-Church Values in Butterfield's Philosophy of History

Although not a trained theologian, Butterfield's historiography is permeated with biblical wisdom. The major Christian doctrines, taken according to classic free-church emphases, were important to Butterfield's historical thought. His philosophy of history was formed in the crucible of a pious Methodist home, early service as a Methodist lay preacher, consistent weekly participation in worship, and humble defense of the faith at the highest reaches of academe. Butterfield developed a reputation as a scientific scholar, a philosopher of history, and a humble preacher of free-church values.

At the center of Butterfield's thought, in both the academy and the church, was his commitment to Jesus Christ. Butterfield's mind was not bound to obscurantism by his beliefs but set free to engage in the most rigorous of intellectual pursuits. His famous ideal for both religion and intellect was: "We can do worse than remember a principle which both gives us a firm Rock and leaves us the maximum elasticity for our minds: the principle: Hold to Christ, and for the rest

---

53 Michael Hobart, "History and Religion in the Thought of Herbert Butterfield," *JHI* 32 (1971): 548, 554.

54 Elton, "Herbert Butterfield and the Study of History," 729–30, 743.

55 Butterfield, *The Whig Interpretation of History*, 90–93, 102–3.

be totally uncommitted."[56] Jesus Christ was the fulcrum in Butterfield's thought. He believed that if one would focus on Christ, then his mind would be granted the freedom necessary for intellectual activity. Personal Christocentrism and a sense of calling to proclaim God's Word[57] allowed Butterfield the personal stability and scholarly liberty to converse with theologians of every Christian tradition as well as intellectuals of every stripe.

Butterfield set out his ideas of the essence of Christianity in a number of places. Because he believed the essence of Christianity is found in the New Testament, he did not speak of a "reformation" of Christianity to some subsequent ideal whether in the early church, the Middle Ages, the Reformation, the Puritans, modernity, or whenever. Rather, the New Testament remained his ideal: "It is better that Christians should be as they were in the New Testament days—humble rather than proud, poor rather than privileged, claiming no rights against society, no rights in the world save that of worshipping the God in Whom they believe and preaching the faith they hold."[58]

The essential concepts in Christianity emanating from the New Testament and working themselves out historically in the lives of individuals begin with love and freedom. These essential concepts become known to individuals, who are the only ones to possess souls, in the "centres of local life," specifically in the "local Church."

> Century after century the minds of people have been soaked with the picture of Christian humility, with the view that mercy is greater than judgment, with the conviction that all men are equal in the sight of God, with the thought that they must remember their own sins before condemning other men, and with the idea that love conquers the hardest heart, that love is the only form of righteousness that matters.[59]

Unfortunately, because of the Christian share in the universal problem of sin, Christian individuals, including clergy, have too often turned to other forms of righteousness. The false righteousness Butterfield especially resents is offered by the state possessed with the "herd-spirit." The Constantinian synthesis of church and state, which gave Christians unprecedented power, led away from New Testament Christianity, for "voluntariness was the very essence of the New Testament religion." Rather than practicing love and personal freedom, Christians became persecutors, practicing the antithesis of true faith.

Far from ignoring the failures of Christians and churches in history, Butterfield agreed with "non-Christian Humanists," who lamented the tyrannies imposed by Europe's churches. Butterfield was not interested in defending Christian failures.

---

[56] Butterfield, *Christianity and History* (London: Bell, 1950), 146. Cp. "Here is one of the reasons why it is well for us if we hold fast to Christ and to spiritual things while retaining great elasticity of mind about everything else." Butterfield, *Christianity in European History*, 42.

[57] "The desire to 'preach the Gospel,' though it has been submerged on occasion, has perhaps been my most constant motor." Butterfield's journal, cited in McIntire, *Herbert Butterfield*, 408.

[58] "The Obstruction to Belief," in *Writings in Christianity and History*, 231–47.

[59] Butterfield, "The Obstruction of Belief," 246.

Neither was he interested in embracing atheism or pluralism. Rather, humility demands that Christians realize their churches often failed to follow Christ's example of love. The only way that Christianity, "a religion claiming exclusiveness," can avoid tyrannizing the world is "to give charity the presiding place in the conduct of mundane affairs."

Butterfield, the dissenting Christian, was thus willing to listen to others, even nonbelieving historians. He also held conversations with Protestant theologians such as Reinhold Niebuhr, whom he criticized for not holding individuals morally accountable,[60] and Rudolf Bultmann, whom he criticized for "divorcing" the Christ of faith from the Jesus of history.[61] Such willingness to converse with other Christians, however, did not dislodge him from his primary commitment to Jesus Christ and New Testament "insurgent Christianity," by which he meant dissent or nonconformity. "The Christian ought to be a nonconformist."[62]

Butterfield was appreciative yet critical of Roman Catholicism, of Protestantism, and of liberalism. His critique of liberalism strikes at the core of its system, an unduly exalted anthropology: "It is not always easy to realise how in modern times we have come to adopt as our initial conception of a human being a pattern that would be more fitting for gods."[63] When Methodists held conversations regarding unification with the Church of England, Butterfield objected loudly. He preferred to increase ties with other dissenting churches, including Presbyterians, Baptists, Congregationalists, and Quakers.

Butterfield's list of Methodist distinctives is similar to that offered in many free churches: personal experience, the witness of the Spirit, works of faith, return to the New Testament, emphasis on the laity, openness to mystery, and opposition to the captivity of the church by the state.[64] But above everything else, for Butterfield, is Jesus Christ. Although Butterfield was primarily a historian of diplomacy, science, and historiography, his values were those of the believers' churches.

A FREE-CHURCH THEOLOGY OF HISTORY

Before reviewing the progress of theology in history, it may be helpful to set out a theology of history. At this point the author admits his utter dependence on the contributions of his forefathers in discerning a theology of history. For deeper acquaintance with general theologies of history, the reader is asked to consider the contributions of Irenaeus of Lyons, Eusebius of Caesarea, Augustine of Hippo, Bonaventure, John Foxe, Adolf Harnack, Ernst Troeltsch, Reinhold Niebuhr, Oscar Cullmann, Jean Daniélou, Gerhard Ebeling, and E. C. Rust, among others.

[60] McIntire, *Herbert Butterfield*, 301–12. Cp. Reinhold Niebuhr, *Faith and History: A Comparison of Christian and Modern Views of History* (London: Nisbet, 1949); Bebbington, *Patterns in History*, 178–80.

[61] McIntire, *Herbert Butterfield*, 196. Butterfield dallied with the historical critical work of Bultmann, but his simple trust in the Bible's veracity asserted itself with his defense of the resurrection. He concluded that biblical critics may not offer final judgments. Cp. Butterfield, *Christianity and History*, 125–28; idem, "The Modern Historian and New Testament History," in *Writings on Christianity and History*, 102–3, 110.

[62] Butterfield's journal, cited in McIntire, *Herbert Butterfield*, 375.

[63] Butterfield, *Christianity and History*, 88.

[64] Ibid., 358–60, 376.

There are two important and large works that every Christian historian should read before daring to attempt relating the progress of God's dealings with the world through his people: Augustine of Hippo's magisterial *The City of God* (*De Civitas Dei*), and Adolf Harnack's *History of Dogma*. Augustine, who is justly claimed by both Roman Catholics and evangelicals, discerns a uniquely Christian view of world history as the intertwined narrative of two distinct communities. Harnack, a liberal evangelical, offers a general introduction to much of Christian history at the same time that he constantly challenges received conventions. Augustine establishes a firm foundation for a Christian theology of history. Harnack warns against naive theological presentations of history.

In keeping with the theological foundation and historiography of the free churches, we note that a theology of history must confess Jesus Christ, particularly with regard to his lordship. Jesus Christ is the Lord of eternity and the Lord of history. As the Lord of history, he is the Lord of both covenants, the Lord of all the churches, and the Lord of all human beings. His lordship extends from eternity and encompasses all of history. The free churches seek to submit themselves and their understanding of all of history, especially of church history, to Jesus Christ, their Lord and Master. They believe that while he is Lord above, the transcendent God has graciously come near in the incarnation. The createdness and fallibility of man, though overcome by God's grace, does not allow the churches to claim infallibility in their doctrinal declarations.

The Lord of Eternity Is the Lord of History

Christianity is a supremely historical religion that views humanity as having a past, present, and future guided by God. The Bible opens with "in the beginning" (Gen 1:1) and closes with Christ's promise to return and bring history to final judgment and renewal, "Surely I am coming quickly" (Rev 22:20). The God of the Bible is He "who is and who was and who is to come." He is "the beginning [*arche*] and the end [*telos*]" and "the first [*protos*] and the last [*eschatos*]" (Rev 1:17; 21:6). The Old Testament teaches that God created the world and placed a man in it with a promise and a warning (Gen 1:16–17). Adam, however, violated God's will, perverting his relationship with God (Gen 3:6), described as "the fall," and the world has since been involved in a long story of corruption (Rom 8:21–22). The context of human history as a movement from creation to corruption to redemption overseen by an eternal God should not be forgotten in any discussion of development. The modern myth of inevitable progress is incompatible with the biblical view of postlapsarian creation and divine providence.

Refuting demythologizing and dehistoricizing tendencies in modern theology, Oscar Cullmann showed, in *Christ and Time*, how the biblical conception of time is linear and centered in the revelation of Jesus Christ. "Salvation is bound to a continuous time process which embraces past, present, and future. Revelation and salvation take place along the course of an ascending time line. . . . All points of this redemptive line are related to the one historical fact at the mid-point. . . . the death and resurrection of Jesus Christ." The kerygma is the center of all of human history as well as of salvation history.[65] There can be little disagreement with Cullmann's rudimentary scheme of history. Jesus Christ is indeed the center of history as well as its beginning and end. The cross and the resurrection of our Lord comprise the gospel that calls all people out of the realm of corruption and death and into the realm of life. The cross with the resurrection is that which places Christ over the ages (Eph 1:19–21).

Unfortunately Cullmann also promotes an idea that has not set well with etymologists, nor with classical theology. In the classic understanding, as perhaps best presented by Augustine, God created time along with everything else.[66] According to modern linguistic research, the New Testament refers to the eternal as that "which transcends time."[67] The existentialism taught by Cullmann's colleagues in the biblical theology movement of the twentieth century stressed the event of salvation and downplayed the continuities between events that are essential to the idea of history. Cullmann disagreed, affirming that the categories of beginning and end, with Christ at the center, demand a linear conception of history. For Cullmann, there is a "movement of history."[68] But while preserving history against existentialism, Cullmann also refuted the supposedly "Hellenistic" view of eternity that he perceived most Christians have adopted. For Cullmann, the eternity that God inhabits, and from which He created and redeems, is an endless time rather than beyond time.

Cullmann's position corrected the exegesis of existentialism but at the expense of classical hermeneutics. James Barr showed that Cullmann was focused on the literalistic meanings of the words used rather than on the way the words were used in the biblical context.[69] John of Damascus, a native Greek speaker, would find Cullmann's project baffling. The Damascene carefully distinguishes the various meanings of age (*aion*) and eternal (*aionios*), including its meaning as "the sort of temporal motion and interval that is co-extensive to things eternal." "For God, Who alone is without beginning, is Himself the Creator of all things, whether age or any other existing thing."[70] William Lane Craig, from a philosophical viewpoint, has shown that the idea of a beginning of time is not a philosophical impossibility.[71] We might point out that biblical references to the end of time imply also the possibility of a beginning of time.[72]

God is "from the beginning" (*arches*), the source from which all things have come into being (1 John 1:1). God is also the one who will roll up all things

[65] Cullmann, *Christ and Time: The Primitive Christian Conception of Time and History*, trans. Floyd V. Filson (Philadelphia: Westminster, 1950), 32–33.

[66] Augustine, *Confessions* 11.11–30; Roger Hazelton, "Time, Eternity, and History," *JR* 33 (1950): 10–12.

[67] Hermann Sasse, "*Aionios*," in *TDNT* 1:208.

[68] Robert D. Elinor, "The End and the Beginning," *JBR* 31 (1963): 11.

[69] James Barr, *Biblical Words for Time* (London: SCM Press, 1962), 145–49.

[70] John of Damascus, *Exposition of the Orthodox Faith* 2.1.

[71] William Lane Craig, "God, Time and Eternity," *RS* 14 (1979): 497–503.

[72] Elinor prefers to speak of an end to history, rather than an end to time, but the disjunction of time and history requires more philosophical subtlety than their juncture. The Bible speaks of the last of time (cp. 1 Pet 1:5) but not the end of history. Elinor, "The End and the Beginning," 14.

and bring them to their intended end. Paul teaches that Christ, at the end of time (*telos*), will take all things and return them to the Father. All of the authority that has been granted to created things will be brought to judgment. The last enemy will be death itself, the ultimate corruption. When he has put "all things" in their proper subjection, Christ will then present them to the Father. Creation will return to the one who is the origin of all things: God will be all in all (1 Cor 15:24–28). If time can be classified as something, and there is no reason to believe otherwise, it too is included in the all things of which Paul writes. All things, including time, come to an end (*telos*) (1 Cor 15:24) in the One who is the end (*telos*) (Rev 21:6). The intersection of eternity and time find their conjunction in Christ.

In the period of the early church, the dominant worldview, found in Greek philosophy or "Hellenism," considered that which is divine to consist "in the unmoved eternal order of Ideas."[73] Eternity or ontology was distinct from history and kept at a great distance, for God could not be corrupted by matter, which was considered evil in substance. Eternal ideas were immutable and should not be corrupted by change; the divine and the material were divided by an extreme dualism. Origen, the most important early systematic theologian in the East, consolidated Christianity with Hellenistic ontology and, in the process, endangered the Christian view of history. The Gnostics went further and actually created a non-Christian religion through syncretism with Neoplatonism.

Adolf Harnack picked up on this problem in the Gnostics, whom he considered the first Greek theologians. He then applied his critique of Hellenization to the entirety of Greek Christianity.[74] Harnack's project was to strip away the husk of Hellenism in order to return to the essence of the gospel.[75] Unfortunately, in the process, Harnack approached the other extreme. If the Gnostics offered an ontology without history, Harnack offered a history without ontology. Both tendencies disconnect history from eternity and Christology suffers as a result. With the Gnostics, Christ became a divine portion of the eternal cosmos. With Harnack, Christ became merely a man.

Unless eternity is relatable to history, there can be no direct creation, much less a divine incarnation to return that creation to intimate fellowship with the divine One who inhabits eternity. In *De Civitas Dei*, Augustine showed how Christianity necessarily embraced both history and eternity. God, from eternity, created history and in Christ entered history to redeem it. Because of the fall, humanity was corrupted, and human reason was perverted; because of redemption, however, history now includes two groups of people—the city of earth (*civitas terrene*) and the city of God (*civitas Dei*). These two cities travel together but to separate destinations. In the final judgment, the city of God will enter heaven; the city of man will be condemned to hell. While adopting a biblical historiography, Augustine carefully

[73] Jean Daniélou, *The Lord of History: Reflections on the Inner Meaning of History*, trans. Nigel Abercrombie (Chicago: Henry Regnery, 1958), 1.

[74] Adolf Harnack, *The History of Dogma*, 3rd ed., trans. Neil Buchanan (repr., Eugene, OR: Wipf and Stock, 1997), 1:227–28.

[75] Harnack stripped not only the Greek husk but gutted the seed of the gospel itself, changing its essence in the process. Harnack, *What Is Christianity?* trans. Thomas Bailey Saunders (New York: Harper, 1900), 13.

weaves the history of Israel, Christ and the apostles, and the postapostolic church in with secular history.[76]

The Lord of All Human Beings Equally

The discipline of history would be impossible without the presupposition that all men share a common nature. The Judeo-Christian doctrine of anthropology and the historian's presupposition regarding a common anthropology thus correlate in a profound way. The Judeo-Christian doctrine of anthropology, however, assigns a sacredness to human personality not necessarily required by secular historiography. Biblical anthropology begins with the creation of human persons, the first major divine act in history: "personalities are the crowning blossom of creation." Butterfield, in *Christianity and History*, is not dismissive of environmental concerns but perceives the creation of humanity as imposing a new order on nature.[77] Theological anthropology is a necessary discipline for the historiographer, yet the theologian and the historian differ, for while the theologian may peer deeply into the human soul, the historian practices restraint.

What then is the form of anthropology proper for history? "History deals with the drama of human life as the affair of individual personalities, possessing self-consciousness, intellect and freedom." In this way Butterfield begins with the individual human, for only human beings have souls. He strongly resisted historical approaches that viewed society as an organism or mechanism, fearing that such approaches overschematize history and depersonalize human beings. Above all, he was anxious to preserve the importance of the human soul in both nature and history. The "Christian view" is "that each individual soul is of eternal moment and has a value incommensurate with the value of anything else in the created universe. Human souls are in this view the purpose and end of the whole story."

Butterfield represents a high view of the human personality that resonates throughout the believers' church tradition from Hubmaier to Helwys to Wesley to Spurgeon to Martin Luther King Jr. As a result, the free-church doctrine of man, especially with regard to the assignation of individual dignity and freedom, is historically higher than that offered by the Catholic and evangelical traditions. According to Butterfield, the development of religious liberty is first found in the Christian tradition but especially among Christian dissenters in the Reformation and early modern period. Moreover, all other modern freedoms have developed from the unrelenting nonconformist demand for freedom of conscience, a demand later taken up by non-Christian humanists, often against the preferences of ecclesiastical traditions such as Roman Catholicism, Lutheranism, and the Reformed.[78]

---

[76] For Augustine's retelling of secular history, see books 1 through 5. Augustine, *The City of God*, trans. Marcus Dods (New York: Modern Library, 1993), 3–180.

[77] Butterfield, "Human Nature in History," in *Christianity and History*, 26–47.

[78] Butterfield, *Historical Development of the Principle of Toleration in British Life* [Robert Waley Cohen Memorial Lecture, 1956] (London: Epworth Press, 1957). See the next section for a fuller treatment of Butterfield's view of the development of freedom.

Butterfield's high view of the dignity of every human personality is coupled with a deep appreciation of the fundamental sinfulness of every human person. In this regard he disputed with Lord Acton, who downplayed the sin of some while excoriating the sins of others.[79] Butterfield believes in the universal kinship of all human beings because of their creation by God and in the universal sinfulness of all human beings because of their share in the fall. As a result of the Christian belief in the creation of all humanity from one couple, history demands a unified approach to humanity that respects all human beings. As a result of the Christian belief in the fallen nature of all humanity, history demands restraint in the exercise of judgment. The human view of sin is different from God's view of sin, for God is the final judge, while the historian must relay the story and the Christian must show mercy.

Divine Providence

Alongside Butterfield's sacred yet realistic anthropology is a high doctrine of divine providence. He recognized that some historians would argue for chance over providence, but Butterfield said that even the modern atheistic historian still posits laws in history. And it is illogical not to proceed to answer the question which immediately follows: whence did the laws come? There are only two possible answers: God or chance.[80] Butterfield answered with God. God created history and guides it to His inscrutable purpose. The Christian historian views the writing of history, therefore, as "a commentary on the ways of Providence."[81]

Butterfield's doctrine of providence, God's guidance of history, has multiple aspects, and nowhere did Butterfield draw together all of these aspects systematically.[82] A review of his writings reveals that he considered providence to manifest itself in the realm of creation, in election, in the promises of the covenants, and in eschatology. Throughout history, providence shows both mercy and judgment. Butterfield identified two forms of divine judgment: in time and in eternity. Sometimes the historian can trace the former, but the latter is in God's hand alone, and the historian must never pretend to cast himself in such a role. The vicissitudes of history reflect divine providence but not always divine judgment, for the end is not yet. Christianity is ultimately a historical religion because it accepts Jesus as the center of history.

While Butterfield was primarily interested in divine providence over universal history, Basil Manly Sr., pastor of the seminal Baptist church in the southern United States, was primarily interested in divine providence over American history. In his history of the Charleston Baptist Church, he outlined the guiding hand of God in terms similar to those offered by Butterfield. God guides the history

[79] Butterfield, "Human Nature in History," 29–30.

[80] Butterfield, "God in History," 8.

[81] Butterfield, *Christianity and History*, 93.

[82] Butterfield's clearest statements regarding providence are found scattered throughout *Christianity and History* and *Writings on Christianity and History*.

of churches and states through both mercy and judgment.[83] God governs history through mercy, which is His "benevolence to sinners," and through judgment, which concerns the "mysterious and afflictive" activity of God. He deals with His people not only in mercy but also in judgment, drawing them to Himself through both activities. Manly believed divine providence was especially operative in the creation of Baptist missionary structures.[84]

The free-church doctrine of providence may be organized temporally in a straight line, because, in explicit agreement with Augustine, it views history not in the Greek sense as cyclical but in the biblical sense as linear. History has come from God and is being led to its end by God.[85] The structure of Augustine's *De Civitas Dei* is informative for the Christian view of history not only as linear but as universal. In books 1 through 5, Augustine established that God was in control of pagan history. In books 6 through 10, he argued that God was also in control of eternity. In books 11 through 22, he turned to a theological explanation of history in temporal terms: 11 through 14 consider the creation of the two cities; 15 through 18, their history; and in 19 through 22, Augustine wrote of their consummation.

After Augustine's *tour de force*, any responsible Christian theology of history must account for divine providence in universal terms over secular history as well as sacred history. A responsible theology of history should also account for divine providence in linear terms from creation to the consummation. Theologically this may entail a consideration of God's intervention in history in three main movements: creation, redemption, eschatology. The Christian God "was," "is," and "will be." He is the Lord of all time. And at the center of time, uniting the beginning with the end and everything in between, is the Lord of history, Jesus Christ. Jesus Christ is Creator, Redeemer, and Consummation. He providentially reveals Himself as Lord of the old covenant as well as the new covenant, is manifesting Himself as Lord of the church, and will be fully manifested as the Lord of the world at the end of time.

The Lord of the Fallible

Even in his scientific historiographical treatise *The Whig Interpretation of History*, Butterfield spoke of "sin" in a religious sense. "The sin in historical composition" is not the possession of personal bias. Rather, the sin is found in not explicitly stating such presuppositions. It is unacceptable for the historian to assume for himself "the voice of God." Acton had demanded that the historian make moral judgments to set right past wrongs, especially with regard to the papacy and religious

[83] Basil Manly, *Mercy and Judgment: A Discourse, Containing Some Fragments of the History of the Baptist Church in Charleston, S.C.* (Charleston, 1837).

[84] Unfortunately Manly also believed divine providence was active in the social structure of the slave-holding society of the southern United States. Ibid., 3–7, 59; cited in Yarnell, "Political Theology at the Foundation of the Southern Baptist Convention," in *First Freedom: The Baptist Perspective on Religious Liberty*, ed. Thomas White, Jason G. Duesing, and Yarnell (Nashville: B&H, 2007), 91–92.

[85] Butterfield, "The Establishment of a Christian Interpretation of World History," in *Writings on Christianity and History*, 129–30. For a comparison of the cyclical view of history with the linear Christian view, see Bebbington, *Patterns in History*, 21–42 and 43–51.

persecution. Butterfield disagreed with Acton but not because he agreed with the papacy or the Protestants. Indeed, he fully agreed with Acton that both Catholics and Protestants engaged inappropriately in religious persecution. Neither did Butterfield disagree with Acton because he saw all men as good. Quite the opposite, Butterfield saw sin as a universal human problem. Because the historian is a sinner and not God, he may neither exonerate nor condemn. It is better for the historian to recognize that human sinfulness "is not really a historical problem at all." Absolute judgments of the sort demanded by Acton are reserved to God alone.[86]

Because Butterfield saw all men as sinners, he refused to interpret history as the opposition between good men and wicked men. Rather, the good and the wicked may be found in the same men. There may be levels of virtue in men and nations that are at war with one another, but no man is entirely lacking in cupidity. Indeed, because of the universality of sin, "wars of righteousness" are driven by an ideology that is in reality a "heresy." The heresy behind the demonization of the enemy and moralistic elevation of the ally is the denial of universal sin.[87] Butterfield was interested in neither exonerating nor condemning anyone. He was more interested in understanding humans as persons individually and as societies collectively so as to glimpse through their lives the ways of providence.

Correcting Acton's work on the rise of religious toleration and religious liberty in history, Butterfield advocated a highly nuanced view of freedom's development.[88] The prophets Jeremiah and Ezekiel taught that the individual is primary in religion, and the early Christians (and the early Methodists) believed the church is a voluntary society with rules of membership intended only for the few. Augustine, however, argued for a unanimous society and opted for religious persecution against the Donatists. The Constantinian and Augustinian ideal of the "State as a Religious Society" or "comprehension" was accepted by most people in the Middle Ages, and during the Reformation by both Roman Catholics and Protestants. Acton demonstrated convincingly that the medieval conflict between the papacy and the empire unexpectedly "tempered the tyranny of both, and reduced both to the necessity of persuading human beings—appealing to an internal arbiter."[89]

Against the Whigs, Butterfield asserted that the Protestants were no more interested in religious liberty than the Catholics. There was a "more tolerant party" in the sixteenth century that stressed the inner life of the individual as a voluntary response to God, but this was a minority view. At first both Catholics and Protestants sought to impose their religion upon their peoples. The system of partition known as *cuius regio eius religio* (whose region, his religion) was considered only a temporary solution until one party gained the ascendancy. However, neither party achieved hegemony. "It was perhaps good for the world that Jesuit and

[86] Butterfield, *The Whig Interpretation of History*, 107, 117–18.

[87] *Christianity, Diplomacy, and War* (London: Epworth, 1953), cited in McIntire, *Herbert Butterfield*, 242–43.

[88] H. Butterfield, *Christianity in European History* (New York: Oxford University Press, 1951); idem, *Historical Development of the Principle of Toleration in British Life*; idem, "Reflections on Religion and Modern Individualism," *JHI* 22 (1961): 33–46; idem, "Toleration in Early Modern Times," *JHI* 38 (1977): 573–84; idem, "The Conflict between Right and Wrong in History," in *Writings on Christianity and History*, 54–74.

[89] Butterfield, "Religion and Modern Individualism," 39.

Calvinist failed to annihilate one another and that under the cover of their conflicts the sects were able to multiply."[90]

Under the systems of toleration that initially arose out of early modern society's sheer exhaustion at religious persecution, minorities were initially turned into second-class citizens. Later, as the nonconformists continued to survive and refused to conform, the idea of full religious liberty, first limited and then universal, developed. This, of course, was not due to any resident virtue on the part of the nonconformists, for had they been able to "establish their own tyranny," they would have done so.[91] The historical service for freedom performed by dissenters was to remain ever in opposition without victory or total defeat.

In this entirely unexpected way, "freedom of conscience" became the basis for all other modern freedoms. There was no historical determinism in the fatalistic sense employed by David Hume or the Marxist historians. Neither was there any battle between the good party (the Protestants) and the evil party (the Catholics), as the Whig historians taught. Rather, good and evil are in all men, including all Christians—Roman Catholic, Protestant, and nonconformist. The battles between men were instrumental in freedom's development, but such battles were providentially unresolved. Moreover, Butterfield humbly recognized that true religious liberty came about only as the nonconformist Christians in England found themselves allied with the secularists. Providentially, it was only with the "Great Secularization" that Christians finally obtained full religious liberty.[92]

The lessons taught by the development of freedom are of universal sin among men and of God's overarching providence. "Of course there is evil in the world. It happens only to be more insidious than people often think, and we are all involved in it more or less, even the moderately virtuous."[93] It has been said that Butterfield's view of sin was Augustinian, making Acton appear almost Pelagian.[94] Although this is a gross simplification, the free-church theologian might make the same argument regarding Catholic or evangelical pretensions at perfection in doctrine.

Butterfield did not address the intricacies of the Catholic idea of the infallible church, for this was diametrically opposed to his idea that all men, including all Christians, and including the institutional church, are sinners. "The Christian Church itself, regarded as a visible and terrestrial institution, has not been exempt from that bias, that curious twist in events, that gravitational pull in human nature, which draws the highest things downwards, mixes them with earth, and taints them with human cupidity."[95] Following the free-church historian, the free-church theologian might conclude that if the church is fallible, its dogma, especially when not taught directly by Scripture, must always remain suspect.

---

[90] Butterfield, *Christianity in European History*, 34.

[91] Butterfield, "The Conflict between Right and Wrong in History," 70.

[92] Butterfield, *Christianity in European History*, 37–38.

[93] Butterfield, "The Conflict between Right and Wrong in History," 57.

[94] Cp. Chadwick, "Acton and Butterfield," 403; McIntire, *Herbert Butterfield*, 164.

[95] Butterfield, *Christianity and History*, 39.

The Lord of Both Covenants

Daniélou noted that a Christian theology of history must not only distinguish itself from the dehistoricizing trend of Greek philosophy, it must also distinguish itself from the alternative historiography of Judaism. Judaism and Christianity agree concerning the basic definition of history. History is composed of events in time made meaningful by their relationship to eternity; the continuity of meaning between various events is provided by divine providence; and the development of events toward the end is set by God. But Judaism has a stalled sense of development, whereas Christianity affirms a progressive revelation. "Jews and Christians agree in believing that the religious institutions of Jewry, such as the circumcision, the Sabbath, and the temple, are of divine origin; but Christians simultaneously hold that Christ abolished these institutions."[96] History for the Jews is still awaiting the Christ, while history for the Christian recognizes that the Christ has come in Jesus. The New Testament presents Jesus as the agent and goal of the creation of the world (Col 2:15–17) and as the fulfillment of Israel's hopes (Matt 16:13–16).

Paul and the author of Hebrews expressed a similar view. According to Paul, there are two covenants, and they must be carefully differentiated, for the sake of salvation. The one covenant is represented in Hagar, the bondwoman, who knows only the law of Mount Sinai and corresponds to Jerusalem today. The children of Hagar are born in the flesh to her bondage. The other covenant is represented in Sarah, the free woman, who carries the promise and corresponds to Jerusalem above. The children of Sarah are born by the Spirit to her freedom. "So then, brethren, we are not children of the bondwoman but of the free" (Gal 4:21–31). According to the author of Hebrews, the new covenant was imperfect and has been replaced by a better covenant. The ordinances of the old covenant were shadows and copies of the new covenant. The new covenant has a perfect priest who has presented a perfect sacrifice. The new covenant participates in eternity itself and thus has put an end to the priesthood, sacrifices, and ordinances of the old covenant (Hebrews 7–10).

The Christian Bible recognizes the Old Testament as Scripture, but Christians also include the New Testament as Scripture. The relationship of the two covenants necessarily raises the issue of the proper Christian interpretation of the Old Testament. Christians interpret the Old Testament according to Jesus Christ, who fulfills the law (Matt 5:17–18; Luke 24:44–45). When it came to interpreting the Bible, the early Christians had diverse hermeneutical models from which to borrow. On the one hand was the allegorical method of the Greeks and of Alexandrian Judaism, which could dismiss history. On the other hand was the literal method of Palestinian Judaism, which retained history but could dismiss theology. The early Christian exegetical schools of Antioch and Alexandria have been popularly identified, respectively, with the literal historical method and the allegorical method.[97] Through its focus on the literal, Antioch faced the problem of theologi-

[96] Daniélou, *The Lord of History*, 4.

[97] T. E. Pollard, "The Origins of Christian Exegesis," *JRH* 1 (1961): 138–47; Bernard Ramm, *Protestant Biblical Interpretation: A Textbook of Hermeneutics*, 3rd rev. ed. (Grand Rapids: Baker, 1970), 24–50.

cal myopia, while Alexandria, through its focus on the spiritual, faced the problem of historical fantasy.[98]

Whatever one's view of allegory, there should be little doubt that typology is required for the Christian interpretation of the Old Testament. "Christians must recognize the legitimacy and necessity of typology, in contrast to allegory, as a way of interpreting the Old Testament which they read in light of the New Testament. They cannot avoid typological exegesis for their devotional and liturgical use of the Old Testament." Pollard considered Christian typology "inescapable" for Christians even to approach the Old Testament. The difference between typology and allegory comes down to the difference between eisegesis, "the art of drawing *into* the sacred text meaning drawn from the interpreter's personal ideas and peculiar brand of philosophy," and exegesis, "the art of drawing *out* of the sacred text its full meaning when read as a whole." Christians may engage in typology because it is "the process of interpreting Scripture by Scripture, the Old Testament in light of the New."[99]

The transition from the old covenant to the new covenant involves a progress, a growth, a development, in revelation. Revelation began with the incomplete revelation to Moses of the law but reached its fulfillment with the complete revelation of Jesus Christ. The New Testament must be read in light of the Old Testament, but the Old Testament is incomplete without the New Testament. Due to its fullness, the witness of Christ and the cowitness of the apostles combine to form the normative revelation. Israel, the people of God in the Old Testament, has been joined with the church, the people of God in the New Testament. The covenants retain their distinctiveness historically, but the old cannot save. The two peoples, formerly divided by hostility, have become one through the reconciling work of Jesus Christ (Eph 2:11–18). In Christ the believing part of Israel enters the church of the new covenant. Paul prophesied that, once the Gentiles had come in, Israel also would have a revival, entering in by faith (Rom 11:20–27). Israel enters into the kingdom through the new covenant, but the church should not be confused with Israel. Maintaining the distinction between Israel and the church is central to avoiding the confusion of the covenants characteristic of Reformed theology.[100]

As Marpeck discovered in his debates with the evangelicals, the discernment of Scripture's historical progress is important for the proper interpretation of Scripture. The Old Testament is best understood as for "yesterday," while the New Testament reveals the gospel of "today" and "tomorrow." The Old Testament may be properly understood only through the incarnation of Jesus Christ. There

---

[98] Maurice F. Wiles, *The Spiritual Gospel: The Interpretation of the Fourth Gospel in the Early Church* (New York: Cambridge University Press, 1960), 31, 38–40, 158–61.

[99] Pollard, "The Origins of Christian Exegesis," 144–45. For an alternative, positive view of precritical exegesis, see David C. Steinmetz, "The Superiority of Pre-Critical Exegesis," *TT* 37 (1980): 27–38; reprinted in Steinmetz, *Memory and Mission: Theological Reflections on the Christian Past* (Nashville: Abingdon Press, 1988), 143–63.

[100] The Reformed confusion of covenants also encourages the replacement theory. Cp. Walter C. Kaiser Jr., "Israel as the People of God," in *The People of God: Essays on the Believers' Church*, ed. Paul Basden and David S. Dockery (Nashville: Broadman, 1991), 99–108.

is a progressive revelation in Scripture, and this progression must be kept in mind in order to avoid serious error in reading and applying Scripture. If progressive revelation in Scripture is not remembered, one may seek to institute the kingdom of God by infant baptism and by the suppression of religious liberty. If discerning history, and Jesus as the Lord of history, is important for the proper interpretation of the Old and New Testaments, it is also important for the proper interpretation of the church's history. The church exists in the time between the times. The kingdom of God has entered and begun the redemption of history through the incarnation, death, and resurrection of Jesus Christ. But the kingdom of God will appear in its fullness only with His visible return to bring eternal judgment. Until then, the church has a missionary mandate to fulfill.

The Lord of All the Churches

According to Gerhard Ebeling, a pioneer in Protestant foundational theology, the only proper form of church history is found in the exposition of Scripture. The priority of biblical interpretation is true not only for the discipline of church history but for all the theological disciplines. "Hence, if any attempt is made to arrange the theological disciplines in order of precedence and value in general, the most that can be said is that every aspect of theological study must subserve the interpretation of Holy Scripture." Ebeling was not arguing that the church historian should ignore the critical skills of historical science, for "above all," those skills must be learned; however, the mere recitation of chronological occurrences (*Historie*), which are discovered according to the skills of historical science, is insufficient. The events must be brought into a pattern of meaning, and until that occurs, there is no history (*Geschichte*) in the proper sense. Again, Ebeling was not arguing for bypassing secular history in the pursuit of sacred history. Rather, all of history must be interpreted with reference to the Word of God.[101]

Paralleling our division of theological foundations in chapter 2 above, Ebeling discerns three main forms for conceiving church history. First, the Roman Catholic conception of church history "makes the history of the Church the direct continuation of the Incarnation and therefore of the history of Jesus Christ." Because the Roman conception of history does not maintain a strong distinction between God and His church in history, its doctrine "can only develop." The only sense of corruption that the Roman church understands is brought about through persecution by the world without and through heresy from within the church. Yet the church and its institutions remain perfect. The Roman conception of church history is historiographically vulnerable to the modern historical method and theologically insufficient with regard to the pervasive nature of depravity.

Second, Ebeling says the "Enthusiastic" concept of church history tends to spiritualize historical events. This concept is "marked by its immediate experience of God. The basic significance of this lies in the fact that the historicity of the Church disap-

[101] Gerhard Ebeling, *The Word of God and Tradition: Historical Studies Interpreting the Divisions of Christianity*, trans. S. H. Hooke (London: Collins, 1968), 11–22.

pears in the essential conception of an invisible Church." Those who hold the Enthusiastic concept tend to make a caricature of church history. The Enthusiastic method uses the tools of historical criticism but only in order to dissolve the visible church. Perhaps Ebeling has in mind the ecclesiastical ruminations of the sixteenth-century historian, Sebastian Franck. For Franck, the true church is entirely invisible, and the visible churches are entirely corrupt.[102] Ebeling is satisfied with neither the enthusiastic "docetic" nor the Roman Catholic "Incarnation" models of church history.

Ebeling's third and preferred form is the Reformed conception of church history. The Reformed conception operates according to a dialectic "of the antithesis between an invisible and a visible Church." Even so, Ebeling recognizes that the Reformed formula is "capable of manifold interpretations" that have not "reached any satisfactory settlement." It tends to splinter into multiple presentations along the lines of particular historical bodies; and it seems to have the problem that many Reformed scholars end up adopting the Enthusiastic concept of church history. The basis of this problem is with "the idea of its [the church's] invisibility." In spite of the problem with the invisible church scenario with regard to providing an adequate church history, Ebeling does not see any way beyond the problematic idea. Unfortunately Ebeling also includes the free churches under the Reformed conception.[103]

Ebeling, reflecting a typical Reformed lacuna, ignores the verity that free-church ecclesiology offers an alternative and arguably more viable conception of Christian history. For instance, the Anabaptists considered the church as in need of restitution rather than reformation. "Restitution" seeks to reinstitute the church of the New Testament, whereas "reformation" seeks to reform the church according to some ideal form, usually defined by an epoch in Christian history.[104] The proponents of reformation too often offer a postbiblical paradigm or extrabiblical philosophy as the proper method for interpreting Scripture. Reformism claims Scripture as a foundation but interprets Scripture according to a tradition or a rationality that limits the work of the Spirit. But the free-church desire for restitution of the New Testament church identifies the invisible church as a Neoplatonic dissolution,[105] the hierarchical visible church as a Dionysian invention,[106] and the national church as an evangelical corruption.[107]

[102] Franck, Letter to John Campanus (1531), in *Spiritual and Anabaptist Writers*, ed. George H. Williams and Angel M. Mergal, LCC (Philadelphia: Westminster, 1957), 147–62.

[103] Ebeling, *The Word of God and Tradition*, 22–26.

[104] Littell, *The Anabaptist View of the Church*, 79.

[105] Augustine's understanding of the church as invisible seems to have been influenced by his appropriation of Plotinus. Phillip Cary, *Augustine's Invention of the Inner Self: The Legacy of a Christian Platonist* (New York: Oxford University Press, 2000), 39, 42, 45–51. His arguments with the Donatists brought him to stress the universal and invisible nature of the church. Peter Brown, *Augustine of Hippo: A Biography* (Los Angeles: University of California Press, 1967), 221–22.

[106] The hierarchical understanding of the church that reached its zenith in the Middle Ages in the West was in part supported by the pseudepigraphical writings of Dionysius. Pseudo-Dionysius envisioned salvation as coming through a scale of levels among both angels and men. The celestial and ecclesiastical hierarchies exist to become one with God through purification, illumination, and perfection. See *The Celestial Hierarchy* and *The Ecclesiastical Hierarchy*, in *Pseudo-Dionysius: The Complete Works*, trans. Colm Luibheid (New York: Paulist, 1987).

[107] The Diet of Speyer, which determined the religion of the prince to be the religion of the people in a territory (*cuius regio eius religio*) also recalled the punishment of death for rebaptism. On the political enforcement of

The New Testament speaks primarily of the church in local terms. Such churches are gathered on the basis of a covenant between God and men (Matt 18:15–20). The historical existence of multiple churches, so disturbing to participants in evangelical and Catholic ecumenical discussions, does not trouble the free churches, for they deem the model biblical. The Jerusalem and Antioch churches were separately governed, even as they intensely sought unity in doctrine (Acts 15). The dominical appeal for unity is understood in eschatological and spiritual terms rather than according to temporary and governmental concepts. Thus there is little impetus for visible union or shared ministries and sacraments among the free churches. That churches become corrupted doctrinally and ethically is seriously lamented and a cause for vigilance. Most of the free churches recognize the universal church, but as it does not gather until the end of time, it is not the primary concern in contemporary history.

The free churches thus bring forward a fourth conception of church history. Because they recognize New Testament doctrine and practice as the norm of orthodoxy, the history of the church is best conceived as the history of local churches. Jesus Christ is the head and foundation of the kingdom of God and of each local church (Col 2:18; 1 Cor 3:11). The emphasis is on a multiplicity of local churches simply because the New Testament treated the local church primarily as local. Believers' church ecclesiology thus flattens any distinctions between the churches, theologically and historically. Christ, by His Spirit, moves among the churches sovereignly and mysteriously. No church has any priority over any other. Every church is ultimately judged by God according to its fidelity to His Word. Ebeling's contention that church historians should adopt "a clear theological definition of the conception of church history" is agreeable even if his definition of "church" is, as is typical among evangelicals, deficient.

Ebeling defined church history as "the history of the interpretation of Holy Scripture." He was careful to distinguish revelation from interpretation and interpretations within history from the contemporary task of interpretation. Moreover, interpretation of Scripture is more than the reading of commentaries or the review of preaching and doctrine. "Interpretation of Scripture finds expression in ritual and prayer, in theological work and in personal decisions, in Church organization and ecclesiastical politics." In other words, the interpretation of Scripture is as much about "doing and suffering" as it is about thinking and speaking.[108] Again the free-church historian finds this a highly laudable conception.

Because the church is comprised of all those of all time who believe in Jesus Christ, church history considers the work of Jesus Christ through Word and Spirit in the lives of Christians of all periods. Such a concept of church history does not privilege Rome over Constantinople, or Wittenberg over Geneva, or London over Nashville, or Dallas over Lagos. Every church is under the direct headship of Jesus Christ and responsible to Him for the way it reads the Bible and follows the Spirit.

the Protestant faith, see Quentin Skinner, *The Foundations of Modern Political Thought* (New York: Cambridge University Press, 1978), 2:89–108.

[108] Ebeling, *The Word of God and Tradition*, 26–28.

This ecclesiastical egalitarianism also encourages a chronological egalitarianism. Sometimes academic historians become enamored with their particular specialty and ecclesiastical historians become enamored with their particular churches, but to cite Butterfield's ruminations regarding the English historiographical debate between "whigs and tories"; all sides are "equally necessary to the picture."[109]

Free-church historiography may stress the history of the dissenting churches, but it may not privilege them. According to his own principles, the free-church historian may not ignore nor may he skew his presentation of churches in other traditions. All historians must recognize that historical ignorance and perverse presentation was practiced in the past. Lamentably, historians covering the Donatists of the early period or the "heretics" of the medieval period or the dissenters of the early modern period largely ignored or misrepresented the thought of their opponents. We know much more about what the medieval persecutor thought than what the Lollard himself thought. Such hostile theological filtering renders the traditional records suspect. If we wish to know what earlier dissenters believed, the heresy trials and historical records of especially the early and medieval periods are simply unreliable. Unfortunately this is, for the most part, the only historical data that the contemporary historian possesses.

Similarly, from a chronological perspective, the free-church historian may not privilege the modern churches over the Reformation churches or the medieval churches over the early churches. There has been talk of a patristic renewal (*ressourcement*) among American evangelicals in recent years, especially with regard to the patristic period.[110] The recovery of patristic theology is welcome, but the reconsideration of the Spirit's work among the churches should not be limited in conception or practice to any one period. As A. N. Williams warned, "The notion that any one period or any one theology is uniquely authoritative necessarily implies a position on the development of doctrine, namely that it halts at some point."[111] In other words, the instantiation of any one postbiblical epoch implicitly denies the continuing work of the Holy Spirit among the people of God and brings the church to a perfection in doctrine that it cannot possess until the *parousia*.

The Rankean principle, reiterated by Butterfield, of reading the past for the sake of the past is helpful here. If history is reading the past for the sake of the past, then theology is reading the past for the sake of the present. Historical reading of the past must seek to read the past for itself. Theological reading of the past must seek to read the past for the present. If the two are confused, one may enthrone the past or the present rather than the Lord of both past and present. Reading the

---

[109] Butterfield, *Christianity and History*, 91.

[110] Marvin W. Anderson, "The Chicago Call: An Appeal to Evangelicals," *Christianity Today*, June 1977, 28–29; Robert E. Webber, "A Call to an Ancient Evangelical Future," *Christianity Today*, September 2006, 57–58; R. R. Reno, "The Return of the Fathers," *FT*, November 2006, 15–20. Some characteristic works include D. H. Williams, *Evangelicals and Tradition: The Formative Influence of the Early Church* (Grand Rapids: Baker, 2005); Russell R. Reno and John J. O'Keefe, *Sanctified Vision: An Introduction to Early Christian Interpretation of the Bible* (Baltimore: Johns Hopkins University Press, 2005).

[111] Williams, "The Future of the Past: The Contemporary Significance of the *Nouvelle Théologie*," *IJST* 7 (2005): 352.

past should be a means of unleashing theological creativity in the present.[112] For the free-church theologian, historical reading is simultaneously fixed by the Word of God and freed by the Spirit of God; nonbiblical history itself lacks a normative function in theology.

Theology should never be fixed by postbiblical developments themselves, although it is extremely wise to listen to the lessons taught in, by, and about our Christian forefathers. Every epoch of history must be read according to the immutable Word illuminated by the Spirit. The free-church theologian may not listen with some Anglicans only to the early fathers, or with some Roman Catholics only to Aquinas, or with some Reformed only to the Puritans, or with some liberals only to modernity. The free-church theologian may not even listen only to the free churches. The free-church theological historian will listen to every theological epoch, discerning the sovereign movement of the Lord among all the churches as they interpret the Word. Jesus Christ is the Lord of all the churches throughout history: patristic, medieval, early modern, modern, and those to come before Christ comes again to call together the universal church for its first gathering.

FROM A THEOLOGY OF HISTORY TO A HISTORY OF THEOLOGY

In this chapter we have surveyed the earlier free-church doctrine of development, with special attention on the "further light" doctrine of the English Separatists and Baptists and on the cross-centered and thus historical nature of Andrew Fuller's prolegomena. We also considered the response of free-church scholars to modern historiography, indicating the compatibility between academic seriousness and dissenting doctrines, as exemplified by Herbert Butterfield. Finally, we offered a free-church theology of history, considering divine providence and giving special attention to Jesus Christ as Lord of history and eternity, as Lord of all human beings equally, as Lord of the fallible, as Lord of both covenants, and as Lord of all the churches. Having defined a theology of history, we are now prepared to propose a pattern and important components within a history of theology.

[112] Ibid., 358.

Chapter Six

THE PATTERN OF THE CROSS AS COMMISSION: *Toward a Free-Church History of Theology*

The previous chapters of this book laid the conceptual framework for the goal of our project, understanding the formation of Christian doctrine. We have considered the problem of theological foundations, examining the various alternatives offered by substantive Christian traditions. We then proposed a particular theological foundation available in the work of a sixteenth-century South German Anabaptist. Upon this theological foundation we examined the predominant alternatives for doctrinal development that have been offered in the past. Then in chapter 5, we proposed a particular view on behalf of free-church historians, especially exemplified by an English Methodist academic historian. In this chapter we take the next step: proposing the pattern of and some important components within a free-church history of theology. This is the shortest chapter in the book and the goal toward which the writer has been driving the entire time. This chapter, however, would be impossible without taking into account the two major aspects of theological method: theological foundation and the development of doctrine.

Responding to the shaking of Christian theological foundations fostered by scholarship since the advance of modernism, James Leo Garrett Jr. recognized the extreme complexity of writing a history of doctrinal development. He surveyed the multiple and divergent approaches that have been taken in the attempt to perceive and record historical theology. Garrett concluded that the best way to approach the complexity of the problem of historical theology is through a coordinated effort among scholars.[1] Indeed, the complexity of history must be recognized and adequately addressed through consistent detailed research accomplished in the community of scholars, but the complexity of a task is no reason to delay engaging in it indefinitely.[2] At some point the general historian must identify, even if only tentatively, the pattern of history he will attempt to follow.

What follows is a preliminary effort to define the pattern of church history according to the free-church commitment to the cross of Jesus Christ. It attempts to define the historical pattern according to the cross as an intimately personal and life-

[1] James Leo Garrett Jr., "The History of Christian Doctrine: Retrospect and Prospect," *RE* 68 (1971): 245–60.

[2] Cp. McIntire's critique of Butterfield's ideal of scientific history and the resultant problem of historical productivity. C. T. McIntire, *Herbert Butterfield: Historian as Dissenter* (New Haven, CN: Yale University Press, 2004), 405.

changing event, rather than as a detached idea. The New Testament focuses on the cross of Jesus Christ and on the demand for human beings to submit to Him as disciples. The call of Christ to take up the cross in discipleship, in imitation of the Master, is contained in many places throughout the Gospels but most conveniently encapsulated in the Great Commission, classically identified with the Matthean version (Matt 28:16–20). Because the New Testament is the literary record that focuses on Jesus Christ, His cross, and its message as taught by His immediate disciples, then church history should properly consider the literary record of those who subsequently responded to the cross. The true believer, a disciple of Jesus Christ, is one who takes up his cross to follow Him (Mark 8:34). A believers' church historiography will seek to relay the story of the true believers, the cross-carrying disciples of Christ.

THE NEW TESTAMENT PATTERN OF HISTORY

As we have seen with both Herbert Butterfield and Andrew Fuller, historians and theologians seek to discern patterns, the patterns of history and the patterns of theological truth. According to many historians and theologians, but especially in the free-church tradition, the cross of Jesus Christ provides the shape of that pattern. Free-church theologians and free-church historians interpret history through the New Testament. A free-church historiography sees all of history—general human history, the broad history of the churches, and the history of the free churches—as being shaped by the central events of the gospel. The gospel is comprised of unique historical events, especially the incarnation, life, death, resurrection, commission, and return of Jesus Christ.

The New Testament Pattern

According to Robert A. Baker (1910–1992), "the New Testament is the pattern and authority for a New Testament Christian." Speaking for a particular denomination among the free churches, he claims, "Both Baptist doctrine and Baptist history stem from this basic truth."[3] Baker, longtime professor of history at Southwestern Baptist Theological Seminary in Fort Worth, Texas, and a leading historian among Southern Baptists, received his PhD from Yale University, having worked with Kenneth Scott Latourette. He has been called a "dean" of Southern Baptist historians. Baker's credentials as an academic historian are impeccable, while his commitments to free-church historiography are incomparable. Like Butterfield, he was noted among his students for his focus on "the facts."[4]

In comparison with Butterfield, Baker was more of a historian and theologian than a philosopher of history or historian of historiography. Yet Baker understood clearly that even scientific history must adopt a pattern of presentation. For Baker, that pattern must come from Scripture, especially the New Testament, rather than from any extrabiblical source. In his presentation of general Christian history,

---

[3] Robert A. Baker, *The Baptist March in History* (Nashville: Convention Press, 1958), 1.

[4] Stephen M. Stookey, "Robert Andrew Baker," in *The Legacy of Southwestern: Writings That Shaped a Tradition*, ed. James Leo Garrett Jr. (North Richland Hills, TX: Smithfield Press, 2002), 109–23.

Baker adopted a summary paradigm in order to guide his students through, in the words of one of his students, John Landers, "the maze" of historical facts.[5]

Baker's summary accords with the classical free-church model. Its historical beginning lay in the establishment of Christ's church, "a local autonomous body where two or three gathering together in prayer could find his presence and power." From a small beginning, His earliest disciples began to establish churches in order to fulfill "the seemingly impossible task contained in the Great Commission."[6] The historical foundation of the churches is found in the commandments of Jesus Christ.

The free-church paradigm in Baker's historiography is unmistakable. It will be remembered that, according to Littell, the Methodist historian of the sixteenth-century Anabaptists, the three major elements of free-church historiography are a "golden age" of the faith, the "fall" of the church, and its "restitution."[7] Baker's "golden age" is the New Testament itself, for he recognizes no proper development in doctrine beyond the New Testament witness. Indeed, corruption, a movement away from the New Testament pattern, is a real problem, and the clergy are far from infallible.

The New Testament pattern included four primary aspects: First, "that salvation comes through simple faith in Jesus Christ." Second, "that a church is a body of persons who have been born again, baptized, and gifted with the Spirit of Christ" and "all churches were on the same level, and each church had authority to govern its own affairs." Third, that "the officers of the local body were two, pastors and deacons." And fourth, that "the ordinances were two, baptism and the Lord's Supper." Worship was simple and direct for every member.[8]

But immediately after the New Testament period, the church began a twofold struggle. From the outside it met with pagan opposition and state persecution. From the inside, it began "struggling to retain its original purity of doctrine and practice."[9] In concert with the Anabaptists and with Butterfield, Baker associates the fall of the church with the conversion of Constantine to Christianity. Baker questions whether Constantine truly became a Christian, asserting that his adoption of Christianity "was more political than religious." Constantine adopted Christianity because he perceived the empire needed "religious unity" in order to strengthen his subjects' "political loyalty."[10]

Constantine's conversion brought to a climax the early church's struggle for purity. In the early centuries Baker found three dilutions of Christianity, four inadequate attempts to understand the Trinity, five pagan corruptions of Christian doctrine and worship, and three reactions to the problem of lowering

---

[5] Landers, "Preface," in Robert A. Baker and John M. Landers, *A Summary of Christian History*, 3rd ed. (Nashville: B&H, 2005), xi.

[6] Ibid., 6.

[7] Franklin H. Littell, *The Anabaptist View of the Church: A Study in the Origins of Sectarian Protestantism* (Boston: Starr King, 1958), 57.

[8] Baker and Landers, *A Summary of Christian History*, 43. Cp. Baker, *The Baptist March in History*, 3–9.

[9] Baker and Landers, *A Summary of Christian History*, 27.

[10] Ibid., 25.

Christian standards.[11] Although he does not pin the entire blame on the emperor, Baker believes that "the New Testament faith became harder to recognize after Constantine."[12]

The corruption of the faith occurred in all four areas: the nature of faith, the nature of the church, the nature of ecclesiastical authority, and the nature of worship. As for faith, salvation was now mediated through the sacraments of the church. As for the church, a third office was added, hierarchy developed, and congregationalism was compromised. As for ecclesiastical authority, Irenaeus, among others, shifted authority from Scripture alone to Scripture and the episcopate. As for worship, the original directness of Christian worship was exchanged for sacramentalism and sacerdotalism, and the original simplicity of worship was corrupted by magic and formality.[13]

The changes in the faith in the early period were definitely "a departure from the New Testament pattern," but there were even more radical changes to come.[14] For instance, the empire based in Constantinople introduced Caesaropapacy, rule of the church by the state. And by the high Middles Ages, the Roman bishop achieved unparalleled authority in both church and state in the West. Scholasticism "intermingled" tradition with Scripture, requiring "a complete redefinition of every doctrine."[15] As a result of such developments, "the golden age of Roman Catholicism contrasts sharply with New Testament Christianity."[16]

Baker is careful not to affirm a hidden succession of dissenting churches from the New Testament to the Reformation. He does note the existence of various dissenting groups in both the early and medieval periods. Unfortunately, "the sparsity of records makes it difficult to judge accurately either the doctrines or the extent of the movements."[17] In spite of such limitations on the evidence, Baker believes that the speed with which the Reformation was accepted suggests that a good number of medieval dissenters were laying the groundwork for the Reformation when it did finally occur.

Baker uses the language of "reform" with regard to the restitution of New Testament Christianity but criticizes the Magisterial reformers for only partially removing the corruptions of the early and medieval periods. While lauding their contributions, he demonstrates their inconsistency in restoring "the scriptural pattern."[18] He also laments the ignorance and gross mischaracterization of the Anabaptists that were subsequently displayed by "the principal historians."[19] With regard to the origins of the early English Baptists, Baker was less concerned with demonstrating a historic succession than with identifying the New Testament pat-

[11] Ibid., 27–42.
[12] Ibid., 43.
[13] Ibid., 44–51. Cp. Baker, *The Baptist March in History*, 13–27.
[14] Baker and Landers, *A Summary of Christian History*, 57.
[15] Ibid., 131.
[16] Ibid., 140.
[17] Ibid., 197.
[18] Ibid., 224.
[19] Ibid., 235, 245–46.

tern as drawing Baptists into existence. "The rediscovery of the New Testament as pattern and authority drew men and women from the Established Church to follow in the train of those whose lineage was marked by the preservation of New Testament principles."[20]

The Pattern of the Cross

The believers' church theology of history bases itself in the New Testament and considers any departure from it to be a fall requiring restitution. But what aspect of New Testament doctrine do free-church historians deem principal? They typically discern the pattern of history according to the cross. The three elements of past Christian history point to a deeper reality, the cross of Jesus Christ.[21] According to Bebbington, "The major claims of Christianity about history are summed up by the cross."[22] According to Latourette, the pattern of history preferred by Christianity focuses upon divine love, and "this love was especially seen in the death of Jesus."[23] According to Baker, the New Testament pattern begins with God as loving and redemptive "so much that he gave his only Son as a revelation of himself and a sacrifice for sin."[24]

According to Butterfield, the Old Testament patterns of history reached their summit in the Suffering Servant. "But the most remarkable of all such types or patterns was the famous picture of the Suffering Servant, who was wounded for transgressions." The Suffering Servant "is a pattern or representation of something which is essential, something which lies at the roots of history." It answers the questions history poses regarding the problem of suffering by giving meaning to the inescapable theme of tragedy. It transforms the concept of righteousness by pointing to God as the one who expiates sins through His own suffering. And the people of God find their meaning in history by participating in His sacrifice: "Israel suffered for all mankind." Through the spectacle of the Suffering Servant, the nations are moved to repent.[25]

The Suffering Servant of the Old Testament was perfectly fulfilled in the cross of Christ in the New Testament. The vicarious suffering of Jesus Christ brings harmony to the dissonances created by human sin in history. Christ achieved the solidarity of humanity by "a principle of love." The cross thus calls for an intimate personal decision, thereby fostering "a heightened conception of personality."[26] The apostle Paul told the Corinthians, "I determined not to know anything among

[20] Baker, *The Baptist March in History*, 42–43.

[21] Augustine also read all of history through the cross, but the consistency of his crucicentrism is cast into doubt by his approval of religious persecution against the Donatists. Peter Iver Kaufman, "Augustine, Martyrs, and Misery," *CH* 63 (1994): 1–14. Toward the end of his life, Augustine began losing his enthusiasm for Christian persecution, but the mold was already set. Peter Brown, *Augustine of Hippo: A Biography* (Los Angeles: University of California Press, 1967), 337–38.

[22] David Bebbington, *Patterns in History: A Christian Perspective on Historical Thought*, 2nd ed. (Vancouver, BC: Regent College Publishing, 1990), 175.

[23] Kenneth Scott Latourette, "The Christian Understanding of History," *AHR* 54 (1949): 265.

[24] Baker, *The Baptist March in History*, 3–4.

[25] Butterfield, *Christianity and History* (London: Bell, 1950), 83–85.

[26] Ibid., 86–87. Cp. Baker, *The Baptist March in History*, 124–26.

you except Jesus Christ and Him crucified" (1 Cor 2:2). Believers' church historians provide the chorus for Paul's profound solo. The dissonances in history find their harmony only in the cross.

The New Testament provides the pattern for both free-church theology and free-church historiography. Jesus Christ and the cross are central to the New Testament. According to the free-church historians, the cross provides the pattern for free-church history, for general church history, indeed for all of human history. It will be remembered that, similarly, the cross provides the pattern for the unfinished systematic theology of Andrew Fuller.[27] More recently Lewis Drummond claimed that "Christ crucified" provides the foundation for Southern Baptist Billy Graham's evangelistic theology.[28] Profoundly, the diverse disciplines of free-church theological studies converge in the cross of Jesus Christ.

From the perspective of leading free-church theologians, historians, and evangelists, human response to Jesus Christ and His cross should determine the pattern for both theology and history. Theologically, the cross is central to the New Testament understanding of God, of salvation, and of community. Historically, the cross is central to the development of the church's understanding of God, of salvation, and of community. Above, we offered a short theology of history; below, we offer a short history of theology. Our suggested pattern is the Great Commission given by Christ for disseminating the message regarding His cross.

SUGGESTED THEMES FOR A FREE-CHURCH HISTORY OF THEOLOGY

The Great Commission is a complex text with multiple historico-theological themes. Five such themes come quickly to mind, two of which have been discussed extensively and often superbly. Kenneth Scott Latourette's multivolume history traced the expansion of the churches through the centuries, addressing international contexts not previously considered by other historians.[29] Due to Christ's universal evangelistic mandate, the churches have sought to take the gospel to the entire world. This primary theme—missions and evangelism—is an absolutely necessary component in any full-fledged history of the theology of the churches.

A second instance would be the composition of church polity as defined through a free-church reading of the Great Commission. The baptizing churches have stressed that the command of Christ to make disciples precedes the command to baptize. The idea that only the regenerate should belong to the church is a fundamental and distinguishing doctrine to many free churches, including the Anabaptists and the Baptists. These same churches often proceed to note that Christ commanded that following baptism the disciples be taught everything that Jesus taught. Of course, this includes commandments regarding the Lord's Supper and church discipline, two other major aspects of church polity.

---

[27] See chapter five.

[28] Lewis Drummond, *The Canvas Cathedral: A Complete History of Evangelism from the Apostle Paul to Billy Graham* (Grand Rapids: Nelson, 2002), 101–5.

[29] Kenneth Scott Latourette, *A History of the Expansion of Christianity* (London: Eyre & Spottiswoode, 1937–45).

Evangelism and church polity as developments of the Great Commission are two dogmatic themes that have received attention and must be considered in any holistic historical theology. However, in the limited space allowed in a book devoted to theological method rather than history proper, we ask the reader to consider three additional themes. These themes have not, perhaps, received the stress they should have in recent years and thus deserve additional attention by future historians. Alongside the doctrinal themes of evangelism and church polity, the reader is encouraged to consider three themes that speak to the character of doctrinal development, especially among the free churches, in their responses to the Great Commission.

In light of the pattern of the cross, a historiography driven by the New Testament will seek to trace the progress and regress of the churches in evangelism and in regenerate church polity. However, it must also seek to answer who Christ is, what He has done for mankind, and what He demands of believers in their relationships with Him and with one another. Those churches that seek to fulfill the final commandment of Christ have thus been led by the Spirit to deal with trinitarian revelation, personal salvation in Christ, and covenantal freedom. These three doctrines are summarily discussed below, indicating how the free churches have come to understand that their doctrine truly does develop from the Scripture illumined by the Spirit and how they must always be ready for correction.

Trinitarian Revelation

The problem of development in doctrine, which first brought Maurice Wiles the international repute he so richly deserved, has exercised the best patristic theologians.[30] Most of the proposals concerning patristic doctrinal development have swirled around biblical exegesis, philosophical background, church tradition, and political interference.[31] Unfortunately no proposal has garnered general agreement as to why trinitarian and Christological orthodoxy developed in the way it did. I argue here that the key to the early church's doctrinal development was Christ's gift of the Great Commission and the church's incorporation of the kerygma with it. First, however, we review the various options put forward.

With regard to philosophical influences, for instance upon "the archetypal heresy" of Arianism, the claims are often contradictory. Early modern commentators considered Plato formative, but Newman identified Aristotle as the culprit. Harnack pointed to both classical philosophers, and Rowan Williams noted the divergences and convergences of Arius with both. More recently, others have pointed to the influence of Stoicism. Wiles opted for the influence of Aristotle, Plato, and the Stoics. Thus, there is little consensus as to whether Arius and the

---

[30] Maurice Wiles, *The Making of Christian Doctrine: A Study in the Principles of Early Doctrinal Development* (New York: Cambridge University Press, 1967). See chapter 2, section 2.

[31] R. P. C. Hanson, *The Search for the Christian Doctrine of God: The Arian Controversy, 318–381* (New York: T&T Clark, 1988; repr., Grand Rapids: Baker, 2005), 824–75. Cp. Lewis Ayres, *Nicaea and Its Legacy: An Approach to Fourth-Century Trinitarian Theology* (New York: Oxford University Press, 2004), 425–29.

Arians were driven by a particular philosophy.[32] If Arianism was driven by philosophy, it was certainly not of any particular type.

With regard to tradition, the situation is little better. Both the Nicene party and the Arians appealed to church tradition. The early supporters of Arius included numerous bishops, the reputed guarantors of tradition, such as Eusebius of Caesarea, father of the discipline of church history.[33] Arius informed his bishop, Alexander of Alexandria, that he had learned his doctrine "from you," by which he probably meant the episcopal office. After carefully reviewing various earlier fathers, Wiles concluded Arius's claim was legitimate.[34] Lewis Ayres agrees with Wiles, especially with regard to Origen, the first systematic theologian in the East. Both the Arian and the Nicene descend from the Origenian tradition.[35] Appeal to tradition is ultimately not the key to orthodoxy.

With regard to political interference, there is little doubt that the emperors sought to favor one party and then another, according to the perceived needs of the day. Constantine himself, after affirming Nicaea, recalled Arius and persecuted Athanasius, the leader of the Nicenes. Athanasius was exiled five times from Alexandria, being generally persecuted by Arian emperors but restored by Nicene emperors and the pagan Julian.[36] George Huntston Williams demonstrated how the Arians accepted the synthesis of church and state more readily, fashioning their Christology and imperial theology accordingly.[37] A later emperor, Theodosius, eventually gave the Nicene party their seemingly critical victory.[38] Yet the Arians, through the barbarians, subsequently ruled much of the empire for centuries. The triumph of Nicene orthodoxy was obviously not due to political interference.

If philosophy, tradition, and politics were not the key to doctrinal development, perhaps the issue was settled by biblical exegesis. Unfortunately a blanket appeal to Scripture's authority is not the answer, for both parties appealed to Scripture. Indeed, this was a battle between conservative believers who regarded the Bible as authoritative.[39] As Robert Grant noted, "In the ancient church theology was generally regarded as the clarification and exposition of the word of God contained in scripture."[40] This was true not only for the Trinitarian controversies

[32] Cp. Hanson, *The Search for the Christian Doctrine of God*, 84–94; Rowan Williams, *Arius: Heresy & Tradition*, rev. ed. (Grand Rapids: Eerdmans, 2001), 197, 226, 231; idem, "The Logic of Arianism," *JTS* 34 (1983): 56–81; Maurice Wiles, *Archetypal Heresy: Arianism through the Centuries* (New York: Oxford University Press, 1996), 23–25.

[33] Hanson, *The Search for the Christian Doctrine of God*, 27–59; Williams, *Arius*, 48–49.

[34] "Arius's appeal to tradition had a broad enough base to warrant a rejection of the description of it as nothing more than 'obsolete traditionalism.'" Wiles, *Archetypal Heresy*, 17–23.

[35] Ayres, *Nicaea and its Legacy*, 20–30, 41–61.

[36] Khaled Anatolios, *Athanasius* (New York: Routledge, 2004), 12–33.

[37] George Huntston Williams, "Christology and Church-State Relations in the Fourth Century," [two parts] *CH* 20.3 (1951): 3–33, and 20.4 (1951): 3–26.

[38] Francis Dvornik, "Emperors, Popes, and General Councils," *Dumbarton Oaks Papers* 6 (1951): 1–23.

[39] James D. Ernest, "Athanasius of Alexandria: The Scope of Scripture in Polemical and Pastoral Context," *VC* 47 (1993): 341. Cp. Wiles, *Archetypal Heresy*, 10–17; Williams, *Arius*, 111–14; Wiles, *The Spiritual Gospel*, 31, 38–40, 158–61.

[40] Robert M. Grant, "The Bible in the Ancient Church," *JR* 26 (1946): 190. Cp. T. E. Pollard, "The Exegesis of Scripture and the Arian Controversy," *BJRL* 41 (1951): 414–29.

of the fourth century but for the Christological controversies of the fifth century, although tradition gained authority over time.[41] The question then becomes the method of interpretation. What was the hermeneutical method that allowed the Nicene party persuasively to carry the churches?

According to Charles Kannengeisser, the hermeneutical method of Athanasius began with Christ, while Arius, along with Origen and Eusebius, engaged in cosmology first. The theological pattern one adopted determined one's interpretation. But would the "pattern" come from Scripture itself or from elsewhere? Reflecting divergent attitudes toward Scripture's sufficiency, Athanasius began with the Christ pattern of Scripture while the Arians began with the cosmological pattern dominating culture. Athanasius "was above all the man of a single battle: he refused a systematic Christology which he did not consider sufficiently inspired by Scripture."[42] Robert Wilken finds a similar reason for the victory of Cyril of Alexandria over Nestorius of Constantinople. Although Nestorius was pro-Nicene, he was more concerned with refuting Arianism according to the "Antiochene pattern of exegesis" than with expounding the Scriptures Christologically. Cyril, on the other hand, focused on the Christ of Scripture, placing the Arian controversy aside.[43]

Ultimately the issue comes down to divine sufficiency. Does God provide the hermeneutical pattern for Scripture or must a pattern be imported from a human source, even a Christian one? Two leading Eastern theologians in fourth-century orthodoxy answered this question in compatible ways. In his lengthy response to Arian exegesis, Athanasius identified "the scope of that faith which we Christians hold, and using it as a rule, apply ourselves, as the apostle teaches, to the reading of Scripture."[44] The scope of Scripture, according to Athanasius, comes from Scripture itself, not from worldly methods.[45] In particular, all passages concerning Jesus Christ must be read according to John 1 and Philippians 2, which teach the "double account" of Christ as both God and man. For Athanasius, Jesus taught that Scripture itself is "a light upon its candlestick": "Search the Scriptures, for they are they which testify of me" (John 5:39).[46]

Where Athanasius solved the problem of hermeneutical sufficiency primarily with reference to the Word, Basil of Caesarea solved it primarily with reference to the Spirit. Scripture's sufficiency is inoperative apart from the Holy Spirit. In his reaction to the *Pneumatomachi* (Spirit-fighters), Basil noted proper interpretation of Scripture was due to "the government of the Holy Spirit."[47] For both Athanasius and Basil, proper hermeneutics is provided only by the Father, who reveals Himself by His Word and Holy Spirit. Unless one is willing to receive the Trinity, one

---

[41] Robert L. Wilken, "Tradition, Exegesis, and the Christological Controversies," *CH* 34 (1965): 123–45.

[42] Charles Kannengeiser, "Athanasius of Alexandria and the Foundation of Traditional Christology," *TS* 34 (1973): 103–13.

[43] Wilken, "Tradition, Exegesis, and the Christological Controversies," 123–45.

[44] Athanasius, *Orationes Contra Arianos* 3.28, *NPNF*², 4:303–431

[45] Andrew Louth, "Reason and Revelation in Saint Athanasius," *SJT* 23 (1970): 385–96.

[46] Athanasius, *Orationes Contra Arianos* 1.9, 3.29.

[47] Basil of Caesarea, *De Spiritu Sancto* 77, in *NPNF*², 1–50.

may not receive the revelation. Athanasius: "For how can he speak truth concerning the Father, who denies the Son that reveals concerning Him?"[48] Basil: "The revelation of mysteries is indeed the peculiar function of the Spirit."[49]

Although their emphases were distinct, both fathers considered both the Word and the Spirit as necessary. Spirit-centered Basil argued that scriptural language must be interpreted according to its own logic, rather than according to the wisdom of the world.[50] Moreover, "he who does not believe the Spirit does not believe in the Son, and he who has not believed in the Son does not believe in the Father."[51] Word-centered Athanasius argued that all the books of Scripture share a common interpretation because "they have but one voice of the Spirit."[52] Basil and Athanasius, of course, merely echo the thoughts of Paul, who believed Scripture was necessarily interpreted by Christ and the Spirit (2 Cor 3:5–6,14; 4:6).

While Scripture illumined by the Spirit was the proper means of interpretation, the proper pattern of interpretation was found in the Great Commission. Christ's baptismal instructions helped Athanasius answer the Arian misinterpretation of Christological passages.[53] But Basil relied upon the Great Commission even more, treating it as the premiere source for Trinitarian dogma, especially with regard to the place of the Holy Spirit.

On the Holy Spirit (*De Spiritu Sancto*) was written in response to the accusation that Basil's doxology went beyond Scripture by ranking the Spirit with the Father and the Son. Because they understood liturgical tradition has a powerful impact upon theology, some objected that Basil's doxology allowed for an alteration of the biblical pattern. Basil had praised God "with the Son together with the Holy Ghost" along with the more literal "through the Son in the Holy Spirit."[54] The critical part of Basil's defense of his trinitarianism was "the foundation of the faith of Christ" that all Christians receive with their baptism. By this he meant the baptismal formula of the Great Commission, the passage that most clearly teaches the Trinity. Christ did not divide the Spirit from the Father and the Son, and neither should we.[55]

The baptismal formula teaches the "connumeration" of the three distinct persons of the Trinity, not their "subnumeration." The "co-ordination" of the three persons in the Great Commission is the beginning of trinitarian doctrine. The scriptural doctrines of the monarchy of the Father (1 John 1:1), the generation of the Son (John 3:16), and the procession of the Spirit (John 15:26) complete the Christian understanding of the "distinction of Persons" and "community of Nature" in the Godhead.[56] The early church's doctrine of the Trinity, which

[48] Athanasius, *Orationes Contra Arianos* 1.8.
[49] Basil, *De Spiritu Sancto* 38.
[50] Ibid., 41.
[51] Ibid., 27.
[52] Athanasius, *Ad Marcellinus de Psalmos* 9.
[53] Athanasius, *Orationes Contra Arianos*, 2.41–42.
[54] Basil, *De Spiritu Sancto* 3. Cp. Eph 2:18.
[55] Ibid., 24–26.
[56] Ibid., 41–46.

reached its confessional apex at the Council of Constantinople, was ultimately dependent on the confession of faith made at baptism. Affirming the Trinity is not merely a cerebral but a moral exercise, for salvation depends on proper confession, baptism follows faithful confession, and the disciple's imitation of Christ is expected as a result.[57]

The trinitarian and Christological conclusions reached in the fourth and fifth centuries were developed in response to the overarching question as to "which side of the fundamental divide between the self-existent and the contingently existent was the Logos to be found."[58] In ranking the Son with the Father, the Great Commission answered that question by correlating the Son with the Father first rather than with creation first. In ranking the Holy Spirit with both the Father and the Son, the same was accomplished in His regard. The commission's baptismal formula not only aided the theologians but also served as the form for the all-important creeds developed in the early church.

At first the baptismal formula given by Christ was administered to new disciples in an interrogatory format. The earliest evidence we have of the interrogatory dates from the late second century and has been found in six versions in four different languages—Arabic, Ethiopic, Coptic, and Latin—spanning almost the entirety of the known Christian world. The threefold structure is striking:

- Do you believe in God the Father Almighty?
  √ I believe.
- Do you believe in Christ Jesus, the Son of God, who was born of the virgin Mary by the Holy Spirit, and was crucified under Pontius Pilate and died and was buried, and was resurrected to life from death on the third day, and ascended to heaven and sits at the right of the Father, from where He will come to judge the living and the dead?
  √ I believe.
- Do you believe in the Holy Spirit, and the holy church, and the resurrection of the flesh?
  √ I believe.[59]

The triune structure was retained as the interrogatory gave way to the *symbolum*. The *symbolum* was a confessional form of identification by which Christians from different areas could recognize one another.[60] The *symbolum* was

[57] Athanasius, *Orationes Contra Arianos* 2.42, 3.19–22; Anatolios, *Athanasius*, 37–38; Basil, *De Spiritu Sancto* 28.

[58] Frances Young, *From Nicaea to Chalcedon: A Guide to the Literature and the Background* (Philadelphia: Fortress, 1983), 178.

[59] The Latin version upon which this author's translation is based has been partially reconstructed, due to the fragility of the ancient Latin fragment, from the other languages by R. H. Connolly. "[Credis in Deum patrem omnipotentem?] Credis in Christum Iesum, filium Dei, qui natus est de Spiritu sancto ex Maria virgine, et crucifixus sub Pontio Pilato et mortuus est et sepultus, et resurrexit die tertia vivus a mortuis, et ascendit in caelis et sedit ad dexteram patris venturus iudicare vivos et mortuos? Credis in Spiritu sancto, et sanctam ecclesiam, et carnis resurrectionem?" Connolly, "On the Text of the Baptismal Creed of Hippolytus," *JTS* 24 (1924): 135.

[60] Rufinus, *A Commentary on the Apostles' Creed*, trans. J. N. D. Kelly, ACW (New York: Newman Press, 1954), 30.

taught to the convert through a catechetical process known as *traditio* and repeated back prior to baptism as *redditio*. Early echoes of the baptismal confession as it developed into creedal form may also be found in the "rule of faith" taught by Irenaeus[61] and Tertullian.[62]

The threefold structure of the baptismal confession was retained in the Old Roman Creed and its descendant, the Apostles' Creed.[63] The baptismal creed of Eusebius of Caesarea was long thought to be the basis of the Nicene Creed,[64] and the baptismal creed of Cyril of Jerusalem may have been the basis for the Nicene-Constantinopolitan Creed.[65] The longer Christological portion of these creeds resulted from the insertion of the kerygma into the trinitarian confession. Early creed critics agree that the creeds owe their theological structure to the Commission's baptismal formula and their Christological content to the kerygma.[66]

Jesus Christ commanded His disciples to go into the world and make disciples by preaching the gospel. He also commanded them to baptize new disciples in the name of the Father, the Son, and the Holy Spirit. The Great Commission brought the kerygma and the baptismal confession together. The postbiblical baptismal interrogatory, *symbolum*, rule of faith, and ultimately the major creeds reflect the influence of the Great Commission. The contributions of Athanasius and Basil verify that the Great Commission is the basis of the Christian development of trinitarian orthodoxy.

Personal Salvation

Not only is the Great Commission the basis of trinitarian orthodoxy, it is also the basis of an orthodox doctrine of personal salvation. In the Great Commission, as retold by Matthew (28:18–20), Jesus Christ explained salvation in terms of discipleship. The disciples of Christ are commanded to go and "make disciples" (*mathēteusate*). The making of Christian disciples is taken to occur along the same lines as the making of the original disciples, through teaching and preaching, personal carrying of the cross, and personal commissioning. The disciple follows his master in all things. The soteriological emphasis in discipleship, therefore, is on faith understood not only as a divine gift but as a living reality. The free churches

[61] Irenaeus, *Adversus Haereses* 1.9.4, 1.10.1–3, in *ANF*, 1:315–567. Cp. *Adversus Haereses* 1.22.1, 2.32.3–4, 3.1.2, 3.4.1–2, 3.3.3, 3.11.1, 3.16.5–6, 3.18.3, 4.9.2, 4.33.7, 5.20.1.

[62] Tertullian, *De Praescriptione Haereticorum* 1.12–19, in *ANF*, 243–68. Cp. *De Praescriptione Haereticorum* 13.36; *De Virginibus Velandis* 1.3; and *Adversus Praxean* 2.1.

[63] H. J. Carpenter, "Creeds and Baptismal Rites in the First Four Centuries," *JTS* 44 (1943): 1–11.

[64] Leo Donald Davis, *The First Seven Ecumenical Councils (325–787): Their History and Theology* (Collegeville, MN: Liturgical, 1990), 59.

[65] Cyril was a radical biblicist whose detailed *traditio* of the creed is extant. *The Works of Saint Cyril of Jerusalem*, trans. Leo P. McCauley and Anthony A. Stephenson, FC (Washington, DC: Catholic University of America Press, 1969).

[66] Hans Lietzmann, "Symbolstudien I–XIV," *ZNE* [five parts] 21 (1922): 1–34; 22 (1923): 257–79; 24 (1925): 193–202; 26 (1927): 75–95; Kirsopp Lake, "The Apostles' Creed," *HTR* 17 (1924): 173–83; D. Larrimore Holland, "The Earliest Text of the Old Roman Symbol: A Debate with Hans Lietzmann and J. N. D. Kelly," *CH* 34.3 (1965): 262–81; J. N. D. Kelly, *Early Christian Creeds*, 3rd ed. (New York: Longman, 1971), 30–61.

have long insisted that true salvation requires a "living faith," a faith that entails a life of discipleship.[67]

The free churches look to the Renaissance as an important contributor to the recovery of personal appropriation of the gospel. Among the medieval scholastic theologians, the New Testament message of salvation by faith had been subtly supplanted with salvation effected by both faith and the sacraments offered by the priesthood.[68] Moreover, theologians began to speak of an "implicit faith," by which the church became the guarantor of the efficacy of the faith of the laity. The laity, especially in mission areas, need not know Christ explicitly but should at least trust in the idea of a mediator.[69]

Erasmus, the leading humanist, firmly rejected the medieval church's idea of implicit faith. He was a scathing critic of superstitious practices and of ignorance and considered the scholastic theologians to be the purveyors of such. Erasmus called Christians to a personal appropriation of the faith. "All was to be focused on piety of mind and heart through the personal conviction and effort of the believer, who should not rely alone on the external rites of a judicially conceived Church since these were by comparison with Scripture poor conductors of spiritual insight."[70]

Erasmus was not antisacramental, but he focused on the spiritual appropriation of the sacraments, insisting on a virtuous life as the Christian layman lives out the *philosophia Christi*.[71] Erasmus also advocated publishing the Bible in the vernacular so that every Christian might become a theologian. His vision was of everyone, even the farmer plowing in the field, knowing the Bible and personally appropriating its message.[72] Erasmus's "philosophy of Christ," especially as expressed in the *Paraclesis*, the preface to his Greek New Testament, was translated into many languages and made a wide impact. Many in the Reformation period began their journey to a fervent, personal faith as a result of Erasmus. He called people to a life of literature, of returning to the sources (*ad fontes*) of the Christian faith, and of personal commitment.[73] But he remained

[67] C. Arnold Snyder, *Anabaptist History and Theology: An Introduction* (Kitchener, ON: Pandora, 1995), 89.

[68] Thomas Aquinas, one of the better medieval theologians, said that while the death of Christ is "the universal cause of salvation," the sacraments were necessary for showing Christ and applying the effects of the cross. Again, the Word is "the first and universal cause of salvation," but the sacraments are the necessary visible signs by which salvation is "applied to men." Aquinas, *Summa Contra Gentiles*, 4.56, trans. Charles J. O'Neil (Notre Dame, IN: University of Notre Dame Press, 1975), 5:246–47. While the cross was necessary in Aquinas's theology, faith and the sacraments were both seen as necessary. The sacraments are necessary "instruments" in salvation. Romanus Cessario, "Aquinas on Christian Salvation," in *Aquinas on Doctrine: A Critical Introduction*, ed. Thomas Weinandy, Daniel Keating, and John Yocum (New York: T&T Clark, 2004), 129–33.

[69] Heiko Obermann, *The Harvest of Medieval Theology: Gabriel Biel and Late Medieval Nominalism* (Grand Rapids: Eerdmans, 1967), 84.

[70] Basil Hall, *Humanists and Protestants, 1500–1900* (Edinburgh: T&T Clark, 1990), 82.

[71] Erasmus, *Handbook of the Militant Christian* (*Enchiridion de Militas Christiani*), trans. John P. Dolan (Notre Dame, IN: Fides Publishers, 1962), 61.

[72] Erasmus, *Paraclesis*, in *Christian Humanism and the Reformation: Selected Writings of Erasmus*, 3rd ed., trans. John C. Olin (New York: Fordham Press, 1987), 101.

[73] Alister E. McGrath, *Reformation Thought: An Introduction,* 3d ed. (Malden, MA: Blackwell, 1999), 39–63.

with the Roman Catholic Church, disputing with Martin Luther regarding grace and free will.

The free churches of the Reformation period agreed with Erasmus concerning the necessity of a personal appropriation of the faith. According to the early Anabaptists, the call to salvation involves both the movement of God's grace in regeneration and the movement of man in obedience. The call of Christ is a call to personal commitment. This personal commitment involves both internal movement and external movement. The distinction between the inner and the outer was common among the South German Anabaptists although they rejected the spiritualist separation of the two. For Marpeck, faith is an internal work of God that should result in the external witness of man, beginning with baptism. Water baptism was an external sign of a deep internal conviction. The regenerate wished to live according to Christ, and the context for such a life was the church fellowship, separated from but ministering to the world.[74]

Abraham Friesen has shown how Erasmus, through his paraphrases of Matthew and Acts, influenced the Anabaptists to understand the Great Commission in personal and orderly terms. The teaching of the Word precedes the internal response of faith, which precedes the external response of baptism, which results in a life of obedience to further teaching of Christ.[75] This understanding of the order of the Christian life, according to the Great Commission and related passages—teaching, faith, baptism, and teaching—was subsequently reaffirmed by the Baptists. The Baptists also recovered the importance of evangelism and missions by focusing on the Great Commission. They believed that the commission was for all Christians, not just the apostles.[76] Indeed, the modern missions movement among modern non-Catholics, especially in the English-speaking world, was galvanized by William Carey's example.

Although drawing much from Erasmus, the free churches of the early modern period primarily agreed with Luther regarding salvation as coming entirely by grace. Free-church theologians affirmed Luther's doctrine of justification by grace through faith in terms of the free imputation of Christ's righteousness to the sinner.[77] This is still true with regard to Anabaptists,[78] Baptists,[79] Methodists,[80]

---

[74] Cp. C. Arnold Snyder, *Following in the Footsteps of Christ: The Anabaptist Tradition* (Maryknoll, NY: Orbis, 2004).

[75] Friesen, *Erasmus, the Anabaptists, and the Great Commission* (Grand Rapids: Eerdmans, 1998), 43–75.

[76] Yarnell, "The Heart of a Baptist," *CTR*, n.s. 4 (2006): 73–87.

[77] Luther, *The Freedom of a Christian* (1520), in *LW* 31: 333–77. The dating of Luther's breakthrough has been debated extensively; his own retelling of it is compelling though conflated. Gordon Rupp, *The Righteousness of God: Luther Studies* (London: Hodder & Stoughton, 1953), 121–37.

[78] Thomas N. Finger, *A Contemporary Anabaptist Theology: Biblical, Historical, Constructive* (Downers Grove, IL: InterVarsity, 2005), 131.

[79] John Piper, *Counted Righteous in Christ: Should We Abandon the Imputation of Christ's Righteousness?* (Wheaton, IL: Crossway, 2002). For a review of the ways in which Baptists have affirmed justification by faith in terms of imputation, see Yarnell, "Christian Justification: A Reformation Baptist View," *CTR*, n.s. 2 (2005): 71–90.

[80] Thomas C. Oden, *Systematic Theology* (1987–1992; repr., Peabody, MA: Prince Press, 2001), 3:128.

and Pentecostals,[81] among others. Alongside Luther, the free churches believe that justification is the article on which the church stands or falls. But they quickly go on to affirm that justification is not the only aspect of salvation. Justification is a necessary part of personal salvation, but it is not alone.

All of the soteriological graces are interconnected. Luther agreed that good works will flow from justification but was wary that they might be mixed with works righteousness. While this is indeed a cause for continuing vigilance, attention must also be placed in another direction. Unfortunately Luther's doctrine of *simul justus et peccator* (at once righteous yet sinful) encouraged not only reliance upon grace but antinomianism among his followers.[82] Understanding that salvation is both static and dynamic, believers' churches are more careful to remember discipleship. "Justification, the declaration of righteousness, and sanctification, growth in righteousness, should neither be separated nor confused."[83]

Later the free churches disputed with scholastic forms of Lutheran and Reformed soteriology, fearing that faith had lost its living quality. The protest against the dead faith of a merely formal Protestantism often swelled the ranks of believers' churches.[84] The words of Philip Jacob Spener, the father of German Pietism, provide a common refrain: "So these preachers, with their own human efforts and without the working of the Holy Spirit, have learned something of the letter of the Scriptures, have comprehended and assented to true doctrine, and have even known how to preach it to others, but they are altogether unacquainted with the true, heavenly light and the life of faith."[85] Similarly, Wesley and the Methodists emphasized personal "experience" as a necessary part of salvation in reaction to the dead formalism they saw in the Church of England.[86] The free churches, responding to Christ's call to discipleship, recognize that salvation must be personally appropriated and personally confessed.

Covenantal Freedom

The Old and New Testaments are replete with the idea of covenant, especially covenants between God and man. In 1 Pet 3:21, the concept of covenant is tied with baptism: "There is also an antitype which now saves us—baptism (not the removal of filth of the flesh, but the answer (*eperotema*) of a good conscience toward God), through the resurrection of Jesus Christ." The Greek word here is used only once in the New Testament and has been translated as either an "answer" or

[81] J. Rodman Williams, *Renewal Theology: Systematic Theology from a Charismatic Perspective* (Grand Rapids: Zondervan, 1988–1992), 2:61–82.

[82] Luther excelled in dialectic and in strong statements. His earlier push against the works-righteousness of medieval theology should also be measured against his later defense of repentance against the antinomians led by Johann Agricola. By this time the persecution of the radicals was in full swing, and the free churches could see Luther only as a sinful persecutor. Bernard Lohse, *Martin Luther's Theology: Its Historical and Systematic Development*, trans. Roy A. Harrisville (Minneapolis: Fortress, 1999), 178–84.

[83] Yarnell, "Christian Justification," 83.

[84] Donald F. Durnbaugh, *The Believers' Church: The History and Character of Radical Protestantism* (Scottdale, PA: Herald, 1984), 118–30.

[85] Spener, *Pia Desideria*, trans. Theodore G. Tappert (Philadelphia: Fortress Press, 1964), 46.

[86] Thomas A. Langford, *Methodist Theology* (Peterborough: Epworth, 1998), 57.

"request," or as a "pledge" or "oath," indicating a confession on the part of the baptizand in response to the question of Christian commitment.[87] Both baptism and the Lord's Supper were considered in the early church to be related to the covenant. Baptism was the pledge to live according to the covenant; the Lord's Supper was an oath renewing the covenant.[88]

During the Reformation period, the concept of the covenant was rediscovered by the Anabaptists. They noted baptism's correlation with the covenant of discipleship to God in the midst of the disciplined community. For instance, Hans Hut, a most powerful evangelist among the Anabaptists who baptized many thousands, stressed the connection between the Great Commission (according to Mark 16:15–16) and baptism as covenant (1 Pet 3:21). In the Great Commission, Christ ordained a particular and inviolable "order." The order was comprised of (1) preaching "the gospel of all creatures"; (2) personal belief; and (3) baptism as "the pledge to bear and suffer all that will be laid upon him from the Father through Christ, and . . . receive the sign of Baptism to a covenant of his resolve before a Christian congregation which has received the covenant from God." Such a pledge and covenant resulted in the granting of divine authority to discipline (Matt 18:15–20).[89]

In the medieval and early modern periods, political authority was understood to be a divine gift. The grant of authority came either from above through sacred kingship, "the great chain of being," or from below through the consent of the people, who appointed their ruler as a representative. In the later sense, "freedom," the exercise of authority by an agent, issued forth from consent to a communal covenant.[90] The Anabaptists understood the church covenant, entered by personal commitment to carry the cross of Jesus Christ, to be the means of divine authorization for church action. The covenant had a God-ward aspect and a man-ward aspect, and involved conditions.[91] The concept of a church covenant was not exclusive to the Continental Anabaptists, however. An earlier concept of covenant in association with the call to human obedience is notable among the medieval Lollards and was picked up by William Tyndale.[92] Robert Browne, the father of English separatism, perhaps borrowing from Dutch Anabaptists who had fled to England, also made the idea fundamental to his ecclesiology.[93]

---

[87] Peter H. Davids, *The Epistle of First Peter*, NICNT (Grand Rapids: Eerdmans, 1990), 144–45; J. Ramsey Michaels, *1 Peter*, WBC (Waco: Word Books, 1988), 214–18; Paige Patterson, *A Pilgrim Priesthood: An Exposition of First Peter* (Nashville: Thomas Nelson, 1982), 146–47.

[88] Charles W. Deweese, *Baptist Church Covenants* (Nashville: Broadman, 1990), 18–19.

[89] Hans Hut, "Of the Mystery of Baptism" (manuscript, ca. 1525), trans. Gordon Rupp in idem, *Patterns of Reformation* (London: Epworth, 1969), 383, 388–89.

[90] Robert Eccleshall, *Order and Reason in Politics: Theories of Absolute and Limited Monarchy in Early Modern England* (New York: Oxford University Press, 1978); Richard Ashcraft, "Locke's Political Philosophy," in *The Cambridge Companion to Locke*, ed. Vere Chappell (New York: Cambridge University Press, 1994), 229–41.

[91] Champlin Burrage, *The Church Covenant Idea: Its Origin and Development* (Philadelphia: American Baptist Publication Society, 1904), 13–25; Deweese, *Baptist Church Covenants*, 20–21.

[92] Yarnell, "Book Note: *The praier and complaynte of the ploweman unto Christe*," *SWJT* 46 (2004): 66–67.

[93] Burrage, *The Church Covenant Idea*, 34–57.

The connection between the internal commitment to follow Jesus Christ pledged externally in baptism, resulting in the divine authorization of the church, was especially emphasized in the early free-church tradition. But the connection between personal commitment and divine authorization is less evident in Reformed theology and among those free churchmen heavily influenced by the Reformed tradition. Ulrich Zwingli not only emphasized divine predestination as a theological foundation but conflated the old and new covenants with each other by identifying circumcision with baptism as a covenant sign. Zwingli did this in order to deny the Anabaptist rediscovery of believers' baptism.[94] Zwingli's successor, Heinrich Bullinger, further developed the idea of the covenant for the Reformed movement.[95] John Knox brought the Reformed idea to Scotland where it had a deep ecclesiological and political impact.[96] Among the English Puritans, the responsibility of human beings to uphold the conditions of the covenant could be diminished by those who were more Reformed.[97]

Covenants were commonly used among the Baptists from their earliest days. Smyth's Gainsborough congregation included the further light doctrine in their covenant. During his transition to Baptist views, John Smyth connected the concept of covenant directly with baptism: "the true forme of the Church is a covenant betwixt God & the Faithful made in baptisme."[98] The popular English Baptist covenant advocated by Benjamin Keach was brought to the middle colonies of America by his son, Elias Keach. The Keach covenant appeals for the assistance of the Holy Spirit, pledges the participants toward God and one another, relates the local church covenant with the universal covenant, and emphasizes living "according to Christ's rule, and the Order of the Gospel."[99]

William Screven, pastor of the Kittery church that became the first Baptist church in the southern colonies, featured the further light doctrine in his covenant: "wherein wee doe Covenant & promise to walk with God & one with another In A dew and faithfull observance of all his most holy & blessed Commandm.tts Ordi-

---

[94] Zwingli, *Of Baptism* (1525), in *Zwingli and Bullinger*, ed. G. W. Bromiley, LCC (Philadelphia: Westminster, 1953), 138.

[95] Relating the conditional nature of covenant theology to double predestination has caused debate within Reformed theology. Cp. Charles S. McCoy and J. Wayne Baker, *Fountainhead of Federalism: Heinrich Bullinger and the Covenant Tradition* (Louisville: Westminster/John Knox Press, 1991); Cornelis P. Venema, *Heinrich Bullinger and the Doctrine of Predestination: Author of the "the Other Reformed Tradition"?* (Grand Rapids: Baker, 2002), 17–34.

[96] Burrage, *The Church Covenant Idea*, 26–33.

[97] Greaves identifies four groups: Antinomians believed God fulfills the covenant, and the moral law is abrogated; Strict Calvinists believed God fulfills the covenant, and moral law is important; Moderate Calvinists believed that God fulfills the covenant, but man must also fulfill the covenant; and, Arminians, whom Greaves identifies as "non-covenant," stressed that man fulfills the covenant. Richard L. Greaves, "John Bunyan and Covenant Thought in the Seventeenth Century," *CH* 36 (1967): 151–69.

[98] Smyth, *The Character of the Beast* (1609), in *The Works of John Smyth, Fellow of Christ's College, 1594–8*, ed. W. T. Whitley (Cambridge: Cambridge University Press, 1915), 2:645.

[99] The Keach Covenant, in *Baptist Church Covenants*, 119–21. Paul Fiddes, in his excellent work on Baptist identity, relates the concept of the universal church to the eternal covenant. It is probably more proper to say that the multiplicity of local covenants participating in the eternal covenant indicates common participation in the kingdom of God rather than the universal church. Paul S. Fiddes, *Tracks and Traces: Baptist Identity in Church and Theology*, SBHT 13 (Waynesboro, GA: Paternoster, 2003), 32.

nances Institutions or Appointments, Revealed to us in his sacred word of ye ould & new Testament and according to ye grac of God & light att present through his grace given us, or here after he shall please to discover & make knowne to us thro his Holy Spirit according to ye same blessed word all ye Dayes of our lives."[100] A contemporary noted that Screven was characterized by the movement of God's "free grace."[101] Screven also stood boldly against the colonial magistrates who sought to enforce infant baptism.[102]

With the Baptists in America, the concept of covenant became a means of freedom in the church and, by example, in the nation. Isaac Backus transitioned from Congregationalism to being a New Light Separate, and ultimately a Separate Baptist. His covenant, adopted by his church in a solemn process, brought a sense of freedom to its participants. They did "solemnly and renewedly sign covenant together; I trust, with some real freedom and sense of divine things."[103] Their palpable sense of "real freedom" came with giving themselves up to God and to one another, and their commitment to be guided by the Spirit in the world, "expecting that he will yet further & more gloriously open his word & the mysteries of his kingdom."[104] The liberating sense of dependence upon the Spirit for further light cast upon God's Word is seen among American Baptists, south and north.[105]

The covenant concept not only fostered a sense of dependence on the Spirit in reading the Word; it also fostered a sense of freedom. Richard Niebuhr has traced the idea of covenant in the rise of American democracy. He notes that there is a "close correspondence and dialectical relationship among the general ideas men hold about their own constitution." The ideas humans hold regarding church and religion naturally reflect upon similar ideas in society and politics. Specifically, the covenant pattern adopted among the congregational churches in the United States encouraged the establishment of American democracy. The covenantal way of thinking, derived from Scripture, became "a *fundamental* pattern in American minds" (author's italics).[106] The pattern of covenant was given authority by the sense of the people that God was providentially active in establishing American freedom. The close correlation of free-church values with the development of American values encouraged by belief in direct providence has been noted by many historians and philosophers.[107]

[100] The Screven Covenant, in Robert A. Baker, *The First Southern Baptists* (Nashville: Broadman, 1966), 29–30.

[101] Humphrey Churchwood to First Baptist Church of Boston (3 January 1682), in ibid., 22.

[102] Records of the Provincial Council at York (13 March 1682), in ibid., 25–26.

[103] Cited in Deweese, *Baptist Church Covenants*, 44.

[104] Covenant of Baptist Church of Middleborough, Massachusetts, in ibid., 139–40.

[105] Cp. Covenant of Cherokee Creek Baptist Church and Covenant of Bent Creek Baptist Church, in ibid., 147, 149. The covenant recommended by the Philadelphia Baptist Association retained the focus on the Word, but the further light doctrine is absent. They did, however, emphasize carrying the cross and following Christ. Ibid., 150–51.

[106] Niebuhr, "The Idea of Covenant and American Democracy," *CH* 23 (1954): 127–30.

[107] Ibid., 132–33; Paul Johnson, "The Almost-Chosen People," *FT* 164 (June/July 2006): 17–22; C. C. Goen, *Broken Churches, Broken Nation: Denominational Schisms and the Coming of the American Civil War* (Macon, GA: Mercer University Press, 1985), 28–32.

Southern Baptists have been among those most convinced that God intended people to live in freedom. They have been promoters not only of "democratic religion" or "egalitarian authority" in the sphere of the church but of religious freedom in the sphere of the state.[108] In their confession they refer to the church as being under the lordship of Christ operating "through democratic processes." "In such a congregation each member is responsible and accountable to Christ as Lord." Their passion for democracy and freedom in the congregation is mirrored in their demand for religious liberty for all people in society. "God alone is Lord of the conscience, and He has left it free from the doctrines and commandments of men which are contrary to His Word or not contained in it. Church and state should be separate."[109]

Unfortunately the free churches have not always been true to their principles. As Francis Wayland lamented, "We have suffered loss, as Baptists, by following the examples of other denominations."[110] Among those principles that Wayland considered dear to Baptists were regenerate church membership, the universal priesthood of all believers, "the absolute right of private judgment in all matters of religion," "the perfect sufficiency of the Scriptures to teach us in all matters pertaining to religion," and the separation of church and state. Under the last principle, Wayland asserted that Baptist "garments have never been defiled by any violation of the rights of conscience."[111] While Wayland was doubtless correct in the first regard—that Baptists suffer when they violate their own principles, he displayed hubris in the second—that Baptists have never been defiled by a lack of respect for personal freedom.

It has been noted that while white Christians cried out for freedom, they refused it to black Christians.[112] Richard Furman, the leading Baptist pastor of the South and first president of the Triennial Convention that brought American Baptists together to fulfill the Great Commission, both cried out for freedom and denied it to his brothers in Christ. Furman was convinced that "Divine Providence" was directly leading America to establish religious and civil freedom. The reason that God was doing so was to preserve "this constitutional principle" against British violations of it. God demanded revolt as a duty in order to preserve "freedom from the domination of arbitrary power." The country's origin was blessed because it was an asylum for those seeking religious liberty. Americans would prosper if they "adhere strictly to the constitution; and let the important principles it contains, have their free and full operation."[113]

---

[108] The phrases are borrowed from Greg Wills, *Democratic Religion: Freedom, Authority, and Church Discipline in the Baptist South, 1785–1900* (New York: Oxford University Press, 1997), 50.

[109] Baptist Faith and Message (2000), arts. vi and xvii. Cp. *Baptist Ideals: For Liberty and Light* (Nashville: Sunday School Board, 1963), 9–11, 20–23.

[110] Francis Wayland, *Notes on the Principles and Practices of Baptist Churches* (New York: Sheldon, Blakeman, 1857), 121.

[111] Ibid., 137.

[112] Mark A. Noll, *A History of Christianity in the United States and America* (Grand Rapids: Eerdmans, 1992), 161.

[113] Furman, "America's Deliverance and Duty" (1802), in *Life and Works of Dr. Richard Furman, D.D.*, ed. G. William Foster (Harrisonburg, VA: Sprinkle, 2004), 389–408. Furman also argued for the revolution to occur

The high principles of full liberty were, however, forsaken by Southern Baptists at their foundation. The Southern Baptist Convention was begun immediately over the violation of Baptist polity by the mission boards that united all American Baptists, but the factor driving the political decisions of both northern and southern Baptists doubtlessly concerned the institution of slavery. The documents of the period indicate that division occurred, from the southern viewpoint, because of the mission boards' neglect to follow convention directives, and from the northern viewpoint, because the mission boards led by northerners could not appoint slaveholders in good conscience.[114] Their support for slavery and slaveholders has been called the "original sin" of Southern Baptists.[115]

The Southern Baptist view of African-Americans was complex. They were definitely considered to be human beings who could and should be evangelized, but they were a "rude" people who should be ruled by despotic means rather than by democracy.[116] In the early Southern Baptist rendition, the normally high anthropology of the free churches gave way to a divided anthropology. The universality of truth, for instance with regard to the consent of the governed, was compromised in favor of racial restrictions.[117] As a result of their deficient anthropology, the political philosophy of the Southern Baptist free churches returned from the covenant basis of authority to the great chain of being of the medieval period.[118]

This is not to say that covenant ecclesiology was lost, but it was compromised. The church covenant was still entered by believers-only baptism, and regenerate church membership was preserved by church discipline.[119] And southerners still spoke of the "equality of rights of citizens" and appealed to divine providence to preserve their rights. God was pictured as the protector of the Confederacy and the "equal rights" of its people.[120] Some have surmised that the dominant Calvinism of the south, which also saw its heyday among Southern Baptists, used the doctrines of providence and predestination to support slavery. God had simply created some people to be slaves and to oppose slavery was working against God. In other words, the southern Reformed doctrine of divine providence willed the restriction of the inalienable rights of some human beings.[121]

because of his belief in constitutional principles prior to the war itself.

[114] *A Baptist Source Book: With Particular Reference to Southern Baptists*, ed. Robert A. Baker (Nashville: Broadman, 1966), 84–122. Cp. Goen, *Broken Churches, Broken Nation*, 90–98.

[115] E. Luther Copeland, *The Southern Baptist Convention and the Judgement of History: The Taint of an Original Sin* (New York: University Press of America, 1995). Slavery was called "the original sin and curse of the country" during the nineteenth century. Goen, *Broken Churches, Broken Nation*, 141.

[116] John L. Dagg, *A Practical View of Christian Ethics* (1859; repr., Harrisonburg, VA: Sprinkle, 2006), 284, 338–41.

[117] Ibid., 286–87.

[118] A. James Fuller, *Chaplain to the Confederacy: Basil Manly and Baptist Life in the Old South* (Baton Rouge: Louisiana State University Press, 2000), 117, 229.

[119] Ibid., 271–72.

[120] Ibid., 291–94.

[121] Dagg, *A Practical View of Christian Ethics*, 285; John H. Leith, "Calvinism," in *The New Encyclopedia of Southern Culture*, vol. 1, *Religion*, ed. Samuel S. Hill (Chapel Hill, NC: University of North Carolina Press, 2006), 44–49; Noll, *The Civil War as a Theological Crisis* (Chapel Hill, NC: University of North Carolina Press, 2006), 81–82.

Not only was there a movement among some Southern Baptists toward Reformed paradigms in order to support slavery, but there was also a movement against the idea of doctrinal development. Richard Fuller, the third president of the Southern Baptist Convention and a lawyer by training, argued eloquently on behalf of slavery in a famous literary debate with the centrist northerner, Francis Wayland.[122] Wayland argued that Scripture contained not only "precepts" but "principles" that God intended His people to follow. Just as the principle of singular fidelity in marriage had led to Christians condemning polygamy, the principle of love toward others should lead to the demise of slavery. "Every one, I think, knows that God has seen fit to enlighten our races progressively; and that he has enlightened different portions in different degrees."[123]

Fuller disagreed and focused on the idea of precepts. Fuller treated Scripture as a static book of law, for people need precepts rather than principles.[124] He also denied that doctrine ever developed. The canon is the "complete rule of faith and practice," and there is never "*an expansion of sense and meaning*." For Fuller, the idea of doctrinal development was unthinkable, for it automatically implies there is error in Scripture.[125] Fuller was unable to distinguish between the immutability of Scripture and the mutability of human interpretation, confusing the Word of God with His perception of the light upon it.[126] His interpretative principles led Fuller to believe the South had been given "a sacred trust" in its responsibilities for the slaves, but they remain slaves nonetheless.[127]

Fortunately the call of the Great Commission to covenantal freedom was not ignored by all free churchmen. Rodney Stark has demonstrated how the end of slavery in the world generally was brought about only in Christianity. Moreover, the impetus in the English-speaking world, which belatedly but eventually led the entire world to ban slave-trading and slavery itself, came from the free churches. The Quakers, driven by their desire to live out the principles of Scripture, led in England and in America for the abolition of slavery. They disciplined their churches to remove slavery and petitioned their governments to do the same. They were subsequently joined in their activities by Methodists, Baptists, and others.[128] Christian confronted Christian, free churchmen confronted free churchmen with the problem of the inconsistency of Christianity and slavery.

David Walker, a black Christian appealed to the Great Commission in his argument against slavery. "You have the Bible in your hands with this very injunction—Have you been to Africa, teaching the inhabitants thereof the words of the

[122] Emir and Ergun Caner, *The Sacred Trust: Sketches of the Southern Baptist Convention Presidents* (Nashville: B&H, 2003), 9–12.

[123] Wayland to Fuller, in *Domestic Slavery Considered as a Scriptural Institution: In a Correspondence Between The Rev. Richard Fuller of Beaufort, S.C., and the Rev. Francis Wayland, of Providence, R.I.* (New York: Lewis Colby, 1845), 52.

[124] Fuller to Wayland, in ibid., 215–17.

[125] Fuller to Wayland, in ibid., 170–73, 185.

[126] Fuller to Wayland, in ibid., 211–12.

[127] Fuller to Wayland, in ibid., 164.

[128] Stark, *For the Glory of God: How Monotheism Led to Reformations, Science, Witch-Hunts, and the End of Slavery* (Princeton, NJ: Princeton University Press, 2003), 339–56.

Lord Jesus?" Southern Baptists could, of course, point to their missionary efforts in Africa, but Walker pressed the issue. He was disgusted with the fact that Americans had been to Africa with a different purpose than the Great Commission, for they caused the Africans, through greed, to turn on one another and sell other Africans into slavery. Slavery was a contradiction of the Great Commission.[129] Greg Wills has detailed the ambiguities experienced by Southern Baptists as they held a "double standard" between the egalitarian or freedom principle alongside the discrimination principle of slavery.[130]

One slave song rings out with condemnation regarding the failure of southern white churches (Baptists, Methodists, and Presbyterians being the most prominent) to grant blacks the freedom they themselves desired:

Am I not a man and a brother?
Ought I not then to be free?
Sell not onc to another.
Take not thus my liberty.
Christ, our Savior,
Died for me as well as thee.[131]

Ultimately, after the Christian appeals were completed, the politicians and generals stepped in and, by divine providence, used a horrible war to bring the southern Christians to their knees. And to their credit the theologians of the Southern Baptist Convention acquiesced, though still with some sense of self-justification. As Jeremiah Jeter wrote, "Slavery, in this country, has been abolished by the overruling providence of God; and I sincerely rejoice in its abolition. Toward the colored race, whether in slavery or in freedom, I have ever cherished the kindest feelings. . . . Let them enjoy their rights, and have full scope for the development of their powers and the improvement of their condition, physical, intellectual, and moral."[132]

And Southern Baptists, displaying a courageous capability publicly to bear the shame of their past, finally indicated unequivocally in 1995 that, although they fervently believe their Bible is without error, their churches certainly may err in its interpretation. In a "Resolution on Racial Reconciliation on the 150th Anniversary of the Southern Baptist Convention," messengers from these free churches publicly recognized the role of slavery in their foundation. They went on to "lament and repudiate," "apologize," "genuinely repent of racism," and "ask forgiveness from our African-American brothers and sisters."

In their resolves, the Southern Baptist Convention highlighted at least two of the great principles of free-church theology, both of which had been compromised in the nineteenth century: first, "that every human life is sacred, and is of equal

[129] Walker, *Appeal, in Four Articles*, ed. Charles M. Wiltse (New York: Hill & Wang, 1965), 42; cited in Noll, *The Civil War as a Theological Crisis*, 68.

[130] Wills, *Democratic Religion*, 59–66.

[131] *The Anti-Slavery Harp* (Boston, 1848), 10; cited in Goen, *Broken Churches, Broken Nation*, 162.

[132] Jeremiah Bell Jeter, *The Recollections of a Long Life* (Richmond, VA: Religious Herald, 1891), 71. Cp. Fuller, *Chaplain to the Confederacy*, 310.

and immeasurable worth, made in God's image, regardless of race or ethnicity (Genesis 1:27)." And second, "That we pledge our commitment to the Great Commission task of making disciples of all people (Matthew 28:19)."[133]

In supporting the wicked institution of racial slavery, the free churches of the Southern Baptist Convention exemplified the truth that the churches may never claim infallibility prior to the second coming of our Lord Jesus Christ. In repenting of that institution and the racism it entailed, those same free churches recommitted themselves to a high anthropology and a high sense of mission, both of which are demanded by the Great Commission of their Lord to which they have been covenanted.

A CONCLUDING EXHORTATION

A true free church may err, but heretical it cannot be, for free churches are willing to be corrected but only by the Word of God illumined by the Holy Spirit of God. A true free churchman believes that the Word of God is perfect but that his or her understanding of Christ and the Bible must always depend on the Spirit. And for the Spirit's illumination, the believers' churches will pray, humbly recognizing that theology is best done in covenantal conversation with other Christians. A free church may fail at times, but such evidence of fallibility will remind it that the grace of God is sufficient for the salvation of sinners. The free churches recognize their utter dependence on divine providence over their history, in which He displays both His judgment and His mercy.

Their principles teach the dissenting churches that they should not be coerced against their consciences, and never should they coerce any other. If faced with persecution, the free churches will prove most unwilling to change, unless they have been convinced by the Word and the Spirit. Following the example of their forefathers, and ultimately their Lord, they must prefer to pay whatever price necessary. In their ever-expanding witness to the truth, as they follow Christ's Great Commission, the believers' churches will zealously take up the cross of confessing their faith in Jesus Christ. The atoning cross of Christ, their Lord and Savior, is why they go, make disciples, baptize, and teach everything He taught. The cross of Christ is also an indicator of why they may ever give their life but never take a life. May free churches follow Christ with ever increasing faithfulness and vigor, until He comes again.

---

[133] Www.sbc.net/resolutions; accessed 26 April 2007.

NAME INDEX

D

E

F

G

H

SUBJECT INDEX

D

E

F

G

H

I

Q

R

S

T

V

W

SCRIPTURE INDEX